Emerging Adults and Substance Use Disorder Treatment

Emerging Adults and Substance Use Disorder Treatment

Developmental Considerations and Innovative Approaches

EDITED BY

DOUGLAS C. SMITH

OXFORD
UNIVERSITY PRESS

OXFORD
UNIVERSITY PRESS

Oxford University Press is a department of the University of Oxford. It furthers
the University's objective of excellence in research, scholarship, and education
by publishing worldwide. Oxford is a registered trade mark of Oxford University
Press in the UK and certain other countries.

Published in the United States of America by Oxford University Press
198 Madison Avenue, New York, NY 10016, United States of America.

Library of Congress Cataloging-in-Publication Data
Names: Smith, Douglas C. (Douglas Cary), editor.
Title: Emerging adults and substance use disorder treatment : developmental considerations
and innovative approaches / edited by Douglas C. Smith.
Description: Oxford ; New York : Oxford University Press, [2018] |
Includes bibliographical references and index.
Identifiers: LCCN 2017029920 (print) | LCCN 2017031329 (ebook) | ISBN 9780190490799 (updf) |
ISBN 9780190672607 (epub) | ISBN 9780190490782 (alk. paper)
Subjects: | MESH: Substance-Related Disorders—therapy | Young Adult
Classification: LCC RC564 (ebook) | LCC RC564 (print) | NLM WM 270 | DDC 616.86/06—dc23
LC record available at https://lccn.loc.gov/2017029920

9 8 7 6 5 4 3 2 1
Printed by Webcom, Inc., Canada

To Carol, Lily, and Delia

CONTENTS

Douglas C. Smith, Ph.D., LCSW, is Associate Professor of Social Work at the University of Illinois at Urbana-Champaign. He has worked in the substance use field for 20 years as a clinician, clinical supervisor, and researcher. Dr. Smith has published numerous scientific articles and his research has been funded by the National Institute of Alcohol Abuse and Alcoholism (NIAAA), the Substance Abuse and Mental Health Services Administration (SAMHSA), and the U.S. Department of Justice. He delights in raising his two daughters and in being an avid Chicago Cubs fan.

Christina M. Andrews
University of South Carolina,
Columbia, SC

Kyle M. Bennett
University of Illinois at
Urbana-Champaign, Urbana, IL

Brandon G. Bergman
Recovery Research Institute,
Massachusetts General Hospital &
Harvard Medical School, Boston, MA

Clifford Bersamira
University of Chicago, Chicago, IL

Jordan Braciszewski
Henry Ford Health System,
Detroit, MI

Sierra Castedo
University of Texas at Austin,
Austin, TX

Heloísa Garcia Claro
University of São Paulo,
São Paulo, Brazil

Jordan P. Davis
University of Illinois at Urbana-
Champaign, Urbana, IL

**Ivan Filipe de Almeida Lopes
Fernandes**
Federal University of ABC,
Santo André, Brazil

**Márcia Aparecida Ferreira
de Oliveira**
University of São Paulo,
São Paulo, Brazil

Michael L. Dennis
Chestnut Health Systems, Normal, IL

Tara M. Dumas
Huron University at Western,
London, Ontario

Nilofar Fallah-Sohy
Recovery Research Institute,
Massachusetts General Hospital &
Harvard Medical School, Boston, MA

Rodney Funk
Chestnut Health Systems, Normal, IL

Frederick X. Gibbons
University of Connecticut, Storrs, CT

Judy Havlicek
University of Illinois at Urbana-
Champaign, Urbana, IL

John F. Kelly
Recovery Research Institute,
Massachusetts General Hospital &
Harvard Medical School, Boston, MA

Mary E. Larimer
University of Washington, Seattle, WA

Jordanna Lembo
University of Houston, Houston, TX

Sarah Makhani
Recovery Research Institute,
Massachusetts General Hospital &
Harvard Medical School, Boston, MA

Clayton Neighbors
University of Houston, Houston, TX

Frank J. Schwebel
University of Washington, Seattle, WA

Douglas C. Smith
University of Illinois at
Urbana-Champaign, Urbana, IL

Lori Holleran Steiker
University of Texas at Austin,
Austin, TX

Rosana Ribeiro Tarifa
University of São Paulo,
São Paulo, Brazil

Melissa Westlake
University of South Carolina,
Columbia, SC

Liliane Cambraia Windsor
University of Illinois at Urbana-
Champaign, Urbana, IL

Emerging Adults and Substance Use Disorder Treatment

Why Should We Focus on Emerging Adults with Substance Use Disorders?

DOUGLAS C. SMITH ■

This book builds on almost two decades of work conceptualizing emerging adulthood, or the period of life from ages 18 to the mid- to late 20s, as a unique life stage. It presents readers with a state-of-the-science review of both this developmental period and substance use disorder (SUD) treatments for emerging adults. Although the study of emerging adulthood has blossomed, there is no up-to-date volume on SUD treatments for emerging adults. This is unfortunate, as there are an estimated 30.6 million emerging adults living in the United States, and 34.5% of them have serious problems with substances that often require clinical treatments. That equates to about 10.5 million emerging adults ages 18–25 in the United States with serious substance use problems (Substance Abuse and Mental Health Services Administration, 2013). In addition, research on SUD treatments for emerging adults lags behind that for adolescents and older adults. This book fills this gap for academics and members of the helping professions.

In this opening chapter we will orient readers to the definitions of emerging adulthood and substance use disorders. We then provide an overview of the major trends of research on development and substance use treatment through an outline of the book.

SOME WORDS ABOUT WORDS: WHAT IS EMERGING ADULTHOOD?

Few individuals would argue with you if you told them that *emerging adults*, or individuals between roughly 18 and 29 years of age, are taking longer in their journeys to become full-fledged adults. Just as we may consider "40 to be the new 30," might we also consider 25 to be the new 16? Fundamental to this question is why we even have a period of adolescence in the first place. Consider the following writing from Erik Erikson (1968) on adolescence:

> As technological advances put more and more time between early school life and the young person's final access to specialized work, the stage of adolescing becomes an even more marked and conscious period, and, as it has always been in some cultures and in some periods, almost a way of life between childhood and adulthood. (p. 128)

Thus, just as the lag between adulthood and childhood was originally used to justify a new concept of adolescence, Arnett's (2000) proposed theory of emerging adulthood is built on this very notion that the time to reaching the so-called specialized work of adulthood has become more elongated. For example, in the United States, roughly 70% of emerging adults in 2009 were attending college, compared to 52% in 1970 (United States Census Bureau, 2014). In essence, college attendance serves a critical role in preventing the full-scale bedlam that would occur if we didn't have institutions to absorb emerging adults who are not fully participating in the labor market. Côté (2006) illustrates this nicely by referring to college as a type of institutionalized moratorium, or a developmental purgatory of sorts where people are mostly physically and mentally mature but are still waiting in line to become adults. Furthermore, the median age of marriage for both men and women has also risen substantially in the past half-century (Arnett, 2000). In short, this lengthier transition to achieving traditional adult milestones, such as marriage, a career-track job, or becoming a parent, has led many scholars to believe that the period of life roughly between 18 and 25 is now a unique developmental stage.

Individuals in this period of life have been referred to as "young adults," "transition age youth," and "emerging adults." Historically, the label *young adults* was used to denote the passage of youth out of adolescence and into adulthood. It conveyed a sense that adolescents had made the transition to adulthood and were now allowed some privileges and increased responsibilities of full adulthood, such as smoking cigarettes, voting, enrolling in the draft, and being tried as an adult in the criminal justice system. Although the term *young adult* conveys a sense of having arrived into adulthood, our laws still acknowledge that individuals in this demographic are not fully developed. For example, the legal drinking age in the United States and some other countries is 21, and research shows that this law is responsible for saving lives and preventing accidents among younger individuals (Kypri et al., 2006; Plunk, Cavazaos-Rehg, Bierut, & Grucza, 2013). So there is something dissatisfying about calling individuals in this age cohort "young adults" when for 3 full years of young adulthood, or ages 18–20, individuals do not have full adult rights for drinking alcohol. The word *young* just doesn't convey the sense that individuals in this age bracket are not quite full-fledged adults.

The term *transition-age youth* is largely popular in the child welfare literature, as this life period is when youth are transitioning out of the foster care system. Recent legislation has supported the need for continuing support of these individuals beyond age 18 because of their multiple risk factors for poor adult outcomes (Courtney, Hook, & Lee, 2012). Again, this moniker acknowledges that its constituent members are not fully developed and are seemingly in need of support to successfully navigate the pathway to adulthood. Despite the popularity of this label, something seems amiss when referring to individuals defined as legal adults in the United States as "youth." Furthermore, the common practice of referring to both adolescents and legal, yet still developing, adults collectively as "youth" further muddies this term. Thus, although the term *transition-age youth* does capture the notion that older teens and those in their mid- to late 20s have not met the milestones of adulthood, it seems inappropriate to use a word that also describes younger teens and pre-teen children (i.e., youth).

In this book, we will describe individuals ages 18–29 as *emerging adults*. This term was first coined by Jeffrey J. Arnett in his highly influential article published in the journal *American Psychologist*, in 2000. At this writing, Google Scholar shows that there are over 8,000 citations to Arnett's (2000) seminal article on emerging adulthood. Perhaps this is because he put into words what the American zeitgeist was already observing: the lengthening of the passage into adulthood. His article described the socioeconomic forces and demographic trends that suggested that it is time to consider emerging adulthood as a unique developmental period, on par with adolescence or other widely recognized life stages. Furthermore, he proposed five broad dimensions, or defining features, of emerging adulthood, describing emerging adulthood as the age of optimism, feeling in-between, instability, identity exploration, and self-focus. Although other developmental scholars are not in full agreement with Dr. Arnett (Côte, 2014), and this book does not endorse all tenets of his theory, we will use the term *emerging adults* to describe individuals who are approximately between the ages of 18 and 29. Chapter 2 includes a more thorough discussion of theories of emerging adulthood, including alternate views of this life period, and discusses how developmental issues may impact substance use and substance use treatment outcomes.

WHAT ARE SUBSTANCE USE DISORDERS?

Just as there are multiple ways to refer to the same age group, there has historically been a wordy menu of terms to describe problematic use of alcohol or drugs (Kelly, 2004). Even as I write out the phrase "problematic use of alcohol or drugs" I contemplate which populations of substance users this describes, what hidden biases are nested within this term, and what baggage may be attached to this phrase. Specifically, the baggage associated with this term is that it has sometimes been used to describe individuals who are not addicted to substances but who are having consequences associated with their use. Another clear sign of terminology run wild is that the *Journal of Studies on Alcohol and Drugs*, a highly regarded scientific journal, has a specific editorial policy restricting the use of the term *substance abuse*—only in reference to the diagnosis of substance abuse that existed in previous versions of the *Diagnostic and Statistical Manual of Mental Disorders*, fourth edition (DSM-IV; American Psychiatric Association, 2000). This editorial policy specifically addressed the problem that the label *substance abuse* has become an umbrella term for a wide range of severity of substance problems, including full-blown, chronic-course addictions.

Table 1.1 presents a list of terms commonly used to describe substance-related problems, excerpts from scientific journals or popular press sources that use these terms, and a critique of the baggage associated with each term. With the publication in the United States of the DSM-5 (American Psychiatric Association, 2013), we should see a new term increasingly infiltrating our menu, *substance use disorders*. Specifically, in the DSM-5, the American Psychiatric Association decided to eliminate the diagnostic category of substance abuse. Instead, three out of four of the criteria for substance abuse were merged with what were previously the substance dependence symptoms from the DSM-IV to form a new diagnosis, called *substance use disorder*. One criterion, the presence of recurring legal problems due to continued substance use, was dropped entirely. Additionally, one symptom, having cravings for the substance, was added. With this background in mind, let's turn our attention to what makes a good or bad descriptive label when referring to a mental health condition and why the label *substance use disorders* may be preferable to older, cloudier ones.

When selecting terms to describe problematic substance use we must be mindful of three major considerations. First, we must consider whether the term in question has the potential to increase stigma for individuals suffering from substance use problems. Research has found that, relative to individuals who smoke cigarettes or are obese, people are more likely to shun (illicit) substance users (Phillips & Shaw, 2013). Thus a key question to consider when thinking about descriptive labels is whether they are tainted with hidden assumptions that may perpetuate stigma. For example, does the term reinforce a negative and dated perspective that substance use problems result from moral failings? Consider the language used by members of Faces and Voices of Recovery (2014), a consumer advocacy group of individuals in long-term recovery from substance use. Rather than referring to themselves as "alcoholics" or "addicts," which are conventions used in 12-step fellowship meetings, they identify themselves as "persons in long-term recovery." This is done deliberately, in that it avoids baggage associated with the terms *alcoholic* and *addict*, resulting in a humanizing effect. In other words, this is an example of "person-first language," which is a core piece of ethical guidelines for publishing research on people with mental illnesses (American Psychological Association, 2010). Second, it communicates a sense of longevity in terms of the amount of time an individual has been living a sober lifestyle. As researchers and health care professionals, we need to be just as deliberate with selecting terms to describe individuals who are still actively suffering from substance use problems, in a way that frames the condition in a humanizing, person-first manner.

Table 1.1. SELECT EXAMPLES OF LABELS USED TO DESCRIBE PROBLEMATIC
SUBSTANCE USE

Label	Example	Critique
Addiction	"A key step in modifying public attitudes and improving how health professionals and policymakers address addiction is to better align the language of addiction with scientific evidence. Unless we clarify the language, those with the disease will continue to experience the stigma. . . ." (Richter & Foster, 2014, p. 60)	Note how the words *addiction* and *disease* are used interchangeably. A value assumption is being made here that addiction is a disease.
Drug dependence	"Obviously, dependent users, by definition (see: Method), would be expected to neglect social and work-related activities in favour of cannabis use and experience reduced control over their use." (Liebregts et al., 2014, p. 3)	The big problem with any label for substance-related problems is that people often think that if you meet criteria for a particular diagnosis that you have all symptoms in that diagnosis. Here, the authors nicely highlight the problem that one can be diagnosed as "dependent" without meeting the criterion for giving up social activities that used to be important to that individual. Substance use disorder in DSM-5 recognizes that no one symptom may be central in the presence of a substance-related problem, and permits grouping people at different severity levels, based on the number of symptoms met.
Substance misuse	"Several efficacious treatments exist for substance-misusing adolescents. . . ." (Smith, Hall, Jang, & Arndt, 2009, p. 101)	This umbrella term describes substance users, substance abusers, and those with dependence. It addresses the problem that some individuals need treatment but don't meet full diagnostic criteria per self-report. It is likely being replaced with DSM-5's substance use disorder, which integrates DSM-IV abuse and dependence diagnoses.

(continued)

Table 1.1. CONTINUED

Label	Example	Critique
Substance abuse	"Chemically dependent persons will show significant psychological, behavioral, and/or physiological impairment. . . . Much of the problem for substance abusers is found in social relationships (love, work play)" (Johnson, 2004, p. 12)	*Substance abuse* is the most entrenched and imprecise label to describe problematic substance use. Notice here how the main distinguishing feature between abuse and dependence is described as a lack of physiological symptoms. Prior thinking was that DSM symptoms of substance abuse would chronologically proceed and be less severe markers of problems than substance dependence symptoms. Research has not supported this idea, prompting the recent revisions in the DSM-5.
Heavy drinking	"Heavy episodic drinking was defined as the consumption of at least five drinks in a row for men and four drinks in a row for women on an occasion during the two weeks prior to the study . . . " (Hingson et al., 2003, p. 24) "In 2012, heavy drinking was reported by 6.5% of the population aged 12 or older, or 17.0 million people. This rate was similar to the rate of heavy drinking in 2011 (6.2%). Heavy drinking is defined as binge drinking on at least 5 days in the past 30 days." (Substance Abuse and Mental Health Services Administration, 2013, p. 3)	As one can see from these different quotes, this term is defined differently in various studies, so one needs to look very closely at each specific definition. Note that the term *heavy drinker* refers to frequency and quantity, not what problems result from this use. In contrast, a substance use disorder is defined as a pattern of leading to "clinically significant impairment" (APA, 2013, p. 490)

This brings us to the second major consideration for selecting terms to describe individuals with substance use problems. The term we select should be precise or accurate in describing the severity of the problem of the individuals involved. Precise language is important to researchers, who need to know to whom their findings apply. Precise labels are also needed so that treatment providers can use common language when discussing clinical severity and the selection of appropriate treatments. Some terms simply may not be extremely precise. For example, who would want to go to an "outpatient chemical dependency unit" if they didn't feel that they were dependent on substances? The effect of such labeling may result in systematically excluding individuals who could benefit from reducing their substance use but who are not physiologically addicted to them. White (2007) also notes how labels are confusing and problematic when describing people who have achieved remission from problematic substance use; White gives specific recommendations for using various labels based on length of and route to recovery.

Furthermore, it may be that at certain levels of severity it makes sense to discuss problematic substance use as a chronic relapsing condition on par with any other medical condition for which relapse is common, such as diabetes or chronic obstructive pulmonary disease (COPD) (McClellan, Lewis, O'Brien, & Kleber, 2000). For decades we have been trying to distinguish who is at most risk for ongoing chronic substance use problems and who may be able to safely return to moderate substance use. In fact, the book *Alcoholics Anonymous*, which was written in 1939, distinguishes between moderate drinkers who could take or leave alcohol, hard drinkers who could still quit if a good enough reason surfaced, and "real alcoholics." Real alcoholics, for whom the original 12-step prescription of reliance on a higher power and lifelong abstinence were developed, were thought to be " . . . beyond human aid" (A.A. World Service, Inc., 1976, p. 24). Thus, it is easy to see how labels such as "hard drinker" and "alcoholic" both try to capture ranges of problem severity and also communicate implicit theories about the nature and course of problematic substance use.

The third consideration is that descriptive labels should complement current efforts to integrate SUD treatment into mainstream healthcare. For too long, individuals suffering from substance use problems were treated outside of healthcare settings, in specialized care settings sometimes referred to as "rehab" settings. The word "rehab" has an increasingly pejorative connotation, reinforcing the shame and stigma associated with having what should be conceptualized as a treatable health condition. The specialization of rehab units resulted in less emphasis on providing services to individuals with lower-severity (but medically and socially damaging) substance use problems. This is disturbing, since the highest social costs are not necessarily borne by those addicted to illegal drugs but rather by the large group of people in the United States who consume more alcohol than is medically advisable (Grant, Dawson, & Moss, 2011). The current drive toward integrating SUD treatments into mainstream healthcare through the Patient Protection and Affordable Care Act's (2010) mandate to cover such treatment is expected to accomplish two things. First, it may increase access to SUD treatment through insurance reimbursement parity. Insurance parity means that reimbursement for substance use disorders must be on par with that for other health problems. Second, it may reduce the stigma of seeking help by reframing substance use problems as treatable medical conditions. Thus, any descriptive labels should be consistent with this major shift in treatment financing.

Against this backdrop, we will describe problematic substance use as *substance use disorders* in this book. We like this term for a couple of reasons. First, the language in the DSM typically tries to stay assumption-free with regard to the etiology and course of mental health problems. The term *substance use disorders* is a big enough tent to capture problems along a continuum of severity, without the baggage of other terms. Second, in initial testing with professionals, the term *substance use disorder* has been viewed more positively than the label *substance abuse* (Kelly & Westerhoff, 2010). That is, Kelly and Westerhoff (2010) randomized continuous education unit (CEU) workshop attendants to receive two different vignettes describing a person with substance-related problems. The only thing that differed in the vignettes was whether the individual was referred to as a "substance abuser" or "person with a substance use disorder." Workshop attendees who received the version describing the individual as a substance abuser endorsed more punitive substance abuse treatment approaches. Although more research should be done on the effects of labels on the stigma surrounding substance use disorders, these preliminary data demonstrate the stigmatizing effects of certain labels. Finally, the DSM-5 conceptualization of substance use disorders has two appealing features. First, it is inclusive enough that individuals with less severe, albeit significant, problems can receive reimbursable treatments in our healthcare system. Second, notwithstanding findings that the overall threshold may be too low in DSM-5 to diagnose chronic-course disorders (Wakefield & Schmitz, 2015), the thresholds for mild, moderate, and severe disorders may be precise enough to provide a common language about severity level and simultaneously expand access to reimbursable services. Chapter 3 presents a more detailed discussion of assessment and diagnosis issues.

WHY FOCUS ON SUBSTANCE USE DISORDER TREATMENTS FOR EMERGING ADULTS?

In addition to the sheer number of emerging adults that could benefit from receiving SUD treatments, other salient reasons exist for focusing on this population. First, emerging adults have been underrepresented in major clinical studies. For example, although emerging adults represent almost one-third of treatment admissions to publicly funded substance use treatments, the largest trial of alcohol use disorder treatments, Project MATCH, included only 74 emerging adults (7.7%) in the outpatient arm sample. Second, a handful of studies have found that emerging adults have poorer treatment outcomes than those of adolescents and older adults when receiving comparable treatments. (See Table 1.2). Third, it could be that substance use during emerging adulthood has lasting health effects. For example, having a persistent SUD during young adulthood predicted health problems at age 64, even when these emerging adults' SUDs were in full remission after emerging adulthood (Haber, Harris-Olenak, Burroughs, & Jacob, 2016). Finally, if the coverage provisions allowing emerging adults to remain on their

Table 1.2. DIRECT COMPARISONS OF EMERGING ADULTS' SUBSTANCE USE DISORDER TREATMENT OUTCOMES WITH THOSE OF OTHER AGE GROUPS

	Sample	Main Findings	Limitations
Satre et al. (2003, 2004)	736 young adults and 468 older adults treated in a large HMO outpatient program	At 6 months and 5 years, 9% and 12% fewer emerging adults were abstinent compared to middle-aged adults and older adults, respectively.	Adults older than age 30 were included in the definition of "young adults." Treatments were not standardized in this study.
Sinha et al. (2003)	171 emerging adults ages 18–25 and 263 older adults ages 26 + who were criminally referred to 12-step-oriented outpatient treatment	30% of emerging adults were drug-free at treatment discharge vs. 70% of older adults. 11% fewer emerging adults completed treatment.	No standardized treatment methods were used.
Smith et al. (2011)	152 emerging adults ages 18–25 and 151 adolescents under age 18 in a national multi-site study on Adolescent Community Reinforcement Approach. Emerging adults and adolescents were matched on 34 variables using propensity score matching.	At last follow-up, 14% fewer emerging adults were abstinent and in remission compared to adolescents. On average, emerging adults used alcohol on 3 days more than adolescents at follow-up.	Although participants were matched well and received a well-supervised, empirically supported treatment, site effects were not accounted for in models.
Davis et al. (2017)	Secondary analysis of emerging ($n = 267$, ages 18–29) and older adults ($n = 1,459$, ages 30+ years) in Project MATCH	Emerging adults randomized to twelve-step facilitation (TSF) had a lower percent of days abstinent and higher number of drinks per drinking day compared to emerging adults in other treatment conditions and older adults in TSF at 12-week follow-up.	This was a well-run randomized trial. However, small sample sizes of emerging adults assigned to three different intervention conditions make testing mediators of these treatment effects difficult, as done in the Sinha et al. (2003) and Satre et al. (2003, 2004) nonexperimental studies.

HMO, health maintenance organization.

parents' insurance are retained in the Patient Protection and Affordable Care Act (2010), it is likely that more emerging adults will present for SUD treatments. Many emerging adults were uninsured before passage of the Patient Protection and Affordable Care Act, likely because they were working in lower-wage jobs that didn't provide health insurance coverage. In short, it is time we take emerging adults' treatment needs seriously.

Treatment Disparities for Emerging Adults

Although we don't know much about how to improve treatments for emerging adults, we do have a chorus of statistical whispers suggesting that we need to do so. As noted earlier, there have been multiple studies showing that emerging adults have inferior treatment outcomes when directly compared to adolescents or older adults. Table 1.2 summarizes studies that have directly compared emerging adult outcomes with older adult outcomes. Additionally, we have reviewed other studies showing the inverse relation between age and substance use: on the whole, older adults use fewer substances than younger adults at long-term follow-up after treatment. These indirect comparison studies, however, cannot speak to specific differences between emerging adults and older adults because of the wide age range of participants in these study samples.

Direct Comparison Studies

Satre and colleagues (Satre, Mertens, Arean, & Weisner, 2003, 2004) completed two of the earliest studies we know of showing differences in emerging adult and older adult SUD treatment outcomes. Furthermore, they also pinpointed some possible variables that accounted for discrepancies in younger and older adults' outcomes. They found that emerging and young adults (ages 18–39; mean age = 30.4) had poorer outcomes than those for older adults at both 1 and 5 years following treatment entry. Compared to older adults (59%), fewer younger adults (50%) were abstinent at 1 year (Satre et al., 2003). The variables that accounted for these differences at 1 year were that younger adults were more hostile, had higher rates of dependence, had shorter lengths of stay in treatment, and had less motivation to remain abstinent. These findings were largely replicated at the 5-year follow-up, with 40% of young adults (ages 18–39) and 52% of older adults achieving abstinence (Satre et al., 2004). These differences in outcomes were explained by young adults having shorter lengths of stay (i.e., about 6 weeks vs. 12 weeks of treatment for older adults), and the presence of at least one individual who encouraged substance use in their social network (17% for young adults vs. 8% in older adults). Although this study was limited in that the age range used for the definition of young adulthood was 18–39 years, it was among the first direct comparisons of younger and older adults in the substance use treatment literature.

An additional study, in the early 2000s, found similar disparities in emerging adult and older adult outcomes, this time in an outpatient program serving individuals referred from criminal justice settings (Sinha, Easton, & Kemp, 2003). Specifically, there was a large difference in the percent of emerging adults (30%) and of older adults (70%) who submitted clean urine samples at the end of treatment. Emerging adults were also less likely to complete treatment. This study improved upon prior work, as it defined emerging adults as persons ages 18–25, more in line with definitions in the emerging adult literature, in which individuals over age 30 are rarely defined as emerging adults.

In my own research, my colleagues and I found that relative to adolescents, 14% fewer emerging adults receiving the Adolescent Community Reinforcement Approach (A-CRA) were abstinent, in early remission, and living in the community (instead of jail or a controlled environment) at follow-up (Smith, Godley, Godley, & Dennis, 2011). A few things about this study bear mentioning. First, we used propensity score matching, an advanced statistical procedure, to carefully match adolescents and emerging adults on 34 variables at baseline that could have potentially influenced outcomes. Thus, findings were not likely due to differences in treatment motivation, symptom severity, or a range of other variables. Second, a novel finding that we did not highlight much in our original report was that emerging adults who were treated in clinics that served a higher concentration of emerging adults tended to have better SUD outcomes. That is, most clinics in this study served younger adolescent populations. The typical emerging adult in this study was seen in a clinic where emerging adults comprised only 16.9% of the total clients. Thus it may be that with more experience with emerging adults (i.e., higher emerging adult caseload), emerging adult treatment outcomes improve. Alternatively, it could be that emerging adults who interact with other emerging adults during treatment may have better outcomes. Finally, because we were highly concerned with comparing apples to apples in our analysis and used statistical matching procedures, we were unable to test which characteristics of emerging adulthood accounted for the differences in outcomes between emerging adults and adolescents.

Finally, Davis, Bergman, Smith, and Kelly (2017) compared the outcomes of emerging adults and older adults in Project MATCH, a well-known study comparing three different treatments for alcohol dependence: twelve-step facilitation (TSF) treatment, cognitive-behavioral therapy (CBT), and motivational enhancement therapy (MET). To our knowledge this is the first study comparing emerging adults' and older adults' outcomes in the context of a randomized trial. The major contribution of this study was that we could see if emerging adults had better outcomes in one treatment condition versus another condition relative to other emerging adults and older adults. In fact, the major finding was that relative to older adults in TSF and emerging adults in CBT or MET, emerging adults in TSF had poorer short-term outcomes. Although outcome differences did not persist at long-term follow-up, this finding implies that initial engagement of emerging adults in TSF could be improved. Additional discussion of emerging adults' involvement in mutual aid societies, such as Alcoholics Anonymous, is discussed in Chapter 8.

Indirect Comparison Studies

In addition to these studies that, for the most part, set out to directly compare emerging adult outcomes with those of older adults, other studies have found that age is associated with outcomes to the extent that they controlled for age in experiments. An example of this is a study comparing mindfulness-based relapse prevention to standard relapse prevention and standard care (Bowen et al., 2014). In most outcome models, age was negatively associated with days of substance use, indicating that older individuals made more substantial reductions in substance use than younger individuals. Additionally, Rossman and colleagues (2011) found a similar association between age and substance use outcomes in their large study on the effectiveness of drug courts. These studies show that outcomes typically are better for older participants in big randomized trials. However, they are unable to state whether emerging adult and older adult outcomes are different, since they did not directly test that hypothesis. These findings underscore the opinions of expert consensus panels which suggest that, whenever possible, we should report differences in outcomes by age for emerging adults and older adults (National Research Council and the Institue of Medicine, 2014).

In summary, there is a small body of research that has shown that emerging adults may have poorer treatment outcomes relative to other age groups. Furthermore, we are just starting to identify why these differences exist. Is it that emerging adults persist in beliefs that they can use substances during this developmental period and easily quit later when they enter the ranks of full adulthood (Arnett, 2005)? Alternatively, are the treatments currently on the market attractive to emerging adults and sensitive to their developmental needs? These are the questions tackled in this book, by reviewing all the available evidence and identifying very critical gaps that could help us improve SUD treatments for emerging adults.

HOW TO USE THIS BOOK

The first half of this book addresses developmental issues associated with emerging adulthood, paying specific attention to how developmental features influence diagnosis and treatment. Chapter 2 reviews several theories about emerging adulthood and presents hypotheses for why substance use prevalence is higher in this population. It is meant to be an in-depth discussion of developmental issues in emerging adulthood and their crossover with SUD. Chapter 3 provides an overview of general SUD assessment and diagnosis, and then highlights issues specific to emerging adults. Those readers with a solid background in assessment and diagnosis may wish to skip the initial portion of the chapter to concentrate on emerging adult–specific issues. In Chapter 4, we provide an exhaustive review of treatments that have the best empirical support for use with emerging adults. One notable feature of this chapter is that we've reviewed the evidence for treatments for both college-attending and non-college-attending samples, as these two groups may be on markedly different developmental trajectories. Typically, little is written about non-college-attending emerging adults (Arnett, 2000). In Chapter 5 we discuss various approaches to ensuring that culturally competent treatments are provided to emerging adults with substance use disorders. Finally, Chapter 6 presents some highlights of the Patient Protection and Affordable Care Act (2010) that could impact treatment for emerging adults.

The second half of the book presents the state of the science for specific interventions and special populations of emerging adults. Topics include the use of peer-based interventions (Chapter 7), twelve-step involvement and treatments for emerging adults (Chapter 8), recovery colleges (Chapter 9), and delivering treatments to child welfare–involved emerging adults (Chapter 10). Chapter 11 provides an international perspective on emerging adults in SUD treatment by presenting findings on Brazilian emerging adults who are served in the public health system. Chapter 12 synthesizes the major themes in this book and looks ahead to major opportunities for advancing SUD treatment services for emerging adults.

REFERENCES

Alcoholics Anonymous World Services, Inc. (1976). *Alcoholics Anonymous: The Story of How Thousands of Men and Women Have Recovered from Alcoholism.* New York: Author.

American Psychological Association (2000). *Diagnostic and Statistical Manual of Mental Disorders,* fourth edition. Washington, DC: Author.

American Psychological Association (2010). *Publication manual of the American Psychological Association,* sixth edition. Washington, DC: Author.

American Psychological Association (2013). *Diagnostic and Statistical Manual of Mental Disorders,* fifth edition. Washington, DC: Author.

Arnett, J. J. (2000). Emerging adulthood: A theory of development from the late teens through the twenties, *American Psychologist, 55,* 469–480.

Arnett, J. J. (2005). The developmental context of substance use in emerging adulthood. *Journal of Drug Issues, 35*(2), 235–254.

Bowen, S., Witkiewitz, K., Clifasefi, S. L., Grow, J., Chawla, N., Hsu, S. H., . . . Larimer, M. E. (2014). Relative efficacy of mindfulness-based relapse prevention, standard relapse prevention, and treatment as usual for substance use disorders: A randomized clinical trial. *JAMA Psychiatry, 71*(5), 547–556.

Côté, J. E. (2006). Emerging adulthood as an institutionalized moratorium: Risks and benefits to identity formation. In J. J. Arnett, & J. L. Tanner (Eds.), *Emerging adults in America: Coming of age in the 21st century* (pp. 85–116). Washington, DC: American Psychological Association. doi: 10.1037/11381-004

Côté, J. E. (2014). The dangerous myth of emerging adulthood: An evidence-based critique of a flawed developmental theory. *Applied Developmental Science, 18*(4), 177–188.

Courtney, M. E. Hook, J. L., & Lee, J. S. (2012). Distinct subgroups of former foster youth during young adulthood: Implications for policy and practice, *Child Care in Practice*, *18*, 409–418.

Davis, J. P., Bergman, B. G., Smith, D. C., & Kelly, J. F. (2017). Testing a matching hypothesis for emerging adults in Project MATCH: During-treatment and 1-year outcomes. *Journal of Studies on Alcohol and Drugs*, *78*, 140–145. http://www.jsad.com/doi/pdf/10.15288/jsad.2017.78.140

Erikson, E. H. (1968). *Identity: Youth and crisis*. New York: Norton & Company.

Faces and Voices of Recovery. (2014). *Recovery messaging for young people in recovery*. Last updated February, 2014. Retrieved from http://www.facesandvoicesofrecovery.org/sites/default/files/Recovery_Messaging_for_Young_People.pdf

Grant, B. F., Dawson, D. A., & Moss, H. B. (2011). Disaggregating the burden of substance dependence in the United States. *Alcoholism: Clinical and Experimental Research*, *35*, 387–388.

Haber, J. R., Harris-Olenak, B., Burroughs, T., & Jacob, T. (2016). Residual effects: Young adult diagnostic drinking predicts late-life health outcomes. *Journal of Studies on Alcohol and Drugs*, *77*(6), 859–867.

Hingson, R., Heeren, T., Zakocs, R., Winter, M., & Wechsler, H. (2003). Age of first intoxication, heavy drinking, driving after drinking, and risk of unintentional injury among U.S. college students. *Journal of Studies on Alcohol and Drugs*, *64*, 23–31.

Johnson, J. L. (2004). *Fundamentals of substance abuse practice*. Belmont, CA: Brooks/Cole, Cengage Learning.

Kelly, J. F. (2004). Toward an addictionary. *Alcoholism Treatment Quarterly*, *22*, 79–87.

Kelly, J. F., & Westerhoff, C. M. (2010). Does it matter how we refer to individuals with substance-related conditions? A randomized study of two commonly used terms. *International Journal of Drug Policy*, *21*, 202–207.

Kypri K., Voas R. B., Langley J. D., Stephenson S. C. R., Begg D. J., Tippetts A. S., & Davie G. S. (2006). Minimum purchasing age for alcohol and traffic crash injuries among 15-to 19-year-olds in New Zealand', *American Journal of Public Health*, *96*, 126–131.

Liebregts, N., van der Pol, P., van Laar, M., de Graaf, R., van den Brink, W., & Korf, D. J. (2014). The role of leisure and delinquency in frequent cannabis use and dependence trajectories among young adults. *International Journal of Drug Policy*, *26*(2), 143–152.

McClellan, A. T., Lewis, D. C., O'Brien, C. P., & Kleber, H. D. (2000). Drug dependence, a chronic medical illness: Implications for treatment, insurance, and outcomes evaluation. *Journal of the American Medical Association, 284*(13), 1689–1695.

National Research Council and the Institue of Medicine. (2014). *Investing in the health and well-being of young adults*. Washington, DC: The National Academic Press.

Patient Protection and Affordable Care Act, 42 U.S.C. § 18001 (2010).

Phillips, L. A., & Shaw, A. (2013). Substance use more stigmatized than smoking and obesity. *Journal of Substance Use, 18*, 247–253.

Plunk, A. D., Cavazaos-Rehg, P., Bierut, L. J., & Grucza, R. A. (2013). The persistent effects of minimum legal drinking age laws on drinking patterns later in life. *Alcoholism: Clinical and Experimental Research*, *37*, 463–469. doi: 10.1111/j.1530-0277.2012.01945.x

Richter, L., & Foster, S. E. (2014). Effectively addressing addiction requires changing the language of addiction. *Journal of Public Health Policy, 35*, 60–64.

Rossman, S. B., Roman, J. K., Zweig, J. M., Rempel, M., & Lindquist, C. H. (Eds.) (2011). *The multi-site adult drug court evaluation: The impact of drug courts.* Washington, DC: The Urban Institute, Justic Policy Center. Retrieved from http://www.urban.org/UploadedPDF/412357-MADCE-The-Impact-of-Drug-Courts.pdf

Satre, D. D., Mertens, J., Arean, P. A., & Weisner, C. (2003). Contrasting outcomes of older versus middle-aged and younger adult chemical dependency patients in a managed care program. *Journal of Studies on Alcohol, 64*, 520–530.

Satre, D., Mertens, J., Arean, P. A., & Weisner, C. (2004). Five-year alcohol and drug treatment outcomes of older adults versus middle-aged and younger adults in a managed care program. *Addiction, 99*(10), 1286–1297. doi: 10.111l/j.1360-0443.2004.00831.x

Sinha, R., Easton, C., & Kemp, K. (2003). Substance abuse treatment characteristics of probation-referred young adults in a community-based outpatient program. *American Journal of Drug and Alcohol Abuse, 29*(3), 585–597.

Smith, D. C., Godley, S. H., Godley, M. D., & Dennis, M. L. (2011). Adolescent community reinforcement approach outcomes differ among emerging adults and adolescents. *Journal of Substance Abuse Treatment, 41*(4), 422–430. doi: 10.1016/j.jsat.2011.06.003

Smith, D. C., Hall, J. A., Jang, M., & Arndt, S. (2009). Therapist adherence to a motivational-interviewing intervention improves treatment entry for substance misusing adolescents with low problem perception. *Journal of Studies on Alcohol and Drugs, 70*(1), 101–105.

Substance Abuse and Mental Health Services Administration. (2013). *Results from the 2012 National Survey on Drug Use and Health: Mental Health Findings*, NSDUH Series H-47, HHS Publication No. (SMA) 13-4805. Rockville, MD: Substance Abuse and Mental Health Services Administration.

United States Census Bureau. (2014). *The 2012 Statistical Abstract-Education: Higher Education: Institutions and Enrollment: College Enrollment of Recent High School Completers.* Retrieved from http://www.census.gov/compendia/statab/2012/tables/12s0277.pdf

Wakefield, J. C., & Schmitz, M. F. (2015). The harmful dysfunction model of alcohol use disorder: Revised criteria to improve the validity of diagnosis and prevalence estimates. *Addiction, 110*, 931–942.

White, W. L. (2007). Addiction recovery: Its definition and conceptual boundaries. *Journal of Substance Abuse Treatment, 33*, 229–241. doi:10.1016/j.jsat.2007.04.015

2

Emerging Adult Development and Substance Use Disorders

DOUGLAS C. SMITH, TARA M. DUMAS,
AND JORDAN P. DAVIS ■

In the first editorial of the journal *Development and Psychopathology*, editor Dante Cichetti (1989) defined the discipline of developmental psychopathology as one that applied developmental principles to the study of deviant behavior. He went on to explain that the highest priority for the field was to identify processes or mechanisms occurring in development associated with the etiology, onset, and course of disorders. The premise of this book is that there are processes occurring in emerging adulthood at the individual, family, community, and larger societal levels that influence the prevalence and features of substance use disorders. Developmental features of emerging adulthood can both be implicated in the onset of new substance use disorders and interact with other processes occurring earlier in the lifespan to exacerbate existing substance use disorders.

This chapter provides an overview of emerging adult developmental issues that may be related to substance use and substance use disorders among emerging adults. We begin by discussing the most well-known theory of emerging adulthood, developed by Jeffrey J. Arnett (2000), and then review salient risk factors for substance use disorders in emerging adulthood.

SUBSTANCE USE IN EMERGING ADULTHOOD

In today's society, we have a culturally ingrained expectation that emerging adults will experiment with alcohol and other substances as part of their journey toward adulthood. For some young people, this experimentation with alcohol and drugs is considered the emerging adult rite of passage (Arnett, 2000). This is so much the case that in 2008 a group of college administrators created the Amethyst Initiative in an attempt to lower the drinking age on college campuses, suggesting that altering binge drinking culture on college campuses was simply too formidable a task (DeJong & Blanchett, 2014). Debates rage about whether it is unhealthy to forego experimentation with substances during emerging adulthood, although some evidence shows that tee-totaling emerging adults appear to be just as emotionally healthy as those using substances moderately (Walton & Roberts, 2004). In short, experimentation with substances is typically viewed as normative for emerging adults.

Consistent with this notion, results from large nationally representative studies demonstrate that well over half (59.6%) of emerging adults in the United States consume alcohol at least monthly (Substance Abuse and Mental Health Services Administration, Center for Behavioral Health Statistics and Quality [SAMHSA], 2015). What is particularly concerning, however, is not the fact that emerging adults drink, but *how* they drink. Moderate alcohol consumption, according to the Dietary Guidelines for Americans, is defined as up to one standard drink (i.e., one 12 oz. bottle of beer, one 5 oz. glass of wine, or 1.5 oz. of spirits) for women and two standard drinks for men per sitting. Yet, during emerging adulthood, people drink over these recommended daily limits more than any other time in life. Compared to older adults (22.5%) and adolescents (6.1%), emerging adults have the highest rates of past-month binge drinking (37.7%) (SAMHSA, 2015).

In North America, *heavier* drinking is considered the norm among emerging adults; it is encouraged within their peer circles and is used as a way to appear socially desirable and to fit in with peers. With drinking among emerging adults, it is not uncommon to have social gatherings centered on consuming large amounts of alcohol—with drinking games, kegs of beer, and perhaps a trip to a local club or bar. For those of us who live among emerging adults in college towns, it is a typical occurrence to witness intoxicated, boisterous emerging adults around the downtown or campus area, on their way to and from drinking events, on almost any day of the week.

In line with this anecdotal evidence, nationally representative statistics indicate that, in 2013, almost 40% of emerging adults engaged in heavy episodic drinking (HED), or consuming a large quantity of drinks in one sitting (4+ for women and 5+ for men) at least monthly (SAMHSA, 2015), again more than any other age group. Further, about 10% of emerging adults who engaged in HED in the last month qualified as being *problematic* drinkers, engaging in HED at least five times in the past month (SAMHSA, 2015). Adolescents (1%) and older adults (ages ≥26; 6.0%) are less likely to be heavy drinkers. This type of drinking contributes to a number of social costs, such as intoxicated driving and interpersonal violence, as well as serious health outcomes, including the approximately 1,700 unintentional injury deaths among individuals ages 18–24 (Chikritzhs, Jonas, Stockwell, Heale, & Dietze, 2001; Hingson, Heeren, Winter, & Wechsler, 2005).

Furthermore, illicit drug use is highest during emerging adulthood, with 22% of 18- to 25-year-olds using an illicit substance in the past month (SAMHSA, 2015). Nationally, 6.6% of emerging adults have an illicit drug use disorder, versus only 1.9% of adults over age 26, and 2.5% of adolescents ages 12–17. Marijuana remains the most common illicitly used substance by emerging adults. At this writing, marijuana use is legal for medicinal use in approximately 30 states and full recreational use in 8 states (Marijuana Policy Project, 2017). Approximately 20% of emerging adults ages 18–25 report using marijuana in the past month. There have also been concerns in the United States surrounding the increase in heroin use. Out of the estimated 31 million emerging adults in the United States in 2013, approximately 250,000 (.08%) were past-year heroin users (SAMHSA, 2015). Although opiate use and addiction can have devastating effects, it remains much rarer among emerging adults relative to alcohol and marijuana use.

Emerging adulthood has become a particularly sensitive time for the onset of substance use disorders. The risk of experiencing a substance use disorder in emerging adulthood (16.3%) is also more than triple that in adolescence (5.0%) and double than that in older adulthood (7.1%; SAMHSA, 2015). In addition, findings from a representative U.S. sample suggest that the prevalence of alcohol use disorders, both 12-month (27%) and lifetime (37%), is highest among young adults (18- to 29-year-olds) as compared to older adults, and the rate of alcohol use disorders in young adulthood is on the rise, increasing significantly from 2001–2002 to 2012–2013 (Grant et al., 2015). Furthermore, for some emerging adults, substance use simply reflects a continuation of problematic use that started earlier in adolescence.

Given its normative nature, it might be easy to dismiss substance use, especially alcohol use, as harmless in emerging adulthood. Many people assume that young people will eventually "grow out of it." Indeed, it is easy to imagine that thriving older adults who drank heavily or experimented with other drugs during emerging adulthood would easily fall into this trap. Yet it would be erroneous to conclude that substance use is harmless for emerging adults. Even at nondiagnosable levels of substance use a myriad of negative consequences may occur for emerging adults, such as unwanted sexual experiences, poor school performance, weight gain, accidents, and increased risks for certain cancers (Callaghan, Allebeck, & Sidorchuck, 2013). These emerging adults can benefit from effective brief interventions that focus on reducing use to healthy levels. National efforts currently exist to widely disseminate such interventions and to mainstream them into primary healthcare. Once emerging adults meet diagnostic thresholds for having alcohol use disorders (see Chapter 3), roughly 30% will continue to have these disorders 3 years later (Vergés et al., 2012). These persistence rates for emerging adults are somewhat lower than for older adults (approximately 40%) for alcohol use disorders, but are similar for illicit drug use disorders (Vergés et al., 2013). Thus we need to be wary of expecting emerging adults to "grow out" of problems once they have met diagnostic thresholds (see Chapter 3), as substance use disorders are as persistent for emerging adults as they are for older adults.

What theories then, can account for this higher substance use among emerging adults? The following sections describe theoretical perspectives on emerging adult substance use, which we critique for their explanatory utility.

ARNETT'S EMERGING ADULTHOOD THEORY AND ITS RELEVANCE TO SUBSTANCE USE BEHAVIOR

In 2000, Jeffrey J. Arnett introduced his theory of emerging adulthood via a publication in *American Psychologist*, which has since been cited over 8,000 times. In his theory, Arnett emphasizes that the age period between 18 and 25 years of age represents a developmentally distinct period of life (Arnett, 2000). Arnett felt it important to distinguish this period of life from young adulthood partly because individuals in both these age groups (and society) tend to not perceive themselves as adults but rather as *moving toward* adulthood. Thus Arnett coined the term *emerging adulthood* to refer to the period in between adolescence and adulthood. Arnett further elaborated on five major themes that help to characterize and distinguish this developmental stage from other periods of life: (1) identity exploration, (2) experimentation and (feelings of endless) possibilities, (3) feeling in between, (4) being self-focused (and thus less other-focused), and (5) negativity and instability. In later writings, Arnett and his colleagues speculated on how these five facets of emerging adulthood serve to explain increased substance use during this period of life (Arnett, 2005; Sussman & Arnett, 2014). In the discussion that follows, we elaborate on Arnett's propositions and describe research that has tested these claims.

First, Arnett emphasized that emerging adulthood is a time of *identity explorations*—a time when it is culturally accepted to postpone adoption of more adult responsibilities (e.g., jobs, marriage, children) to explore oneself, where one fits in, and where one is going in life. This may manifest in extended periods of education, travel, or, as Arnett proposed, substance use. Arnett believes that emerging adults might engage in substance use as a form of identity exploration, a way of trying new things and gaining new experiences. On a similar note, Arnett proposed that emerging adulthood is a time of feeling-in-between. Indeed, most individuals in this developmental period tend to perceive themselves not yet as "full adults" (Arnett, 2003). Without the responsibilities associated with later stages of life, and with a culture that emphasizes personal exploration and growth as the most important psychosocial task for emerging adulthood, this period of time becomes one of heightened self-focus (and, thus, less other-focus). Arnett argues that in no other time in life do individuals have more personal freedom and lack of responsibility; emerging adults lack both the parental oversight characteristic of adolescence and the structure provided by family responsibilities in adulthood. With few people depending on them, Arnett argued, emerging adults have more freedom to engage in substance use and can rationalize certain substance use behaviors more than people of other ages (e.g., older adults who are needed at home to care for their families). On top of this, Arnett proposed that the increased optimism and positive expectations for life that are associated with emerging adulthood (Weinstein, 1989) may make emerging adults overconfident in their ability to use substances without negative consequences and to quit or reduce their use once this period of life is over.

Additionally, Arnett hypothesized that substance use among emerging adults occurs in response to developmental stressors resulting from the *instability* characteristic of this time in life—with many emerging adults experiencing multiple transitions in work, school, romantic relationships, and residence. Moreover, because identity development—or the task of arriving at a coherent, well-explored self-definition—can often be an arduous task, Arnett felt that some emerging adults may engage in substance use as a way to lessen the stress associated with this process and the associated identity confusion.

Research Support for Emerging Adult Theory

Many studies have tested associations between Arnett's five features of emerging adulthood and substance use. Nelson and Barry (2005) compared individuals ($n = 232$, mean age = 21) who identified as self-perceived adults to their emerging adult counterparts, finding that those who felt they hadn't reached adulthood engaged in more frequent drinking to intoxication. Overall, nearly 70% of individuals reported they had reached adulthood "in some ways but not in others." More recently, several studies have used Reiffman, Arnett, and Colwell's (2007) Inventory of Dimension of Emerging Adulthood (IDEA) to predict substance use (see Table 2.1). Results from these studies are mixed and demonstrate various associations between IDEA scores and substance use. For example, Allem, Lisha, Soto, Baezconde-Garbanati, and Unger (2013) investigated the association between emerging adulthood dimensions and role transitions on alcohol and marijuana use among 1,390 Hispanic emerging adults. Participants were part of a larger longitudinal study (Project RED; Lorenzo-Blanco, Unger, Baezconde-Garbanati, Ritt-Olson, & Soto, 2012) and were assessed during adolescence and again during emerging adulthood. Substance use in adolescence was used as a predictor of role transitions (e.g., marriage, job, having a child, loss of relationship). Individuals who felt as though emerging adulthood was a time of focusing on others were less likely to report marijuana use and less likely to engage in binge drinking in the past month. No other dimensions were significantly associated with substance use. Baggio, Iglesias, Studer, and Gmel (2015) assessed the psychometric properties of a short, 8-item version of the IDEA among 5,223 emerging adults entering the Swiss National Military. To assess the validity of the short version, participants were split into two groups, with one receiving the IDEA-31 and the other receiving the IDEA-8. Scoring higher on either IDEA measure was associated with more risky single-occasion drinking ($r = .058 - .062$, $p < .001$), hazardous cannabis use ($r = .047 - .057$, $p < .001$), use of illicit drugs ($r = .065 - .078$, $p < .001$), alcohol dependence ($r = .124 - .158$, $p < .001$), and cannabis use disorder ($r = .125 - .131$, $p < .001$).

To date, only one study has investigated the dimensions of emerging adulthood and its association with substance use in a clinical sample. Smith, Bahar, Cleeland, and Davis (2014) recruited 105 emerging adults screened for substance use problems in a not-for-profit community setting. The sample was diverse in terms of

Table 2.1. Inventory of Dimensions of Emerging Adulthood (IDEA)

Is this period of your life a . . .	Strongly Disagree (1)	Somewhat Disagree (2)	Somewhat Agree (3)	Strongly Agree (4)
1. time of many possibilities?				
2. time of exploration?				
3. time of confusion?				
4. time of experimentation?				
5. time of personal freedom?				
6. time of feeling restricted?				
7. time of responsibility for yourself?				
8. time of feeling stressed out?				
9. time of instability?				
10. time of optimism?				
11. time of high pressure?				
12. time of finding out who you are?				
13. time of settling down?				
14. time of responsibility for others?				
15. time of independence?				
16. time of open choices?				
17. time of unpredictability?				
18. time of commitments to others?				

(continued)

Table 2.1. CONTINUED

Is this period of your life a . . .	Strongly Disagree (1)	Somewhat Disagree (2)	Somewhat Agree (3)	Strongly Agree (4)
19. time of self-sufficiency?				
20. time of many worries?				
21. time of trying out new things?				
22. time of focusing on yourself?				
23. time of separating from parents?				
24. time of defining yourself?				
25. time of planning for the future?				
26. time of seeking a sense of meaning?				
27. time of deciding on your own beliefs and values?				
28. time of learning to think for yourself?				
29. time of feeling adult in some ways but not others?				
30. time of gradually becoming an adult?				
31. time of being not sure whether you have reached full adulthood?				

NOTE: The instrument instructions are as follows: "First, please think about *this time in your life*. By 'time in your life,' we are referring to the *present* time, *plus* the *last few years* that have gone by, and the *next few years* to come, as you see them. In short, you should think about a roughly five-year period, with the present time right in the middle."

SOURCE: http://www.webpages.ttu.edu/areifman/IDEA_instrument.htm. Reprinted with permission of the author.

race/ethnicity (>45% non-White), income (past 90-day income = $2,657), and educational status (3% enrolled in school). None of the dimensions of emerging adulthood were associated with substance frequency (e.g., days of use). However, feeling in-between was positively associated with substance-related problems.

Some studies posit that emerging adults may have less motivation for treatment as they associate their substance use as "normative" and in line with what they are "supposed" to be doing (Arnett, 2005). This notion of normative risky behaviors is in line with two of Arnett's dimensions—identity exploration and experimentation. Goodman, Henderson, Peterson-Badali, and Goldstein (2015) recruited 164 treatment-referred emerging adults. Those who reported being more other-focused, or having a life that was more directed at responsibility for others, were more likely to report intrinsic reasons for seeking treatment. Interestingly, individuals who reported feeling more in-between were more likely to report seeking treatment for introjected reasons (e.g., entering treatment due to feelings of guilt or shame). Emerging adults were more likely to seek treatment if they reported emerging adulthood as a time of more self-focus and experimentation. In subsequent multivariate analyses, the only dimension associated with both identified and introjected motivation to enter treatment was being other-focused.

In summary, research on Arnett's (2005) emerging adult dimensions produces mixed findings, with feeling in between and other-focus being the most consistent correlates of substance use and treatment motivation (Allem et al., 2013; Goodman et al., 2015; Smith et al., 2014). Additionally, Baggio et al. (2015) found that composite scores on the IDEA-8 were associated with more substance use. Thus, although Arnett's emerging adulthood theory is well known and his hypotheses about how the dimensions of emerging adulthood would increase substance use (Arnett, 2005, Sussman & Arnett, 2014), additional research is needed.

We make three recommendations for future lines of inquiry. First, these inconsistent findings could indicate that Arnett's hypotheses (2005) are more applicable to substance use initiated during emerging adulthood. Many emerging adults in substance use disorder treatment (61%) use substances before age 15 (Dennis, White, & Ives, 2009), with approximately 4 1/2 years of use prior to treatment entry (Smith, Godley, Godley, & Dennis, 2011). Thus, causal explanations of use should focus on how age of onset interacts with features of emerging adulthood. Second, we should improve the measurement of the dimensions of emerging adulthood. Across studies noted earlier, internal consistency (α) values for the IDEA range from 0.58 to 0.88. Additionally, the items on the IDEA are very general and the instructions ask people to consider a 5-year period of life when formulating their responses (see Table 2.1). Thus, younger emerging adults could be responding to items on the basis of their adolescent experiences. To address these potential measurement issues, Smith, Davis, and Dumas (2016) developed the Emerging Adult Reasons for Substance Use (EARS) measure, finding some initial evidence that the subscales discriminate between emerging and older adults and correlate with substance use (see Table 2.2) Finally, we need a richer understanding of whether biological, intrapersonal, or environmental processes explain associations between emerging adult status and substance use. For example, personality

Table 2.2. EMERGING ADULT REASONS FOR SUBSTANCE USE (EARS)

You use substances because . . .	Strongly Disagree	Disagree	Neutral	Agree	Strongly Agree
1. At your age, you can do what you want.	1	2	3	4	5
2. At your age, you can make your own decisions.	1	2	3	4	5
3. You think substance use is a rite of passage.	1	2	3	4	5
4. It won't throw your life off track.	1	2	3	4	5
5. At your age, substance use does not hurt other people.	1	2	3	4	5
6. You are in no rush to grow up.	1	2	3	4	5
7. It is what people your age are supposed to do before they grow up.	1	2	3	4	5
8. You don't have many serious responsibilities in life.	1	2	3	4	5
9. You're not ready to settle down yet.	1	2	3	4	5
10. You are getting all your partying done before you start a family.	1	2	3	4	5
11. It will not affect your future.	1	2	3	4	5
12. You have a lot of free time.	1	2	3	4	5

Table 2.2. Continued

You use substances because . . .	Strongly Disagree	Disagree	Neutral	Agree	Strongly Agree
13. You've been through a lot of changes recently in housing, relationships and jobs.	1	2	3	4	5
14. Things are changing so fast during this time of your life.	1	2	3	4	5
15. This part of your life is a difficult period of time.	1	2	3	4	5
16. There are few people who depend on you at this point in your life.	1	2	3	4	5
17. You are focusing on your wants and needs.	1	2	3	4	5
18. This is just a phase.	1	2	3	4	5
19. Nothing bad will happen.	1	2	3	4	5
20. There won't be any long-term consequences.	1	2	3	4	5
21. There hasn't been a lot of consistency during this time of your life.	1	2	3	4	5
22. You don't feel stable at this age.	1	2	3	4	5
23. So many things are "up in the air" during this stage of your life.	1	2	3	4	5

(continued)

Table 2.2. CONTINUED

You use substances because . . .	Strongly Disagree	Disagree	Neutral	Agree	Strongly Agree
24. It helps you to lessen the strain from trying to figure out what you want in your life.	1	2	3	4	5
25. It helps you take your mind off of the pressures of making choices about the future.	1	2	3	4	5
26. It is stressful to explore what you want your life to be like.	1	2	3	4	5
27. It's overwhelming to sort out all your choices in life.	1	2	3	4	5
28. You don't know what to expect in your future.	1	2	3	4	5
29. You are not a "full" adult yet.	1	2	3	4	5
30. Because you won't have a chance to do this when you're older.	1	2	3	4	5
31. Because it won't be acceptable for you to do this when you're older.	1	2	3	4	5

NOTE: Instructions given to participants are as follows: "Below is a list of reasons people sometimes give for drinking alcohol and using other drugs. Thinking of times you drink or use drugs, how much would you agree or disagree with each of the following reasons for your substance use?"

trait associations with age are different after controlling for IDEA scores (Roberts and Davis, 2016). Also, Gates, Corbin, and Fromme (2016) found that the associations between some IDEA scales and substance use were diminished when adding impulsivity and sensation seeking measures.

RELATED DEVELOPMENTAL THEORIES AND CRITICISMS OF ARNETT

Role Overload Theory

The negativity/instability subscale on the IDEA measures perceived instability. That is, it contains items such as "Is this time of your life a time of instability?" and "a time of high pressure." Arnett's (2005) hypotheses on the association between the number of work, residential, and romantic transitions (i.e., instability) and substance use are grounded in prior theory suggesting that coping resources may be inadequate in the presences of an increasing number of changes. Coping motives for substance use clearly predict emerging adults' progression of substance use (Van der Pol et al., 2013) and mediate the association between social anxiety and alcohol use for emerging adults (Clerkin, Werntz, Magee, Lindgren, & Teachman, 2014). However, it is unclear if developmentally induced instability as conceptualized by Arnett (2005) places a strain on emerging adults' coping responses and results in higher substance use.

Schulenberg, O'Malley, Bachman, and Johnston (2005) tested whether emerging adult instability, measured by a higher number of transitions by ages 19 and 20, predicted future emerging adult substance use. Emerging adults with the most transitions had the greatest decline in substance use, and the authors noted that the specific patterns and types of transitions may be more important than the sheer number of changes implicated in the instability–coping model. Better differentiation of types of emerging adult instability is also needed because instability may vary by socioeconomic status. For example, housing changes most frequently described in support of Arnett's emerging adult theory (2000) are associated with leaving home and going to college, switching apartments frequently prior to home ownership, or picking up and moving to a new region of the country as part of one's identity explorations. Instability for emerging adults who are living in poverty may include brushes with homelessness or moving to different cities where social welfare benefits may be better. Emerging adult instability may influence substance use, but through different mechanisms, depending on the type of instability.

Life Course Theory

One major critique of Arnett's theory is that it applies mainly to emerging adults in industrialized countries in the current sociopolitical era. Life course theory emphasizes that development occurs in a macro-historical context (Shanahan, Miech, & Elder Jr., 1998). Thus developmental theories explaining substance use among contemporary emerging adults would be remiss not to consider how contemporary society influences development. For example, longitudinal epidemiological studies show that while the general increase in substance use during the late teens and early 20s transcends generational cohorts, the amounts of substance use were higher in the late 1970s than in the 1980s and early 1990s (Schulenberg et al., 2005). So clearly, historical and macro-level influences can affect emerging adult substance use.

Perceived disapproval of substance use seems to vary across generations and is one predictor of increased prevalence of substance use. Although liberalization of marijuana policy has not yet impacted disapproval of marijuana use or prevalence of marijuana use among adolescents, marijuana use disapproval decreased significantly among emerging adults from 2002 to 2013 (Hasin et al., 2015; Salas-Wright, Vaughn, Todic, Córdova, & Perron, 2015). Specifically, whereas 40.5% of emerging adults strongly disapproved of marijuana use in 2002, only 22.6% did so in 2013 (Salas-Wright et al., 2015). It is currently unclear how state laws on medical or recreational use will impact perceived disapproval. One major problem in determining this is that states that have enacted more liberal policies had higher prevalence of use and approval for marijuana use before passing these state referenda. Nevertheless, the historical context of when one becomes an emerging adult may influence substance use either through shifts in legislation or massive public health campaigns that raise awareness about dangers of certain substances.

One informative and amusing list of such influences is the annual Mindset List, published by Beloit College. It lists popular culture references and historical events that may or may not have been experienced by the incoming freshman class. The Class of 2019 Beloit College Mindset list has several interesting historical references, such as "They have never licked a postage stamp" and "The therapeutic use of marijuana has always been legal in a growing number of American states." The current rendition also notes some interesting alcohol and drug references used by current emerging adults, such as "dankrupt," or out of weed, and "slurring 'textroverts'," or people who text nonsensical messages when under the influence (Mindset Lists of American History, 2017).

The current liberalization of drug policy in the United States and rapid developments in mobile technology are but two societal-level factors that may influence emerging adult substance use. For example, very soon, American emerging adults will never have lived in a world with the original twin towers of the World Trade Center, which were demolished in terrorist attacks on September 11, 2001. In 2014, there remain approximately three-quarters of a million emerging adults in active-duty and reserve units, and 37% of all active-duty military personnel are emerging adults (Federal Interagency Forum on Child and Family Statistics, 2014). Finally, emerging adults of the late 2000s coped with the economic downturn of the Great Recession. The recession was associated with increases in binge drinking, especially among unmarried and unemployed White emerging adults (Bor, Basu, Coutts, McKee, & Stuckler, 2013).

In summary, multiple historical factors occurring during one's period of emerging adulthood are likely to influence substance use.

BIOLOGICAL AND INTRAPERSONAL INFLUENCES

Biological Explanations for Substance Use

A number of biological processes likely interact with environmental influences of substance use in emerging adulthood. Here we focus on brain development and genetic predisposition toward substance use.

Brain development processes during adolescence and emerging adulthood may partially explain why substance use and substance use disorders are common in emerging adulthood. Adolescents may be particularly sensitive to the rewarding properties of substances (i.e., dopaminergic system). Plus, the area of the brain associated with risk-taking behavior and goal-directed behavior (i.e., frontal cortex) continually matures throughout emerging adulthood. For example, emerging adults ages 23–25 have more frontal cortex activation during a neurocognitive task than emerging adults ages 18–19 (Veroude, Jolles, Croiset, & Krabbendam, 2013). The brain development hypothesis may explain why early onset of substance use in adolescence consistently confers greater risk for substance dependence and related problems during emerging adulthood (Hingson, Heeren, Zakocs, Winter, & Wechsler, 2003). For example, Weiland and colleagues (2014) found that emerging adults were more likely to have smaller frontal gray matter volume if they experienced an early-adolescent onset of substance use, had substance-related problems by age 17, or had a history of externalizing behavior in adolescence. Findings held even when controlling for family history of substance use and current use as an emerging adult. Additionally, Price et al. (2015) found that emerging adults' past-year marijuana use was associated with smaller medial orbitofrontal cortex volumes.

In general, researchers measuring brain volume or activity use small sample sizes and fail to use longitudinal designs. We cannot currently discern under what circumstances frontal lobe maturity is a risk factor for emerging adult onset of substance use disorders or simply a byproduct of use that was already initiated earlier during adolescence. Against this backdrop, the U.S. National Institutes of Health (NIH) is currently funding a study called the Adolescent Brain and Cognitive Development Study (ABCD) that will provide the largest sample ($n = 10,000$) of preadolescent brain images and complete follow-up testing through emerging adulthood.

Some individuals simply have a higher genetic predisposition for developing substance use disorders regardless of age. However, we are learning much more about the circumstances under which such genetic risk is heightened for emerging adults. Early-adolescent onset of substance use combined with a particular dopamine transporter genotype predicted substance use during emerging adulthood (Schmid et al., 2009). Furthermore, when comparing co-twins discordant for college attendance, those who went to college were found to have higher heavy alcohol consumption (Slutske et al., 2004). As twins have the same genetic liability for substance use, this suggests that environmental influences, and college attendance specifically, may moderate the genetic expression of alcohol use behaviors and associated problems for emerging adults.

Self-Medication of Negative Affective States

Whereas Arnett's (2005) hypotheses implicate coping to deal with numerous life transitions during emerging adulthood, there is a long history of conceptualizing maladaptive substance use as a response to underlying psychopathology regardless of the developmental challenges within a life stage. Stone, Becker, Huber, and Catalano's (2012) review concluded that there is robust evidence to suggest that early signs of externalizing behavior (i.e., delinquency, aggression, conduct disorder) are associated with emerging adult substance use. In their review, internalizing disorders were inconsistent predictors of emerging adult substance use in prospective longitudinal research.

Notwithstanding the lack of clarity on causality, emerging adults reporting that they use for emotional coping typically exhibit higher psychopathology. For example, marijuana-using emerging adults that used it to cope with negative affect had higher psychopathology than that of both non-users and marijuana users who used primarily for social reasons. Emerging adults with social anxiety have also reported using substances more for coping-related reasons than for social reasons (Buckner, Bonn-Miller, Zvolensky, & Schmidt, 2007). Coping motives also explained the association between depression and alcohol use among college students (Gonzalez, Reynolds, & Skewes, 2011). Importantly, in one study a reduction in coping-related use partially explained the association between age-related decreases in neuroticism and alcohol use from age 18 to age 35 (Littlefield, Sher, & Wood, 2010).

Religiosity

One's level of religiosity is also frequently implicated as a protective factor against emerging adult substance use or substance use disorders (Stone et al., 2012) and can provide a buffer against increases in drinking during the transition from high school to college (White et al., 2006). In fact, one meta-analysis found that religiosity was a stronger protective factor against substance use for emerging adults than for adolescents (Yonker, Schnabelrauch, & DeHaan, 2012).

However, religiosity may operate differently, depending on other factors. For example, one study showed that heterosexual emerging adults higher on religiosity were less likely to binge drink or use marijuana, but this was not the case for emerging adults who identified as sexual minorities (Rostosky, Danner, & Riggle,

2007). Subsequent analyses revealed that religiosity was protective for all emerging adult men, regardless of sexuality, as well as for heterosexual females. However, for lesbian females, high religiosity predicted higher alcohol use and heavy episodic drinking (Rostosky, Danner, & Riggle, 2010). For African-Americans emerging adults, however, religiosity predicts lower substance use, with the effects mediated through drug refusal self-efficacy, or the ability to assertively decline a substance use offer (Nasim, Utsey, Corona, & Belgrave, 2006). The effects of religiosity on emerging adults' substance-using behaviors are well documented and likely vary depending on other factors.

ENVIRONMENTAL INFLUENCES

Peers

Emerging adults' peers exert significant influence on their alcohol- and other substance-using behaviors (Andrews, Tildesley, Hops, & Li, 2002). Peer influences are likely bidirectional, as individuals with a higher propensity toward drinking are likely to select pro-substance-using peers (i.e., homophily), who, in turn, influence their substance use. For example, drinking prior to college entry predicted the presence of more pro-drinking peers in the first semester of college, which then predicted subsequent drinking (White, Fleming, Kim, Catalano, & McMorris, 2008). Peer risks, however, are complex and may depend on the context or the individual's liability for developing a substance use problem. For example, peer alcohol use in high school predicted alcohol use in emerging adulthood, but peer alcohol use during emerging adulthood only predicted alcohol use in one's 30s among individuals with the long allele of the DRD4 dopamine receptor gene (Mrug & Windle, 2014).

Regardless of the mechanisms or individual liability, it would be erroneous to ignore the role of peers on emerging adults' drinking and drug use behavior. The network density of peers who approve of and use alcohol or drugs regularly is typically related to emerging adults' drinking behaviors in both college (Borsari & Carey, 2001) and non-college samples (Lau-Barraco & Collins, 2011). Interestingly, these associations may not be limited to an emerging adults' local peer networks, as substance use by their online peers is also associated with their substance use (Cook, Bauermeister, Gordon-Messer, & Zimmerman, 2013). Clinical scientists are currently translating these findings into clinical models that integrate peers, into treatment models for emerging adults.

College Attendance

Attending college appears to confer risk for drinking. As noted, co-twins who attended college attendance drank more, indicating that the college environment predicted heavy drinking even after accounting for genetic predisposition (Slutske et al., 2004). As emerging adults in college settings are surrounded by similarly aged peers and live in communities that may have lax alcohol control policies (Nelson, Naimi, Brewer, & Wechsler, 2005), it is not surprising that college attendance is a risk factor for heavy drinking.

Parental Use and Parental Disapproval

Parental substance use is clearly related to substance use by emerging adults. Emerging adults whose parents have alcohol use disorders had an elevated risk for substance use disorders themselves (Chassin, Pitts, DeLucia, & Todd, 1999). However, the mechanisms through which parental alcoholism elevates risks for substance use during emerging adulthood are unclear. For example, the effects of parental alcoholism on emerging adults' substance use were largely mediated by behavioral under-control and parenting (King & Chassin, 2004).

In the United States, we have cultural ambivalence about how much of an active role parents should take in their emerging adult children's lives. Nonetheless, parenting practices during emerging adulthood appear to be associated with substance use. Maternal knowledge of their emerging adults' daily activities was associated with less substance use by emerging adults (Padilla-Walker, Nelson, Madsen, & Barry, 2008). Emotional closeness and support from parents was associated with less heavy drinking, both when initially measured during emerging adulthood and 5 years later (Serido, Lawry, Li, Conger, & Russell, 2014). Furthermore, in one study, emerging adults in substance use disorder treatment indicated that they had less interpersonal pressure to quit using than did adolescents, which was mediated by the number of days of being in trouble with one's family due to substance use (Smith, Cleeland, & Dennis, 2010). This could indicate a gradual decrease in parental sanctions for emerging adult substance use relative to adolescent substance use.

SUMMARY AND CONCLUSIONS

There are a number of explanations for emerging adults using substances more than any other age group. Research has produced mixed findings on Arnett's (2005) hypotheses about the developmental features of emerging adulthood that are associated with substance use. At the same time, Arnett's (2000, 2005) theory and hypotheses are spurring new research on emerging adult substance use. As no single theory is likely to account for all substance use within this developmental period, the next generation of research will need to examine the complex interplay of processes occurring both before and during emerging adulthood.

REFERENCES

Allem, J. P., Lisha, N. E., Soto, D. W., Baezconde-Garbanati, L., & Unger, J. B. (2013). Emerging adulthood themes, role transitions and substance use among Hispanics in Southern California. *Addictive Behaviors, 38*(12), 2797–2800.

Andrews, J. A., Tildesley, E., Hops, H., & Li, F. (2002). The influence of peers on young adult substance use. *Health Psychology, 21*(4), 349–357.

Arnett, J. J. (2000). Emerging adulthood: A theory of development from the late teens through the twenties. *American Psychologist, 55*(5), 469–480.

Arnett, J. J. (2003). Conceptions of the transiton to adulthood among emerging adults in American ethnic groups. *New Directions in Child and Adolescent Development, 100,* 63–75.

Arnett, J. J. (2005). The developmental context of substance use in emerging adulthood. *Journal of Drug Issues, 35,* 235–254.

Baggio, S., Iglesias, K., Studer, J., & Gmel, G. (2015). An 8-item short form of the Inventory of Dimensions of Emerging Adulthood (IDEA) among young Swiss men. *Evaluation & the Health Professions, 38*(2), 246–254.

Bor, J., Basu, S., Coutts, A., McKee, M., & Stuckler, D. (2013). Alcohol use during the Great Recession of 2008–2009. *Alcohol and Alcoholism, 48,* 343–348.

Borsari, B., & Carey, K. B. (2001). Peer influences on college drinking: A review of the research. *Journal of Substance Abuse, 13*(4), 391–424.

Buckner, J. D., Bonn-Miller, M. O., Zvolensky, M. J., & Schmidt, N. B. (2007). Marijuana use motives and social anxiety among marijuana-using young adults. *Addictive Behaviors, 32*(10), 2238–2252.

Callaghan, R. C., Allebeck, P., & Sidorchuk, A. (2013). Marijuana use and risk of lung cancer: A 40-year cohort study. *Cancer Causes & Control, 24*(10), 1811–1820.

Chassin, L., Pitts, S. C., DeLucia, C., & Todd, M. (1999). A longitudinal study of children of alcoholics: Predicting young adult substance use disorders, anxiety, and depression. *Journal of Abnormal Psychology, 108*(1), 106–119.

Chikritzhs, T. N., Jonas, H. A., Stockwell, T. R., Heale, P. F., & Dietze, P. M. (2001). Mortality and life-years lost due to alcohol: A comparison of acute and chronic causes. *Medical Journal of Australia, 174*(6), 281–284.

Cicchetti, D. (1989). Developmental psychopathology: Some thoughts on its evolution. *Development and Psychopathology, 1*(01), 1–4.

Clerkin, E. M., Werntz, A., Magee, J., Lindgren, K. P., & Teachman, B. (2014). Evaluating age differences in coping motives as a mediator of the link between social anxiety symptom and alcohol problems. *Psychology of Addictive Behaviors, 28,* 880–886.

Cook, S. H., Bauermeister, J. A., Gordon-Messer, D., & Zimmerman, M. A. (2013). Online network influences on emerging adults' alcohol and drug use. *Journal of Youth and Adolescence, 42*(11), 1674–1686.

DeJong, W., & Blanchette, J. (2014). Case closed: Research evidence on the positive public health impact of the age 21 minimum legal drinking age in the United States. *Journal of Studies on Alcohol and Drugs, Supplement,* (s17), 108–115.

Dennis, M. L., White, M. K., & Ives, M. L. (2009). Individual characteristics and needs associated with substance misuse of adolescents and young adults in addiction treatment. In C. G. Leukefeld, T. P. Gullotta, & M. Staton-Tindall (Eds.). *Adolescent* substance abuse: Evidence-based approaches to prevention and treatment (pp. 45–72) New York: Springer.

Federal Interagency Forum on Child and Family Statistics. (2014). America's Young Adults: Special Issue, 2014. Washington, DC: U.S. Government Printing Office. Retreived from http://www.childstats.gov/pubs/pubs.asp?PlacementID=2&SlpgID=27

Gates, J. R., Corbin, W. R., & Fromme, K. (2016). Emerging adult identity development, alcohol use, and alcohol-related problems during the transition out of college. Psychology of Addictive Behaviors, 30(3), 345–355.

Gonzalez, V. M., Reynolds, B., & Skewes, M. C. (2011). Role of impulsivity in the relationship between depression and alcohol problems among emerging adult college drinkers. Experimental and Clinical Psychopharmacology, 19(4), 303–313.

Goodman, I., Henderson, J., Peterson-Badali, M., & Goldstein, A. L. (2015). The relationship between psychosocial features of emerging adulthood and substance use change motivation in youth. Journal of Substance Abuse Treatment, 52, 58–66.

Grant, B. F., Goldstein, R. B., Saha, T. D., Chou, S. P., Jung, J., Zhang, H., . . . Hasin, D. S. (2015). Epidemiology of DSM-5 alcohol use disorder: Results from the National Epidemiologic Survey on Alcohol and Related Conditions III. JAMA Psychiatry, 72(8), 757–766.

Hasin, D. S., Wall, M., Keyes, K. M., Cerdá, M., Schulenberg, J., O'Malley, P. M., . . . Feng, T. (2015). Medical marijuana laws and adolescent marijuana use in the USA from 1991 to 2014: Results from annual, repeated cross-sectional surveys. Lancet Psychiatry, 2, 601–608.

Hingson, R., Heeren, T., Winter, M., & Wechsler, H. (2005). Magnitude of alcohol-related mortality and morbidity among US college students ages 18–24: Changes from 1998 to 2001. Annual Review of Public Health, 26, 259–279.

Hingson, R., Heeren, T., Zakocs, R., Winter, M., & Wechsler, H. (2003). Age of first intoxication, heavy drinking, driving after drinking and risk of unintentional injury among US college students. Journal of Studies on Alcohol, 64(1), 23–31.

King, K. M., & Chassin, L. (2004). Mediating and moderated effects of adolescent behavioral undercontrol and parenting in the prediction of drug use disorders in emerging adulthood. Psychology of Addictive Behaviors, 18(3), 239–249.

Lau-Barraco, C., & Collins, R. L. (2011). Social networks and alcohol use among nonstudent emerging adults: A preliminary study. Addictive Behaviors, 36(1), 47–54.

Littlefield, A. K., Sher, K. J., & Wood, P. K. (2010). Do changes in drinking motives mediate the relation between personality change and "maturing out" of problem drinking? Journal of Abnormal Psychology, 119(1), 93–105.

Lorenzo-Blanco, E. I., Unger, J. B., Baezconde-Garbanati, L., Ritt-Olson, A., & Soto, D. (2012). Acculturation, enculturation, and symptoms of depression in Hispanic youth: The roles of gender, Hispanic cultural values, and family functioning. Journal of Youth and Adolescence, 41(10), 1350–1365.

Marijuana Policy Project. (2017). State policy. Retrieved from https://www.mpp.org/states/

Mindset Lists of American History. (2017). The Beloit College mindset list: Class of 2019 (Born 1997!). Retrieved from http://themindsetlist.com/2015/08/the-beloit-college-mindset-list-class-of-2019-born-1997/

Mrug, S., & Windle, M. (2014). DRD4 and susceptibility to peer influence on alcohol use from adolescence to adulthood. Drug and Alcohol Dependence, 145, 168–173.

Nasim, A., Utsey, S. O., Corona, R., & Belgrave, F. Z. (2006). Religiosity, refusal efficacy, and substance use among African-American adolescents and young adults. *Journal of Ethnicity in Substance Abuse, 5*(3), 29–49.

Nelson, L. J., & Barry, C. M. (2005). Distinguishing features of emerging adulthood the role of self-classification as an adult. *Journal of Adolescent Research, 20*(2), 242–262.

Nelson, T. F., Naimi, T. S., Brewer, R. D., & Wechsler, H. (2005). The state sets the rate: The relationship among state-specific college binge drinking, state binge drinking rates, and selected state alcohol control policies. *American Journal of Public Health, 95*(3), 441–446.

Padilla-Walker, L. M., Nelson, L. J., Madsen, S. D., & Barry, C. M. (2008). The role of perceived parental knowledge on emerging adults' risk behaviors. *Journal of Youth and Adolescence, 37*(7), 847–859.

Price, J. S., McQueeny, T., Shollenbarger, S., Browning, E. L., Wieser, J., & Lisdahl, K. M. (2015). Effects of marijuana use on prefrontal and parietal volumes and cognition in emerging adults. *Psychopharmacology, 232*(16), 2939–2950.

Reifman, A., Arnett, J. J., & Colwell, M. J. (2007). Emerging adulthood: Theory, assessment, and application. *Journal of Youth Development, 2,* 1–12. Retrieved from http://jyd.pitt.edu/ojs/jyd/article/view/359

Roberts, B. W., & Davis, J. P. (2016). Young adulthood is the crucible of personality development. *Emerging Adulthood, 4*(5), 318–326.

Rostosky, S. S., Danner, F., & Riggle, E. D. (2007). Is religiosity a protective factor against substance use in young adulthood? Only if you're straight! *Journal of Adolescent Health, 40*(5), 440–447.

Rostosky, S. S., Danner, F., & Riggle, E. D. (2010). Religiosity as a protective factor against heavy episodic drinking (HED) in heterosexual, bisexual, gay, and lesbian young adults. *Journal of Homosexuality, 57*(8), 1039–1050.

Salas-Wright, C. P., Vaughn, M. G., Todic, J., & Córdova, D. (2015). Trends in the disapproval and use of marijuana among adolescents and young adults in the United States: 2002–2013. *American Journal of Drug and Alcohol Abuse, 41,* 392–404.

Schmid, B., Blomeyer, D., Becker, K., Treutlein, J., Zimmermann, U. S., Buchmann, A. F., . . . & Laucht, M. (2009). The interaction between the dopamine transporter gene and age at onset in relation to tobacco and alcohol use among 19-year-olds. *Addiction Biology, 14*(4), 489–499.

Schulenberg, J., O'Malley, P. M., Bachman, J. G., & Johnston, L. D. (2005). Early adult transitions and their relation to well-being and substance use. In R. A. Settersten, Jr., F. F. Furstenberg, Jr., & R. G. Rubén (Eds.), *On the frontier of adulthood: Theory, research, and public policy* (pp. 417–453). Chicago: University of Chicago Press.

Serido, J., Lawry, C., Li, G., Conger, K. J., & Russell, S. T. (2014). The associations of financial stress and parenting support factors with alcohol behaviors during young adulthood. *Journal of Family and Economic Issues, 35*(3), 339–350.

Shanahan, M. J., Miech, R. A., & Elder Jr., G. H. (1998). Changing pathways to attainment in men's lives: Historical patterns of school, work, and social class. *Social Forces, 77*(1), 231–256.

Slutske, W. S., Hunt-Carter, E. E., Nabors-Oberg, R. E., Sher, K. J., Bucholz, K. K., Madden, P. A., . . . Heath, A. C. (2004). Do college students drink more than their non-college-attending peers? Evidence from a population-based longitudinal female twin study. *Journal of Abnormal Psychology, 113*(4), 530.

Smith, D. C., Bahar, O.S., Cleeland, L. R., & Davis, J. P. (2014). Self-perceived emerging adult status and substance use. *Psychology of Addictive Behaviors, 28,* 935–941. doi: 10.1037/a0035900

Smith, D. C., Cleeland, L., & Dennis, M. L. (2010). Reasons for quitting among emerging adults and adolescents in substance-use-disorder treatment. *Journal of Studies on Alcohol and Drugs, 71*(3), 400–409.

Smith, D. C., Davis, J. P., & Dumas, T. M. (2016). What's development got to do with it? A new measure of emerging adults motives for substance use. *Alcoholism Clinical and Experimental Research, 40,* 247A.

Smith, D. C., Godley, S. H., Godley, M. D., & Dennis, M. L. (2011) Adolescent Community Reinforcement Approach (A-CRA) outcomes differ among emerging adults and adolescents. *Journal of Substance Abuse Treatment, 41,* 422–430.

Stone, A. L., Becker, L. G., Huber, A. M., & Catalano, R. F. (2012). Review of risk and protective factors of substance use and problem use in emerging adulthood. *Addictive Behaviors, 37*(7), 747–775.

Substance Abuse and Mental Health Services Administration (SAMHSA), Center for Behavioral Health Statistics and Quality. (2015). *Behavioral health trends in the United States: Results from the 2014 National Survey on Drug Use and Health* (HHS Publication No. SMA 15-4927, NSDUH Series H-50). Rockville, MD: Author. Retrieved from http://www.samhsa.gov/data/

Sussman, S., & Arnett, J. J. (2014). Emerging adulthood: Developmental period facilitative of the addictions. *Evaluation & the Health Professions, 37,* 147–155 doi: 10.1177/0163278714521812

Van der Pol, P., Liebregts, N., de Graaf, R., Korf, D. J., van, den Brink., W., & van Laar, M. (2013). Predicting the transition from frequent cannabis use to cannabis dependence: A three-year prospective study. *Drug and Alcohol Dependence, 133*(2), 352–359. doi: 10.1016/j.drugalcdep.2013.06.009

Vergés, A., Haeny, A. M., Jackson, K. M., Bucholz, K. K., Grant, J. D., Trull, T. J., . . . Sher, K. J. (2013). Refining the notion of maturing out: Results from the National Epidemiologic Survey on Alcohol and Related Conditions. *American Journal of Public Health, 103*(12), e67–e73.

Vergés, A., Jackson, K. M., Bucholz, K. K., Grant, J. D., Trull, T. J., Wood, P. K., & Sher, K. J. (2012). Deconstructing the age-prevalence curve of alcohol dependence: Why "maturing out" is only a small piece of the puzzle. *Journal of Abnormal Psychology, 121*(2), 511.

Veroude, K., Jolles, J., Croiset, G., & Krabbendam, L. (2013). Changes in neural mechanisms of cognitive control during the transition from late adolescence to young adulthood. *Developmental Cognitive Neuroscience, 5,* 63–70.

Walton, K. E., & Roberts, B. W. (2004). On the relationship between substance use and personality traits: Abstainers are not maladjusted. *Journal of Research in Personality, 38*(6), 515–535.

Weiland, B. J., Korycinski, S. T., Soules, M., Zubieta, J. K., Zucker, R. A., & Heitzeg, M. M. (2014). Substance abuse risk in emerging adults associated with smaller frontal gray matter volumes and higher externalizing behaviors. *Drug and Alcohol Dependence, 137,* 68–75.

Weinstein, N. D. (1989). Optimistic biases about personal risks. *Science, 246*(4935), 1232–1233.

White, H. R., Fleming, C. B., Kim, M. J., Catalano, R. F., & McMorris, B. J. (2008). Identifying two potential mechanisms for changes in alcohol use among college-attending and non-college-attending emerging adults. *Developmental Psychology*, *44*(6), 1625–1639.

White, H. R., McMorris, B. J., Catalano, R. F., Fleming, C. B., Haggerty, K. P., & Abbott, R. D. (2006). Increases in alcohol and marijuana use during the transition out of high school into emerging adulthood: The effects of leaving home, going to college, and high school protective factors. *Journal of Studies on Alcohol*, *67*(6), 810–822.

Yonker, J. E., Schnabelrauch, C. A., & DeHaan, L. G. (2012). The relationship between spirituality and religiosity on psychological outcomes in adolescents and emerging adults: A meta-analytic review. *Journal of Adolescence*, *35*(2), 299–314.

3

Screening, Assessment, and Diagnosis of Substance Use Disorders among Emerging Adults

DOUGLAS C. SMITH, KYLE M. BENNETT,
MICHAEL L. DENNIS, AND RODNEY FUNK ■

Substance use problems among emerging adults exist along a continuum rang-ing from infrequent use with minimal consequences, to heavier use, to bona fide addiction with a high potential for chronicity. Disagreements about where thresholds lie for emerging adults are nested within the larger debate on the exact nature of substance use problems. The bottom line is that substance use is devel-opmentally normative for emerging adults. This chapter tackles the difficult task of determining precisely when an emerging adult's substance use falls outside the parameters of developmentally normative use.

WHAT IS A SUBSTANCE USE DISORDER?

From Substance Abuse and Dependence to Substance Use Disorder

Although a litany of terms describe problematic substance use, our preferred term is *substance use disorder (SUD)*. The benefits of this substance use disor-der moniker rest in its lower potential for perpetuating stigma than prior labels, the possibility of expanded treatment access for emerging adults due to lowering the symptom count threshold, and the conceptualization of SUD existing on a continuum ranging from mild to severe. On the other hand, this new conceptu-alization of SUD may muddy the waters in the age-old chronicity and typology debate by lowering the symptom threshold from three symptoms in the *Diagnostic and Statistical Manual for Mental Disorders*, fourth edition (DSM-IV) to two in the fifth edition (DSM-5).

The DSM-5 requires that an individual report a minimum of 2 of 11 of the following criteria in order to qualify for this diagnosis (American Psychiatric Association, 2013). The criteria include (1) losing control over the time spent using or amounts one is using; (2) having a persistent desire to quit or unsuccessful quit attempts; (3) having one's life revolve around obtaining, using, or recovering from the effects of a substance; (4) having cravings or strong urges to use; (5) failing to meet one's core obligations at work, school, or home because of ongoing use; (6) using despite having social and relationship problems caused or made worse by substance use; (7) withdrawing from social or occupational activities due to use; (8) using in situations that could result in bodily harm; (9) using despite health or behavioral health problems that are caused or affected by substance use; (10) greater tolerance of the substance; and (11) experiencing a withdrawal syn-drome if one stops using or maintaining one's use to avoid the unpleasant pros-pect of experiencing withdrawal. In addition to meeting the criteria, individuals are said to have mild, moderate, or severe substance use disorders at symptom counts of two to three, four to five, or six and higher, respectively.

Before the DSM-5's publication, in 2013, there existed two major diagnoses, substance abuse and substance dependence (American Psychiatric Association, 2000). For substance abuse, an individual had to meet one of four criteria in the past year (i.e., legal problems, failure to meet obligations, social problems, and use in hazardous situations), and for substance dependence an individual needed to meet three of seven criteria (i.e., tolerance, withdrawal, loss of control, greater time spent, use despite health/behavioral health problems, withdrawal from social activities, desire to quit/unsuccessful efforts) in the past year. In DSM-5, these two categories were collapsed into one major category, called *substance use disorder*, and the threshold was set at a minimum of two criteria. A symptom on craving was added. Finally, the DSM-IV substance abuse criterion pertaining to repeated legal problems due to substance use was removed (Hasin et al., 2013).

Why Change to Substance Use Disorder?

The decision to collapse DSM-IV substance abuse and substance dependence into a single diagnosis in the DSM-5, substance use disorder, was based on research showing that the abuse and dependence criteria were, in fact, unidimensional. Basically, some abuse symptoms were as severe as dependence symptoms. This conflicted with the prior notion that the diagnostic category of abuse represented a less severe form of harmful use that could progress into dependence. For example, the decision rules in DSM-IV were that if one had dependence, one could not be diagnosed with abuse because we defaulted to the more serious, and ostensibly more chronic and intractable disorder.

However, research with emerging adults did not support this idea that abuse would progress into dependence. For example, Grant, Stinson, and Harford (2001) found that emerging adults' alcohol abuse diagnoses rarely progressed into alcohol dependence diagnoses over the course of 5 years. Additionally, findings from a large nationally representative epidemiological study that oversampled emerging adults also showed that some abuse items were indicative of more severe problems and some dependence items were associated with less severity (Hasin et al., 2013). These empirical findings contradicted the logic that abuse was a less severe precursor to dependence. In short, the changes in DSM-5 appear to have a solid empirical footing for emerging adults.

ISSUES IN APPLYING DSM CRITERIA TO EMERGING ADULTS

Here we address three major questions surrounding the application of these DSM-5 criteria to emerging adults. First, do these criteria predict emerging adults' problem severity as well as they do for other age groups? That is, at the same symptom count thresholds are emerging adults' problems less severe, as severe, or more severe than those for other age groups? We also discuss item-level idiosyncrasies among the DSM-5 criteria for emerging adults to inform clinicians about when to exercise caution when interpreting emerging adults' assessments. Second, what DSM-5 symptoms are the most common among emerging adults? We explore this with two large data sets, including the National Survey of Drug Use and Health, and the Global Appraisal of Individual Needs' Coordinating Center (GAIN GCC) data. Using these data sets we address the potential consequences specific to emerging adults that result from shifting to DSM-5, such as whether the shift results in more emerging adults qualifying for SUD treatment. Third, what screening and assessment instruments have empirical support for use with emerging adults? We review such instruments.

How Well Does the DSM-5 Capture Emerging Adult Problem Severity?

As mentioned, research with emerging adults has justified the changes in DSM-5. One concern with any assessment tool such as the DSM-5 is whether it performs equally well at characterizing emerging adult SUD severity as well as it does for individuals in other age groups. There appears to be consensus that when the criteria are taken as a whole they work as well for emerging adults as for other age groups. This is important, as some have argued that the high prevalence of substance use disorders among emerging adults is related to diagnostic bias. That is, some criteria may be reported more frequently by emerging adults because of developmental processes more common for this age group and thus may not be as indicative of substance use severity for them. Large epidemiological research, however, generally shows that diagnostic bias is unlikely to account for the differentially high prevalence rates of substance use and SUD among emerging adults (Delforterie et al., 2015; Mewton, Teesson, & Slade, 2010).

Although the full criteria set seems to be working as well for emerging adults as for other age groups, some items appear to operate differently for emerging adults than they do for other age groups. For example, Conrad, Dennis, Bezruczko, Funk, and Riley (2007) compared the differential item functioning of DSM-IV symptoms between adolescents (n = 5,366), emerging adults (n = 749), and adults (n = 1,293). Differential item functioning indicates whether an item is rarer and more severe for one subgroup, such as emerging adults, than another. In this study, all DSM-IV items were of comparable severity between adolescents and emerging adults. However, a non-DSM-IV item on hiding use was more common among adolescents than for emerging adults, which makes sense, as substance use is more normative among emerging adults, and alcohol use is legal for those emerging adults over age 21. When comparing emerging adults to older adults, two items were more common and less severe among emerging adults: the legal trouble and social/interpersonal trouble criteria. Practically speaking, this does not indicate that these are not useful items in diagnosing substance use problems among emerging adults, but simply that they are indicative of more severe problems among older adults, for whom these are less common symptoms. A second major finding from this study was support for collapsing the abuse and dependence diagnoses of DSM-IV. Kahler and Strong (2006) also found similar evidence for merging substance abuse and dependence items for emerging adults. Indeed, the overall conclusion was that the 33-item Alcohol Use Disorders and Associated Disabilities Interview Schedule (AUDADIS; Grant, Dawson, & Hasin, 2001) did well capturing alcohol problem severity across a wide continuum. Further, the tolerance symptoms appeared to be low-severity items for emerging adults (ages 18–24) relative to older adults (ages 25+). Because emerging adults are more likely to be heavy episodic drinkers, tolerance to alcohol alone should not be used in isolation to conclude that an emerging adult will have chronic alcohol problems. Finally, an Australian study on cannabis use disorders found that the harmful-use criterion (i.e., recurrent substance use in situations that are physically hazardous) was indicative of more severe problems among individuals ages 18–24 than for those ages 25 and older. Further, more men report this criterion, which could explain gender differences between males and females in cannabis use disorder prevalence rates (Mewton et al., 2010). A recent U.S. study, however, failed to replicate this finding that the harmful use criterion was indicative of more severe problems among emerging adults (Delforterie et al., 2015).

In addition to the items just described that appear to perform differently for emerging adults, the DSM criterion of using for a longer time or in larger amounts than intended also merits more research attention. This criterion is supposed to measure increasingly compulsive use and the inability to moderate use. However, when asked later what they were thinking about when responding to this criterion, the majority of emerging adults said they drank more than intended to for social reasons, such as matching their peers' drinking levels (Slade et al., 2013). Fewer of them gave responses indicating a loss of control over drinking. As this is a commonly stated criterion by emerging adults both in the United States (see Table 3.2) and internationally (Pabst, Kraus, Piontek, & Baumeister, 2012), caution must be exercised when interviewing emerging adults to ensure they are understanding the criteria and to also contextualize it with frequency and quantity data. That is, episodic binge-drinking emerging adults stating this criterion may not be experiencing a loss of control, which is considered to be a symptom that is more indicative of a potentially more severe SUD.

Should Frequency/Quantity Measures be Added to the Substance Use Disorder Criteria?

In addition to a higher proportion of emerging adults meeting criteria for substance use disorders, emerging adults also use substances more frequently than other age groups. Because of this, the debate over whether or not to integrate measures of quantity and frequency into the SUD criteria is highly relevant to emerging adults. Frequent binge drinking was not included in DSM-5 as a criterion, in part because doing so would have resulted in diagnosing fewer women and minorities with alcohol use disorders (Keyes, Geier, Grant, & Hasin, 2009). This appears to have been a good decision for emerging adults as well. With emerging adults, for whom alcohol is the most commonly used substance, it may in fact be that alcohol use frequency and quantity is not as good a marker of problem severity. Kahler, Hoeppner, and Jackson (2009) found evidence for differential item severity for several quantity and frequency items such as "weekly drinking," "monthly drinking," and been "hung over." All of these types of questions reflected less severity for emerging adults but were indicative of more severe alcohol problems for adolescents. Thus, for alcohol problems specifically, it is unclear whether adding a frequency/quantity criterion to the DSM would have added valuable information when diagnosing emerging adults. Although information about the quantity and frequency of substance use is highly relevant because of the potential health and social consequences, high frequency and quantity should not be confused with disordered use.

In summary, multiple studies with emerging adults justify the decision by the DSM-5 committee to eliminate the substance abuse diagnosis for alcohol. There appear to be some nuances in item functioning for emerging adults that should be taken into consideration when assessing emerging adults. Specifically, tolerance and drinking frequency are less "difficult" items for emerging adults, indicating less of an association with problem severity. Conversely, hiding use is a higher severity item for emerging adults relative to adolescents. Despite these idiosyncrasies in individual criteria for emerging adults, research supports the idea of a unidimensional SUD construct for emerging adults. One caveat, however, is that most of these studies are limited to research on alcohol. More research is needed on the cannabis use disorder criteria in light of recent evidence suggesting that emerging adult males with DSM-IV cannabis abuse would have no diagnoses in DSM-5 (Mewton, Slade, & Teesson, 2013).

Prevalence of Substance Use Disorder and Symptom Patterns among Emerging Adults

Table 3.1 presents the prevalence of substance use disorders, as well as specific symptom-level data for emerging adults ages 18–25 from two large national data sets. The first data set, the National Survey of Drug Use and Health (NSDUH), is a nationally representative survey of substance use and related behaviors among non-institutionalized U.S. citizens (Substance Abuse and Mental Health Services Administration, [SAMHSA] Center for Behavioral Health Statistics and Quality, 2013). Also displayed in Table 3.1 are data from a pooled data set of emerging adults receiving SUD treatments (i.e., clinical sample) who completed the Global Appraisal of Individual Needs (GAIN; Dennis, Titus, White, Unsicker, & Hodgkins, 2003), a widely used, reliable, and valid SUD assessment. This data set represents the largest sample of emerging adults in treatment in the United States (Hunter, Griffin, Booth, Ramchand, and McCaffrey, 2014); the characteristics of these emerging adults are reported elsewhere (Dennis, White, & Ives, 2009; Smith, Bennett, Dennis, & Funk, 2017). Table 3.2 contains data from the same two data sources but expands the definition of emerging adults to those ages 18–29.

PREVALENCE AMONG EMERGING ADULTS AGES 18–25

Not surprisingly, the prevalence of DSM-IV abuse and dependence for any substance is higher among those in the clinical sample of 18- to 25-years-olds (20.7% and 58.7%) than among nationally representative youth (8.2% and 10.7%). The estimated prevalence rates of DSM-5 SUD are also higher in the clinical sample (11% mild SUD, 9.6% moderate SUD, and 53.2% severe SUD) than in the NSDUH sample (11.2% mild SUD, 6.6% moderate SUD, and 12.5% severe SUD). What is notable is that the majority of the 18- to 25-year-olds in the clinical sample had a severe SUD. Among the NSDUH community sample, the most commonly reported SUD symptoms for any substance among 18- to 25-year-olds were spending a lot of time getting the substance (28.4%), tolerance (26.1%), and interpersonal problems due to use (17%). In the clinical sample, a majority of emerging adults reported all but three symptoms, including withdrawal from activities (47%), persistent use in light of health problems (45.5%), and physical withdrawal (39.1%).

Finally, one interesting thing to note is that the percent of diagnostic orphans goes down in the NSDUH sample if we apply the DSM-5 criteria (11.9%) instead of the DSM-IV criteria (16.4%). Diagnostic orphans under DSM-IV were those that reported less than three dependence symptoms but no abuse symptoms. Under DSM-5, any individual meeting two criteria would be reclassified as having

Table 3.1. PAST YEAR USE, SYMPTOMS, AND DISORDERS FOR EMERGING ADULTS (AGE 18–25) FROM A NATIONAL (NSDUH 2012) AND CLINICAL (GAIN-I 2012 SUPER DATA) SAMPLE

Sample	Any Substance		Alcohol		Cannabis		Other Drugs	
	Community	Clinical	Community	Clinical	Community	Clinical	Community	Clinical
Sample size[a]	34,589,954	9,808	34,589,954	9,808	34,589,954	9,808	34,589,954	9,808
Days of use[b]								
None	21.7%	15.5%	22.8%	38.6%	69.1%	41.4%	82.7%	54.4%
Monthly (1–25 days)	22.3%	14.8%	27.4%	29.7%	12.2%	15.1%	10.6%	10.7%
Weekly (26–182 days)	36.2%	22.1%	42.3%	22.7%	8.4%	18.9%	4.6%	12.1%
Daily (183–365 days)	19.7%	47.5%	7.4%	9.1%	10.3%	24.6%	2.1%	22.8%
DSM-IV symptoms								
Repeated use caused you to not meet your responsibilities	5.5%	54.9%	3.2%	17.3%	1.8%	23.2%	1.7%	29.9%
Used repeatedly in unsafe situations	10.8%	54.9%	9.1%	18.4%	1.4%	20.5%	1.8%	28.3%
Your use caused you to have problems with the law	2.6%	53.6%	1.8%	18.0%	0.7%	21.9%	0.5%	24.2%
You have needed more to get high	26.1%	52.2%	19.1%	15.4%	9.2%	21.0%	4.5%	30.2%
You have had withdrawal problems[c]	16.3%	39.1%	2.1%	9.2%	NA	7.8%	14.9%	26.7%
You used longer than you meant to	16.0%	55.9%	4.0%	17.3%	2.0%	21.6%	11.9%	31.1%
You were unable to cut down or quit using	14.1%	54.3%	2.7%	15.1%	13.5%	22.9%	11.1%	29.8%

You spent a lot of time getting substance or using it	28.4%	61.4%	19.8%	15.9%	1.7%	28.0%	3.9%	32.1%
Use caused you to give up or reduce activities	7.7%	47.0%	4.2%	13.3%	2.9%	17.5%	1.9%	28.0%
You kept using despite medical, psychological or emotional problems	17.9%	45.5%	4.7%	12.5%	1.9%	14.0%	14.2%	27.0%
DSM-IV disorder								
Abuse	8.2%	20.7%	8.0%	17.2%	1.9%	17.7%	0.9%	7.5%
Dependence	10.7%	58.7%	6.3%	17.5%	3.7%	25.3%	2.5%	35.1%
DSM-V disorder								
Mild (2–3 symptoms)	11.2%	11.0%	12.3%	9.3%	7.4%	11.7%	1.7%	5.1%
Moderate (4–5)	6.6%	9.6%	3.5%	5.8%	1.8%	9.4%	9.8%	4.1%
Severe (6–11)	12.5%	53.2%	2.2%	15.8%	0.9%	18.5%	3.8%	32.1%
Diagnostic orphans								
DSM-IV (1–2 dependence symptoms, no abuse)	16.4%	2.8%	17.8%	3.6%	10.2%	5.5%	0.7%	3.6%
DSM-V (1 symptom)	11.9%	7.7%	14.1%	8.2%	5.8%	9.0%	0.6%	4.9%

GAIN, Global Appraisal of Individual Needs; NSDUH, National Household Survey of Drug Use and Health.

[a] The community sample size is from NSDUH 2012 data and is the weighted population estimate of young adults ages 18–25.

[b] For the clinical sample, it is days of use in the past 90 days while in the community (excludes days in a controlled environment) prior to interview. This number was multiplied times 4 to get annual days of use.

[c] Withdrawal from marijuana use was not asked about in the community sample.

Table 3.2. Past Year Use, Symptoms, and Disorders for Emerging Adults (Age 18–29) from a National (NSDUH 2012) and Clinical (GAIN-I 2012 Super Data) Sample

Sample	Any Substance		Alcohol		Cannabis		Other Drugs	
	Community	Clinical	Community	Clinical	Community	Clinical	Community	Clinical
Sample size[a]	34,589,954	9,808	51,987,802	13,776	51,987,802	13,776	51,987,802	13,776
Days of use[b]								
None	20.0%	15.6%	20.9%	39.0%	72.8%	45.6%	83.8%	51.8%
Monthly (1–25 days)	23.1%	15.0%	27.6%	28.8%	11.0%	15.3%	9.8%	10.8%
Weekly (26–182 days)	38.0%	21.7%	43.2%	22.2%	7.4%	17.3%	4.6%	12.4%
Daily (183–365 days)	18.9%	47.6%	8.3%	10.0%	8.8%	21.8%	1.9%	25.0%
DSM-IV symptoms								
Repeated use caused you to not meet your responsibilities	5.0%	56.5%	3.1%	18.4%	1.3%	20.6%	1.6%	32.7%
Used repeatedly in unsafe situations	10.4%	56.4%	9.1%	22.6%	1.1%	17.9%	1.8%	30.8%
Your use caused you to have problems with the law	2.4%	54.0%	1.7%	18.9%	0.5%	18.8%	0.5%	26.1%
You have needed more to get high	23.4%	53.1%	17.4%	15.6%	7.4%	18.4%	4.2%	32.3%
You have had withdrawal problems[c]	14.8%	41.4%	2.5%	10.4%	NA	6.9%	13.2%	28.7%
You used longer than you meant to	15.1%	57.6%	4.3%	18.8%	1.7%	19.2%	10.9%	33.6%
You were unable to cut down or quit using	13.2%	56.1%	3.2%	16.6%	1.4%	20.3%	9.9%	32.5%
You spent a lot of time getting substance or using it	25.5%	61.9%	18.3%	16.9%	10.9%	24.2%	3.7%	34.5%

Use caused you to give up or reduce activities	7.2%	49.0%	4.3%	14.7%	2.4%	15.4%	1.9%	30.8%
You kept using despite medical, psychological, or emotional problems	16.5%	48.4%	5.0%	14.0%	1.5%	12.9%	12.8%	29.7%
DSM-IV disorder								
Abuse	7.5%	19.6%	7.3%	16.5%	1.4%	15.8%	1.2%	7.6%
Dependence	9.9%	60.1%	6.2%	19.0%	3.0%	22.1%	12.4%	37.8%
DSM-V disorder								
Mild (2–3 symptoms)	10.2%	10.6%	11.0%	8.8%	5.9%	10.5%	1.5%	5.0%
Moderate (4–5)	6.3%	9.0%	3.3%	5.5%	1.4%	8.0%	8.8%	3.9%
Severe (6–11)	11.2%	54.9%	2.4%	16.6%	0.6%	16.1%	3.5%	35.0%
Diagnostic orphans								
DSM-IV (1–2 dependence symptoms, no abuse)	16.2%	2.6%	17.2%	3.3%	8.7%	5.1%	0.7%	3.1%
DSM-V (1 symptom)	12.1%	6.6%	14.1%	7.7%	5.1%	8.3%	0.5%	4.7%

GAIN, Global Appraisal of Individual Needs; NSDUH, National Household Survey of Drug Use and Health.

a The community sample size is from NSDUH 2012 data and is the weighted population estimate of young adults ages 18–25.

b For the clinical sample, it is days of use in the past 90 days while in the community (excludes days in a controlled environment) prior to interview. This number was multiplied times 4 to get annual days of use.

c Withdrawal from marijuana use was not asked about in the community sample.

a mild SUD. Because diagnosis often drives reimbursement for specialty treatment, this is encouraging news. However, the percent of diagnostic orphans go up in the clinical sample under DSM-5 criteria (7.7%) versus under DSM-IV criteria (2.8%). This may be accounted for by eliminating the criterion of having repeated trouble with the law, given that many programs in this data set relied on criminal justice–referred emerging adults.

PREVALENCE AMONG EMERGING ADULTS AGES 18–29

The prevalence rates for any SUD in 18- to 29-year-olds in the clinical and national sample are remarkably similar to those in the sample of 18- to 25-year-olds (see Table 3.2). Approximately 80% of those in the clinical sample had a DSM-IV diagnosis of either abuse or dependence. Additionally, the percent of individuals with mild, moderate, or severe SUD in both the NSDUH and clinical samples rarely differed by more than a few percentage points when changing the age range. Furthermore, the rank order of the most commonly reported substances in the NSDUH sample remained the same, including spending a lot of time getting the substance (25.5%), tolerance (23.4%), and interpersonal problems due to use (15.3%). The overall percentage of individuals in the sample of 18- to 29-year-olds reporting each of these three criteria dropped a couple percentage points for each criterion. Finally, a similar pattern emerged among 18- to 29-year-olds: there were fewer diagnostic orphans in the NSDUH sample under DSM-5 (16.2%) versus DSM-IV (12.1%) rules, but the reverse was true for the clinical sample (2.6% in DSM-IV, 6.6% in DSM-5).

Summary

Among emerging adults nationally, those who enter specialty treatment have much more severe problems, with approximately 80% having an SUD and much higher percentages of weekly use of substances other than alcohol. However, one can also see that among emerging adults in the nationally representative sample, somewhere between 19% and 30% of 18- to 29-year-olds meet criteria for any SUD, depending on which version of the DSM you use. Because community-dwelling emerging adults have a roughly 10% chance of receiving treatments such as those used in the clinical sample, widespread implementation of screening emerging adults for substance use and SUD is important.

SCREENING AND ASSESSMENT

Evidence-Based Screening

New changes to healthcare laws may expand the number of emerging adults eligible for SUD screening and treatment services. New demand may challenge the capacity of the currently underfunded treatment system, so efficient use of treatment and prevention resources is important. A current systems-level transformation involves providing screening and brief interventions (i.e., 15–60 minutes) in opportunistic settings such as primary care (Babor et al., 2007). Optimizing the detection of substance use and delivery of such interventions for emerging adults requires the availability of evidence-based screeners, or those that have a demonstrated ability to correctly classify emerging adults' substance use risk levels (Smith et al., 2017).

Screening, or rapid identification of people in need of further assessment and/or treatment, aids in such resource management. The best screeners will use very few questions while efficiently predicting which emerging adults are most likely to need additional services. In other words, good screeners produce few false negatives or false positives. A false negative occurs when an individual is screened as being in need of further assessment or treatment, but further assessment concludes that there is not a problem worthy of intervention. A false positive, on the other hand, indicates that an individual was screened as not needing further attention but in reality did need more assessment or intervention. Research studies measure screeners' efficiency by calculating the percent of false positives and false negatives at certain cut points. A screener is said to be sensitive if it correctly identifies a high percentage of true positives, and specific if it is able to correctly exclude a high percentage of true negatives (Dennis, Chan, & Funk, 2006).

Good screening instruments can dramatically outperform professional judgement in predicting risky substance use (Vinson, Turner, Manning, & Galliher, 2013). In other words, knowing what questions to systematically ask is vitally important, and there is virtually no reason a healthcare or social service agency should make up their own screening questions given the availability of screeners known to have high sensitivity and specificity for emerging adult populations. Using questions that have marginally or unknown predictive power in determining which emerging adults are suffering from substance use disorders reflects poor and, perhaps, unethical practice. That is, multiple professional societies value using state-of-the-art science in informing care decisions, and failure to identify emerging adults in need of substance use treatment will perpetuate their already low treatment engagement (Acevedo, Garnick, Ritter, Horgan, & Lundgren, 2015; Wu, Pilowsky, Schlenger, & Hasin, 2007).

In addition to sensitivity and specificity, there are other considerations when selecting a screener for emerging adult populations. First, some settings, such as primary care offices or organizations, prefer screeners to be as short as possible. This may also be the case in settings where the primary purpose is not substance use treatment (e.g., mental health agency, domestic violence shelter). In these settings, substance use screening questions may be slipped in among a litany of other psychosocial assessment questions. Second, it is critical to know if screeners have been validated on diverse populations. For example, gender can impact the performance of screeners (Kelly, Donovan, Chung, Bukstein, & Cornelius, 2009). Thus, the best screeners are those with known specificity and sensitivity that have been tested in large diverse samples.

With these considerations in mind, Table 3.3 displays a number of screeners that have been used with emerging adults. It displays several features of each

Table 3.3. Empirically Supported Screeners for Use with Emerging Adults

Screener Name	# of Items	High Sensitivity/Specificity[a]	Norms for Emerging Adults Available[b] (n > 1,000)	Settings	Minority Populations[c]	International Samples or Translations[c]	Predicts SUDs?[d]
AUDIT	10	Yes (80% sensitivity, 78% specificity @ 6+)	Yes	Clinical/school, research	Yes	Yes	Yes
AUDIT-C	3	Yes (78% sensitivity, 79% specificity @ 5+)	Yes	Clinical/school	Yes	Yes	Yes
GAIN-SS	5	Yes (83% sensitivity, 95% specificity @ 2+)	No	Clinical/nonclinical, research	No	No	Yes
MAST	24	No	No	Primary health care, clinical settings	Yes	No	No
CRAFFT	6	Yes (sensitivity = .95, specificity = .86)	Yes	Clinical/nonclinical, research	Yes—American Indian, Alaskan Native	Yes	Yes
CAGE	4	No	Yes	Clinical/nonclinical, research	Yes	No	No
DAST	28	Yes (sensitivity 81%–96%, specificity 71%–94% @ 6+)	No	Clinical screening, research	Yes	Yes (Chinese, Spanish...)	Yes

ASSIST	8	No	No	Clinical settings, research	Yes	Yes	No
YAAPST	27	No	Yes	School/clinical	Yes	No	No

For full names of screeners, see text.

[a] Sensitivity and specificity scores were included in the table, along with cut-off scores when reported, if scholarly publications reported scores higher than 70% for each.

[b] Emerging adult norms were considered available if a screener had been used with samples greater than 1,000 emerging adults and reported average scores on the screener with the emerging adult sample.

[c] A screener received a "yes" if multiple studies had been conducted with international samples and international translations, with samples consisting of mostly minority participants.

[d] 1+ study predicting substance use disorders for emerging adults.

screener, including the number of items, sample characteristics, and sensitivity and specificity estimates. Here, for inclusion as a substance use screener in this chapter, multiple studies must report sensitivity and specificity scores of 75% or higher.

THE ALCOHOL USE DISORDERS AND IDENTIFICATION TEST (AUDIT)

Initially developed in collaboration with the World Health Organization (WHO) (Saunders, Aasland, Babor, De la Fuente, & Grant, 1993), the AUDIT is one of the most widely used and recognizable screeners for risky alcohol use. Two versions of the AUDIT have been tested with emerging adults, the full version of the AUDIT (i.e., 10 items) and the AUDIT-C (Consumption), which only uses three items pertaining to alcohol use consumption.

Both the AUDIT and AUDIT-C are better at predicting risky drinking among emerging adults than for alcohol use disorders. For example, Kokotailo and colleagues (2004) found high sensitivity (91%) and reasonable specificity (60%) when predicting risky drinking at a cutoff score of 6, and recommended a cutoff between 6 and 8. Risky drinking was defined as exceeding a set number of drinks (i.e., 57 + for men, 29 + for women) or having four or more binge drinking days (i.e., 5 + drinks on one occasion for men, 4 + drinks on one occasion for women) over the course of the past month. However, when predicting alcohol use diagnoses from the same cutoff, both sensitivity (78%) and specificity (57%) were lower. In this study, the internal consistency of the AUDIT was good (Cronbach's α = .81). DeMartini and Carey (2012) found that the optimal cutoff point for the AUDIT was 8 for both males. Zamboanga and colleagues (2007) found AUDIT scores of 5 and 6 were optimal for predicting women's involvement in drinking games.

The AUDIT-Consumption, or AUDIT-C, has also been used in several studies with emerging adults. Interestingly, the AUDIT-C performs better than the AUDIT for women in detecting heavy drinking, defined as exceeding weekly drinking limits or having four or more binge drinking episodes in the past month (DeMartini & Carey, 2012). At a cutoff of 5, the AUDIT-C had .82 specificity and .82 sensitivity in detecting heavy drinking. For males, however, the recommended cutoff was a score of 7, which resulted in 80% sensitivity and 88% specificity. Similarly, Kelly and colleagues' (2009) emergency department study found that the optimal cutoff was 6 for males (77% sensitivity, 68% specificity) and 5 for females (77% sensitivity, 78% specificity) in detecting alcohol use disorders. The AUDIT-C had better specificity and sensitivity in detecting alcohol use disorders in this sample than in prior studies, but it did not perform as well as a screener that simply included two of the DSM-IV's alcohol use disorder criteria (i.e., drinking in hazardous situations, longer times/larger amounts; 88% sensitivity, 90% specificity).

In summary, there are important considerations for using the AUDIT and AUDIT-C with emerging adults. First, although both screeners appear to have high sensitivity and specificity for predicting risky drinking patterns among emerging adults, they generally appear less efficient at predicting alcohol use disorders. Thus, in settings where the goal is to screen for potentially disordered use, alternative measures may be advised for emerging adults. Second, slightly lower cutoffs should be used for female than for male emerging adults. Third, cutoffs for emerging adults can sometimes be lower, not higher, than the cutoff of 8 initially recommended by the AUDIT's developers (Kokotailo et al., 2004; Saunders et al., 1993; Zamboanga et al., 2007). Implementing a screening protocol with higher cutoffs under the auspices that emerging adult drinking is "normative" would result in failure to identify many emerging adults in need of brief interventions and/or referral to treatment. Finally, practically all emerging adult–specific studies on the AUDIT have relied on college-attending samples in the United States.

MAST, B-MAST, S-MAST

The Michigan Alcohol Screening Test (MAST), developed in 1971, was the first standardized measure to screen for alcohol-related issues among clinical populations (Devos-Comby & Lange, 2008; Gibbs, 1983; Maisto, Connors, & Allen, 1995). The MAST can be utilized with a wide variety of populations and consists of 26 items designed to determine an individual's lifetime experiences with alcohol consumption. Like the AUDIT, the MAST can be used to screen for risky or problematic drinking behaviors and also includes items relating to DSM criteria for substance use disorders. Unlike assessment tools like the AUDIT or the Addiction Severity Index (ASI), however, the MAST was not designed to diagnose individuals who may present symptoms related to substance use disorders (Devos-Comby & Lange, 2008). The MAST differs from other screening tools like the Rutgers Alcohol Problem Index (RAPI) in that its original design was to screen for alcohol-related issues among adults rather than adolescents or traditionally aged college students, although researchers have conducted a number of validation studies among college students as well (Clements, 1998; Martin, Leipman, & Young, 1990; Svanum & McGrew, 1995).

Some studies raise concerns about the MAST's ability to positively identify individuals with alcohol-related issues and correctly reject individuals who do not present significant levels of alcohol-related issues. Studies conducted by Svanum and McGrew (1995) and Martin et al. (1990) included sensitivity scores of 63% and 100%, respectively. Specificity scores for those two studies varied from 36% to 70% (2008). One final example comes from a study conducted at a large public university in the Midwest where undergraduate psychology students participated in a project that identified 52% of them as "alcoholics," which, as the author indicates, seems unrealistically high considering the sample (Devos-Comby & Lange, 2008; Myerholtz & Rosenberg, 1998).

Shorter versions of the MAST include the Brief MAST (B-MAST) and the Short MAST (S-MAST), which contain 10 and 13 items, respectively. According to Devos-Comby and Lange (2008), these two screening tools have been particularly ineffective in identifying individuals with substance use disorders, especially college students. Some researchers propose reasons for this ineffectiveness are that the B-MAST lacks items that correspond to current diagnostic criteria for substance use disorders, and although the S-MAST incorporated items relating to help-seeking behavior, social/interpersonal problems, and legal issues and thus performed better in correctly classifying some male populations as having a substance use disorder or not, none of the items in the S-MAST correspond to current criteria of substance use disorders (Devos-Comby & Lange, 2008). Considering their design as screening tools rather than as standardized assessments, this finding is not necessarily surprising, but when tasked with identifying individuals who engage in risky or problematic drinking, the B-MAST did not demonstrate acceptable levels of sensitivity and specificity (Smith, Collins, Kreisberg, Volpicelli, & Alterman, 1987). The S-MAST performed comparatively better, obtaining sensitivity and specificity scores of 83% and 87%, respectively, with a joint sample of emerging adult college students and non–emerging adult clinical populations (Hays & Revetto, 1992). Ultimately, some researchers question the capability of the MAST instruments to accurately and consistently screen for alcohol-related issues or indices of symptoms relating to DSM diagnoses of substance use disorders specifically among college students and other emerging adult populations (Devos-Comby & Lange, 2008; Larimer, Cronce, Lee, & Kilmer, 2004).

CAGE

The CAGE questionnaire, developed in 1984 as a screening tool for alcohol-related issues among clinical populations, comprises four dichotomous questions to determine an individual's lifetime experiences regarding four potentially inter-related dimensions of alcohol consumption. Based on an individual's response to these four scored items, such as "Have you ever felt you should cut down on your drinking?" or "Have you ever felt bad or guilty about your drinking?," the CAGE is simple to administer and score. A CAGE score of ≥1 is widely considered to be a valid predictor of an individual who has some alcohol-related issue (Demirbaş, 2015). The CAGE is shorter than the full AUDIT and the MAST instruments.

Regarding the CAGE as a screening tool for emerging adults, it has been used in some validation studies, although mostly with college students, limiting the generalizability of these studies' findings (Boyd, McCabe, & d'Arcy, 2003; Clements, 1998; Clements & Heintz, 2002; Heck & Williams, 1995; Ross & Tisdall, 1994). CAGE data regarding sensitivity and specificity indicate varying degrees of reliability, with some studies reporting sensitivity and specificity levels of 77% and 83%, respectively (Ross & Tisdall, 1994), and others reporting levels of 57% and 85% (Smith et al., 1987). The diversity of samples across research studies is of note, however, as some studies examined clinical samples of students (Ross & Tisdall, 1994) while others gathered more general samples of undergraduate college students (Boyd et al., 2003). Most studies and researchers corroborate the ineffectiveness of the CAGE in screening for risky or problematic alcohol consumption among college students or emerging adults. Devos-Comby and Lange (2008) suggest that the CAGE does not address the alcohol-related issues deemed most relevant by students. The items included within the CAGE ". . . presume an awareness and willingness to admit to a drinking problem, cognitions that may not be those of many students, especially those who get drunk the most often" (2008, p. 354).

CRAFFT

Slightly longer than the CAGE, the CRAFFT substance use screening test comprises six items, with each letter in the acronym representing a particular type of substance-related consequence (i.e., Car, Relax, Alone, Forget, Friends, Trouble). Researchers designed the CRAFFT for use with adolescents (ages 14–18) seen in primary care settings who may be presenting with alcohol-related issues (Knight et al., 1999). Previous research with these populations has obtained sensitivity and specificity scores for identifying any problem as 76% and 94%, respectively, and for identifying any disorder as 80% and 86%, respectively (Knight, Sherritt, Shrier, Harris, & Chang, 2002). In addition, studies have determined that, in general, a CRAFFT score ≥2 is ideal for identifying any substance-related problem (2002). For adolescents, the CRAFFT effectively identifies substance use disorders.

Unlike the CAGE, MAST, and AUDIT, the CRAFFT's strength lies in its ability to screen for issues relating to substances other than alcohol. Although its designers constructed the items to be more developmentally appropriate for adolescents than for traditionally aged college students or emerging adults (Knight et al., 2002), some researchers have used the CRAFFT questionnaire as part of larger studies with older adolescents and emerging adults (Bernstein et al., 2009, 2010; Kelly et al., 2009). For example, from a sample of 18- to 20-year-olds treated in emergency departments ($n = 181$), researchers determined the CRAFFT to have sensitivity and specificity levels of .69 and .73, respectively, at a cut point of 3 (Kelly et al., 2009). Other CRAFFT research done with emerging adults found evidence for high sensitivity (83.7%) but low specificity (48.6%) at a cut-off of 4 or higher (Bagley, Anderson, & Stein, 2017). When screening for alcohol use disorders at the same cut-off point, sensitivity (81.4%) and specificity (45.3%) scores were similar (2017).

In summary, cut-offs for the CRAFT for emerging adults are higher than for adolescents, and the screener does well identifying true positives (i.e., sensitivity) for substance use disorders, but it comes at the cost of tolerating some false positives.

GLOBAL APPRAISAL OF INDIVIDUAL NEEDS SHORT SCREENER (GAIN SS)

Derived from its parent instrument, the GAIN SS includes a substance disorder screener (Past Year Substance Disorder Screener [SDSCrY]) that was developed with rapid screening in mind. Unlike the alcohol-specific instruments that include consumption-based items, it consists solely of five items consistent with DSM criteria. As such, it has been found to do a better job at predicting the presence of substance use disorders than other screeners. Dennis and colleagues (2006) found that a cut-off of 2 or higher resulted in high sensitivity and specificity across the lifespan. More recently, a large emerging adult–specific study ($n = 9,808$) replicated these findings, also finding high sensitivity (83%) and specificity (95%) at a cut-off of 2 or higher (Smith et al., 2017). Both studies predicted the presence of any past-year DSM-IV substance use disorder, because the samples used included much heterogeneity in terms of specific SUD.

Alcohol, Smoking, and Substance Involvement Screening Test (ASSIST)

The ASSIST is a brief screening instrument designed to identify an individual's use of various psychoactive substances. Initially developed by the WHO and substance use researchers in 1997, the brief interviewer-administered ASSIST consists of eight items and screens for tobacco, alcohol, cannabis, cocaine, hallucinogens, and other drugs (Henry-Edwards, Humeniuk, Ali, Poznyak, & Monteiro, 2003). In addition to screening for multiple substances, the ASSIST measures lifetime and past 3-month use, problems pertaining to substance use, and risks associated with use. While studies focusing on emerging adults report sensitivity and/or specificity scores, the ASSIST has been validated extensively with diverse populations of various ages (Barreto, Christoff, & Boerngen-Lacerda, 2014; Humeniuk et al., 2008; Kahn et al., 2012). The screener has demonstrated consistently good levels of concurrent validity and internal consistency, an ability to identify individuals' use of various substances, and for those reporting it, acceptable levels of sensitivity (66.7%–100%) and specificity (83.5%–97.1%) (Barreto, Christoff, & Boerngen-Lacerda, 2014; Henry-Edwards et al., 2003; Humeniuk et al., 2008; Khan et al., 2012). Reliability scores have been shown to range from good to excellent as well (Henry-Edwards et al., 2003; Tiburcio et al., 2015).

A shorter version of the ASSIST, the ASSIST-Lite, has been developed for use in fast-paced medical settings. While still preliminary in nature and not used with exclusively emerging adult samples, findings suggest high levels of sensitivity and specificity for certain items in the scale. More validations studies are necessary to advance the ASSIST-Lite as a reliable and efficient screener for substance use issues with emerging adults (Ali, Meena, Eastwood, Richards, & Marsden, 2013).

Drug Abuse Screening Test (DAST)

The DAST and its variations (DAST-28, DAST-20, DAST-10) are self-reported measures of substance use for individuals used primarily for treatment research and clinical screening purposes (Yudko, Lozhkina, & Fouts, 2007). Each version measures the severity of consequences associated with an individual's substance use, typically those experienced in the past year. The DAST has been translated into many languages and used to screen diverse populations in numerous research studies, including some with emerging adults (Goodman, Henderson, Peterson-Badali, & Goldstein, 2015). Despite its widespread use in clinical settings, however, the DAST has rarely been used with exclusively emerging adult samples. The primary study we identified that used the DAST with a sample of emerging adults was focused on identification of comorbid bipolar spectrum disorders and depression (Smith, Harrison, Muir, & Blackwood, 2005). Here the authors found that emerging adults with a bipolar spectrum disorder scored significantly higher on the DAST than their peers without the diagnosis (2005). All versions of the DAST have demonstrated good to excellent levels of internal consistency and test-retest reliability (Yudko et al., 2007).

Sensitivity and specificity scores for the DAST-28, at a cut-off score of 6, ranged from 80.9% to 96% and 71% to 93.9%, respectively (Yudko et al., 2007).

The DAST-20 scored comparatively lower, with sensitivity scores ranging from 74% to 89% and specificity scores ranging from 68% to 83%. These scores were achieved at various cut-off points (e.g., at 2 or 3 vs. 5 or 6). The shortest of the three versions of the DAST, the DAST-10, achieved sensitivity scores of 41% to 95% and specificity scores of 68% to 99% (2007). Worth noting is that when the highest specificity value of 99% and the lowest sensitivity value of 41% are dropped from the analysis, the overall range of specificity and sensitivity scores for the DAST-10 is comparable to that from the DAST-28, which is indicative of its potential utility as a shorter screener for emerging adults (2007). Finally, the DAST-A, a version of the screener for adolescents, achieved sensitivity scores of 78.6% and specificity scores of 84.5% when using diagnostic criteria from the DSM-IV (2007).

YOUNG ADULT ALCOHOL PROBLEMS SCREENING TEST (YAAPST)
The YAAPST questionnaire (Hurlbut & Sher, 1992) is an assessment/screening tool that measures lifetime, past-year, and frequency of past-year negative consequences associated with alcohol use among college students. It measures both traditional consequences associated with alcohol use (e.g., hangovers) and consequences typically prone to occur at higher rates among populations of emerging adult college students (e.g., missing class). It may be used as a screening tool in clinical settings for recent and lifetime alcohol use and may be used for diagnostic purposes as well. The YAAPST has demonstrated good levels of internal consistency for measuring past-year adverse consequences ($\alpha = .83$) and past-year severity ($\alpha = .84$) as well as lifetime adverse consequences ($\alpha = .87$) due to alcohol use (Devos-Comby & Lange, 2008). In addition, a Spanish version of the YAAPST has been validated with an emerging adult sample in South America (González, Riveros, Uribe, & Luna, 2006)

WHAT IS AN EMPIRICALLY SUPPORTED ASSESSMENT?

Empirically supported assessments are typically designed to diagnose individuals who are in need of specialized care and/or measure the extent of substance-related problems. The key considerations in selecting an assessment are (1) whether you need diagnostic information, (2) the allowable length of administration, and (3) and the extent to which you want to collect data on co-occurring problems (i.e., legal, psychiatric, social). Comprehensive biopsychosocial assessments are those that permit both making diagnoses and collection of extensive information on co-occurring problems. In short, comprehensive biopsychosocial assessments are most useful for facilitating level-of-care placement decisions (i.e., outpatient, intensive outpatient, residential) or for treatment planning. Additionally, we review surveys that have been used in large epidemiological studies with emerging adults, with varying levels of market readiness. More limited assessments may be used for research purposes or simply in situations where diagnosis and treatment planning are not necessary.

Market-Ready Comprehensive Biopsychosocial Assessments

ADDICTION SEVERITY INDEX (ASI)

The ASI is one of the most well-established SUD assessments (McClellan et al., 1992; McClellan, Cacciola, Alterman, Rikoon, & Carise, 2006). It is a multidimensional assessment that includes composite scores for psychiatric functioning, medical problems, substance use, legal problems, and employment. It has found to be a reliable and valid measure in multiple studies using diverse samples (McClellan et al., 2006). It can be administered via paper and pencil as an interview, or as a computer-assisted interview. One study ($n = 88$) estimated the ASI administration time at approximately 50 minutes (Cacciola, Alterman, McLellan, Lin, & Lynch, 2007). Importantly, the ASI has been used in some emerging adult–focused treatment outcome studies. A research version of the ASI exists, and the developers also have updated their computer administration software for those who need to make diagnoses per DSM-5 guidelines. More information about the ASI is available on the developer's website (http://www.tresearch.org/tools/download-asi-instruments-manuals).

The ASI has been used in multiple emerging adult–focused clinical trials (Carroll et al., 2006; Gonzalez et al., 2015; Marlowe et al., 2003; Santis et al., 2013), in studies comparing emerging and older adults' clinical characteristics and treatment outcomes (Chi et al., 2014; Morse, Watson, MacMaster, & Bride, 2015), and in studies on how frequency of alcohol and marijuana use interacts to predict higher marijuana problem severity (Stein, Caviness, & Anderson, 2014). Additionally, emerging adult–specific validity data are available for the ASI. Specifically, Delucchi, Matzger, and Weisner (2008) showed that all but one of the ASI composite scores (i.e., medical composite score) were higher among emerging adults with alcohol dependency than for those exhibiting problematic drinking.

GLOBAL APPRAISAL OF INDIVIDUAL NEEDS (GAIN)

The full version of the GAIN, called the GAIN-Intake version, is a full biopsychosocial assessment that can be used for research, placement decisions, and treatment planning (Dennis et al., 2003). It is divided into eight separate areas: substance use, background and treatment arrangements, risk behaviors, physical health, mental health, environmental factors, legal issues, and vocational functioning. It has over 100 scales and variables, which have been validated with diverse individuals across the lifespan, including emerging adults (Dennis, Funk, Godley, Godley, & Waldron, 2004; Lennox, Dennis, Scott, & Funk, 2006) Information on the GAIN's reliability and norms for emerging adults is widely available (Dennis et al., 2009). The GAIN has a validated training model ($n = 15,858$) that has been shown to increase the reliability of data collection and can often be administered in approximately 90 minutes (Titus et al., 2012). The GAIN is typically administered as an interviewer-assisted assessment, with computer administration and printable report features available from the developer (http://gaincc.org/).

There are numerous emerging adult studies that have used the GAIN's core scales to track emerging adults' outcomes (Smith, Davis, Dumas, & Ureche, 2016), compare the outcomes of emerging adults and adolescents (Smith, Godley, Godley, & Dennis, 2011), document that marijuana withdrawal predicts faster relapse on cannabis (Davis, Smith, Morphew, Lei, & Zhang, 2016), evaluate the impact of victimization and trauma on substance use (Davis, Merrin et al., 2016; Garner, Hunter, Smith, Smith, & Godley, 2014), document that emerging adults have fewer interpersonal reasons for quitting use of substances (i.e., pressure from family) (Smith, Cleeland, & Dennis, 2010), and demonstrate that developmental features of emerging adulthood correlate with substance-related problems (Smith, Bahar, Cleeland, & Davis, 2014). Additionally, Chan, Dennis, and Funk (2008) have shown the high levels of psychiatric comorbidity in emerging adults receiving treatment, as well as the age-related prevalence differences for co-occurring disorders.

Assessments Used in National Epidemiological Research

THE STRUCTURED CLINICAL INTERVIEW FOR THE DSM (SCID)

The SCID (First, 1995) is an interview protocol for which both clinician and researcher versions exist. It has been used as an expert administered interview against which diagnoses from lay interviewers were calibrated in the U.S. National Comorbidity Survey-Replication (NCS-R) study, a large, nationally representative epidemiological study (Kessler, Berglund, et al., 2005; Kessler, Chiu, Demler, & Walters, 2005). Emerging adults ages 18–29 comprised 23% of the weighted sample (Degenhardt, Chiu, Sampson, Kessler, & Anthony, 2007). Studies using the SCID that are exclusively focused on emerging adults are difficult to locate, with the exception of one emerging adult–focused epidemiological study completed in Ireland (Harley et al., 2015). Interrater reliability can range from moderate to high in some samples, including international replication studies (Lobbestael, Leurgans, & Arntz, 2011). The SCID is a comprehensive diagnostic system allowing diagnoses of both Axis I and Axis II disorders, with administration time ranging from 60 to 90 minutes depending on whether it is being administered to a community or clinical sample, respectively (First, 1995).

The SCID is available for use by clinicians and researchers. More information about the DSM-5 version of the SCID, as well as costs associated with using the SCID, is available on the developer's website (https://www.appi.org/products/structured-clinical-interview-for-dsm-5-scid-5).

ALCOHOL USE DISORDER AND ASSOCIATED DISABILITIES INTERVIEW SCHEDULE (AUDASIS)

The AUDASIS was specifically designed as an epidemiological survey for the National Epidemiologic Survey on Alcohol and Related Conditions (NESARC; Hasin & Grant, 2015). In addition to modules on substance use, the AUDASIS includes modules for common psychiatric problems (e.g., posttraumatic stress disorder) and risk factors for substance use (i.e., acculturation, adverse childhood experiences, stigma, intimate partner violence). The reliability and validity of the AUDASIS were initially established in the NESARC, a large study that oversampled emerging adults ages 18–24 (Grant et al., 2003). The DSM-5 version of the AUDASIS was also validated more recently (Grant et al., 2015) among a community sample that included emerging adults ($n = 98$; about 10% of sample). One potential caveat exists when using the AUDASIS with emerging adults: Boness Lane, and Sher (2016) found that emerging adult diagnosis rates could potentially be inflated when using the AUDASIS because the items on withdrawal capture hangovers.

Administration time estimates for the AUDASIS were not readily available. However, as administration times for an abbreviated version of the AUDASIS ranged from 50 to 80 minutes (Pull et al., 1997), it seems likely that using the full AUDASIS would take a minimum of 2 to 3 hours. The full set of AUDASIS questionnaires is publicly available from the National Institute of Alcohol Abuse and Alcoholism (NIAAA) at https://niaaa.nih.gov/research/nesarc-iii/questionnaire.

Limited, Shorter Assessments

THE RUTGERS ALCOHOL PROBLEM INDEX (RAPI)

The RAPI addresses consequences associated with alcohol consumption, focusing specifically on risky or problematic drinking. Thus, its strength is in assessing alcohol-related harm in populations of emerging adults with subclinical alcohol-related problems. There is a strong need for such an instrument for emerging adults in both college and non-college contexts. It is a very effective tool for identifying "clinically significant alcohol-related consequences" (Neal, Corbin, & Fromme, 2006, p. 412).

The RAPI has 23 five-point Likert scale items and identifies problematic alcohol use over the course of the individual's life and during the past 3 years. It has been used in studies revolving around program evaluation (Borsari & Carey, 2005; Collins & Carey, 2005), empirical measures of alcohol-related issues (Ham & Hope, 2005; Pagan et al., 2006), and effective screening tools for alcohol misuse (Neal & Carey, 2004). Data derived from a variety of studies have identified the RAPI as having good to excellent levels of internal consistency (.85 to .95) and positive correlations with other indices of alcohol use ($.28 < r < .70$) (Devos-Comby & Lange, 2008; Monti et al., 2007; Segatto, Andreoni, de Souza e Silva, Diehl, & Pinksy, 2010).

More contemporary research utilizing the RAPI has focused on drinking problems and patterns with undergraduate students in the United States and identified levels of internal consistency that ranged from .68 to .83 (Martens, Neighbors, Dams-O'Connor, Lee, & Larimer, 2007; Neal et al., 2006). The project conducted by Martens et al. (2007) in particular involved three data sets totaling 5,000 undergraduate students from multiple, large public U.S. universities (2007). Criticisms of the RAPI include the fact that developers constructed the tool with a sample that included a large number of adolescents under the age of 15, which has led some to question the applicability and external validity of portions of the measure (Devos-Comby & Lange, 2008). Additionally, some researchers have suggested that the RAPI omits items that may be more relevant to college students, such as problems relating to driving under the influence of alcohol or engaging in risky sexual activities (2008).

Other studies have identified differences in responses to various items in the RAPI based on the gender of the individual respondent (Earleywine, LaBrie, & Pedersen, 2008). Their research included an analysis of over 2,000 college students who identified themselves as consumers of alcohol, and the study determined ultimately that some items functioned differently for women than for men. For example, items relating to alcohol interfering with work and school obligations or items relating to alcohol consumption leading to arguments with family members appeared biased toward women, while items relating to alcohol contributing to social and interpersonal problems with friends or items relating to the consumption of alcohol beyond what was intended or planned appeared biased toward men (2008). These observations are supported by other research that indicates some consistent differences in responses to various items based on the respondent's gender, such as items involving spending too much money on alcohol being a more severe item for men (Neal et al., 2006). Ultimately, the researchers concluded that a shorter version of the RAPI that did not include the problematic items, or that only included some items for specific samples or types of research, would wield greater utility across genders in general (Earleywine et al., 2008; Neal et al., 2006). Notwithstanding these critiques, the RAPI is a viable instrument for measuring alcohol-related consequences experienced by emerging adults.

Leed's Dependence Questionnaire (LDQ)
The LDQ (Raistrick et al., 1994) is a brief, 10-item measure of substance dependency. Given the short administration time, it is an ideal instrument for researchers with serious assessment time constraints in need of identifying substance use disorders among emerging adults. However, it should be noted that it does not include the full DSM-5 criteria set, which may make it of limited use in practice settings where full diagnostic information is necessary. Kelly, Magill, Slaymaker, and Kahler (2010) found that the LDQ was reliable and valid for emerging adults. It was only moderately correlated with SCID-generated DSM symptom counts. However, their findings were not surprising, because the LDQ does not have tolerance or withdrawal items. The LDQ is a public domain instrument made freely available from the developer at http://www.dual-diagnosis.org.uk/Leeds%20 Dependency%20Questionnaire.pdf.

Young Adult Alcohol Consequences Questionnaire (YAACQ)
The YAACQ (Read, Kahler, Strong, & Colder, 2006) is a self-administered questionnaire and assessment tool designed to measure a wide range of alcohol-related consequences experienced by both male and female college students. The YAACQ assesses all symptoms of alcohol use disorders defined by the DSM and

is strongly correlated with the RAPI ($r = .79$) (Devos-Comby & Lange, 2008). The total score derived from the administration of the assessment represents a spectrum of adverse consequences and contains useful information focusing on specific domains of consequences. These domains include impaired control, self-perception, self-care, social and interpersonal consequences, risk behaviors, academic and/or occupational consequences, physical consequences of excessive drinking such as heightened tolerance and withdrawals, and mental effects such as experiencing blackouts.

Preliminary validation studies have suggested the YAACQ demonstrates good concurrent validity with other indicators of risky alcohol use and its items appear to function equally well across genders (Devos-Comby & Lange, 2008; Keough, O-Connor, & Read, 2016; Read, Merrill, Kahler, & Strong, 2007). In addition, the assessment has demonstrated adequate test-retest reliability ($r = .86$) and internal consistency, with scores ranging from .75 to .95 (Devos-Comby & Lange, 2008; Read et al., 2007). Scores of self-reported problems associated with alcohol use range from 14.7 to 8.7 across studies (Devos-Comby & Lange, 2008; Read et al., 2007).

A shorter version of the YAACQ, the Brief Young Adult Alcohol Consequences Questionnaire (B-YAACQ), exists and has shown adequate to good levels of internal consistency (Devos-Comby & Lange, 2008; Kahler, Hustad, Barnett, Strong, & Borsari, 2008). In addition, the B-YAACQ has demonstrated excellent distributional properties, contains items that match well to varying severities of alcohol use in emerging adult samples, covers the full spectrum of problem severity, and appears highly efficient in capturing all the significant variance initially described by its larger parent scale, the YAACQ (Kahler, Strong, & Read, 2005). Finally, multiple translations of both the YAACQ and the B-YAACQ, including Spanish, Portuguese, and Danish versions, have been adapted and validated in cross-national studies (Ferreira, Martins, Coelho, & Kahler, 2014; Pilatti et al., 2014; Pilatti, Read, & Caneto, 2016; Verster, van Herwijnen, Olivier, & Kahler, 2009).

SUMMARY

Many challenges exist with regard to screening for and assessing substance use disorders among emerging adults. A chief concern is that research has shown that some items are misinterpreted by emerging adults. Thus caution should be exercised with these items, and additional research should focus on improving the wording of such items (i.e., withdrawal, longer/larger criteria). Notwithstanding these nuances, there is a substantial amount of research that applies the DSM-5 criteria to emerging adults, and recent changes appear justified for this population. Several empirically supported screeners and assessments exist and can be used in various contexts, depending on the needs of researchers or clinicians. We encourage practitioners to use empirically validated screeners and assessments, as they have been shown to outperform professional judgment in identifying individuals in need of substance use treatment.

REFERENCES

Acevedo, A., Garnick, D., Ritter, G., Horgan, C., & Lundgren, L. (2015). Race/ethnicity and quality indicators for outpatient treatment for substance use disorders. *American Journal on Addictions, 24*(6), 523–531.

Ali, R., Meena, S., Eastwood, B., Richards, I., & Marsden, J. (2013). Ultra-rapid screening for substance-use disorders: the Alcohol, Smoking and Substance Involvement Screening Test (ASSIST-Lite). *Drug and Alcohol Dependence, 132*(1), 352–361.

American Psychiatric Association (2000). *Diagnostic and Statistical Manual of Mental Disorders*, fourth edition. Washington, DC: Author.

American Psychiatric Association (2013). *Diagnostic and Statistical Manual of Mental Disorders*, fifth edition. Washington, DC: Author.

Babor, T. F., McRee, B. G., Kassebaum, P. A., Grimaldi, P. L., Ahmed, K., & Bray, J. (2007). Screening, Brief Intervention, and Referral to Treatment (SBIRT) toward a public health approach to the management of substance abuse. *Substance Abuse, 28*(3), 7–30.

Bagley, S. M., Anderson, B. J., & Stein, M. D. (2017). Usefulness of the CRAFFT to diagnose alcohol or cannabis use disorders in a sample of emerging adults with past-month alcohol or caanabis use. *Journal of Child & Adolescent Substance Abuse, 26*, 18–23.

Barreto, H. A., Christoff, A. O., & Boerngen-Lacerda, R. (2014). Development of a self-report format of ASSIST with university students. *Addictive Behaviors, 39*(7), 1152–1158.

Bernstein, E., Edwards, E., Dorfman, D., Heeren, T., Bliss, C., & Bernstein, J. (2009). Screening and brief intervention to reduce marijuana use among youth and young adults in a pediatric emergency department. *Society for Academic Emergency Medicine, 16*(11), 1174–1185.

Bernstein, J., Heeren, T., Edward, E., Dorfman, D., Bliss, C., Winter, M., & Bernstein, E. (2010). A brief motivational interview in a pediatric emergency department, plus 10-day telephone follow-up, increases attempts to quit drinking among youth and young adults who screen positive for problematic drinking. *Academy of Emergency Medicine, 17*(8), 890–902.

Boness, C. L., Lane, S. P., & Sher, K. J. (2016). Assessment of withdrawal and hangover is confounded in the Alcohol Use Disorder and Associated Disabilities Interview Schedule: Withdrawal prevalence is likely inflated. *Alcoholism: Clinical and Experimental Research, 40*(8), 1691–1699.

Borsari, B., & Carey, K. B. (2005). Two brief alcohol interventions for mandated college students. *Psychology of Addictive Behaviors, 19*(3), 296–302.

Boyd, C. J., McCabe, S. E., & d'Arcy, H. (2003). A modified version of the CAGE as an indicator of alcohol abuse and its consequences among undergraduate drinkers. *Substance Abuse, 24*(4), 221–232.

Cacciola, J. S., Alterman, A. I., McLellan, A. T., Lin, Y. T., & Lynch, K. G. (2007). Initial evidence for the reliability and validity of a "lite" version of the Addiction Severity Index. *Drug and Alcohol Dependence, 87*(2), 297–302.

Carroll, K. M., Easton, C. J., Nich, C., Hunkele, K. A., Neavins, T. M., Sinha, R., . . . Rounsaville, B. J. (2006). The use of contingency management and motivational/skills-building therapy to treat young adults with marijuana dependence. *Journal of Consulting and Clinical Psychology, 74*(5), 955–966.

Chi, F. W., Weisner, C., Grella, C. E., Hser, Y. I., Moore, C., & Mertens, J. (2014). Does age at first treatment episode make a difference in outcomes over 11 years? *Journal of Substance Abuse Treatment, 46*(4), 482–490.

Clements, R. (1998). A critical evaluation of several alcohol screening instruments using the CIDI-SAM as a criterion measure. *Alcoholism: Clinical and Experimental Research, 22*(5), 985–993.

Clements, R., & Heintz, J. M. (2002). Diagnostic accuracy and factor structure of the AAS and APS scales of the MMPI-2. *Journal of Personality Assessment, 79*(3), 564–582.

Collins, S. E., & Carey, K. B. (2005). Lack of effect for decisional balance as a brief motivational intervention for at-risk college drinkers. *Addictive Behaviors, 30*(7), 1425–1430.

Conrad, K. J., Dennis, M. L., Bezruczko, N., Funk, R. R., & Riley, B. B. (2007). Substance use disorder symptoms: Evidence of differential item functioning by age. *Journal of Applied Measurement, 8*(4), 373–387.

Chan, Y. F., Dennis, M. L., & Funk, R. R. (2008). Prevalence and comorbidity of major internalizing and externalizing problems among adolescents and adults presenting to substance abuse treatment. *Journal of Substance Abuse Treatment, 34*(1), 14–24.

Davis, J. P., Merrin, G. J., Berry D. J., Dumas, T. M., Hong, J. S., & Smith, D. C. (2016). Examining within-person and between-person effects of victimization and social risk on cannabis use among emerging adults in substance-use treatment. *Psychology of Addictive Behaviors, 30*, 52–63.

Davis, J. P., Smith, D. C. Morphew, J. W., Lei, X., & Zhang, S. (2016). Cannabis withdrawal, post-treatment abstinence, and days to first cannabis use among emerging adults in substance use treatment: A prospective study. *Journal of Drug Issues, 46*, 64–83.

Degenhardt, L., Chiu, W. T., Sampson, N., Kessler, R. C., & Anthony, J. C. (2007). Epidemiological patterns of extra-medical drug use in the United States: Evidence from the National Comorbidity Survey Replication, 2001–2003. *Drug and Alcohol Dependence, 90*(2), 210–223.

Delforterie, M. J., Creemers, H. E., Agrawal, A., Lynskey, M. T., Jak, S., & Huizink, A. C. (2015). The influence of age and gender on the likelihood of endorsing cannabis abuse/dependence criteria. *Addictive Behaviors, 42*, 172–175.

Delucchi, K. L., Matzger, H., & Weisner, C. (2008). Alcohol in emerging adulthood: 7-year study of problem and dependent drinkers. *Addictive Behaviors, 33*(1), 134–142.

DeMartini, K. S., & Carey, K. B. (2012). Optimizing the use of the AUDIT for alcohol screening in college students. *Psychological Assessment, 24*(4), 954–963.

Demirbaş, H. (2015). Substance and alcohol use in young adults in Turkey as indicated by the CAGE questionnaire and drinking frequency. *Archives of Neuropsychiatry, 52*(1), 29–35.

Dennis, M. L., Chan, Y. F., & Funk, R. R. (2006). Development and validation of the GAIN Short Screener (GSS) for internalizing, externalizing and substance use disorders and crime/violence problems among adolescents and adults. *American Journal on Addictions, 15*(s1), 80–91.

Dennis, M. L., Funk, R., Godley, S. H., Godley, M. D., & Waldron, H. (2004). Cross-validation of the alcohol and cannabis use measures in the Global Appraisal of Individual Needs (GAIN) and Timeline Followback (TLFB; Form 90) among adolescents in substance abuse treatment. *Addiction, 99*(s2), 120–128.

Dennis, M. L., Titus, J. C., White, M. K., Unsicker, J. I., & Hodgkins, D. (2003). *Global Appraisal of Individual Needs_Initial (GAIN-I)*. Bloomington, IL: Chestnut Health Systems.

Dennis, M. L., White, M. K., & Ives, M. L. (2009). Individual characteristics and needs associated with substance misuse of adolescents and young adults in addiction treatment. In C. Leukefeld, T. P. Gulotta, & M. Statton-Tindall (eds.), *Adolescent Substance Abuse* (pp. 45–72). New York: Springer.

Devos-Comby, L., & Lange, J. E. (2008). Standardized measures of alcohol-related problems: A review of their use among college students. *Psychology of Addictive Behaviors*, *22*(3), 349–361.

Earleywine, M., Labrie, J. W., & Pedersen, E. R. (2008). A brief Rutgers Alcohol Problem Index with less potential for bias. *Addictive Behaviors*, *33*(9), 1249–1253.

Ferreira, J. A., Martins, J. S., Coelho, M. S., & Kahler, C. W. (2014). Validation of Brief Young Adult Alcohol Consequences Questionnaire (B-YAACQ): Portuguese version. *Spanish Journal of Psychology*, *17*, E71.

First, M. B. (1995). *Structured clinical interview for the DSM (SCID)*. New York: John Wiley & Sons.

Garner, B. R., Hunter, B. D., Smith, D. C., Smith, J. E., & Godley, M. D. (2014). The relationship between child maltreatment and substance abuse treatment outcomes among emerging adults and adolescents. *Child Maltreatment*, *19*, 261–269. doi: 10.1177/1077559514547264

Gibbs, L. E. (1983). Validity and reliability of the Michigan Alcoholism Screening Test: A review. *Drug and Alcohol Dependence*, *12*(3), 279–285.

Gonzalez, G., DiGirolamo, G., Romero-Gonzalez, M., Smelson, D., Ziedonis, D., & Kolodziej, M. (2015). Memantine improves buprenorphine/naloxone treatment for opioid dependent young adults. *Drug and Alcohol Dependence*, *156*, 243–253.

González, M. C. T., Riveros, M. M. P., Uribe, J. I., & Luna, S. M. (2006). Validation of the Young Adult Alcohol Problems Screening Test "YAAPST" in a group of undergraduate students of the Pontifica Universidad Javeriana. *Universitas Psychologica*, *5*(1), 175–190.

Goodman, I., Henderson, J., Peterson-Badali, M., & Goldstein, A. L. (2015). The relationship between psychosocial features of emerging adulthood and substance use change motivation in youth. *Journal of Substance Abuse Treatment*, *52*, 58–66.

Grant, B. F., Dawson, D. A., & Hasin, D. S. (2001). *The Alcohol Use Disorders and Associated Disabilities Interview Schedule—version for DSM-IV (AUDADIS-IV)*. Bethesda, MD: National Institute on Alcohol Abuse and Alcoholism.

Grant, B. F., Dawson, D. A., Stinson, F. S., Chou, P. S., Kay, W., & Pickering, R. (2003). The Alcohol Use Disorder and Associated Disabilities Interview Schedule-IV (AUDADIS-IV): Reliability of alcohol consumption, tobacco use, family history of depression and psychiatric diagnostic modules in a general population sample. *Drug and Alcohol Dependence*, *71*(1), 7–16.

Grant, B. F., Goldstein, R. B., Saha, T. D., Chou, S. P., Jung, J., Zhang, H., . . . Hasin, D. S. (2015). Epidemiology of DSM-5 alcohol use disorder: Results from the National Epidemiologic Survey on Alcohol and Related Conditions III. *JAMA Psychiatry*, *72*(8), 757–766.

Grant, B. F., Stinson, F. S., & Harford, T. (2001). The 5-year course of alcohol abuse among young adults. *Journal of Substance Abuse*, *13*(3), 229–238.

Ham, L. S., & Hope, D. A. (2005). Incorporating social anxiety into a model of college student problematic drinking. *Addictive Behaviors, 30*(1), 127–150.

Harley, M. E., Connor, D., Clarke, M. C., Kelleher, I., Coughlan, H., Lynch, F., . . . Cannon, M. (2015). Prevalence of mental disorder among young adults in Ireland: A population based study. *Irish Journal of Psychological Medicine, 32*(1), 79–91.

Hasin, D. S., & Grant, B. F. (2015). The National Epidemiologic Survey on Alcohol and Related Conditions (NESARC) Waves 1 and 2: Review and summary of findings. *Social Psychiatry and Psychiatric Epidemiology, 50*(11):1609–1640. doi: 10.1007/s00127-015-1088-0

Hasin, D. S., O'Brien, C. P., Auriacombe, M., Borges, G., Bucholz, K., Budney, A., . . . Grant, B. F. (2013). DSM-5 criteria for substance use disorders: Recommendations and rationale. *American Journal of Psychiatry, 170*(8), 834–851. doi: 10.1176/appi.ajp.2013.12060782

Hays, R. D., & Revetto, J. P. (1992). Old and new MMPI-derived scales and the Short-MAST as screening tools for alcohol disorder. *Alcohol and Alcoholism, 27*(6), 685–695.

Heck, E. J., & Williams, M. D. (1995). Using the CAGE to screen for drinking-related problems in college students. *Journal of Studies on Alcohol, 56*(3), 282–286.

Henry-Edwards, S., Humeniuk, R., Ali, R., Poznyak, V., & Monteiro, M. (2003). *The Alcohol, Smoking and Substance Involvement Screening Test (ASSIST): Guidelines for use in primary care.* Geneva: World Health Organization.

Humeniuk, R., Ali, R., Babor, T. F., Farrell, M., Formigoni, M. L., Jittiwutikarn, J., ... Simon, S. (2008). Validation of the Alcohol, Smoking, and Substance Involvement Screening Test (ASSIST). *Addiction, 103*(6), 1039–1047 .

Hunter, S. B., Griffin, B. A., Booth, M. S., Ramchand, R., & McCaffrey, D. F. (2014). Assessing the generalizability of the CSAT-sponsored GAIN dataset: Are the CSAT sites representative of adolescent treatment programs in the US? *Journal of Substance Abuse Treatment, 46*(2), 238–243.

Hurlbut, S. C., & Sher, K. J. (1992). Assessing alcohol problems in college students. *Journal of American College Health, 41*(2), 49–58.

Kahler, C. W., Hoeppner, B. B., & Jackson, K. M. (2009). A Rasch model analysis of alcohol consumption and problems across adolescence and young adulthood. *Alcoholism: Clinical and Experimental Research, 33*(4), 663–673.

Kahler, C. W., Hustad, J., Barnett, N. P., Strong, D. R., & Borsari, B. (2008). Validation of the 30-day version of the Brief Young Adult Alcohol Consequences Questionnaire for use in longitudinal studies. *Journal of Studies on Alcohol & Drugs, 69*(4), 611–615.

Kahler, C. W., & Strong, D. R. (2006). A Rasch model analysis of DSM-IV alcohol abuse and dependence items in the National Epidemiological Survey on Alcohol and Related Conditions. *Alcoholism: Clinical and Experimental Research, 30*(7), 1165–1175.

Kahler, C. W., Strong, D. R., & Read, J. P. (2005). Toward efficient and comprehensive measurement of the alcohol problems continuum in college students: The Brief Young Adult Alcohol Consequences Questionnaire. *Alcoholism: Clinical & Experimental Research, 29*(7), 1180–1189.

Kahn, R., Chatton, A., Thorens, G., Achab, S., Nallet, A., Broers, B., . . . Khazaal, Y. (2012). Validation of the French version of the Alcohol, Smoking, and Substance Involvement Screening Test (ASSIST) in the elderly. *Substance Abuse Treatment, Prevention, and Policy, 7*(14), 1–7.

Kelly, J. F., Magill, M., Slaymaker, V., & Kahler, C. (2010). Psychometric validation of the Leeds Dependence Questionnaire (LDQ) in a young adult clinical sample. *Addictive Behaviors*, *35*(4), 331–336.

Kelly, T. M., Donovan, J. E., Chung, T., Bukstein, O. G., & Cornelius, J. R. (2009). Brief screens for detecting alcohol use disorder among 18–20 year old young adults in emergency departments: Comparing AUDIT-C, CRAFFT, RAPS4-QF, FAST, RUFT-Cut, and DSM-IV 2-Item Scale. *Addictive Behaviors*, *34*(8), 668–674. doi: 10.1016/j.addbeh.2009.03.038

Keough, M. T., O-Connor, R. M., & Read, J. P. (2016). Replication and validation of the Young Adult Alcohol Consequences Questionnaire in a large sample of Canadian undergraduates. *Alcoholism: Clinical & Experimental Research*, *40*(5), 1093–1099

Kessler, R. C., Berglund, P., Demler, O., Jin, R., Merikangas, K. R., & Walters, E. E. (2005). Lifetime prevalence and age-of-onset distributions of DSM-IV disorders in the National Comorbidity Survey Replication. *Archives of General Psychiatry*, *62*(6), 593–602.

Kessler, R. C., Chiu, W. T., Demler, O., & Walters, E. E. (2005). Prevalence, severity, and comorbidity of 12-month DSM-IV disorders in the National Comorbidity Survey Replication. *Archives of General Psychiatry*, *62*(6), 617–627.

Keyes, K. M., Geier, T., Grant, B. F., & Hasin, D. S. (2009). Influence of a drinking quantity and frequency measure on the prevalence and demographic correlates of DSM-IV alcohol dependence. *Alcoholism: Clinical and Experimental Research*, *33*(5), 761–771. doi: 10.1111/j.1530-0277.2009.00894.x

Khan, R., Chatton, A., Thorens, G., Achab, S., Nallet, A., Broers, B., . . . & Khazaal, Y. (2012). Validation of the French version of the alcohol, smoking and substance involvement screening test (ASSIST) in the elderly. *Substance Abuse Treatment, Prevention, and Policy*, *7*(1), 14.

Knight, J. R., Sherritt, L., Shrier, L. A., Harris, S. K., & Chang, G. (2002). Validity of the CRAFFT substance abuse screening test among adolescent clinic patients. *Archives of Pediatrics and Adolescent Medicine*, *156*(6), 607–614.

Knight, J. R., Shrier, L., Bravender, T., Farrell, M., Vanderbilt, J., & Shaffer, H. A. (1999). A new brief screen for adolescent substance abuse. *Archives of Pediatrics and Adolescent Medicine*, *15*(3), 591–596.

Kokotailo, P. K., Egan, J., Gangnon, R., Brown, D., Mundt, M., & Fleming, M. (2004). Validity of the Alcohol Use Disorders Identification Test in college students. *Alcoholism: Clinical and Experimental Research*, *28*(6), 914–920. doi: 10.1097/01.ALC.0000128239.87611.F5

Larimer, M. E., Cronce, J. M., Lee, C. M., & Kilmer, J. R. (2004). Brief intervention in college settings. *Alcohol Research & Health*, *28*(2), 94–104.

Lennox, R., Dennis, M. L., Scott, C. K., & Funk, R. (2006). Combining psychometric and biometric measures of substance use. *Drug and Alcohol Dependence*, *83*(2), 95–103.

Lobbestael, J., Leurgans, M., & Arntz, A. (2011). Inter-rater reliability of the Structured Clinical Interview for DSM-IV Axis I disorders (SCID I) and Axis II disorders (SCID II). *Clinical Psychology & Psychotherapy*, *18*(1), 75–79.

Maisto, S. A., Connors, G. J., & Allen, J. P. (1995). Contrasting self-report screens for alcohol problems: A review. *Clinical and Experimental Research*, *19*(6), 1510–1516.

Marlowe, D. B., Festinger, D. S., Lee, P. A., Schepise, M. M., Hazzard, J. E., Merrill, J. C., . . . McLellan, A. T. (2003). Are judicial status hearings a key component of drug court? During-treatment data from a randomized trial. *Criminal Justice and Behavior, 30*(2), 141–162.

Martens, M. P., Neighbors, C., Dams-O'Connor, K., Lee, C. M., & Larimer, M. E. (2007). The factor structure of a dichotomously scored Rutgers Alcohol Problem Index. *Journal of Studies on Alcohol and Drugs, 68*(4), 597–606.

Martin, C. S., Liepman, M. R., & Young, C. M. (1990). The Michigan Alcoholism Screening Test: False positives in a college student sample. *Alcoholism: Clinical and Experimental Research, 14*(6), 853–855.

McLellan, A. T., Cacciola, J. C., Alterman, A. I., Rikoon, S. H., & Carise, D. (2006). The Addiction Severity Index at 25: Origins, contributions and transitions. *American Journal on Addictions, 15*(2), 113–124.

McLellan, A. T., Kushner, H., Metzger, D., Peters, R., Smith, I., Grissom, G., . . . Argeriou, M. (1992). The fifth edition of the Addiction Severity Index. *Journal of Substance Abuse Treatment, 9*(3), 199–213.

Mewton, L., Slade, T., & Teesson, M. (2013). An evaluation of the proposed DSM-5 cannabis use disorder criteria using Australian national survey data. *Journal of Studies on Alcohol and Drugs, 74*(4), 614–621.

Mewton, L., Teesson, M., & Slade, T. (2010). "Youthful epidemic" or diagnostic bias? Differential item functioning of DSM-IV cannabis use criteria in an Australian general population survey. *Addictive Behaviors, 35*(5), 408–413.

Monti, P. M., Barnett, N. P., Colby, S. M., Gwaltney, C. J., Spirito, A., Rohsenow, D. J., & Woolard, R. (2007). Motivational interviewing versus feedback only in emergency care for young adult problem drinking. *Society for the Study of Addiction, 102*, 1234–1243.

Morse, S. A., Watson, C., MacMaster, S. A., & Bride, B. E. (2015). Differences between older and younger adults in residential treatment for co-occurring disorders. *Journal of Dual Diagnosis, 11*(1), 75–82.

Myerholtz, L., & Rosenberg, H. (1998). Screening college students for alcohol problems: Psychometric assessment of the SASSI-2. *Journal of Studies on Alcohol, 59*(4), 439–446.

Neal, D. J., & Carey, K. B. (2004). Developing discrepancy within self-regulation theory: Use of personalized normative feedback and personal strivings with heavy-drinking college students. *Addictive Behaviors, 29*(2), 281–297.

Neal, D. J., Corbin, W. R., & Fromme, K. (2006). Measurement of alcohol-related consequences among high school and college students: Application of item response models to the Rutgers Alcohol Problem Index. *Psychological Assessment, 18*(4), 402–414.

Pabst, A., Kraus, L., Piontek, D., & Baumeister, S. E. (2012). Age differences in diagnostic criteria of DSM-IV alcohol dependence among adults with similar drinking behaviour. *Addiction, 107*(2), 331–338.

Pagan, J. L., Rose, R. J., Viken, R. J., Pulkkinen, L., Kaprio, J., & Dick, D. M. (2006). Genetic and environmental influences on stages of alcohol use across adolescence and into young adulthood. *Behavior Genetics, 36*(4), 483–497.

Pilatti, A., Read, J. P., & Caneto, F. (2016). Validation of the Spanish version of the Young Adult Alcohol Consequences Questionnaire (S-YAACQ). *Psychological Assessment, 28*(5), E49.

Pilatti, A., Read, J. P., Vera, B. D. V., Caneto, F., Garimaldi, J. A., & Kahler, C. W. (2014). The Spanish version of the Brief Young Adult Alcohol Consequences Questionnaire (B-YAACQ): A Rasch model analysis. *Addictive Behaviors*, *39*(5), 842–847.

Pull, C. B., Saunders, J. B., Mavreas, V., Cottler, L. B., Grant, B. F., Hasin, D. S., . . . Üstün, B. T. (1997). Concordance between ICD-10 alcohol and drug use disorder criteria and diagnoses as measured by the AUDADIS-ADR, CIDI and SCAN: Results of a cross-national study. *Drug and Alcohol Dependence*, *47*(3), 207–216.

Raistrick, D., Bradshaw, J., Tober, G., Weiner, J., Allison, J., & Healey, C. (1994). Development of the Leeds Dependence Questionnaire (LDQ): A questionnaire to measure alcohol and opiate dependence in the context of a treatment evaluation package. *Addiction*, *89*(5), 563–572.

Read, J. P., Kahler, C. W., Strong, D. R., & Colder, C. R. (2006). Development and preliminary validation of the Young Adult Alcohol Consequences Questionnaire. *Journal of Studies on Alcohol*, *67*(1), 169–177.

Read, J. P., Merrill, J. E., Kahler, C. W., & Strong, D. R. (2007). Predicting functional outcomes among college drinkers: Reliability and predictive validity of the Young Adult Alcohol Consequences Questionnaire. *Addictive Behaviors*, *32*(11), 2597–2610.

Ross, H. E., & Tisdall, G. W. (1994). Identification of alcohol disorders at a university mental health centre, using the CAGE. *Journal of Alcohol and Drug Education*, *39*(3), 119–126.

Santis, R., Hidalgo, C. G., Jaramillo, A., Hayden, V., Armijo, I., & Lasagna, A. (2013). A family outreach intervention for engaging young out-of-treatment drug users: Pre- versus post-treatment comparison. *Journal of Substance Abuse Treatment*, *44*(1), 61–70.

Saunders, J. B., Aasland, O. G., Babor, T. F., De la Fuente, J. R., & Grant, M. (1993). Development of the Alcohol Use Disorders Identification Test (AUDIT): WHO collaborative project on early detection of persons with harmful alcohol consumption-II. *Addiction*, *88*(6), 791–804.

Segatto, M. L., Andreoni, S., de Souza e Silva, R., Diehl, A., & Pinsky, I. (2010). Brief motivational interview and educational brochure in emergency room settings for adolescents and young adults with alcohol-related problems: A randomized single-blind clinical trial. *Revista Brasileira de Psiquiatria*, *33*(3), 225–233.

Slade, T., Teesson, M., Mewton, L., Memedovic, S., & Krueger, R. F. (2013). Do young adults interpret the DSM diagnostic criteria for alcohol use disorders as intended? A cognitive interviewing study. *Alcoholism: Clinical and Experimental Research*, *37*(6), 1001–1007.

Smith, D. C., Bahar, O.S., Cleeland, L. R., & Davis, J. P. (2014). Self-perceived emerging adult status and substance use. *Psychology of Addictive Behaviors*, *28*, 935–941. doi: 10.1037/a0035900

Smith, D. C., Bennett, K. M., Dennis, M. L., & Funk, R. R. (2017). Sensitivity and specificity of the gain short-screener for predicting substance use disorders in a large national sample of emerging adults. *Addictive Behaviors*, *68*, 14–17.

Smith, D. C., Cleeland, L., & Dennis, M. L. (2010) Reasons for quitting among emerging adults and adolescents in substance use disorder treatment. *Journal of Studies on Alcohol and Drugs*, *71*, *3*, 400–409.

Smith, D. C., Davis, J. P., Dumas, T., & Ureche, D. J. (2016). Six-month outcomes of a peer-enhanced community reinforcement approach for emerging adults with substance misuse: A preliminary study. *Journal of Substance Abuse Treatment*, *61*, 66–73.

Smith, D. C., Godley, S. H., Godley, M. D., & Dennis, M. L. (2011) Adolescent Community Reinforcement Approach (A-CRA) outcomes differ among emerging adults and adolescents. *Journal of Substance Abuse Treatment*, *41*, 422–430.

Smith, D. J., Harrison, N., Muir, W., & Blackwood, D. H. (2005). The high prevalence of bipolar spectrum disorders in young adults with recurrent depression: Toward an innovative diagnostic framework. *Journal of Affective Disorders*, *84*(2), 167–178.

Smith, D. S., Collins, M., Kreisberg, J. P., Volpicelli, J. R., & Alterman, A. I. (1987). Screening for problem drinking in college freshmen. *Journal of American College Health*, *36*, 89–94.

Stein, M. D., Caviness, C. M., & Anderson, B. J. (2014). Alcohol use potentiates marijuana problem severity in young adult women. *Women's Health Issues*, *24*(1), e77–e82.

Substance Abuse and Mental Health Services Administration (SAMSHA). Center for Behavioral Health Statistics and Quality. (2013). National survey on drug use and health, 2012. ICPSR34933-v1. doi: 10.3886/ICPSR34933.v1

Svanum, S., & McGrew, J. (1995). Prospective screening of substance dependence: The advantages of directness. *Addictive Behaviors. 20*(2), 205–213.

Tiburcio, S. M., Rosete-Mohedano, M. G., Natera, R. G., Martínez, V. N., Carreño, G. S., & Pérez, C. D. (2015). Validity and reliability of the Alcohol, Smoking, and Substance Involvement Screening Test (ASSIST) in university students. *Adicciones*, *28*(1), 19–27.

Titus, J. C., Smith, D. C., Dennis, M. L., Ives, M., Twanow, L., & White, M. K. (2012). Impact of a training and certification program on the quality of interviewer-collected self-report assessment data. *Journal of Substance Abuse Treatment*, *42*(2), 201–212.

Verster, J. C., van Herwijnen, J., Olivier, B., & Kahler, C. W. (2009). Validation of the Dutch version of the Brief Young Adult Alcohol Consequences Questionnaire (B-YAACQ). *Addictive Behaviors*, *34*(5), 411–414.

Vinson, D. C., Turner, B. J., Manning, B. K., & Galliher, J. M. (2013). Clinician suspicion of an alcohol problem: An observational study from the AAFP National Research Network. *Annals of Family Medicine*, *11*(1), 53–59.

Wu, L. T., Pilowsky, D. J., Schlenger, W. E., & Hasin, D. (2007). Alcohol use disorders and the use of treatment services among college-age young adults. *Psychiatric Services*, *58*(2), 192–200.

Yudko, E., Lozhkina, O., & Fouts, A. (2007). A comprehensive review of the psychometric properties of the Drug Abuse Screening Test. *Journal of Substance Abuse Treatment*, *32*(2), 189–198.

Zamboanga, B. L., Horton, N. J., Tyler, K. M. B., O'Riordan, S. S., Calvert, B. D., & McCollum, E. C. (2007). The utility of the AUDIT in screening for drinking game involvement among female college students. *Journal of Adolescent Health*, *40*(4), 359–361. doi: 10.1016/j.jadohealth.2006.11.139

4

What Is the State of the Art in Preventing and Treating Substance Use Disorders among Emerging Adults?

DOUGLAS C. SMITH, CLAYTON NEIGHBORS, AND JORDANNA LEMBO ■

INTRODUCTION

This chapter provides an in-depth and up-to-date summary of empirically supported interventions for substance use among both college-attending and non-college-attending emerging adults. We begin by focusing on approaches that address the "binge drinking culture" on college campuses. Many individual-level interventions directly target the internalized myth among heavily drinking students that such drinking is done by most students on college campuses; indeed, it is not. For example, a subset of frequent binge drinkers consumes most alcohol on campus, such as the 30% of students who drink five or more drinks more than three times monthly (Wechsler & Nelson, 2008). The second half of the chapter focuses on non-college-attending emerging adults, a group sometimes referred to as "the forgotten half" of emerging adults (Arnett, 2000). Emerging adults who do not attend college are underrepresented in clinical trials and sometimes have different life trajectories than those of college students (Mitchell & Syed, 2015). Such emerging adults may present specific challenges for substance use disorder treatment professionals.

INTERVENING WITH COLLEGE STUDENTS

In 2005, there were 1,825 alcohol-related deaths among college students (Hingson, Zha, & Weitzman, 2009). Thus it is no surprise that substantial efforts have been expended in addressing alcohol and other substance use on college campuses. All colleges in the United States have policies regarding alcohol and other substance use and include a wide range of strategies designed to support these policies. The National Institute on Alcohol Abuse and Alcoholism (NIAAA) has actively promoted the development, evaluation, and dissemination of effective strategies for addressing problem drinking among college students. Noteworthy contributions include the formation of a task force in 1999 of experts who collaborated on a comprehensive report, "A Call to Action: Changing the Culture of Drinking at U.S. Colleges" (NIAAA, 2002), which was designed to inform and assist college administrators in addressing drinking on their campuses. The task force also produced a number of high-quality reviews published in a special issue of the *Journal of Studies on Alcohol* in 2002. Subsequently, the NIAAA created an initiative entitled "Rapid Response to College Drinking Problems" in which five teams of intervention experts were partnered with 15 campuses chosen to receive support in the design and implementation of intervention programs on their campuses. Results of this initiative included the evaluation of 15 specific intervention programs, a dedicated special issue of the *Journal of Studies on Alcohol and Drugs* in 2009, a number of additional related publications not included in the special issue, and the formation of productive and enduring collaborative relationships, which continue to contribute to the advancement of prevention and treatment approaches for alcohol and other substance use. Most recently, the NIAAA has undertaken the College Alcohol Intervention Matrix (College AIM) initiative. Most materials related to NIAAA initiatives can be found on their website dedicated to this issue: http://www.collegedrinkingprevention.gov/. The College AIM initiative reviews individual and environmental interventions targeting college drinking. These two categories roughly overlap with the primary foci of this portion of the chapter: (1) discussion of the Brief Alcohol Screening and Intervention for College Students (BASICS; Dimeff, Baer, Kivlahan, & Marlatt, 1999) and adaptations of BASICS, motivational interviewing, and personalized feedback interventions, and (2) macro-level prevention models.

BASICS and Personalized Feedback Interventions

Treatments for college student substance use include individually focused interventions, group-based interventions, and macro-level prevention models. Of these, individually focused interventions are most frequently evaluated in the literature. The Brief Alcohol Screening and Intervention for College Students (BASICS; Dimeff et al., 1999) continues to serve as the prototype and gold standard of brief intervention for drinking among college students. Most, but not all, individually focused interventions are direct descendants of this approach. Individually focused interventions of primary focus include BASICS and BASICS-like interventions, motivational interviewing (MI), and personalized feedback intervention (PFI).

A Brief History of BASICS

In 1982, Marlatt and colleagues received funding from the NIAAA to develop and evaluate interventions for problem drinking among college students. The first of these was a group-based intervention entitled the Alcohol Skills Training Program (ASTP; Fromme, Marlatt, Baer, & Kivlahan, 1994). The ASTP was originally presented as an 8-week moderation-oriented, cognitive-behavioral alcohol skills training class. Each class was 90 minutes. The ASTP was evaluated relatve to a didactic alcohol information class and an assessment-only control condition. Results showed promising effects of ASTP relative to both comparison groups, but with only 36 participants in the trial, the study was not powered to detect significant differences. The ASTP format was subsequently streamlined to a six-session group format and compared to a single session of personalized feedback and advice, which was a prototype of BASICS (Baer et al., 1992). Both groups showed significant and comparable declines in drinking over a 2-year follow-up. Results suggested that the single individual intervention worked as well as the six-session group intervention, but the absence of a control group limited causal inference. The seminal evaluation of BASICS was a fully powered randomized controlled trial that revealed significant reductions in drinking and related problems over 2 years relative to controls (Marlatt et al., 1998). The BASICS manual was published shortly thereafter (Dimeff et al., 1999). To date, BASICS continues as the gold standard for college alcohol interventions. Its efficacy has been supported in many trials by a number of different research groups (see Fachini, Aliane, Martinez, & Furtado [2012] for a meta-analysis).

Summary of Content

BASICS is the prototype of what has since been more generally referred to as a personalized feedback intervention (PFI). In its original format students first completed an in-person interview during which they were asked questions about their drinking patterns, perceptions of typical drinking by peers (i.e., perceived norms), family history, symptoms of abuse and dependence, beliefs about the effects of alcohol (i.e., expectancies), level of concern about their drinking, and perceived level of risk for experiencing future alcohol-related consequences. The BASICS session was administered in a subsequent 1-hour session during which participants received personalized feedback related to each of these content areas. Peronalized feedback was summarized in the form of a printed report, which the intervention provider used to structure the intervention session. It is important to note that all intervention providers first received extensive training in the content and in motivation interviewing (MI; Miller & Rollnick, 1991) as the delivery format.

Motivational interviewering (Miller & Rollnick, 2012) is a client-centered, goal-oriented, therapeutic technique designed to help individuals resolve ambivalence about a specific issue (e.g., drinking). Essential to this approach is the perspective that the provider is there to listen, empathize, help clarify, reflect, and summarize in a way that may facilitate resolution of ambivalence about change; it is not the provider's job to prescribe, persuade, dictate, label, or judge. Rather, the provider is presented as a partner in the effort to help the receipient achieve his or her goals, whatever those goals might be.

EXTENSIONS AND ADAPTATIONS

A large number of interventions have been developed and evaluated since the development of BASICS that have been directly or indirectly adapted from BASICS. *Personalized feedback intervention* is the broad term often used to describe these adaptations. These adapted PFIs are similar in that recipients first respond to questions related to their drinking and related constructs and are then provided feedback that is personalized on the basis of their responses. Specific categories of adaptation include single or subsets of components, such as personalized norms feedback only (e.g., meta-analysis; Dotson, Dunn, & Bowers, 2015) and personalized norms feedback + protective behavior strategies (Martens, Smith, & Murphy, 2013). Researchers have examined the impact of novel content not origianlly considered in the BASICS framework, such as behavioral economic components (Murphy, Dennhardt, et al., 2012; Murphy, Skidmore, et al., 2012) and adaptation to specific events, such as one's 21st birthday (Neighbors et al., 2012; Neighbors, Lee, Lewis, Fossos, & Walter, 2009) and spring break (Lee et al., 2014; Patrick, Lee, & Neighbors, 2014). In addition to content and focus, effective BASICS adaptations have been developed for specific high-risk groups, including Greek letter organizations (Larimer et al., 2001), mandated students (meta-analysis; Carey, Scott-Sheldon, Garey, Elliott, & Carey, 2016), and college athletes (Martens, Kilmer, Beck, & Zamboanga, 2010).

Among the constants in this work is that feedback regarding the recipient's personal drinking pattern and comparison with perceived and actual norms (i.e., personalized normative feedback) is included in virtually all PFIs, and this feedback is the only consistently supported mediator of PFIs (Reid & Carey, 2015). Other commonly included components (reviewed in Miller et al., 2013; Walters & Neighbors, 2005) include didactic information; risk factors (e.g., tolerance and family history); personalized blood alcohol concentration (BAC) charts; protective behavior strategies; review of alcohol-related consequences; costs of drinking (e.g., money spent, calories consumed, time spent); referral information; expectancies and evidence of placebo effects on social facilitation; and decisional balance excercises (pros of cons of current drinking and reducing drinking).

Finally, it is worth noting that electronically delivered interventions have become increasingly frequent. Despite common perceptions among some intervention researchers that computer-delivered feedback performs equally well as therapist-delivered feedback, meta-analyses have demonstrated that therapist-delivered feedback outperforms computer-delivered feedback (Carey, Scott-Sheldon, Elliott, Garey, & Carey, 2012). While computer-delivered interventions have been found to be effective in meta-analyses, potential explanations on why computer-delivered feedback may be less efficacious relative to in-person feedback are only now emerging. The location where students access the intervention may account for such differences, considering that in some studies the computer-delivered intervention is administered in person (i.e., students have an appointment to attend and complete the Web/computer-based intervention), and in other studies administration occurs remotely (i.e., students complete the intervention remotely at the time and location of their choice) (Carey et al., 2012; Riper et al., 2009). This is an important distinction given recent findings suggesting that computer/Web-delivered interventions (i.e., with no therapist) have stronger and/or longer effects when administered in person than when Web-delivered feedback interventions are done remotely (Cadigan et al., 2015; Rodriguez et al., 2015). This difference in effect appears to be due in large part to participants' distractions and lack of attention when interventions are administered remotely. In a recent randomized control trial of Web-based PFIs, many students reported simultaneously engaging in multiple tasks unrelated to the intervention, including watching TV/listening to music (26.9%); emailing, messaging, or surfing the Web (23.6%); studying or doing classwork (23.2%); and being on the phone or texting (15%), among other activities (Lewis & Neighbors, 2015). Furthermore, students reported that level of attention to the intervention moderated its effect relative to control.

In summary, BASICS administered in person by a trained intervention provider remains the gold-standard intervention for college students who drink heavily. Many variations of BASICS have also been found to be effective. Remotely delivered computer/Web-based PFIs are less effective than commonly assumed, partly because meta-analytic evaluations have included them in the same category as computer/Web-based PFIs administered in person. Moving forward, it will be important to consider methods controlling, reducing, or at least monitoring the level of distraction and attention in remotely delivered interventions, particularly for students who are not motivated to reduce their drinking to begin with. It is also important to note that while electronic interventions are likely to be less expensive and have greater reach, they may never completely replace an actual intervention provider giving feedback using MI skills. Given the differential resources and effect sizes, it would seem prudent to continue pursuing remotely delivered interventions with added structures facilitating active involement and to have therapist-delivered BASICS as an option for students who do not respond to lower-threshold interventions.

Community-Level Interventions

Many alcohol prevention efforts on college campuses have focused on intrapersonal factors, group processes, and institutional factors (DeJong & Langford, 2002). Equally important, however, are community-level preventions. Community-level, or macro-level, alcohol preventions focus on a broader effort, one that is designed to target the physical, legal, social, and economic factors that promote college drinking (DeJong & Hingson, 1998). There are five subgroups included within community-level preventions: (1) promoting and offering social, extracurricular, recreational, and public service options that do not involve alcohol; (2) creating a residential, social, and campus environment that supports positive health norms; (3) limiting alcohol availability, both on- and off-campus; (4) restricting the marketing and promotion of alcohol both on- and off-campus; and (5) developing and enforcing campus policies and local, state, and federal laws (Neighbors et al., 2007).

College students, while technically adults, typically have few adult responsibilities and ample unstructured free time. Without social and recreational options available, some students may turn to alcohol and other drugs. Thus an objective of community-level prevention programs is to develop and offer social, extracurricular, recreational, and public service options that are alcohol- and drug-free. Examples of this strategy include creating and promoting new, alcohol-free events and activities (e.g., on-campus concerts and movies, scavenger hunts, game nights); creating and publicizing volunteer opportunities; requiring community service as part of the curriculum; having a student center, coffeehouse, and other alcohol-free locations; expanding hours for student centers, coffee houses, and other alcohol-free locations; and promoting the consumption of nonalcoholic beverages at events (DeJong & Langford, 2002; Neighbors et al., 2007). Much of the literature on this strategy has examined associations between substance-free activities and substance use without actually manipulating availability of alternative activities. In a study that examined the relationship between substance-free activity enjoyment and alcohol use among college students, researchers found that female students who reported greater enjoyment from substance-free evenings also reported significantly less drinking over the past month. Additionally, the researchers found, regardless of gender, that students who reported greater enjoyment from substance-free activities were more likely to be actively considering changing their alcohol consumption (Murphy, Barnett, Goldstein, & Colby, 2007).

Fewer empirical studies have evaluated substance-free activities as intervention strategies for reducing alcohol and other substance use. In a randomized controlled study, Correia, Benson, and Carey (2005) assigned 133 undergraduates who reported recent substance use to one of three conditions: a substance reduction group, an activity increase group, and a no-change control group. Participants in the substance reduction group were instructed to decrease their substance use over the next 4 weeks by 50% (e.g., if they reported 12 days of substance use, they were instructed to use substances on no more than 6 days of the following 4 weeks). Participants assigned to the activity increase group were instructed to increase the amount of days that they both exercised and engaged in artistic/creative activities by 50%. The researchers found that participants within the substance reduction and activity increase groups reported a significant decrease in substance use (Correia et al., 2005). In another study, Murphy et al. (2005) had college student heavy drinkers complete a single-session motivational intervention. While the findings suggest that only women experienced a significant reduction in drinking at 6-month follow-up, the authors found that participants who reduced their drinking displayed an increase in reinforcement from substance-free activities (Murphy et al., 2005).

Most UW students have LESS than 2 Alcoholic beverages on a given weekend evening*

*Note: This information comes from a 2007 self-report study which included a random sample of 1,876 UW students.

Figure 4.1 Example of advertisement used in social norms marketing campaign.

SOCIAL NORMS MARKETING

Another issue that contributes to substance use on college campuses stems from students' beliefs that using alcohol and other drugs is a normal part of the college experience. Research has consistently found that college students overestimate alcohol and drug use among their peers (Lewis et al., 2010; Martens et al., 2006; Neighbors et al, 2007). Community-level preventions aim to address this problem by creating a social, residential, and academic environment that promotes positive health norms. Also known as social norms marketing (SNM) campaigns, examples of this strategy include modifying the academic schedule, increasing academic standards, offering "dry" residence options, increasing faculty–student contact, and creating programs to correct misperceptions of substance use norms (Dejong & Langford, 2002). Sometimes advertisements are used in visible campus locations (e.g., on campus buses) that aim to inform students that heavy drinking may be less rampant than they think (see Figure 4.1).

Research on SNM campaigns that target college drinking have rendered inconsistent results. In the most rigorous evaluation of SNM campaigns, DeJong et al. (2006) conducted an 18-site randomized trial in which universities were randomly assigned to either a treatment or control group. In the treatment group, the universities implemented an SNM campaign that included school-specific and data-driven messages. Students were surveyed at baseline and 3 years following the campaign. The researchers found that students who attended the universities with SNM campaigns had a lower risk of alcohol consumption than students at the control group institutions (DeJong et al., 2006). In another promising SNM campaign study, Turner, Perkins, and Bauerle (2008) followed randomly selected undergraduate students over the course of 6 years. During the course of their education, these students were exposed to portions of the SNM campaign. The campaign included monthly dorm posters, newspaper and Facebook ads, emails, and an annual music event. The researchers found that first-year students who recalled exposure to the campaign experienced less negative consequences relating to alcohol and were also less likely to experience a BAC level higher than .08. Additionally, over the 6 study years, the odds of all participants having never experienced any of 10 negative alcohol-related consequences nearly doubled (Turner et al., 2008).

Other studies have not found support for SNM campaigns. Werch and colleagues (2000) implemented a social norm intervention designed to prevent binge drinking in first-year college students. Students were randomly assigned to a control group, where they received the standard campus prevention program, or to the intervention group. The intervention took place over two semesters: in the fall, participants received three greeting cards that included prevention messages based on social norms, and in the spring they completed a telephone survey that reinforced the same prevention messages. The researchers found that there were no differences in alcohol use between participants within the control and experimental group (Werch et al., 2000). In a study at a large urban public university, Clapp, Lange, Russell, Shillington, and Voas (2003) randomly selected one residence hall to receive the SNM, and another hall served as a comparison group. The SNM campaign included posters, stickers, bookmarks, and notepads being distributed to students in the residence hall, while students in the comparison group were provided with an address book that contained information on alcohol. The researchers found that while the SNM campaign was successful in improving misperceptions of drinking norms, there were no effects on drinking behaviors (Clapp et al., 2003).

SUPPLY REDUCTION

An additional problem that leads to substance use in a college environment is alcohol availability. Alcohol is often easily accessible and inexpensive for college students. To address this issue, community-level prevention efforts aim to limit the availability of alcohol on campus and within the immediate community. Examples of this strategy include banning alcohol on campus, designing guidelines for off-campus parties, keg registrations, prohibiting alcohol use in public spaces, limiting the number of alcohol outlets near campus, limiting the days and hours of alcohol sales, increasing state alcohol taxes, and increasing the cost of alcohol sales licenses (DeJong & Langford, 2002).

Research on this strategy has rendered promising findings. Wechsler, Lee, Gledhill-Hoyt, and Nelson (2001) examined student alcohol use at colleges that banned alcohol on campus. Over 11,000 college students completed a survey in which they were asked about their alcohol use and behaviors. The responses of students enrolled at "ban" schools were compared to those of students at "non-ban" schools. The researchers found that students enrolled at "ban" schools were significantly less likely to be classified as a heavy episodic drinker. However, feasibility of this approach might be associated with school characteristics (e.g., a religious institution that has a non-alcohol policy for students). Additionally, fewer students at "ban" schools experienced second-hand effects of the drinking of their peers (Wechsler et al., 2001). Williams, Chaloupka, and Wechsler (2005) examined the role that alcohol price plays in college drinking behaviors. Using a nationally representative sample, student drinking behavior, price paid per drink, and college alcohol policies were surveyed. The researchers found that students who faced higher prices for alcohol were less likely to transition from an abstainer to a moderate drinker, and from a moderate drinker to a heavy drinker (Williams et al., 2005).

The marketing and promotion of alcohol can also lead to problematic substance use both on and off campus. Bars, restaurants, and liquor stores within college communities often use aggressive tactics and promotions to target college drinkers. In order to combat this issue, community-level preventions aim to restrict the marketing and promotion of alcohol on and off campus. Examples of this strategy on campus include banning or restricting the advertising of alcohol, banning or restricting alcohol sponsors for on-campus events, and limiting the content used within event announcements. Off campus, this strategy can be used through the banning of alcohol promotions that show drinking in high-risk contexts and that have special appeal to underage drinkers; instituting requirements for pro-health messages to counterbalance alcohol advertising; and designing agreements with bars, restaurants, and liquor stores to institute minimum pricing and limit special drink promotions (Dejong & Langford, 2002).

Research on reducing alcohol marketing has produced promising findings on alcohol consumption. Saffer and Dave (2000) examined the relationship between alcohol advertisement bans and alcohol consumption. In examining a pooled time series data set from 20 countries over 26 years, Saffer found that alcohol advertising bans decreased alcohol consumption. More specifically, the results showed that an increase of one ban could reduce alcohol consumption by up to 8% (Saffer and Dave, 2000). In a study on a community coalition, Gebhardt and colleagues (2000) implemented several strategies, including developing an advertising and beverage-service agreement with local bar owners. In this study, bar owners signed voluntary agreements to follow advertisement guidelines that included a reminder to be respectful to neighborhood residents and behave responsibly, to emphasize the legal drinking age, to avoid language that promotes heavy episodic drinking episodes (e.g., "Toxic Thursdays), and to promote nonalcoholic drinks and food specials as often as alcoholic beverage specials. The researchers found that the advertisement campaign and several other community initiatives were associated with a decrease in the number of alcohol-related problems in the college community, as indicated by a decline in off-campus noise ordinance reports filed by police and in the number of calls to a university-held hotline for reporting off-campus issues (Gebhardt et al., 2000).

Lastly, a systemic issue that can lead to greater substance use in college communities is lack of consistency in the enforcement of campus policies and of local, state, and federal laws. Community-level prevention efforts seek to amend this issue through the development and enforcement of campus policies and laws. Some examples of this strategy on campuses include the revision and dissemination of the campus alcohol and other drug (AOD) policy; requiring on-campus functions to be registered; implementing ID checks at on-campus events; increasing disciplinary sanctions for and criminal prosecution of violation of campus AOD policy and alcohol-related offenses; implementing decoy operations at campus functions; and increasing patrols near on-campus parties. Off campus, this strategy could involve imposing driver's license penalties for minors who violate alcohol laws; increasing ID checks at off-campus bars and liquor stores; enforcing laws against buying alcohol for minors; educating sellers and servers about legal liability; increasing the enforcement of DUI laws; and passing ordinances to restrict noise level and open-house assemblies (Dejong & Langford, 2002).

Research supports these strategies. Saltz and colleagues (2010) implemented environmental prevention strategies at large public universities in California. In total, 14 schools participated in the study, and 7 were randomly assigned to receive the intervention. The intervention combined heavy publicity (e.g., website, emails, newspaper articles) with alcohol control measures. The enforcement consisted of the following: DUI checks, police compliance checks using decoys to enforce laws on alcohol sales, and "party patrols" that enforced laws regarding the distribution of alcohol to minors and disturbing the peace. The researchers found that, compared to control schools, intervention universities experienced a significant decrease in the likelihood of intoxication at bars and off-campus parties. Additionally, students at the intervention universities had a lower likelihood of intoxication the last time they drank at an off-campus party, a bar, or any other setting (Saltz et al., 2010).

In a similar study, Wolfson et al. (2012) implemented a randomized trial involving 10 universities in North Carolina. The five schools randomly assigned to the intervention were given a campus organizer who was hired to form a campus–community coalition and develop and implement a plan to use community strategies to reduce drinking. These strategies included compliance checks and alcohol enforcement; increased sanctions for student alcohol violations; interdepartmental procedures for reporting; judicial policies to target off-campus behavior; clarity on the student code of conduct; party patrols; and DUI checkpoints. The researchers found that, compared to the control group, the intervention group experienced a significant decrease in consequences and injuries related to alcohol.

Community-level preventions have been found to be effective at reducing college drinking and related consequences. These community strategies should continue to be researched and implemented on campuses nationwide to combat alcohol-related issues.

INTERVENING WITH EMERGING ADULTS NOT IN COLLEGE

Delivering substance use treatment and prevention to non-college-attending emerging adults presents several challenges, such as high heterogeneity in substances used and severity, varied or minimal institutional affiliations, and lower readiness to change relative to older adults. These factors make summarizing the literature on treating and preventing substance use among non-college-attending emerging adults a rather daunting task. Yet it is an important one, as about 12.5 million emerging adults ages 18–24 (40%) in the United States are not enrolled in college (United States Department of Education, 2015). Twice as many non-college-attending emerging adults smoke marijuana on a daily basis as college students, and they drink alcohol at approximately the same rates. In addition to differences in substance use patterns and sociodemographic backgrounds, emerging adults in non-college settings do not respond as well to PFIs as they do to other types of interventions (Davis, Smith, & Briley, 2017). The remainder of this chapter discusses these challenges in treating emerging adults and reviews what we know and don't know about treating non-college-attending emerging adults.

Challenges in Treating Non-College-Attending Emerging Adults

As described earlier, most research on college-attending emerging adults focuses on alcohol use. However, emerging adults consume more opioids and marijuana than any other age group. Relative to college-attending emerging adults, those not in college are more likely to use illicit drugs. There is also large heterogeneity in the places where they may access treatment. Such locations may include public health clinics, criminal justice settings, primary care settings, the military, private practice, or specialized substance use disorder treatment facilities. Treatment settings may make a difference in treatment response, as some settings may be confounded with higher psychosocial risks. For example, Worden and McGrady (2013) argued that individuals treated in publicly funded clinics may have poorer responses to treatment because of heightened risk factors (e.g., poverty, higher psychological comorbidity). Location of service receipt may also depend on individuals' assessed severity level. The American Society of Addiction Medicine (ASAM) developed a widely used patient placement criteria guide specifying guidelines on when to provide prevention, outpatient, intensive outpatient, or residential/medically monitored inpatient services (Mee-Lee, 2013). It is important to recognize that treatment and prevention services vary in duration and intensity.

Empirically Supported Interventions

There are a wide variety of treatments used for emerging adults outside of the college context. We will focus this review on those that have the most empirical evidence for use with non-college-attending emerging adults, such as twelve-step-oriented therapy, motivational interviewing, and cognitive-behavioral therapy.

We will also discuss the current evidence for brief interventions delivered in healthcare settings, as well as technology-assisted interventions. These primary-care and technology-based interventions represent new frontiers in treating emerging adults.

TWELVE-STEP-ORIENTED TREATMENTS

Twelve-step facilitation treatments are influenced by the philosophy of Alcoholics Anonymous and other twelve step organizations that substance use disorders are chronic conditions for which only remission may be achieved (Alcoholics Anonymous World Services, 2001). These self-help organizations prescribe a spiritual solution. Individuals first admit they can never drink again, then they come to terms with a higher power and pursue a more spiritual life, proceed to analyze the damage from their substance use and take personal responsibility for it, and, ultimately, help others as they were helped. Alcoholics Anonymous boasts 115,000 groups worldwide, with 12% of members being under 30 years of age (Alcoholics Anonymous World Services, 2014).

Remarkably, despite the large influence of twelve-step philosophy on substance use disorder treatment in the United States, there are practically no trials of twelve-step facilitation (TSF) treatment that have specifically focused on emerging adults. That is, no randomized studies have compared twelve-step-based treatments to other treatments for emerging adults specifically. Emerging adults were also conspicuously underrepresented in the largest trial of TSF, Project MATCH. Whereas emerging adults have the highest prevalence of alcohol dependence nationally, less than 10% of the participants in Project MATCH were emerging adults. Emerging adults in Project MATCH did benefit from TSF (Hoeppner, Hoeppner, & Kelly, 2014) but, relative to older adults, had a poorer response to TSF during the 8 weeks in which they were receiving treatment. However, this difference was not apparent at long-term follow-up (Davis, Bergman, Smith, & Kelly, 2017).

To be clear, there are numerous emerging adult–focused studies on the effects of twelve-step meeting participation, and also on the mechanisms of action through which such participation produces its effects. Many of these studies were completed by John F. Kelly and his colleagues, who summarize their work and that of others in Chapter 8 of this volume. Yet more work remains to be done, as much of their work comes from one sample ($n = 302$) of emerging adults who received residential treatment.

What does this mean for using TSF with emerging adults? Notwithstanding the concerns about emerging adults' low religiosity and poorer initial response to TSF (Davis, Bergman, et al., 2017), emerging adults have been receiving TSF in treatment settings for many years as part of eclectic practice that we in the scientific community affectionately label "treatment as usual." In other words, eclectic practice driven by an overarching twelve step philosophy is likely the current standard of practice against which other treatments are judged. Since empirically tested treatments often do as well or only slightly better than treatment as usual, there is reason for optimism in using TSF with emerging adults.

Besides the effectiveness of TSF being hidden in these unspecified treatment-as-usual conditions, the effects of twelve-step participation for emerging adults may be obscured in studies on empirically supported treatments. For example, drug courts are widely available programs that often require participants to attend twelve-step-based support groups as a condition of program involvement. Drug courts are intensive programs for individuals involved with the criminal justice system who are nonviolent and have serious substance use problems. Drug courts rely on intensive treatment combined with regular court supervision (i.e., weekly meetings with judges) and rapid sanctions when individuals are not maintaining sobriety (Rossman, Roman, Zweig, Rempel, & Lindquist, 2011). To our knowledge, only one drug court program has been tested specifically with emerging adults (Marlowe, Festinger, Dugosh, & Lee, 2005), which found that emerging adults receiving more regularly scheduled court hearings had similar substance use outcomes to those having "as needed" hearings. It is unclear how twelve-step attendance influences drug court outcomes for emerging adults, but such attendance is a common requirement in these models.

In summary, practically no trials of TSF exist specifically for emerging adults, and the treatment outcomes of emerging adults who have received TSF are often buried in clinical trials with large age ranges, treatment-as-usual conditions, or multicomponent empirically supported treatments such as drug courts. However, emerging adults do benefit from TSF; while they experience poorer initial outcomes than those of older adults, they have outcomes equivalent to those of older adults at long-term follow-up (Davis, Bergman, et al., 2017). More studies are needed that (1) compare emerging adults receiving TSF to emerging adults receiving other treatments, (2) develop modifications to TSF that may make it more developmentally appropriate for emerging adults, and (3) test the mechanisms of action of TSF for emerging adults.

MOTIVATIONAL INTERVIEWING

Perhaps no intervention has received such widespread testing in the addiction field as motivational interviewing (MI). Initially developed in 1983 by William R. Miller, MI is an empathic, nonconfrontational counseling method designed to assist individuals in reducing ambivalence about changing their substance use through directive focus on clients' change language. *Change language* is defined as in-session speech by the client in favor of change as opposed to speech about the status quo (i.e., sustain talk). In other words, MI involves a discussion in which the clinician demonstrates empathy and uses active listening skills in a manner that results in client change talk. This is all done in hopes of moving toward a decision about substance use reduction. As of 2009, there were approximately 200 trials testing the efficacy of MI among substance users and among those ambivalent about making changes in other health behaviors (Miller & Rose, 2009). By extension, MI remains one of the few treatments with extensive testing among non-collegiate emerging adults. About one-third of all studies treating emerging adults for substance use in non-college settings involved MI (Davis, Smith, & Briley, 2017) or adaptations of MI called motivational enhancement therapy (MET). This may be an underestimate if one considers the literature on brief adaptations of MI delivered in healthcare settings (see later discussion).

These studies largely support the efficacy of MI with emerging adults outside of the college context, across a wide variety of substance use severity levels and practice settings. For example, MET combined with cognitive-behavioral therapy (CBT) and contingency management had the largest impact on marijuana use among marijuana-dependent emerging adults referred from the criminal justice system (Carroll et al., 2006). Naar-King and colleagues (2008) found greater reductions in alcohol use at 6 months for emerging adults living with HIV who received MET than for those randomized to treatment as usual. Among Swiss army conscripts, MI produced small reductions across multiple substance use measures, only producing superior reductions in marijuana use relative to control participants (Gmel, Gaume, Bertholet, Flückiger, & Daeppen, 2013). Finally, Slesnick, Guo, Brakenhoff, and Bantchevska (2015) found significant reductions in substance use for emerging adults receiving MET at homeless shelters, with equivalent outcomes compared to two other active treatment comparison groups (i.e., community reinforcement approach, contingency management). Although it would be beyond the scope of this chapter to review all studies on MI with non-college-attending emerging adults, these studies highlight MI's efficacy across a variety of substances and practice settings.

COGNITIVE-BEHAVIORAL TREATMENTS

Generally speaking, CBT models are widely used and efficacious approaches for individuals receiving substance use disorder treatment (Magill & Ray, 2009). For emerging adults treated in non-college settings, the most commonly used CBT models are variations of the community reinforcement approach (CRA; Meyers & Smith, 1995) or CBT combined with MI.

In the CRA model, clinicians flexibly use several core and recommended procedures depending on client needs, including functional analysis of the antecedents and consequences of substance use, functional analysis of prosocial activities, goal setting, happiness scaling to track progress on goals, substance refusal skills training, problem solving, communication skills training, and job seeking. The overarching philosophy of this model is that individuals will remain substance-free if sobriety becomes more rewarding than substance use. Another emblematic feature of CRA is the use of role-play by the clinician to demonstrate skills. Such role-playing is often followed by in vitro role-play practice by the clients, which in turn is praised and critiqued by the clinician.

Studies have shown that emerging adults receiving CRA reduce their substance use over time (Smith, Godley, Godley, & Dennis, 2011) and exhibit substance use outcomes just as good as those among emerging adults receiving MI or contingency management (Slesnick et al., 2015). Furthermore, a peer-enhanced version of CRA delivered to emerging adults treated in a publicly funded treatment center was shown to increase the percentage of days of abstinence for both the identified client emerging adult and their peer (Smith, Davis, Dumas, & Ureche, 2016). Notably, these studies were conducted mainly in publicly funded treatment centers (Smith et al., 2011, 2016) or with emerging adults receiving services in homeless shelters (Slesnick et al., 2015).

BRIEF MOTIVATIONAL INTERVENTIONS IN HEALTHCARE SETTINGS

There is currently a national emphasis on mainstreaming substance use services into general health services. Historically, individuals in need of substance use disorder services accessed services in specialized treatment centers that were not well integrated with primary care. This is problematic from a public health perspective in that only a small percentage of individuals in need of services ever access services in a dedicated "rehab" facility (i.e., specialized treatment center). In addition, this service delivery system is set up for only intervening with individuals with diagnosed substance use disorders. Thus, one method of mainstreaming substance use services is to train healthcare professionals to deliver brief interviews during emergency room or primary care visits. These interventions go by many names, such as brief motivational intervention (BMI), Screening Brief Intervention and Referral to Treatment (SBIRT), and brief physician advice (BPA) interventions. They all include a rapid screening with psychometrically sound cut-offs for identifying problems, discussion of the client's motivation for making changes, and attempts to engage the individual in setting a substance use reduction goal. These interventions can be as short at 10–30 minutes so that they can be integrated into routine medical appointments, or they can last up to an hour when done in research protocols.

Most studies on delivering BMIs to emerging adults in healthcare settings have done so in the emergency room. In an early study, Monti and colleagues (1999) found that emerging adults experiencing alcohol-related emergency room visits had better alcohol-related outcomes if they were randomized to a BMI (30–45 minutes) versus standard care. These results have been replicated in subsequent studies by the same investigators (Monti et al., 2007) as well as an independent team (Bernstein et al., 2010). Additionally, findings have been extended to marijuana-related outcomes (Bernstein et al., 2009; Magill, Barnett, Apodaca, Rohsenow, & Monti, 2009). Bernstein and colleagues' (2010) sample was highly diverse (26% White; 55% female), and it is also notable that their 20- to 30-minute intervention was delivered to emergency room patients by peer educators.

To our knowledge, only two emerging adult–focused studies delivered a BMI or SBIRT model in outpatient primary care facilities. Grossberg, Brown, and Fleming (2004) found some impressive 4-year post-intervention effects: emerging adults receiving BMI had fewer motor vehicle crashes, arrests, drinks per occasion, and number of past 30-day binge drinking episodes relative to those in the control condition. Additionally, a South African study found lower ASSIST scores (for alcohol only) for emerging adults receiving BMI in a public health clinic (Mertens, Ward, Bresick, Broder, & Weisner, 2013). Thus, it is currently unclear if BMIs delivered in outpatient healthcare settings can also reduce marijuana or other drug use among emerging adults.

To summarize, a handful of studies support the use of BMIs with non-college-attending emerging adults. Most studies have been conducted in emergency room settings, and findings apply to alcohol and marijuana, the two most commonly used substances by emerging adults. Additional research, however, is needed with emerging adults presenting to Federally Qualified Health Centers (FQHCs) that serve more impoverished emerging adults. Additionally, more research is needed on whether the benefits of these interventions extend to those emerging adults crossing the threshold for having substance use disorders, and whether referrals to subsequent specialized treatment are needed to achieve these effects (Glass et al., 2015).

TECHNOLOGY-ASSISTED INTERVENTIONS

About 20% of studies (11/50) in a recent meta-analysis on emerging adults in non-college settings included technology-assisted interventions (Davis, Smith & Briley, 2017). However, many of these studies are by the same investigators who report findings on the same intervention with either a different subset of clients (Bertholet et al., 2015a, 2015b) or at different follow-up periods (Gonzales, Ang, Murphy, Glik, & Anglin, 2014; Gonzales, Hernandez, Murphy, & Ang, 2016; Suffoletto, Callaway, Kristan, Kraemer, & Clark, 2012; Suffoletto et al., 2014, 2015). Thus much more work is needed. Below we review this small literature and highlight important issues surrounding the use of technology-assisted interventions with emerging adults in non-college settings.

STAND-ALONE WEB-BASED INTERVENTIONS

Several studies have invited emerging adults to participate in stand-alone brief interventions delivered on the Internet. These interventions are typically delivered to emerging adults who are heavy or low-risk drinkers. Although it is not always clear if such emerging adults meet formal criteria for alcohol use disorders, these interventions can be widely disseminated.

Two Swiss studies used the same online PFI with both low- and high-risk drinkers. The Internet-based intervention included personalized feedback on caloric content of alcohol and alcohol use norms and made recommendations to participants on low-risk drinking guidelines. In their study on low-risk Swiss emerging adults, there were no differences in drinks per week between those receiving a Web-based feedback intervention or a control condition (Bertholet et al., 2015a). However, a smaller percentage of those receiving the Web-based PFI (14.4%) binge drank at 1 month compared to the control participants (19%). In a separate report focused on higher-risk drinkers, Bertholet and colleagues (2015b) randomized Swiss emerging adults to the very same intervention or a control group. Those receiving the Web-based intervention had lower alcohol consumption and AUDIT scores compared to controls, but there were no differences in binge drinking or alcohol-related consequences.

In addition to these Swiss studies, one Dutch study tested the efficacy of a similar Web-based intervention (Spijkerman et al., 2010). These researchers sought to determine if providing normative feedback (i.e., contrast of the individual's personal substance use amounts to a large normative sample) would be more effective than simply giving recommendations to reduce current drinking to established national risk guidelines. Study findings were positive for the normative feedback condition, but reductions in drinking were limited to males. Additionally, this study suffered a major methodological limitation in that a large proportion of participants (48%) never completed follow-up surveys.

CLINICAL AND OPPORTUNISTIC SETTINGS

Some studies have delivered technology-assisted interventions to emerging adults where they initially present for face-to-face services. Because some investigators have questioned whether freestanding technology-assisted interventions produce meaningful change, future research is likely to focus on integrating such interventions into typical face-to-face service settings (Dedert et al., 2015).

Doumas and Hannah (2008) recruited emerging adults through companies' human resources departments and investigated the added benefit of in-person MI when combined with a Web-based brief intervention. Participants were randomized to receive either a Web-based PFI only, the same Web-based feedback plus a 15-minute in-person MI session, or a waiting list condition. Both Web-based feedback and Web-based feedback plus MI were better than the control condition at reducing drinking, but neither was superior relative to the other. Importantly, participants in this study were mostly (69%) low-risk drinkers, defined as not having binge drank in the past 2 weeks prior to the study.

A series of three separate studies examined the effects of an interactive text messaging intervention for heavily drinking emerging adults presenting to emergency departments. The intervention collected data via text messaging on drinking and, in response, texted back tailored messages to participants. For example, individuals reporting binge drinking would receive messages expressing concern, be provided data on healthy drinking limits recommended by the NIAAA, and be asked if they would be willing to set a drinking reduction goal. In an initial pilot study, Suffoletto and colleagues (2012) found that those randomized to a text messaging intervention ($n = 14$) had fewer heavy drinking days and drinks per drinking day at follow-up relative to participants receiving ongoing the text-based assessments only ($n = 12$) condition. A control group received no ongoing text-based assessments ($n = 13$). Two subsequent follow-up studies using the same intervention and design reported positive outcomes at 3 (Suffoletto et al., 2014) and 9 months (Suffoletto et al., 2015).

Gonzales and colleagues (2014) randomly assigned emerging adults finishing residential or outpatient treatment to either a text messaging–based aftercare condition or aftercare as usual. Daily text messages were sent to participants that focused on self-monitoring, general wellness, and substance use education/social support. Emerging adults receiving the text-messaging condition were less likely to relapse at 3 months compared to those in the control condition. These findings held at 9 months as well (Gonzales et al., 2016).

SUMMARY OF TECHNOLOGY-ASSISTED INTERVENTIONS

There are two major limitations in the current literature on technology-assisted interventions. First, the vast majority of technology-assisted interventions used with non-college-attending emerging adults are preventative in nature. With the exception of one study on a text messaging–based aftercare model (Gonzales et al., 2014, 2016), most studies target emerging adults without substance use disorders. Second, these studies are mostly limited to targeting alcohol use. Given the higher prevalence of marijuana and other illicit drug use among emerging adults, interventions are needed that target users of these substances. Finally, with few exceptions, these studies mostly used technology-assisted interventions as stand-alone interventions (Doumas and Hannah, 2008; Gonzales et al., 2014, 2016). More research is needed on integrating technology-assisted interventions into face-to-face clinical care.

META-ANALYTIC FINDINGS FOR NON-COLLEGE-ATTENDING EMERGING ADULTS

Davis, Smith, and colleagues' (2017) meta-analysis on emerging adult substance abuse treatment in non-college settings included some encouraging and surprising findings. First, they found evidence of small clinical effects that were highly comparable to those found in the collegiate drinking literature. Thus, despite the wide heterogeneity in treatment settings, substances used, and interventions, treatment effectiveness appears similar for emerging adults treated in non-college settings. Second, interventions that included personalized feedback were not as effective as interventions without personalized feedback. This was surprising given the strong track record of PFIs in the collegiate literature.

Many brief interventions rely on such personalized feedback as contrasting an individual's use against a normative sample or discussing what percent of individuals meet criteria for disordered use (Smith et al., 2016). It is currently difficult to know if this means that personalized feedback itself is ineffective for students in non-college settings or if this really means that brief interventions in which they appear are less effective. This is potentially concerning as the United States is moving toward widespread integration of brief interventions into primary care. We may need to rethink whether PFIs are the best bet for reducing substance use among emerging adults treated in non-college settings. It is possible that additional services beyond brief treatment may be needed to ameliorate the substance use of these emerging adults, and it is also possible that feedback is more effective among college students. College students may especially benefit from PFIs because, with culturally ingrained expectations about college drinking, they may be more surprised to learn that not all their fellow students are using as heavily as they are.

SUMMARY

Numerous intervention approaches exist for emerging adults that can be used on or off college campuses. There is extensive research on reducing collegiate binge drinking and the associated consequences. The evidence supports the use of personalized feedback approaches with college students, which can be combined with drinking reduction strategies (i.e., alternating drinks) and delivered in either individual or group sessions. Environmental approaches to college drinking such as compliance checks and interventions that address alcohol marketing to students enjoy some support, but campus-level social-norming campaigns have mixed support. There is less research with emerging adults treated in non-campus settings, with large heterogeneity in clinical settings, substances used, and treatments implemented. In general, treatment effects for emerging adults in non-college settings appear similar to those of college students. However, there are some questions about whether personalized feedback will work as well as it does with students. Additionally, more research is needed on technology-assisted treatments with non-college students.

REFERENCES

Alcoholics Anonymous World Services (2001). *Alcoholics anonymous* (4th ed.). New York: Author.

Alcoholics Anonymous World Services (2014). *Alcoholics anonymous 2014 membership survey*. New York: Author. Available on-line at http://www.aa.org/assets/en_US/p-48_membershipsurvey.pdf. Last accessed on June 9th, 2016

Arnett, J. J. (2000). Emerging adulthood: A theory of development from the late teens through the twenties. *American Psychologist, 55*, 469–480.

Baer, J. S., Marlatt, G. A., Kivlahan, D. R., Fromme, K., Larimer, M. E., & Williams, E. (1992). An experimental test of three methods of alcohol risk reduction with young adults. *Journal of Consulting and Clinical Psychology, 60*, 974–979.

Bernstein, E., Edwards, E., Dorfman, D., Heeren, T., Bliss, C., & Bernstein, J. (2009). Screening and brief intervention to reduce marijuana use among youth and young adults in a pediatric emergency department. *Academic Emergency Medicine, 16*(11), 1174–1185.

Bernstein, J., Heeren, T., Edward, E., Dorfman, D., Bliss, C., Winter, M., & Bernstein, E. (2010). A brief motivational interview in a pediatric emergency department, plus 10-day telephone follow-up, increases attempts to quit drinking among youth and young adults who screen positive for problematic drinking. *Academic Emergency Medicine, 17*(8), 890–902.

Bertholet, N., Cunningham, J. A., Faouzi, M., Gaume, J., Gmel, G., Burnand, B., & Daeppen, J. B. (2015a). Internet-based brief intervention to prevent unhealthy alcohol use among young men: A randomized controlled trial. *PLoS one, 10*(12), e0144146.

Bertholet, N., Cunningham, J. A., Faouzi, M., Gaume, J., Gmel, G., Burnand, B., & Daeppen, J. B. (2015b). Internet-based brief intervention for young men with unhealthy alcohol use: A randomized controlled trial in a general population sample. *Addiction, 110*(11), 1735–1743.

Cadigan, J. M., Haeny, A. M., Martens, M. P., Weaver, C. C., Takamatsu, S. K., & Arterberry, B. J. (2015). Personalized drinking feedback: A meta-analysis of in-person versus computer-delivered interventions, 83, 430–437.

Carey, K. B., Scott-Sheldon, L. A., Elliott, J. C., Garey, L., & Carey, M. P. (2012). Face-to-face versus computer-delivered alcohol interventions for college drinkers: A meta-analytic review, 1998 to 2010. *Clinical psychology review, 32*(8), 690–703.

Carey, K. B., Scott-Sheldon, L. A. J., Garey, L., Elliott, J. C., & Carey, M. P. (2016). Alcohol interventions for mandated college students: A meta-analytic review. *Journal of Consulting and Clinical Psychology, 84*(7), 619–632. doi:10.1037/a0040275

Carroll, K. M., Easton, C. J., Nich, C., Hunkele, K. A., Neavins, T. M., Sinha, R., . . . Rounsaville, B. J. (2006). The use of contingency management and motivational/skills-building therapy to treat young adults with marijuana dependence. *Journal of Consulting and Clinical Psychology, 74*(5), 955–966.

Clapp, J. D., Lange, J. E., Russell, C., Shillington, A., & Voas, R. B. (2003). A failed norms social marketing campaign. *Journal of studies on alcohol, 64*(3), 409–414.

Correia, C. J., Benson, T. A., & Carey, K. B. (2005). Decreased substance use following increases in alternative behaviors: A preliminary investigation. *Addictive behaviors, 30*(1), 19–27.

Davis, J. P., Bergman, B. G., Smith, D. C., Kelly, J. F. (2017). Testing a matching hypothesis for emerging adults in Project MATCH: During-treatment and 1-year outcomes. *Journal of Studies on Alcohol and Drugs, 78*, 140–145.

Davis, J. P., Smith, D. C., & Briley, D. (2017). Substance use prevention and treatment outcomes for emerging adults in non-college settings: A meta-analysis. *Psychology of Addictive Behavior, 31*(3), 242–254. doi: 10.1037/adb0000267

Dedert, E. A., McDuffie, J. R., Stein, R., McNiel, J. M., Kosinski, A. S., Freiermuth, C. E., . . . Williams, J. W. (2015). Electronic interventions for alcohol misuse and alcohol use disorders: A systematic review. *Annals of Internal Medicine, 163*(3), 205–214.

DeJong, W., & Hingson, R. (1998). Strategies to reduce driving under the influence of alcohol. *Annual review of public health, 19*(1), 359–378.

DeJong, W., & Langford, L. M. (2002). A typology for campus-based alcohol prevention: Moving toward environmental management strategies. *Journal of Studies on Alcohol, Supplement*, (14), 140–147.

DeJong, W., Schneider, S. K., Towvim, L. G., Murphy, M. J., Doerr, E. E., Simonsen, N. R., . . . Scribner, R. A. (2006). A multisite randomized trial of social norms marketing campaigns to reduce college student drinking. *Journal of Studies on Alcohol, 67*(6), 868–879.

Dimeff, L. A., Baer, J. S., Kivlahan, D. R., & Marlatt, G. A. (1999). *BASICS: Brief Alcohol Screening and Intervention for College Students: A harm reduction approach.* New York: Guilford Press.

Dotson, K. B., Dunn, M. E., & Bowers, C. A. (2015). Stand-alone personalized normative feedback for college student drinkers: A meta-analytic review, 2004 to 2014. *PloS One, 10*(10), e0139518.

Doumas, D. M., & Hannah, E. (2008). Preventing high-risk drinking in youth in the workplace: A Web-based normative feedback program. *Journal of Substance Abuse Treatment, 34*(3), 263–271.

Fachini, A., Aliane, P. P., Martinez, E. Z., & Furtado, E. F. (2012). Efficacy of Brief Alcohol Screening Intervention for College Students (BASICS): A meta-analysis of randomized controlled trials. *Substance Abuse Treatment, Prevention, and Policy, 7*(1), 1.

Fromme, K., Marlatt, G. A., Baer, J. S., & Kivlahan, D. R. (1994). The alcohol skills training program: A group intervention for young adult drinkers. *Journal of Substance Abuse Treatment, 11*(2), 143–154.

Gebhardt, T. L., Kaphingst, K., & DeJong, W. (2000). A campus-community coalition to control alcohol-related problems off campus: An environmental management case study. *Journal of American College Health*, 48(5), 211–215.

Glass, J. E., Hamilton, A. M., Powell, B. J., Perron, B. E., Brown, R. T., & Ilgen, M. A. (2015). Specialty substance use disorder services following brief alcohol intervention: A meta-analysis of randomized controlled trials. *Addiction*, 110(9), 1404–1415.

Gmel, G., Gaume, J., Bertholet, N., Flückiger, J., & Daeppen, J. B. (2013). Effectiveness of a brief integrative multiple substance use intervention among young men with and without booster sessions. *Journal of Substance Abuse Treatment*, 44(2), 231–240.

Gonzales, R., Ang, A., Murphy, D. A., Glik, D. C., & Anglin, M. D. (2014). Substance use recovery outcomes among a cohort of youth participating in a mobile-based texting aftercare pilot program. *Journal of Substance Abuse Treatment*, 47(1), 20–26.

Gonzales, R., Hernandez, M., Murphy, D. A., & Ang, A. (2016). Youth recovery outcomes at 6 and 9 months following participation in a mobile texting recovery support aftercare pilot study. *American Journal on Addictions*, 25(1), 62–68.

Grossberg, P. M., Brown, D. D., & Fleming, M. F. (2004). Brief physician advice for high-risk drinking among young adults. *Annals of Family Medicine*, 2(5), 474–480.

Hingson, R. W., Zha, W., & Weitzman, E. R. (2009). Magnitude of and trends in alcohol-related mortality and morbidity among US college students ages 18–24, 1998–2005. *Journal of Studies on Alcohol and Drugs, Supplement*, (16), 12–20.

Hoeppner, B. B., Hoeppner, S. S., & Kelly, J. F. (2014). Do young people benefit from AA as much, and in the same ways, as adult aged 30? A moderated multiple mediation analysis. *Drug and Alcohol Dependence*, 143, 181–188.

Kivlahan, D. R., Marlatt, G. A., Fromme, K., Coppel, D. B., & Williams, E. (1990). Secondary prevention with college drinkers: Evaluation of an alcohol skills training program. *Journal of Consulting and Clinical Psychology*, 58, 805–810.

Larimer, M. E., Turner, A. P., Anderson, B. K., Fader, J. S., Kilmer, J. R., Palmer, R. S., & Cronce, J. M. (2001). Evaluating a brief alcohol intervention with fraternities. *Journal of Studies on Alcohol*, 62(3), 370–380. doi: 10.15288/jsa.2001.62.370

Lee, C. M., Neighbors, C., Lewis, M. A., Kaysen, D., Mittmann, A., Geisner, I. M., ... Larimer, M. E. (2014). Randomized controlled trial of a spring break intervention to reduce high-risk drinking. *Journal of Consulting and Clinical Psychology*, 82(2), 189–201. doi:10.1037/a0035743

Lewis, M. A., & Neighbors, C. (2015). An examination of college student activities and attentiveness during a Web-delivered personalized normative feedback intervention. *Psychology of Addictive Behaviors*, 29(1), 162–167. doi: 10.1037/adb0000003

Lewis, M. A., Neighbors, C., Geisner, I. M., Lee, C. M., Kilmer, J. R., & Atkins, D. C. (2010). Examining the associations among severity of injunctive drinking norms, alcohol consumption, and alcohol-related negative consequences: The moderating roles of alcohol consumption and identity. *Psychology of Addictive Behaviors*, 24(2), 177–189.

Magill, M., Barnett, N. P., Apodaca, T. R., Rohsenow, D. J., & Monti, P. M. (2009). The role of marijuana use in brief motivational intervention with young adult drinkers treated in an emergency department. *Journal of Studies on Alcohol and Drugs*, 70(3), 409–413.

Magill, M., & Ray, L. A. (2009). Cognitive-behavioral treatment with adult alcohol and illicit drug users: A meta-analysis of randomized controlled trials. *Journal of Studies on Alcohol and Drugs, 70*(4), 516–527.

Marlatt, G. A., Baer, J. S., Kivlahan, D. R., Dimeff, L. A., Larimer, M. E., Quigley, L. A., ... Williams, E. (1998). Screening and brief intervention for high-risk college student drinkers: Results from a 2-year follow-up assessment. *Journal of Consulting and Clinical Psychology, 66*(4), 604–615.

Marlowe, D. B., Festinger, D. S., Dugosh, K. L., & Lee, P. A. (2005). Are judicial status hearings a "key component" of drug court?: Six and twelve months outcomes. *Drug and Alcohol Dependence, 79*(2), 145–155.

Martens, M. P., Kilmer, J. R., Beck, N. C., & Zamboanga, B. L. (2010). The efficacy of a targeted personalized drinking feedback intervention among intercollegiate athletes: A randomized controlled trial. *Psychology of Addictive Behaviors, 24*(4), 660–669. doi: 10.1037/a0020299

Martens, M. P., Page, J. C., Mowry, E. S., Damann, K. M., Taylor, K. K., & Cimini, M. D. (2006). Differences between actual and perceived student norms: An examination of alcohol use, drug use, and sexual behavior. *Journal of American College Health, 54*(5), 295–300.

Martens, M. P., Smith, A. E., & Murphy, J. G. (2013). The efficacy of single-component brief motivational interventions among at-risk college drinkers. *Journal of Consulting and Clinical Psychology, 81*(4), 691–701.

Mee-Lee, D. (Ed.) (2013). *The ASAM criteria: Treatment criteria for addictive, substance-related, and co-occurring conditions*, third edition. Chevy Chase, MD: American Society of Addiction Medicine.

Mertens, J. R., Ward, C. L., Bresick, G. F., Broder, T., & Weisner, C. M. (2013). Effectiveness of nurse-practitioner-delivered brief motivational intervention for young adult alcohol and drug use in primary care in South Africa: A randomized clinical trial. *Alcohol and Alcoholism, 49*(4), 430–438.

Meyers, R. J., & Smith, J. E. (1995). *Clinical guide to alcohol treatment: The community reinforcement approach*. New York: Guilford Press.

Miller, M. B., Leffingwell, T., Claborn, K., Meier, E., Walters, S., & Neighbors, C. (2013). Personalized feedback interventions for college alcohol misuse: An update of Walters & Neighbors (2005). *Psychology of Addictive Behaviors, 27*(4), 909–920. doi: 10.1037/a0031174

Miller, W. R., & Rollnick, S. (1991). *Motivational interviewing: Preparing people to change addictive behavior*. New York: Guilford Press.

Miller, W. R., & Rollnick, S. (2012). *Motivational interviewing: Helping people change*. New York: Guilford Press.

Miller, W. R., & Rose, G. S. (2009). Toward a theory of motivational interviewing. *American Psychologist, 64*(6), 527–537.

Mitchell, L. L., & Syed, M. (2015). Does college matter for emerging adulthood? Comparing developmental trajectories of educational groups. *Journal of Youth and Adolescence, 44*, 2012–2027.

Monti, P. M., Barnett, N. P., Colby, S. M., Gwaltney, C. J., Spirito, A., Rohsenow, D. J., & Woolard, R. (2007). Motivational interviewing versus feedback only in emergency care for young adult problem drinking. *Addiction, 102*(8), 1234–1243.

Monti, P. M., Colby, S. M., Barnett, N. P., Spirito, A., Rohsenow, D. J., Myers, M., . . . Lewander, W. (1999). Brief intervention for harm reduction with alcohol-positive older adolescents in a hospital emergency department. *Journal of Consulting and Clinical Psychology*, 67(6), 989–994. doi: 10.1037/0022-006X.67.6.989

Murphy, J. G., Barnett, N. P., Goldstein, A. L., & Colby, S. M. (2007). Gender moderates the relationship between substance-free activity enjoyment and alcohol use. *Psychology of Addictive Behaviors*, 21(2), 261–265.

Murphy, J. G., Correia, C. J., Colby, S. M., & Vuchinich, R. E. (2005). Using behavioral theories of choice to predict drinking outcomes following a brief intervention. *Experimental and Clinical Psychopharmacology*, 13(2), 93–101.

Murphy, J. G., Dennhardt, A. A., Skidmore, J. R., Borsari, B., Barnett, N. P., Colby, S. M., & Martens, M. P. (2012). A randomized controlled trial of a behavioral economic supplement to brief motivational interventions for college drinking. *Journal of Consulting and Clinical Psychology*, 80(5), 876–886. doi: 10.1037/a0028763

Murphy, J. G., Skidmore, J. R., Dennhardt, A. A., Martens, M. P., Borsari, B., Barnett, N. P., & Colby, S. M. (2012). A behavioral economic supplement to brief motivational interventions for college drinking. *Addiction Research & Theory*, 20(6), 456–465. doi: 10.3109/16066359.2012.665965

Naar-King, S., Lam, P., Wang, B., Wright, K., Parsons, J. T., & Frey, M. A. (2008). Maintenance of effects of motivational enhancement therapy to improve risk behaviors and HIV-related health in a randomized controlled trial of youth living with HIV. *Journal of Pediatric Psychology*, 33(4), 441–445.

National Institute on Alcohol Abuse and Alcoholism. (2002). A call to action: Changing the culture of drinking at US colleges. Bethesda, MD.

Neighbors, C., Lee, C. M., Atkins, D. C., Lewis, M. A., Kaysen, D., Mittmann, A., . . . Larimer, M. E. (2012). A randomized controlled trial of event-specific prevention strategies for reducing problematic drinking associated with 21st birthday celebrations. *Journal of Consulting and Clinical Psychology*, 80(5), 850–862. doi: 10.1037/a0029480

Neighbors, C., Lee, C. M., Lewis, M. A., Fossos, N., & Larimer, M. E. (2007). Are social norms the best predictor of outcomes among heavy-drinking college students? *Journal of Studies on Alcohol and Drugs*, 68(4), 556–565.

Neighbors, C., Lee, C. M., Lewis, M. A., Fossos, N., & Walter, T. (2009). Internet-based personalized feedback to reduce 21st-birthday drinking: A randomized controlled trial of an event-specific prevention intervention. *Journal of Consulting and Clinical Psychology*, 77(1), 51–63. doi: 10.1037/a0014386

Patrick, M. E., Lee, C. M., & Neighbors, C. (2014). Web-based intervention to change perceived norms of college student alcohol use and sexual behavior on spring break. *Addictive Behaviors*, 39(3), 600–606. doi: 10.1016/j.addbeh.2013.11.014

Reid, A. E., & Carey, K. B. (2015). Interventions to reduce college student drinking: State of the evidence for mechanisms of behavior change. *Clinical Psychology Review*, 40, 213–224.

Riper, H., van Straten, A., Keuken, M., Smit, F., Schippers, G., & Cuijpers, P. (2009). Curbing problem drinking with personalized-feedback interventions: A meta-analysis. *American Journal of Preventive Medicine*, 36(3), 247–255.

Rodriguez, L. M., Neighbors, C., Rinker, D. V., Lewis, M. A., Lazorwitz, B., Gonzales, R. G., & Larimer, M. E. (2015). Remote versus in-lab computer-delivered personalized normative feedback interventions for college student drinking. *Journal of Consulting and Clinical Psychology, 83*, 455–463.

Rossman, S. B., Roman, J. K., Zweig, J. M., Rempel, M., & Lindquist, C. H. (Eds.) (2011). The multi-site adult drug court evaluation: The impact of drug courts. The Urban Institute, Justic Policy Center, Washington, DC. Retrieved from http://www.urban.org/UploadedPDF/412357-MADCE-The-Impact-of-Drug-Courts.pdf

Saffer, H., & Dave, D. (2002). Alcohol consumption and alcohol advertising bans. *Applied Economics, 34*(11), 1325–1334.

Saltz, R. F., Paschall, M. J., McGaffigan, R. P., & Nygaard, P. M. (2010). Alcohol risk management in college settings: the safer California universities randomized trial. *American Journal of Preventive Medicine, 39*(6), 491–499.

Slesnick, N., Guo, X., Brakenhoff, B., & Bantchevska, D. (2015). A Comparison of three interventions for homeless youth evidencing substance use disorders: Results of a randomized clinical trial. *Journal of Substance Abuse Treatment, 54*, 1–13.

Smith, D. C., Davis, J. P., Dumas, T., & Ureche, D. J. (2016). Six-month outcomes of a peer-enhanced community reinforcement approach for emerging adults with substance misuse: A preliminary study. *Journal of Substance Abuse Treatment, 61*, 66–73.

Smith, D. C., Godley, S. H., Godley, M. D., & Dennis, M. L. (2011) Adolescent Community Reinforcement Approach (A-CRA) outcomes differ among emerging adults and adolescents. *Journal of Substance Abuse Treatment, 41*, 422–430.

Spijkerman, R., Roek, M. A., Vermulst, A., Lemmers, L., Huiberts, A., & Engels, R. C. (2010). Effectiveness of a Web-based brief alcohol intervention and added value of normative feedback in reducing underage drinking: A randomized controlled trial. *Journal of Medical Internet Research, 12*(5), e65.

Suffoletto, B., Callaway, C., Kristan, J., Kraemer, K., & Clark, D. B. (2012). Text-message-based drinking assessments and brief interventions for young adults discharged from the emergency department. *Alcoholism: Clinical and Experimental Research, 36*(3), 552–560.

Suffoletto, B., Kristan, J., Callaway, C., Kim, K. H., Chung, T., Monti, P. M., & Clark, D. B. (2014). A text message alcohol intervention for young adult emergency department patients: A randomized clinical trial. *Annals of Emergency Medicine, 64*(6), 664–672.

Suffoletto, B., Kristan, J., Chung, T., Jeong, K., Fabio, A., Monti, P., & Clark, D. B. (2015). An interactive text message intervention to reduce binge drinking in young adults: A randomized controlled trial with 9-month outcomes. *PloS One, 10*(11), e0142877.

Turner, J., Perkins, H.W., & Bauerle, J. (2008). Declining negative consequences related to alcohol misuse among students exposed to social norms marketing intervention on a college campus. *Journal of American College Health, 57*(1), 85–94.

United States Department of Education. (2015). Digest of educational statistics. Available online at https://nces.ed.gov/programs/digest/d15/tables/dt15_302.60.asp?current=yes

Walters, S. T., & Neighbors, C. (2005). Feedback interventions for college alcohol misuse: What, why and for whom? *Addictive Behaviors, 30*(6), 1168–1182. doi: 10.1016/j.addbeh.2004.12.005

Wechsler, H., Lee, J. E., Gledhill-Hoyt, J., & Nelson, T. F. (2001). Alcohol use and problems at colleges banning alcohol: Results of a national survey. *Journal of Studies on Alcohol, 62*(2), 133–141.

Wechsler, H., & Nelson, T. F. (2008). What we have learned from the Harvard School of Public Health Alcohol Study: Focusing attention on college student alcohol consumption and the environmental conditions that promote it. *Journal of Studies on Alcohol and Drugs, 69*, 481–490.

Werch, C. E., Pappas, D. M., Carlson, J. M., DiClemente, C. C., Chally, P. S., & Sinder, J. A. (2000). Results of a social norm intervention to prevent binge drinking among first-year residential college students. *Journal of American College Health, 49*(2), 85–92.

Williams, J., Chaloupka, F. J., & Wechsler, H. (2005). Are there differential effects of price and policy on college students' drinking intensity?. *Contemporary Economic Policy, 23*(1), 78–90.

Wolfson, M., Champion, H., McCoy, T. P., Rhodes, S. D., Ip, E. H., Blocker, J. N., . . . & Mitra, A. (2012). Impact of a Randomized Campus/Community Trial to Prevent High-Risk Drinking Among College Students. *Alcoholism: Clinical and Experimental Research, 36*(10), 1767–1778.

Worden, B. L., & McCrady, B. S. (2013). Effectiveness of a feedback-based brief intervention to reduce alcohol use in community substance use disorders treatment. *Alcoholism Treatment Quarterly, 31*(2), 186–205.

5

Substance Use Disorder Treatments

Addressing the Needs of Emerging Adults from Privileged and Marginalized Backgrounds

LILIANE CAMBRAIA WINDSOR, DOUGLAS C. SMITH,
KYLE M. BENNETT, AND FREDERICK X. GIBBONS ∎

INTRODUCTION

Emerging adults in the United States (those whose age ranges from 18 to 25) represent 9.9% of the total population in the United States (U.S. Census Bureau, 2015). They are one of America's most diverse generations with slightly over 40% being members of marginalized racial groups, approximately half being women, and an estimated 1.03% being members of the LGBT community (The Williams Institute–UCLA School of Law, 2016). It is also known that emerging adults have significantly higher rates of alcohol and illicit substance misuse than those for other age groups (Substance Abuse and Mental Health Services Administration, 2015a). Yet, according to the latest available data, in 2013, only 8% of all emerging adults who needed treatment for a substance use disorder received it at a specialty facility (Substance Abuse and Mental Health Services Administration [SAMHSA], 2014).

In the late 1980s, significant critiques emerged about the lack of inclusion of marginalized groups in health research and in treatment (Allmark, 2004; Amaro, Raj, Vega, Mangione, & Perez, 2001; National Institute on Drug Abuse, 2003). Such critiques highlighted the need to engage and retain diverse populations including racial and gender minorities in research and treatment (U.S. Department of Health and Human Services, 2000). As a result, funders such as the National Institutes of Health (NIH) developed agendas that specifically focused on engaging and retaining marginalized populations in research (both as participants and as researchers) and in treatment (U.S. Department of Health and Human Services, 2000, 2010). Many researchers responded by adapting and testing existing evidence-based interventions with marginalized populations (Craig, Austin, & Alessi, 2013; Hall, 2001; Lau, 2006). Others proposed to develop brand new culturally tailored treatment approaches (Prado et al., 2007; Windsor, Pinto, Benoit, Jessell, & Jemal, 2014). Many others implemented strategies to increase the engagement and retention of marginalized groups in research testing the effectiveness of interventions and conducting analyses controlling for demographic variables, such as race, gender, age, and socioeconomic status (SES) (Allmark, 2004; Collins, 1992; Windsor, Jessell, Lassiter, & Benoit, 2015).

After three decades of efforts to reduce substance use–related health inequalities in the United States, few studies focused on emerging adults from marginalized groups (Brody, Yu, Chen, Kogan, & Smith, 2012; Smith, Godley, Godley, & Dennis, 2011). The goal of this chapter is to examine existing literature on development and effectiveness of culturally relevant substance use disorder treatments for emerging adults and make recommendations for future research and best practices.

Notably, we question the assumption that every marginalized group has unique *culturally driven mediators*, defined here as culture-bound intervention targets, which if altered by culturally adapted interventions, can reduce substance misuse and treat substance use disorders. Said another way, it seems unclear that there are unique and culturally determined processes requiring a new treatment manual for every possible marginalized group. Consider the advice from classic texts on psychotherapy with Latinos that recommended inclusion of priests in Latino interventions because of the higher religiosity of Latinos (McGoldrick, 2005). Yet, the adoption of this strategy is likely impractical in many settings and ignores intragroup variation in religiosity (i.e., some Latinos are less religious). There are also few trials that ever examine some of the inherent assumptions in this proposed culturally adaptive treatment model. For example, this proposition that priests would enhance the treatment outcomes for Latinos assumes that Treatment A that includes priests would outperform Treatment B that did not include priests. Such designs are rarely used (Miller, Villanueva, Tonigan, & Cuzmar, 2007).

In this chapter we argue that instead of focusing on modifying culture-bound intervention targets and developing specific interventions for specific cultural groups, researchers and practitioners concerned with equitably serving privileged and marginalized emerging adults should consider (1) developing and adopting interventions that target social determinants of health, (2) developing and adopting inclusive interventions that are responsive to cultural contexts, and (3) investing in therapist training to be effective with diverse groups.

DEFINITIONS: PRIVILEGE AND MARGINALIZATION IN THE UNITED STATES

Here we define *privileged* emerging adults as those who are between the ages of 18 and 25, White, male, heterosexual, living above the poverty line, and/or being able-bodied. Privileged emerging adults enjoy advantages in the United States in the form of access to power and resources that act as protective factors against substance use frequency, severity, or the consequences of substance use (e.g., incarceration, HIV prevalence). Some would even say that privileged emerging adults from high socioeconomic backgrounds in developed countries are uniquely able to afford the experience of emerging adulthood (Côté, 2014; Hendry & Kloep, 2010). That is, access to financial resources may facilitate the delayed onset of adult roles and self-exploration (Côté, 2014). *Marginalized* groups are those with shared characteristics that have been historically and systematically excluded from enjoying equitable opportunities in the United States through systemic discrimination, biased policies, and lack of access to power and resources. As there are many such groups (i.e., racial/ethnic minorities, sexual minorities, individuals from lower socioeconomic backgrounds), it is beyond the scope of this chapter to describe all possible intersections with emerging adulthood. Simply describing the shared commonalities among marginalized subgroups may also contribute to creating or perpetuating stereotypes (Stuart, 2004). That is, it is of paramount importance to recognize that there is diversity within specific subgroups and that no two individuals are identical. These groups may be marginalized because of gender, racial, economic, social, or disability discrimination. The common thread that ties these diverse marginalized groups together are inequalities that impact health outcomes, including substance misuse patterns and consequences. For instance, Blacks and Latinos are overrepresented in the criminal justice system despite showing similar rates of drug use when compared to their White counterparts (Binswanger, Redmond, Steiner, & Hicks, 2012). Research shows that Black and Latino youth are more likely to be convicted of a drug charge, owing to systematic racial bias in the criminal justice system (Alexander, 2010; Dumont, Allen, Brockmann, Alexander, & Rich, 2013). Thus, for the purposes of this chapter, emerging adults from marginalized groups include any subgroup that has historically been systematically excluded from full civic, social, and economic participation in the United States.

SOCIAL DETERMINANTS OF HEALTH, SUBSTANCE USE DISORDERS, AND EMERGING ADULTS FROM MARGINALIZED GROUPS

Social determinants of health are macro-level variables that help explain health inequalities between privileged and marginalized emerging adults (Trinh-Shevrin, Islam, Nadkarni, Park, & Kwon, 2015). In this chapter, we will focus on acculturation, discrimination, and treatment access as being directly linked with substance use frequency, severity, and consequences of substance, use as displayed in Figure 5.1. Widespread adoption of certain treatment approaches and therapist cultural competence training could possibly moderate the associations between these social determinants of health and substance use outcomes.

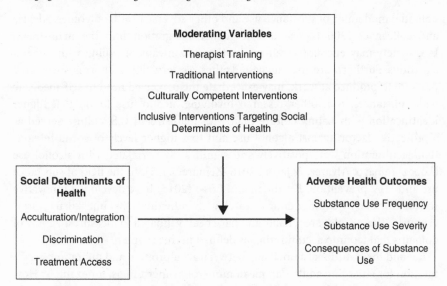

Figure 5.1 Proposed model for moderating the association between characteristics of marginalized emerging adults and substance use outcomes.

Acculturation

Acculturation is defined here as the degree to which a given emerging adult subscribes to values, beliefs, and behaviors of their cultural in-group. *Cultural context* refers to a set of demographic characteristics, bound to a specific location and time, in conjunction with values, beliefs, and behaviors a particular emerging adult may subscribe to. This is in line with a trend where scholars have operationalized acculturation in ways that are more pragmatic when considering analyzing health outcomes for migrant populations. Modern critics of acculturation studies cite the lack of context within which such processes occur as problematic for research findings (Arcia, Skinner, Bailey, & Correa, 2001; Viruell-Fuentes, 2007). Still others believe modern acculturation studies dismiss the economic, historical, or sociopolitical contexts that drive migration, or that culture as a concept is socially constructed rather than inherent to various social groups or populations (Hunt, Schneider, & Comer, 2004; Viruell-Fuentes, Morenoff, Williams, & House, 2013). In response to some of these critiques, some researchers have proposed new models of analyzing health that place social and psychological factors ahead of biological ones (Chae, Nuru-Jeter, Lincoln, & Francis, 2011). These newer models and frameworks for defining and analyzing acculturation and inequalities in health are important because, although they acknowledge the importance of biological and psychological health in determining health outcomes, they recognize the importance of social inequities and histories of oppression that predict racial disparities in health as well (Chae et al., 2011; Phelan, Link, & Tehranifar, 2010).

Identifying the importance of social inequities is important because acculturation, or more appropriately social integration, plays an important role as a potential moderator of substance use and other adverse health outcomes. Alegría and colleagues (2008) posited that greater integration into the mainstream U.S. society may encourage self-medication as a means of coping with difficult situations. Furthermore, they suggested other Western cultural norms, such as the pressure to produce at work, may exacerbate the perceived need to self-medicate with substances. Still other research involving alcohol use found that higher identification with Latinx culture than with mainstream U.S. culture served as a protective factor against alcohol use and that higher levels of social integration/acculturation were positively and significantly correlated with alcohol use (Lopez-Tamayo, Alvarez, & Jason, 2016; Zemore, 2005). In the field of substance use and HIV prevention, Friedman and Rossi (2015) have developed innovative scales informed by ethnographic research with individuals that inject drugs intravenously. These scales are reliable and have been validated to measure a variety of domains that tap into acculturation as defined in this chapter.

Beyond the traditional association between acculturation and migration, acculturation for emerging adults can mean numerous other things, for example: How does one adjust to changes in age or professional cultures, or in what ways do emerging adults with substance use disorders engage in and adapt to the particularities of treatment cultures? According to Jeffrey Arnett's now famous emerging adulthood concept and theory, individuals between the ages of 18 and 25 experience a developmental period that is unique and distinct from adolescence and older adulthood. Individuals in this age group experience greater independence from traditional social roles and from societally normative expectations than adolescents (Arnett, 2000). With such freedoms come enhanced responsibilities and opportunities for engaging in risky behaviors that will be moderated by the cultural contexts just discussed. Thus interventions that work well for both marginalized and privileged emerging adults must take acculturation into account.

Discrimination

A great deal of research has examined psychological variables as possible causes and consequences of substance use among emerging adults from marginalized groups (Clark, 2014; Gibbons, Gerrard, Cleveland, Wills, & Brody, 2004; Shavers et al., 2012). Among these variables, perceived racial discrimination is one of the most studied and most critical variables thought to affect substance use disorders among emerging adults from marginalized racial groups (Gibbons et al., 2004). There is consensus among researchers in the area that there are two primary paths of influence from perceived discrimination to health. The first is direct: The stress produced by discrimination is associated with a variety of health markers and outcomes, both acute (e.g., blood pressure elevation) and chronic (inflammation, metabolic syndrome) (Lewis, Aiello, Leurgans, Kelly, & Barnes, 2010; Ryan, Gee, & Laflamme, 2006). The second pathway is indirect, through behaviors such as substance use, which are an attempt to ameliorate the stress reaction but, in the process, increase health risk (Clark, 2014; Gibbons et al., 2004; Pascoe & Smart Richman, 2009).

It is important to note that despite the increased stress suffered through perceived racial discrimination, emerging adults from *marginalized racial groups* generally use less drugs than their privileged counterparts (SAMHSA, 2015a). Several explanations have been offered for this tendency for less use early in life, including differences in acculturation, religiosity, family ties, and discretionary income (Ding & Crawley, 2010; Lorenzo-Blanco, Unger, Ritt-Olson, Soto, & Baezconde-Garbanati, 2011; Ritt-Olson et al., 2004; Rote & Taylor, 2014; Unger, Schwartz, Huh, Soto, & Baezconde-Garbanati, 2014). Finally, in part because marginalized groups do use substances less frequently, substance use is less a part of their culture (Pugh & Bry, 2007).

Research has shown that these factors protecting emerging adults from marginalized racial groups from developing substance use disorders diminish in early adulthood and, in fact, appear to reverse. This "racial crossover" (Kandel, Schaffran, Hu, & Thomas, 2011) is consistent, but it does vary somewhat as a function of the type of substance. For instance, alcohol use rates tend to remain lower for Blacks than for Whites into adulthood, but among those who do drink, there appears to be a higher likelihood of alcohol-related problems for Blacks than for Whites (Caetano & Clark, 1998; Witbrodt, Mulia, Zemore, & Kerr, 2014). The crossover is more pronounced for smoking and marijuana use. Kandel et al. (2011) reported that Black smoking rates begin exceeding those of Whites sometime around age 29. Chen and Jacobson (2012) found higher rates among Black adults for both smoking and marijuana, whereas Keyes et al. (2015) also found higher rates of marijuana use for Blacks, especially females. The primary reason for this crossover has to do with the fact that Whites and other racial/ethnic groups show a significant decline in use in their early 20s, coinciding with significant life changes signaling more responsibility (employment, marriage, having children). In other words, those who are using begin to cut back or stop when they leave home or graduate from college, a process typically referred to as "maturing out" (Finlay, White, Mun, Cronley, & Lee, 2012).

Treatment Access

In addition to having higher rates of substance use disorders and risky substance use behaviors, emerging adults in the United States have worse treatment engagement rates than all older adult demographics (SAMHSA, 2015b). According to the Substance Abuse and Mental Health Services Administration (2015a), only 1.9% of emerging adults in the United States without health insurance received substance use treatment during the past year. The numbers for insured emerging adults are only slightly higher, with 2.3% receiving substance use treatment during the past year (2015). Adams, Knopf, and Park (2014), in their nationally representative sample of emerging adults (*n* = 19,312), found that 11% of those who had been diagnosed with a substance use disorder received related treatment. This population's increased vulnerability and lack of access to age-appropriate and culturally considerate treatments compared to other age groups is supported by prior studies as well (Mulye et al., 2009). Hence, it is critical to increase substance use disorder treatment access to all emerging adults.

While overall, the majority of emerging adults who need services never receive them, there are currently no racial differences on access to treatment between marginalized emerging adults and their privileged counterparts (SAMHSA, 2015a). Moreover, research has shown an inverse relationship between low SES and access to treatment (Fisher, Silver, & Wolff, 2006; Wu, Ringwalt, & Williams, 2003). Specifically, the lower one's SES, the more likely one is to receive substance use disorder treatment. This seems counterintuitive, considering the number of individuals who cite inability to afford services as one of the main reasons for not seeking treatment. However, individuals from marginalized racial groups are much more likely to be arrested and convicted for drug offenses than privileged individuals (Alexander, 2010; Raphael, 2011; Schnittker, Massoglia, & Uggen, 2011). Since a large portion of existing substance use disorder treatment is court ordered and provided at no or low cost (17.5%) (SAMHSA, 2015a), incarceration may have an unintended effect of making substance use disorder treatment more accessible to marginalized racial groups (Lê Cook & Alegría, 2011). Public assistance is another potential explanation for the increased treatment access enjoyed by emerging adults from marginalized groups. Medicare, Medicaid, and other public sources of funding pay for substance use disorder treatment, increasing financial access to these services. Indeed, public assistance covered 63% of all substance use disorder treatment episodes for emerging adults in 2014 (SAMHSA, 2015a).

Despite the more similar access rates between many marginalized emerging adults and their counterparts, it is unfortunate that what may explain this access in large part lies within a very oppressive system of incarceration and poverty. Moreover, recent research challenges the data just discussed, suggesting that Latinx individuals are less likely to seek substance use treatment, have significantly decreased access to treatment and receive fewer services, and report overall lower levels of treatment satisfaction compared to U.S.-born, non-Latinx White individuals (Guerrero, Marsh, Khachikian, Amaro, & Vega, 2013). These findings regarding the utilization of substance use treatments across racial/ethnic groups are corroborated by other studies as well (Acevedo et al., 2012; Mancini, Salas-Wright, & Vaughn, 2015). Moreover, with the shrinking of incarceration rates due to decriminalization of marijuana, and the dismantling of the Affordable Care Act, the future of substance abuse treatment access is uncertain in the United States.

SUBSTANCE USE DISORDER TREATMENTS AND EMERGING ADULTS

Efficacy of Mainstream Interventions for Emerging Adults

Historically, mainstream treatments for substance use disorders have been developed and tested for and with predominantly White, heterosexual, and middle to upper class populations (Amaro et al., 2001; Baquet, Commiskey, Mullins, &

Mishra, 2006; Pinto, Campbell, Hien, Yu, & Gorroochurn, 2011; Sheikh, 2006; Windsor, Jemal, & Alessi, 2015). *Mainstream interventions* are those with no special emphasis on social determinants of health or inclusivity. The challenges that scientists have faced in better establishing the effectiveness of substance use disorder treatments among diverse groups include methodological limitations, declining funding streams, and challenges engaging and retaining marginalized groups in research (Collins, 1992; Krohn & Thornberry, 1998; Pinto et al., 2011; Sheikh, 2006; Strycker, Duncan, Duncan, Haiou, & Desai, 2006). For instance, a large and diverse sample along with a great deal of resources is needed in order to conduct a rigorous randomized clinical trial to establish the effectiveness of substance use disorder treatment among diverse groups while controlling for differences in age, gender, race, sexual orientation, and socioeconomic impact. Currently, most of the existing treatment effectiveness research focuses on adolescents. There are very few studies that examine substance use disorder treatments, with most of the literature on emerging adults dedicated to binge drinking prevention studies in college settings. To our knowledge there are only 10 randomized studies in non-college settings that include a substantial amount of emerging adults from racial/ethnic minority backgrounds (Davis, Smith & Briley, 2017). Much of what we know about emerging adults in some treatment areas (i.e., residential and twelve-step outcomes) comes from predominantly White male samples (Bergman, Hoeppner, Nelson, Slaymaker, & Kelly, 2015; Kelly, Urbanoski, Hoeppner, & Slaymaker, 2012; Schuman-Olivier, Claire Greene, Bergman, & Kelly, 2014; Schuman-Olivier, Weiss, Hoeppner, Borodovsky, & Albanese, 2014).

The broader literature on mainstream treatments comparing effectiveness among individuals from marginalized and privileged backgrounds presents mixed results. Some studies show improved outcomes, and other studies show little to no differences in outcomes when comparing marginalized populations with their privileged counterparts (Craig et al., 2013; Mawson, Best, Beckwith, Dingle, & Lubman, 2015; Santisteban, Mena, & McCabe, 2011; Windsor, Jemal, & Alessi, 2015). Research seems to attribute most of the treatment effects to general treatment components such as therapist alliance, support networks, and treatment engagement (Hawke, Hennen, & Gallione, 2005; Hogue, Dauber, Stambaugh, Cecero, & Liddle, 2006; Mawson et al., 2015; Pinto et al., 2011). Women tend to have poorer outcomes at baseline and better outcomes at follow-up when compared to men, indicating that they may benefit most from substance use disorder treatments (Green, 2006). More research is critically needed that assesses and compares treatment outcomes between emerging adults from marginalized groups and their privileged counterparts.

Efforts to Develop Culturally Competent Substance Use Disorders Programs

Culturally competent treatment refers to early and broader attempts to develop approaches that would increase retention in substance abuse treatment programs and increase effectiveness in reducing substance use among individuals from marginalized groups. These programs attempted to respond to characteristics that were unique to specific marginalized groups (e.g., Latino youth) and often focused on the provision of bilingual services, creating environments that displayed diverse cultures through pictures and food, training staff on providing services to specific groups, and making specific attempts to recruit individuals from the target populations (Hernandez, Nesman, Mowery, Acevedo-Polakovich, & Callejas, 2009).

We could not locate any attempt to define or evaluate culturally competent treatments for emerging adults. An example from the broader literature on culturally competent substance use disorder treatments is the frameworks developed by Shorkey and Windsor (Shorkey, Windsor, & Spence, 2009a, 2009b). These frameworks enable programs and researchers to evaluate and plan culturally competent services in the provision of substance use disorder treatment to Latino and African American clients by providing a tool that assesses how much a program incorporates services and activities in several dimensions. For instance, dimensions of cultural competence for programs targeting African Americans include family involvement, staff and program cultural diversity, counselor traits, linkage to other relevant services, community/faith services, and agency culture.

These approaches were informed by research that attempted to identify barriers to treatment and describe unique characteristics of specific marginalized groups. This body of literature was important in identifying and addressing barriers to treatment, recognizing the role of extended families, the impact of stigma, and the importance of providing bilingual services. However, this approach has been criticized for unwittingly creating or perpetuating stereotypes and assuming that marginalized groups are homogeneous.

Culturally Relevant or Culturally Tailored Interventions

Culturally relevant or culturally tailored interventions are often used interchangeably with culturally competent interventions in the literature. For the purposes of this chapter, *culturally relevant interventions* are those that were systematically developed and went beyond responding to unique characteristics of marginalized groups to incorporate the voices and views of the groups being targeted. For example, Griner and Smith (2006) noted that the most common types of cultural adaptations integrate the values and cultural concepts into interventions (84%). This goes beyond what some refer to as "surface structure" changes in interventions (i.e., bilingual services) (Castro, Barerra, & Holleran-Steiker, 2010). As noted earlier in the chapter, the rationale for developing culturally relevant treatments is the belief that there are specific culturally driven mediators, that if modified, would result in better improvements for the target populations. Thus, the content of these interventions was purposefully developed by researchers, on the basis of extensive and systematic work, to understand the marginalized group of interest and attempt to impact culturally driven mediators. However, we note that research designs rarely test whether culturally relevant treatments work better than non-adapted treatments (Miller et al., 2007) and whether culturally driven mediators account for any outcome differences between treatment conditions.

An example of a culturally tailored evidence-based intervention is Familias Unidas. This intervention was developed to help reduce risk behaviors such as substance use among Hispanic adolescents in the United States. It takes into consideration deeply rooted Hispanic cultural values such as the importance of family, the impact of acculturation, and immigrant experiences that can create conflicts between parents and adolescents (Prado et al., 2007). These approaches show excellent treatment outcomes among their target populations. However, as mentioned earlier, they can be difficult and expensive to develop, as each marginalized group would need a unique intervention. These approaches also run the risk of segregating groups of people based on their demographic characteristic. Again, to our knowledge, there are no studies on *culturally relevant interventions* for emerging adults with substance use disorders (Davis et al., 2017).

Culturally Adapted Interventions

Culturally adapted substance use disorder treatment interventions are not as expensive as culturally tailored interventions because they are developed through the adaptation of existing, evidence-based interventions. For instance, cognitive-behavioral treatment has been adapted to reduce substance use among ethnoracial- and gender-marginalized groups (Craig et al., 2013; Hinton, Rivera, Hofmann, Barlow, & Otto, 2012). These interventions incorporate the cultural values of the client (Flaskerud & Nyamanthi, 2000; Rowe & Grills, 1993) and try to match the clinician with the race/ethnicity or native language of the client (Lam & Sue, 2001; Sue et al., 2009). Two meta-analytic studies have shown that culturally adapted mental health interventions have an overall positive effect, and that culturally adapted mental health interventions may be more efficacious when these adaptations are specific or targeted to a particular racial/ethnic group (Benish, Quintana, & Wampold, 2011; Griner & Smith, 2006). However, we also note that Griner and Smith's (2006) meta-analysis on culturally adapted treatments ($k = 76$) only included four studies targeting substance use. As with the cultural adaptation literature, no culturally competent and culturally relevant substance use interventions were identified during our literature search for emerging adults from marginalized groups.

.Culturally adapted interventions may increase treatment engagement among emerging adults from marginalized groups, as they may be more appealing to groups that are typically unlikely to seek treatment, they may be more effective at meeting the unique needs of specific groups, and they conserve resources by building upon existing evidence-based interventions. However, culturally adapted interventions may also be expensive to develop, may only apply to a single target population (e.g., African-American emerging adults in substance use treatment, emerging adults who identify as sexual and gender minorities), and may ultimately create or perpetuate stereotypes and segregate groups of people.

Given these limitations, very stringent criteria should be used before embarking on developing intervention content for culturally tailored or adapted interventions. Castro et al. (2010) argued that four conditions should be met before adapting interventions for special populations: the marginalized group exhibits (1) poorer clinical engagement in treatment, (2) unique risk or protective factors, (3) a unique presentation of the clinical problem, and (4) lower intervention efficacy when using non-tailored interventions. We would like to propose two additional criteria for judging culturally tailored treatments: (1) any tailored treatment must be feasible to implement in typical treatment settings, and (2) research shows that culturally driven mediators account for outcomes in the tailored treatment.

MOVING TOWARD INCLUSIVE AND SUSTAINABLE INTERVENTIONS FOR EMERGING ADULTS

The typical approach in developing a substance use disorder intervention consists of first testing the intervention's efficacy in a highly controlled environment and only bringing it to the real world once this intervention is shown to be efficacious under the best possible conditions. This is an important step in testing whether the intervention works. However, interventions are usually less effective when studied in real-world settings, possibly in part owing to the involvement of more marginalized populations in study samples. In fact, Davis and colleagues (2017) found that the percentage of college students in treatment outcome study samples moderated effect sizes. That is, those studies with larger proportions of students had better substance use treatment outcomes, which may be partially accounted for by the relative privilege of college students. In other instances, interventions may not be feasible because of resource limitations. An example is an intervention that requires a 1-hour session but for which Medicaid only covers 30 minutes of the intervention delivery. Agencies that rely on Medicaid payments may, therefore, have no choice but to cut the intervention in half, potentially reducing its effectiveness. Marginalized groups are disproportionately covered by Medicaid (Centers for Medicare and Medicaid Services, 2015). In order to minimize this challenge, researchers have started considering sustainability in the early stages of intervention development. One increasingly popular strategy has been working with community members as partners, conducting efficacy trials in community agencies, and adding a qualitative component to the intervention development methodology. These strategies are particularly important when considering intervention cultural adaptations and cultural grounding as they inform the developers about what type of activities are acceptable and feasible for implementation in the real world.

Intervention development and delivery cost is an important consideration when developing sustainable interventions. In order to serve all marginalized groups with specific interventions, developers must create and test several different interventions that can only be used with significantly smaller numbers of people. For instance, a culturally adapted intervention for low-income Native American emerging adults would only be delivered to this group. Training therapists to deliver these types of evidence-based interventions is very expensive and it takes time. Thus, developing effective and inclusive interventions that can be delivered to diverse groups may be a more feasible option.

Inclusive Interventions that Seem Equally Effective Across Marginalized Groups

Perhaps, and paradoxically, the most effective and sustainable strategy to retain and treat emerging adults from marginalized groups with substance use disorders is to adopt interventions that work for a large number of diverse individuals. Such interventions are designed to allow therapists to "meet the client where the client is." A great example of such an intervention approach is motivational interviewing (MI). MI was designed to work with "resistant" clients, but it has been shown to be effective with a wide variety of groups (Lundahl, Kunz, Brownell, Tollefson, & Burke, 2010). The rationale for this success can be explained by several MI principles that may be inclusive, in other words, relevant to all people. For instance, the therapist respects the autonomy of all clients, leaving decisions about behavior change up to clients (Miller & Rollnick, 2012). This empowers clients to consider their own cultural values in the decision-making process, and in-depth listening represents an easy way to avoid the trap of stereotyping individual clients on the basis of data about any marginalized groups to which they belong (Stuart, 2004). The use of reflections allows the therapist to empathetically reflect back the client's world views to help the client draw his or her own conclusions, and likely reflects advanced culturally competent practice (Miller et al., 2007).

Another intervention that may be considered inclusive when properly implemented is the community reinforcement approach (CRA). Because the CRA also allows individuals a large degree of self-determination in choosing intervention goals, it too may be considered culturally inclusive. Meta-analyses have found the CRA to be a particularly effective treatment, and one large national study ($n = 1,819$) found that adolescent-focused CRA was equally effective for males and females, as well as for individuals from diverse racial/ethnic minority backgrounds (Godley, Hedges, & Hunter, 2011). This study, however, only included a small percentage of emerging adults, so replication efforts are needed to see if the CRA works equally as well for emerging adults from marginalized backgrounds.

Substance Use Disorder Interventions that Target Social Determinants of Health

While there is a great deal of literature on the impact of perceived discrimination and micro-aggressions on substance use disorders, there is a dearth of evidence-based substance use interventions that include components specifically designed to address racism, classism, and sexism. *Community Wise*, a manualized multilevel group intervention aimed at reducing health inequalities related to alcohol and illicit drug use, was developed to address this gap, although it was designed and pilot tested with adults (Windsor, Jemal, & Benoit, 2014; Windsor, Jessell, Lassiter, & Benoit, 2015). Community Wise is still being developed by the authors of this chapter and it seems like a promising approach. It addresses social determinants of health at the *micro-level* (e.g., cognitive and behavioral processes), *meso-level* (e.g., relationships with individuals and organizations), and *macro-level* (e.g., political and cultural processes) by raising critical consciousness. *Critical consciousness* is an individual's ability to understand the structural roots of personal and societal problems (which include racism, classism, and sexism) and to address social determinants of health while changing individual behaviors (e.g., reducing substance use frequency) (Windsor, Pinto, et al., 2014). The intervention includes a component called *Critical Dialogue*, which is designed to engage participants in discussions about structural and internalized oppression and how these forces may contribute to substance use and inequalities. Participants compare their lived experiences with racism, classism, and sexism with existing literature on social determinants of heath and state and federal policies. Pilot results with a small sample of 56 individuals showed increases in critical consciousness and pre-post reductions in alcohol and illicit substance use. The intervention is yet to be evaluated for efficacy in a randomized clinical trial.

Interventions that address social determinants of health may be more generalizable across marginalized populations. Further, an intervention like Community Wise is modular and could easily be integrated with existing substance use treatment approaches. In short, developing broad-based, multilevel interventions that address social determinants of health may be one new approach to increasing cultural competence for emerging adults with substance use disorders (Gorin, Badr, Krebs, & Prabhu Das, 2012).

Reaching Emerging Adults from Privileged and Marginalized Groups through Therapist Training

Little is known about what practitioners know about particular marginalized groups and whether they can harness such knowledge to either develop effective culturally adapted treatments (i.e., modules) or use such knowledge in interventions such as MI. The former approach would entail developing actual intervention content to attempt to address a culturally driven outcomes mediator. For example, a practitioner would develop an intervention module specifically to address oppression, which may increase the comfort of individuals from marginalized backgrounds and result in better outcomes. On the other hand, a more inclusive approach would be an infusion approach, in which cultural knowledge is represented in actual clinical skills that could be used with or without specific culturally tailored intervention content. For example, we have a concept of an *accurate clinician reflection*, defined as a clinician statement that adroitly captures the client's intended meaning and perhaps deepens the conversation. But currently we have no construct of a *culturally accurate reflection*, which could be defined as a clinician statement that accurately captures potentially cultural-specific content discussed by clients. Given the emphasis on cultural humility and making hypotheses in reflective-listening statements that appears in both the cultural competence and MI literature (Miller et al., 2007; Stuart, 2004), one wonders if clinicians' cultural knowledge is ever expressed in clinicians' guesses about client experiences. For example, consider a clinician working with an African American emerging adult in substance use disorder treatment. During the course of a session, the clinician uses the reflection: "You are angry by the way the cops treat people of color in your neighborhood, and you personally want to stay away from drugs to give them less ammunition." Notice how this reflection serves the dual role of overtly acknowledging racial oppression experienced by a marginalized group and the client's personal substance use, the focus of the intervention.

Preparing students as clinicians to infuse *culturally accurate reflections* in day-to-day practice would possibly require both knowledge building about various marginalized groups and opportunities for skills training practice on applying cultural knowledge in simulated therapeutic interactions. That is, there is growing recognition that training in empirically supported models such as MI requires didactic learning on the intervention, practice, and supervised feedback on the intervention delivery (Smith, 2012). Such training can be accomplished during coursework but requires an institutional commitment to employ experts in MI who are willing to complete audio-recorded reviews with their students. We anticipate much anxiety on the part of students completing assignments applying reflective-listening skills to case scenarios with overt marginalization themes. Yet, intentional works attempts to train clinicians to translate their cultural knowledge into actual clinical practice skills, such as culturally accurate reflections, could prepare students to better address marginalization.

RECOMMENDATIONS FOR PRACTICE AND FUTURE RESEARCH

This chapter highlights the scarcity of research focusing on treating emerging adults in general and calls for the development, testing, and adoption of substance use disorder treatments that are inclusive and sustainable, target social determinants of health, and train therapists to provide effective treatment to diverse groups. Our primary recommendation is a call for further research on substance use disorder treatment outcomes to test the recommendations presented in this chapter that consider potential differences between privileged emerging adults and their marginalized counterparts. Following is a summary of our recommendations, the rationale to support them, and proposed future research questions:

1) *Development of interventions that target social determinants of health.* Since research clearly demonstrates the negative impact of stigma and discrimination on health (Major, Dovidio, & Link, in press), it is critical that interventions be developed and tested for their effectiveness to mitigate these negative effects on substance use outcomes. What kinds of strategies are the most effective in addressing stigma in treatment? How can we improve engagement and retention in substance use disorder treatment for diverse groups without opening these doors through incarceration or the welfare system? And what interventions can we develop to minimize the disproportionately more severe consequences of drug use experienced by marginalized groups?

2) *Development of inclusive strategies that make treatment welcoming to diverse groups.* How can we isolate intervention components including therapist characteristics that seem to meet the client where the client is and add these components to existing traditional substance use disorder treatments? More research is needed specifically on whether treatments with potentially universally curative components (e.g., MI, CRA) would improve outcomes among marginalized emerging adults. Study designs should test whether these treatments work through universal processes common to both marginalized and privileged emerging adults or operate through culturally driven mediators.

3) *Interventions that consider sustainability.* Interventions must be grounded in the literature but developed with direct input from the community-based agencies that will be delivering the interventions and from the groups of clients likely to benefit, namely emerging adults from diverse groups. Using community-based participatory research methods where the community works with researchers as partners in every stage of the research may be a useful approach to maximize sustainability. Testing interventions in the real world and including qualitative components in the methodology where people can provide direct feedback to researchers is also recommended.

4) *More training for practitioners.* Because we know so little about how students in clinical training apply knowledge about marginalized groups in practice, additional research could focus on whether client outcomes differ on the basis of different levels of student training. For example, students could be randomized to receive additional content on addressing cultural themes through typical active-listening practices associated with MI as described earlier. Alternatively, practitioners in the field already expert in practices such as MI could be randomized to training on life course issues associated with emerging adulthood

and marginalization to see if such training resulted in higher levels of culturally and developmentally accurate reflections on their audio-recorded work samples. Such studies may comprise a different approach to training practitioners to address diversity issues with marginalized emerging adults with substance use disorders.

CONCLUSION

This chapter examined the current literature on development and effectiveness of existing culturally relevant substance use disorder treatments focusing on emerging adults and made recommendations for future research and best practices. We have argued that there is a dearth of literature focusing on substance use disorders and substance use disorder treatments for emerging adults, especially those from marginalized backgrounds. We suggest that the field move forward by (1) developing and adopting interventions that target social determinants of health, (2) developing and adopting inclusive interventions that are responsive to cultural context, and (3) investing in therapist training.

REFERENCES

Acevedo, A., Garnick, D. W., Lee, M. T., Horgan, C. M., Ritter, G., Panas, L., . . . Reynolds, M. (2012). Racial and ethnic differences in substance abuse treatment initiation and engagement. *Journal of Ethnicity in Substance Abuse, 11*(1), 1–21.

Adams, S. H., Knopf, D. K., & Park, M. J. (2014). Prevalence and treatment of mental health and substance use problems in the early emerging adult years in the United States: Findings from the 2010 National Survey on Drug Use and Health. *Emerging Adulthood, 2*(3), 163–172.

Alegría, M., Canino, G., Shrout, P. E., Woo, M., Duan, D., Vila, D. . . . Meng, X.L. (2008). Prevalence of mental illness in immigrant and non-immigrant U.S. Latino groups. *American Journal of Psychiatry, 165*(3), 359–369.

Alexander, M. (2010). *The new Jim Crow: Mass incarceration in the age of colorblindness.* New York: The New Press.

Allmark, P. (2004). Should research samples reflect the diversity of the population? *Journal of Medical Ethics, 30*(2), 185–189.

Amaro, H., Raj, A., Vega, R. R., Mangione, T. W., & Perez, L. N. (2001). Racial/ethnic disparities in the HIV and substance abuse epidemics: Communities responding to the need. *Public Health Reports, 116*(5), 434.

Arcia, E., Skinner, M., Bailey, D., & Correa, V. (2001). Models of acculturation and health behaviors among Latino immigrants to the US. *Social Science & Medicine, 53*(1), 41–53.

Arnett, J. J. (2000). Emerging adulthood: A theory of development from the late teens through the twenties, *American Psychologist, 55*, 469–480.

Baquet, C. R., Commiskey, P., Mullins, C. D., & Mishra, S. I. (2006). Recruitment and partici pation in clinical trials: Socio-demographic, rural/urban, and health care access predictors. *Cancer Detection & Prevention, 30,* 24–33. doi: 10.1016/j.cdp.2005.12.001

Benish, S. G., Quintana, S., & Wampold, B. E. (2011). Culturally adapted psychotherapy and the legitimacy of myth: A direct-comparison meta-analysis. *Journal of Counseling Psychology, 58,* 279–289.

Bergman, B. G., Hoeppner, B. B., Nelson, L. M., Slaymaker, V., & Kelly, J. F. (2015). The effects of continuing care on emerging adult outcomes following residential addiction treatment. *Drug and Alcohol Dependence, 153,* 207–214. doi: 10.1016/j.drugalcdep.2015.05.017

Binswanger, I. A., Redmond, N., Steiner, J. F., & Hicks, L. S. (2012). Health disparities and the criminal justice system: An agenda for further research and action. *Journal of Urban Health: Bulletin of the New York Academy of Medicine, 89*(1), 98–107. doi: 10.1007/s11524-011-9614-1

Brody, G. H., Yu, T., Chen, Y., Kogan, S. M., & Smith, K. (2012). The Adults in the Making program: Long-term protective stabilizing effects on alcohol use and substance use problems for rural African American emerging adults. *Journal of Consulting and Clinical Psychology, 80*(1), 17–28. doi: 10.1037/a0026592

Caetano, R., & Clark, C. L. (1998). Trends in alcohol-related problems among whites, blacks, and Hispanics: 1984-1995. *Alcoholism, Clinical and Experimental Research, 22*(2), 534–538.

Castro, F. G., Barrera Jr, M., & Holleran Steiker, L. K. (2010). Issues and challenges in the design of culturally adapted evidence-based interventions. *Annual Review of Clinical Psychology, 6,* 213–239.

Centers for Medicare and Medicaid Services (2015). 2015 CMS statistics. Retrieved from https://www.cms.gov/Research-Statistics-Data-and-Systems/Statistics-Trends-and-Reports/CMS-Statistics-Reference-Booklet/Downloads/2015CMSStatistics.pdf

Chae, D. H., Nuru-Jeter, A. M., Lincoln, K. D., & Francis, D. D. (2011). Conceptualizing racial disparities in health. *DuBois Review: Social Science Research on Race, 8*(1), 63–77.

Chen, P., & Jacobson, K. C. (2012). Developmental trajectories of substance use from early adolescence to young adulthood: Gender and racial/ethnic differences. *Journal of Adolescent Health, 50*(2), 154–163. doi: 10.1016/j.jadohealth.2011.05.013

Clark, T. T. (2014). Perceived discrimination, depressive symptoms, and substance use in young adulthood. *Addictive Behaviors, 39*(6), 1021–1025. doi: 10.1016/j.addbeh.2014.01.013

Collins, R. L. (1992). Methodological issues in conducting substance abuse research on ethnic minority populations. *Drugs & Society, 6*(1), 59–78.

Côté, J. E. (2014). The dangerous myth of emerging adulthood: An evidence-based critique of a flawed developmental theory. *Applied Developmental Science, 18*(4), 177–188.

Craig, S. C., Austin, A., & Alessi, E. (2013). Gay affirmative cognitive behavioral therapy for sexual minority youth: A clinical adaptation. *Clinical Social Work Journal, 41,* 258–266. doi: 10.1007/s10615-012-0427-9

Davis, J. P., Smith, D. C., & Briley, D. (2017) Substance use prevention and treatment outcomes for emerging adults in non-college settings: A meta-analysis. *Psychology of Addictive Behaviors,* doi: 10.1037/adb0000267

Ding, K., & Crawley, M. B. (2010). Drug use among African American teenagers and their mental health. *Home Health Care Management & Practice, 22*(7), 492–498. doi: 10.1177/1084822310370944

Dumont, D. M., Allen, S. A., Brockmann, B. W., Alexander, N. E., & Rich, J. D. (2013). Incarceration, community health, and racial disparities. *Journal of Health Care for the Poor and Underserved, 24*(1), 78–88. doi: 10.1353/hpu.2013.0000

Finlay, A. K., White, H. R., Mun, E.-Y., Cronley, C. C., & Lee, C. (2012). Racial differences in trajectories of heavy drinking and regular marijuana use from ages 13 to 24 among African-American and white males. *Drug and Alcohol Dependence, 121*(1–2), 118–123. doi: 10.1016/j.drugalcdep.2011.08.020

Fisher, W. H., Silver, E., & Wolff, N. (2006). Beyond criminalization: Toward a criminologically informed framework for mental health policy and services research. *Administration and Policy in Mental Health, 33*(5), 544–557. doi: 10.1007/s10488-006-0072-0

Flaskerud, J. H., & Nyamathi, A. M. (2000). Attaining gender and ethnic diversity in health intervention research: Cultural responsiveness versus resource provision. *Advances in Nursing Science, 22*(4), 1–15. Retrieved from http://www.ncbi.nlm.nih.gov/pubmed/10852665

Friedman, S. R., & Rossi, D. (2015). Some musings about big events and the past and future of drug use and of HIV and other epidemics. *Substance Use & Misuse, 50*(7), 899–902. doi: 10.3109/10826084.2015.1018752

Gibbons, F. X., Gerrard, M., Cleveland, M. J., Wills, T. A., & Brody, G. (2004). Perceived discrimination and substance use in African American parents and their children: A panel study. *Jounral of Personality and Social Psychology, 86*(4), 517–529.

Godley, S. H., Hedges, K., & Hunter, B. (2011). Gender and racial differences in treatment process and outcome among participants in the adolescent community reinforcement approach. *Psychology of Addictive Behaviors, 25*(1), 143–154.

Gorin, S. S., Badr, H., Krebs, P., & Prabhu Das, I. (2012). Multilevel interventions and racial/ethnic health disparities. *Journal of the National Cancer Institute Monographs, 2012*(44), 100–111. doi: 10.1093/jncimonographs/lgs015

Green, C. A. (2006). Gender and use of substance abuse treatment services. *Alcohol Research & Health, 29*(1), 55–62.

Griner, D., & Smith, T. B. (2006). Culturally adapted mental health intervention: A meta-analytic review. *Psychotherapy (Chicago, Ill.), 43*, 531–548.

Guerrero, E. G., Marsh, J. C., Khachikian, T., Amaro, H., & Vega, W. A. (2013). Disparities in Latino substance use, service use, and treatment: Implications for culturally and evidence-based interventions under health care reform. *Drug and Alcohol Dependence, 133*, 805–813.

Hall, G. C. N. (2001). Psychotherapy research with ethnic minorities: Empirical, ethical, and conceptual issues. *Journal of Consulting and Clinical Psychology, 69*, 502–510. doi: 10.1037/0022-006X.69.3.502

Hawke, J. M., Hennen, J., & Gallione, P. (2005). Correlates of therapeutic involvement among adolescents in residential drug treatment. *American Journal of Drug and Alcohol Abuse, 31*(1), 163–177.

Hendry, L. B., & Kloep, M. (2010). How universal is emerging adult-hood? An empirical example. *Journal of Youth Studies, 13*, 169–179.

Hernandez, M., Nesman, T., Mowery, D., Acevedo-Polakovich, I. D., & Callejas, L. M. (2009). Cultural competence: A literature review and conceptual model for mental health services. *Psychiatric Services*, *60*(8), 1046–1050. doi: 10.1176/ps.2009.60.8.1046

Hinton, D. E., Rivera, E. I., Hofmann, S. G., Barlow, D. H., & Otto, M. W. (2012). Adapting CBT for traumatized refugees and ethnic minority patients: Examples from culturally adapted CBT (CA-CBT). *Transcultural Psychiatry*, *49*, 340–365. doi: 10.1177/1363461512441595

Hogue, A., Dauber, S., Stambaugh, L. F., Cecero, J. J., & Liddle, H. A. (2006). Early therapeutic alliance and treatment outcome in individual and family therapy for adolescent behavior problems. *Journal of Consulting and Clinical Psychology*, *74*(1), 121–129.

Hunt, L. M., Schneider, S., & Comer, B. (2004). Should "acculturation" be a variable in health research? A critical review of research on US Hispanics. *Social Science & Medicine*, *59*(5), 973–986.

Kandel, D., Schaffran, C., Hu, M.-C., & Thomas, Y. (2011). Age-related differences in cigarette smoking among whites and African-Americans: Evidence for the crossover hypothesis. *Drug and Alcohol Dependence*, *118*(2–3), 280–287. doi: 10.1016/j.drugalcdep.2011.04.008

Kelly, J. F., Urbanoski, K. A., Hoeppner, B. B., & Slaymaker, V. (2012). "Ready, willing, and (not) able" to change: Young adults' response to residential treatment. *Drug and Alcohol Dependence*, *121*(3), 224–230. doi: 10.1016/j.drugalcdep.2011.09.003

Keyes, K. M., Vo, T., Wall, M. M., Caetano, R., Suglia, S. F., Martins, S. S., . . . Hasin, D. (2015). Racial/ethnic differences in use of alcohol, tobacco, and marijuana: Is there a cross-over from adolescence to adulthood? *Social Science & Medicine (1982)*, *124*, 132–141. doi: 10.1016/j.socscimed.2014.11.035

Krohn, M. D., & Thornberry, T. P. (1998). Retention of minority populations in panel studies of drug use. *Drugs & Society*, *14*(1), 185–207.

Lam, A. G., & Sue, S. (2001). Client diversity. *Psychotherapy: Theory, Research, Practice Training*, *38*, 479–486. https://doi.org/10.1037/0033-3204.38.4.479

Lau, A. S. (2006). Making the case for selective and directed cultural adaptations of evidence-based treatments: Examples from parent training. *Clinical Psychology: Science & Practice*, *13*(4), 295–310.

Lê Cook, B., & Alegría, M. (2011). Racial-ethnic disparities in substance abuse treatment: The role of criminal history and socioeconomic status. *Psychiatric Services*, *62*(11), 1273–1281. doi: 10.1176/ps.62.11.pss6211_1273

Lewis, T. T., Aiello, A. E., Leurgans, S., Kelly, J., & Barnes, L. L. (2010). Self-reported experiences of everyday discrimination are associated with elevated C-reactive protein levels in older African-American adults. *Brain, Behavior, and Immunity*, *24*(3), 438–443. doi: 10.1016/j.bbi.2009.11.011

Lopez-Tamayo, R., Alvarez, J., & Jason, L. A. (2016). Testing a multidimensional acculturation model on Latinos who completed substance abuse treatment. *Journal of Drug Abuse*, *2*(2).

Lorenzo-Blanco, E. I., Unger, J. B., Ritt-Olson, A., Soto, D., & Baezconde-Garbanati, L. (2011). Acculturation, gender, depression, and cigarette smoking among U.S. Hispanic youth: The mediating role of perceived discrimination. *Journal of Youth and Adolescence*, *40*(11), 1519–1533. doi: 10.1007/s10964-011-9633-y

Lundahl, B. W., Kunz, C., Brownell, C., Tollefson, D., & Burke, B. L. (2010). A meta-analysis of motivational interviewing: Twenty-five years of empirical studies. *Research on Social Work Practice, 20,* 137–160.

Major, B., Dovidio, J. F., & Link, B. G. (Eds.). (in press). *The Oxford Handbook of Stigma, Discrimination, and Health.* New York: Oxford University Press.

Mancini, M. A., Salas-Wright, C. P., & Vaughn, M. G. (2015). Drug use and service utilization among Hispanics in the United States. *Social Psychiatry and Psychiatric Epidemiology, 50*(11), 1679–1689.

Mawson, E., Best, D., Beckwith, M., Dingle, G. A., & Lubman, D. I. (2015). Social identity, social networks and recovery capital in emerging adulthood: A pilot study. *Substance Abuse Treatment, Prevention, and Policy, 10*(1), 45. doi: 10.1186/s13011-015-0041-2

McGoldrick, M., Giordano, J., & Garcia-Petro, N. (Eds.). (2005). *Ethnicity & family therapy.* New York: Guilford Press.

Miller, W. R., & Rollnick, S. (2012). *Motivational interviewing: Helping people change.* New York: Guilford Press.

Miller, W. R., Villanueva, M., Tonigan, J. S., & Cuzmar, I. (2007). Are special treatments needed for special populations? *Alcoholism Treatment Quarterly, 25*(4), 63–78.

Mulye, T. P., Park, M. J., Nelson, C. D., Adams, S. H., Irwin, C. E., & Brindis, C. D. (2009). Trends and adolescent and young adult health in the United States. *Journal of Adolescent Health, 45,* 8–24.

National Institute on Drug Abuse. (2003). *Minority report on racial minorities* (Vol. 2012).

Pascoe, E. A., & Smart Richman, L. (2009). Perceived discrimination and health: A meta-analytic review. *Psychological Bulletin, 135*(4), 531–554. doi: org/10.1037/a0016059

Phelan, J. C., Link, B. G., & Tehranifar, P. (2010). Social conditions as fundamental causes of health inequalities: Theory, evidence, and policy implications. *Journal of Health and Social Behavior, 51,* S28–S40.

Pinto, R. M., Campbell, A. N. C., Hien, D. A., Yu, G., & Gorroochurn, P. (2011). Retention in the National Institute on Drug Abuse clinical trials network women and trauma study: Implications for posttrial implementation. *American Journal of Orthopsychiatry, 81,* 211–217. doi: 10.1111/j.1939-0025.2011.01090.x

Prado, G., Pantin, H., Briones, E., Schwartz, S. J., Feaster, D., Shi, H., . . . Szapocznik, J. (2007). A randomized controlled trial of a parent-centered intervention in preventing substance use and HIV risk behaviors in Hispanic adolescents. *Journal of Consulting & Clinical Psychology, 75*(6), 914–926.

Pugh, L. A., & Bry, B. H. (2007). The protective effects of ethnic identity for alcohol and marijuana use among Black young adults. *Cultural Diversity & Ethnic Minority Psychology, 13*(2), 187–193. doi: 10.1037/1099-9809.13.2.187

Raphael, S. (2011). Incarceration and prisoner re-entry in the United States. *Annals of the American Academy of Political and Social Science, 635*(1), 192–215. doi: 10.1177/0002716210393321

Ritt-Olson, A., Milam, J., Unger, J. B., Trinidad, D., Teran, L., Dent, C. W., & Sussman, S. (2004). The protective influence of spirituality and "health-as-a-value" against monthly substance use among adolescents varying in risk. *Journal of Adolescent Health, 34*(3), 192–199.

Rote, S. M., & Taylor, J. (2014). Black/white differences in adolescent drug use: A test of six hypotheses. *Journal of Child & Adolescent Substance Abuse, 23*(5), 282–290. doi: 10.1080/1067828X.2013.869133

Rowe, D., & Grills, C. (1993). African-centered drug treatment: An alternative conceptual paradigm for drug counseling with African-American clients. *Journal of Psychoactive Drugs, 25*, 21–33. https://doi.org/10.1080/02791072.1993.10472588

Ryan, A. M., Gee, G. C., & Laflamme, D. F. (2006). The association between self-reported discrimination, physical health and blood pressure: Findings from African Americans, black immigrants, and Latino immigrants in New Hampshire. *Journal of Health Care for the Poor and Underserved, 17*(2 Suppl.), 116–132. doi: 10.1353/hpu.2006.0092

Santisteban, D. A., Mena, M. P., & McCabe, B. E. (2011). Preliminary results for an adaptive family treatment for drug abuse in Hispanic youth. *Journal of Family Psychology, 25*(4), 610–614. doi: 10.1037/a0024016

Schnittker, J., Massoglia, M., & Uggen, C. (2011). Incarceration and health of the African American community. *Du Bois Review, 8*(1), 1–9.

Schuman-Olivier, Z., Claire Greene, M., Bergman, B. G., & Kelly, J. F. (2014). Is residential treatment effective for opioid use disorders? A longitudinal comparison of treatment outcomes among opioid dependent, opioid misusing, and non-opioid using emerging adults with substance use disorder. *Drug and Alcohol Dependence, 144*, 178–185. doi: 10.1016/j.drugalcdep.2014.09.009

Schuman-Olivier, Z., Weiss, R. D., Hoeppner, B. B., Borodovsky, J., & Albanese, M. J. (2014). Emerging adult age status predicts poor buprenorphine treatment retention. *Journal of Substance Abuse Treatment, 47*(3), 202–212. doi: 10.1016/j.jsat.2014.04.006

Shavers, V. L., Fagan, P., Jones, D., Klein, W. M. P., Boyington, J., Moten, C., & Rorie, E. (2012). The state of research on racial/ethnic discrimination in the receipt of health care. *American Journal of Public Health, 102*(5), 953–966. doi: 10.2105/AJPH.2012.300773

Sheikh, A. (2006). Why are ethnic minorities under-represented in U.S. research studies? *PLoS Medicine, 3*, 166–167. doi: 10.1371/journal.pmed.0030049

Shorkey, C., Windsor, L., & Spence, R. (2009a). Assessing and developing cultural competence/relevance in chemical dependence treatment organizations that serve Mexican American clients and their families. *Journal of Behavioral Health Services & Research, 36*(1), 61–74.

Shorkey, C., Windsor, L., & Spence, R. (2009b). Systematic assessment of culturally competent chemical dependence treatment services for African Americans. *Journal of Ethnicity in Substance Abuse, 8*(2), 113–128.

Smith, D. C. (2012). Jacquelines of all trades or masters of some: Negative implications of focusing on common factors. *Social Work, 57*(3), 283–287. doi: 10.1093/sw/sws038

Smith, D. C., Godley, S. H., Godley, M. D., & Dennis, M. L. (2011). Adolescent community reinforcement approach outcomes differ among emerging adults and adolescents. *Journal of Substance Abuse Treatment, 41*(4), 422–430. doi: 10.1016/j.jsat.2011.06.003

Stuart, R. B. (2004). Twelve practical suggestions for achieving multicultural competence. *Professional Psychology: Research and Practice, 35*(1), 3–9.

Strycker, L. A., Duncan, S. C., Duncan, T. E., Haiou, H., & Desai, N. (2006). Retention of African-American and white youth in a longitudinal substance use study. *Journal of Ethnicity in Substance Abuse, 5*, 119–131.

Substance Abuse and Mental Health Services Administration (SAMHSA). (2014). National Survey on Drug Use and Health. Population data. Retrieved from http://www.samhsa.gov/data/population-data-nsduh/reports?tab=32

Substance Abuse and Mental Health Services Administration (SAMHSA). (2015a). *Behavioral health trends: Results from the 2014 National Survey on Drug Use and Health*. Retrieved from https://www.samhsa.gov/data/sites/default/files/NSDUH-FRR1-2014/NSDUH-FRR1-2014.pdf

Substance Abuse and Mental Health Services Administration (SAMHSA). (2015b). Behavioral health barometer: United States, 2015. HHS Publication No. SMA–16–Baro–2015. Rockville, MD: Substance Abuse and Mental Health Services Administration.

Sue, S., Zane, N., Hall, G., & Berger, L. (2009). The case for cultural competency in psychotherapeutic interventions. *Annual Review of Psychology, 60*, 525–48. https://doi.org/10.1146/annurev.psych.60.110707.163651

The Williams Institute–UCLA School of Law. (2016). Same-sex couple and LGBT demographic data interactive. Retrieved from http://williamsinstitute.law.ucla.edu/visualization/lgbt-stats/?topic=LGBT&compare=percentage#comparison

Trinh-Shevrin, C., Islam, N. S., Nadkarni, S., Park, R., & Kwon, S. C. (2015). Defining an integrative approach for health promotion and disease prevention: A population health equity framework. *Journal of Health Care for the Poor and Underserved, 26*(2 Suppl.), 146–163. doi: 10.1353/hpu.2015.0067

Unger, J. B., Schwartz, S. J., Huh, J., Soto, D. W., & Baezconde-Garbanati, L. (2014). Acculturation and perceived discrimination: Predictors of substance use trajectories from adolescence to emerging adulthood among Hispanics. *Addictive Behaviors, 39*(9), 1293–1296. doi: 10.1016/j.addbeh.2014.04.014

U.S. Census Bureau. (2015). Millennials outnumber baby boomers and are far more diverse. Retrieved from https://www.census.gov/newsroom/press-releases/2015/cb15-113.html

U.S. Department of Health and Human Services. (2000). *Healthy people 2010: Understanding and improving health*. Retrieved from http://www.healthypeople.gov

U.S. Department of Health and Human Services. (2010). *Healthy people 2020*. Retrieved from http://www.healthypeople.gov/2020/about/default.aspx

Viruell-Fuentes, E. A. (2007). Beyond acculturation: Immigration, discrimination, and health research among Mexicans in the United States. *Social Science and Medicine, 65*(7), 1524–1535.

Viruell-Fuentes, E. A., Morenoff, J. D., Williams, D. R., & House, J. S. (2013). Contextualizing nativity status, social ties, and ethnic enclaves: Implications for understanding immigrant and Latino health paradoxes. *Ethnicity & Health, 18*(6), 586–609.

Windsor, L., Jemal, A., & Alessi, E. (2015). Cognitive behavioral therapy: A meta-analysis of race and substance use outcomes. *Cultural Diversity & Ethnic Minority Psychology, 21*(2), 300–313. doi: 10.1037/a0037929

Windsor, L., Jemal, A., Benoit, E. (2014). Community Wise: Paving the way for empowerment in community reentry. *International Journal of Law and Psychiatry, 37*(5), 501–511.

Windsor, L., Jessell, L., Lassiter, T., & Benoit, E. (2015). Community Wise: A formative evaluation of a community based health intervention. *International Public Health Journal, 7*(1), 79–90.

Windsor, L., Pinto, R. M., Benoit, E., Jessell, L., & Jemal, A. (2014). Community Wise: Development of a model to address oppression in order to promote individual and community health. *Journal of Social Work Practice in the Addictions, 14*(4), 405–420. doi: 10.1080/1533256X.2014.962141

Witbrodt, J., Mulia, N., Zemore, S. E., & Kerr, W. C. (2014). Racial/ethnic disparities in alcohol-related problems: Differences by gender and level of heavy drinking. *Alcoholism, Clinical and Experimental Research, 38*(6), 1662–1670. doi: 10.1111/acer.12398

Wu, L.-T., Ringwalt, C. L., & Williams, C. E. (2003). Use of substance abuse treatment services by persons with mental health and substance use problems. *Psychiatric Services, 54*(3), 363–369. doi: 10.1176/appi.ps.54.3.363

Zemore, S. E. (2005). Re-examining whether and why acculturation relates to drinking outcomes in a rigorous, national survey of Latinos. *Alcoholism: Clinical and Experimental Research, 29*, 2144–2153. doi: 10.1097/01.alc.0000191775.01148.c0

6

The Impact of the Affordable Care Act on Substance Use Disorder Treatment for Emerging Adults

CHRISTINA M. ANDREWS, CLIFFORD BERSAMIRA, AND MELISSA WESTLAKE ∎

INTRODUCTION

Emerging adults have the highest prevalence of substance use disorders (SUDs) of any age group in the United States. Yet historically, few emerging adults who need SUD treatment—defined here as targeted services to address SUDs that go beyond brief intervention—ever receive it. While the reasons for poor access to treatment are multifaceted and complex, inability to pay is consistently cited as a major barrier to accessing treatment. Enacted in 2010, the Patient Protection and Affordable Care Act (ACA) includes a number of provisions designed to address these challenges. Provisions of the ACA, including the expansion of Medicaid eligibility requirements, the dependent coverage mandate permitting children to stay on their parents' health plans until age 26, and the creation of insurance marketplace exchanges, have already demonstrated success, as evidenced by a significant drop in the percentage of uninsured emerging adults. Moreover, the ACA requires many health insurance plans to provide at least some coverage for SUD treatment, expanding the reach of federal parity requirements originally limited to large private health insurance plans. Finally, the ACA establishes new incentives for the integration of SUD treatment into mainstream medical care to respond to long-standing challenges in treatment quality and coordination. Taken together, these changes have already resulted in major improvements in the accessibility and quality of SUD treatment for emerging adults. However, to fully realize the ACA's promise, it will be critical to address ongoing challenges to effective implementation, including inadequate SUD treatment supply, variation in treatment access and quality, and long-standing socioeconomic disparities.

SUD TREATMENT PRIOR TO HEALTH REFORM

In the era prior to the ACA, the financing and organization of SUD treatment were rather different than that of general medical care. Unlike general healthcare, the SUD treatment system was heavily reliant on public sector payment (Frank, McGuire, Regier, Manderscheid, & Woodward, 1994). Spending for SUD treatment in the decades before the ACA was marked by periods of growth and retraction. During the 1980s, health insurance coverage for SUD treatment expanded and access improved. However, during the mid- and late 1980s, with mounting employer concerns about growing healthcare costs, many health insurance plans reduced or eliminated coverage for SUD treatment and imposed new controls on service utilization, primarily via managed care (Mark, Levit, Vandivort-Warren, Buck, & Coffey, 2011).

The overall trend in the 30 years before ACA implementation was slow but steady growth in SUD treatment spending. According to the Substance Abuse and Mental Health Services Administration (SAMHSA) (2013a), SUD treatment spending doubled from $12 billion in 1997 to $24 billion in 2009 (Mark et al., 2000). Yet, this spending has not kept pace with spending in other areas of healthcare, and consequently, spending for SUD treatment has represented a declining proportion of all-health spending for most payers (Mark et al., 2011).

On the eve of the implementation of the ACA's major insurance expansions in later 2013, public payers accounted for 69% of all SUD treatment spending, with Substance Abuse Prevention and Treatment (SAPT) block grants administered by the SAMHSA accounting for 40% of all SUD treatment spending. State and local payers (excluding state contributions to Medicaid) accounted for 31% (SAMHSA, 2013a). Medicaid accounted for 21% of SUD treatment spending and private insurance accounted for 16%. In the section below, we describe each of the major pre-ACA sources of funding for SUD treatment in greater detail.

Medicaid

Medicaid is the nation's largest public health insurance program for low-income people. It is a jointly financed intergovernmental program, largely administered by states under a set of federal regulations (Centers for Medicare & Medicaid Services [CMS], 2005). States are responsible for administering Medicaid programs and develop their own eligibility requirements and benefits packages within broad federal guidelines (Stewart & Hogan, 2011). Prior to the ACA, Medicaid eligibility was based on a combination of financial and categorical eligibility requirements. Beneficiaries had to be low income, although states made separate determinations of income thresholds. States were required by federal law to cover children up to age 6 who were under 133% federal poverty level (FPL) and those aged 7–18 under 100% of FPL; pregnant women and infants up to 133% FPL; poor disabled and elderly (65+ years of age) recipients of Supplemental Security Income (SSI); and poor families with dependent children eligible for Temporary Assistance for Needy Families (TANF). States also have the option to extend coverage to other populations and receive the federal contribution. Federal spending levels for Medicaid are determined by the number of people participating, the extent to which enrollees use services, and the scope of services covered.

Medicaid expenditures for SUD treatment increased over the past three decades as a result of expansions in state Medicaid programs' eligibility and benefits for SUD treatment. Historically, states have had great discretion with regard to Medicaid coverage for SUD treatment. Federal guidelines were vague: While they did not include coverage for SUD treatment, they also did not exclude it. Consequently, states varied greatly with regard to what coverage they provided and who could receive it (Coughlin & Zuckerman, 2002). Some states covered no SUD treatment, and among those that did, there was great variation in the specific types of treatment services covered and reimbursement rates for them. Moreover, states differed with regard to the criteria used to determine eligibility for Medicaid. Some states extend eligibility only to mandatory categories stipulated by federal program guidelines, while others have used Medicaid as a vehicle through which to extend healthcare coverage to a range of vulnerable populations, including low-income, medically needy, and working disabled individuals.

Programmatic barriers to access to SUD treatment for Medicaid enrollees have been well documented (Abraham, Knudsen, Rieckmann, & Roman, 2013). At the time of the ACA's passage, only about half of SUD treatment programs in the United States accepted Medicaid enrollees, creating potential challenges to treatment availability (Andrews, 2014; Terry-McElrath, Chriqui, & McBride, 2011). Additionally, reimbursement rates for Medicaid in comparison with rates for private insurance have historically been low, making it undesirable to a significant sector of private treatment programs that cater to the insured population. Other programs face different kinds of disincentives to accept Medicaid, including significant challenges in meeting the staffing and technological requirements of many state Medicaid programs to become Medicaid-billable providers. Moreover, many Medicaid programs use managed care to oversee SUD treatment financing and reimbursement, and consequently, many SUD treatment services are subject to a variety of utilization controls, including preauthorization, cost-sharing, and limits of intensity and frequency of services used (Maglione & Ridgeley, 2006). In the vast majority of cases, requirements imposed on SUD treatment have been more restrictive than those placed on other medical services (Garfield, Lave, & Donohue, 2010).

However, the literature on the effects of managed care on SUD treatment access is mixed. After the transition from a fee-for-service to managed care system, treatment access increased considerably in Oregon and Iowa (Deck, McFarland, Titus, Laws, & Gabriel, 2000; McCarty & Argeriou, 2003) and stayed the same in Maryland and Massachusetts (Callahan, Shepard, Beinecke, Larson, & Cavanaugh,

1995; Ettner, Denmead, Dilonardo, Cao, & Belanger, 2003). Only in Michigan was the transition to managed care associated with a decrease in Medicaid beneficiaries receiving treatment (Hodgkin, Shepard, Anthony, & Strickler, 2004). Finally, a national study on the impact of publicly funded managed care on treatment outcomes found that Medicaid behavioral health carve-outs were associated with greater use of treatment (Chuang, Wells & Alexander, 2011).

Private Insurance

The first private health insurance plans began to cover treatment for alcoholism in the 1960s. However, these plans were generally reluctant to offer coverage at similar levels to that of other medical and surgical services (Scott, Greenberg, & Pizzaro, 1992). In the 1970s, advocates for emerging SUD treatment communities attempted to persuade health insurance providers to extend coverage, but with only limited success. To push back at the health insurance industry's early resistance to covering SUD treatment, some states turned to insurance mandates requiring insurance plans to provide coverage for SUD treatment or offer enrollees the option to purchase it separately. By 1991, 41 states had enacted SUD treatment mandates (Scott et al., 1992). As a consequence of these mandates, private health insurance funding for SUD treatment rose rapidly to account for one-third of all spending for SUD treatment by the 1990s (Rogowski, 1992; Scott et al., 1992). By 1990, 96% of private health plan beneficiaries had access to SUD treatment benefits (Rogowski, 1992).

However, private financing of SUD treatment began to decline shortly thereafter, as managed care organizations (MCOs) reached dominance in the private insurance market (Stewart & Horgan, 2011). As a cost-saving measure, many large group health insurance plans elected to rely on MCOs in response to rapidly rising costs of healthcare across the industry, and the SUD treatment industry was no exception. Enrollment rapidly expanded from 48 million in the early 1990s to about 120 million by the middle of the decade, with the majority insured through private employer-sponsored plans (Institute of Medicine, 1996). Generally, lifetime limits on behavioral healthcare were rare—only 6% of plans used them. However *annual* limits on behavioral health service utilization were more common; 93% of outpatient SUD treatment placed some kind of limit on use of SUD treatment services in a single year (Hodgkin, Horgan, Garnick, & Merrick, 2009).

From 1986 to 2003, private spending for SUD treatment fell by 8%, to $2.2 billion (Mark & Vandivort-Warren, 2012). Just prior to the ACA implementation, about one-third of enrollees in individual private health insurance plans and 12% of enrollees in employer-sponsored health insurance plans lacked any coverage for SUD treatment (Association for Behavioral Health and Wellness [ASPE], 2011). Moreover, enrollees in plans that did cover SUD treatment typically faced higher cost-sharing and service limits for SUD treatment than other medical and surgical services, particularly within managed care carve-outs (Gabel et al., 2007; Levit et al., 2008). By 2003, managed care plans enrolled 95% of privately insured

SUD patients (Hodgkin et al., 2009). MCOs employed a number of strategies to monitor and regulate treatment utilization, including use of preauthorization of service requirements, utilization review, and limits on the frequency, length, and number of treatment sessions (Sosin, 2002). MCOs appear to have had the greatest impact on the frequency and length of SUD treatment provided. SUD treatment programs reporting significant involvement with managed care also reported shorter treatment duration and provided an average of 10 fewer individual sessions than treatment programs with less involvement with managed care (Lemak & Alexander, 2001). From 1992 to 2001, the percentage of private insurance enrollees using SUD treatment declined by 23% (Mark & Coffey, 2004).

Block Grants

The block grant was initially created in 1992, as part of the Alcohol, Drug Abuse, and Mental Health Administration Reorganization Act of 1992. The purpose of the block grant is to provide financial assistance to states, tribes, and other U.S. jurisdictions, including for the development and implementation of SUD prevention, treatment, and recovery services (United States Government Publishing Office, 2017). States have the ability to spend grant funds at their discretion in order to meet the objectives of the SAPT block grant within the context of its statutory language. The SAPT block grant is unique in that there is no state match requirement, as there is with Medicaid.

The block grant was developed in the 1980s as a means of distributing federal funds to states to purchase SUD treatment services, while permitting state flexibility in the design and administration of services and limiting the federal government's role (Stewart & Horgan, 2011). Congress decides on the grant amount on an annual basis, which is then distributed among the states according to a formula (Stewart & Horgan, 2011). The block grant is administered by SAMHSA, the federal agency responsible for overseeing mental health and SUD treatment and funding. SAMHSA allocates block grant funds to the state government agencies, who are in turn responsible for distributing the funds to local agencies to provide SUD treatment.

Block grant funds finance SUD treatment for 2.5 million Americans annually (National Association of State Alcohol and Drug Abuse Directors [NASADAD], 2016). In particular, block grant funds are intended to provide services to people without access to insurance coverage. Additionally, some block grant funds are earmarked for treatment of vulnerable populations, including pregnant and parenting women, intravenous drug users, individuals with HIV/AIDS, and individuals with tuberculosis (United States Government Publishing Office, 2017).

Prior to the ACA, the SAPT block grant constituted approximately 40% of all SUD treatment spending in the United States and was the largest source of state funding for the SUD treatment system (Cowell, McCarty, & Woodward, 2003; NASADAD, 2016). Sixteen states reported that more than half of their spending on SUD prevention and treatment came from the block grant. However, block grant funds have not kept up with healthcare inflation, resulting in a 26% reduction in purchasing value (or $483 million decrease) over the past decade (NASADAD, 2016). From 2009—the period just prior to the implementation of ACA—to 2016, SAPT block grant funding has maintained roughly level funding, from $1.779 billion to $1.858 billion (non-inflation-adjusted dollars). It is also important to note how reliant many SUD treatment providers and states are on SAPT block grant funds. Sixteen states reported relying on the block grant for more than 50% of their SUD prevention and treatment funding.

Other Funding

Additional funding for SUD treatment comes from state and local spending and client out-of-pocket spending. State and local spending on SUD services varies geographically, but, on average, constitutes about 6% of SUD treatment spending (Stewart & Horgan, 2011). In contrast, out-of-pocket spending constituted 11% of spending on SUD treatment in 2009 (SAMHSA, 2013a). Between 1986 and 2003, out-of-pocket spending increased from $1.2 billion to $1.7 billion, at an annual rate of 1.5% (Mark et al., 2007).

CHALLENGES TO TREATMENT ACCESS AND QUALITY

Treatment Access

In the era before the ACA, access to SUD treatment for emerging adults—along with just about every other demographic population in the United States—was poor. Just prior to the passage of the ACA, in 2010, only 7.7% of emerging adults who needed SUD treatment reported receiving it (SAMHSA, 2012b). Low rates of treatment receipt among this population are particularly concerning, as 20.3% of all individuals aged 18–25 were classified as needing treatment in 2010, compared to 7.5% of youth ages 12–17, and 7.4% of individuals 26 and older (SAMHSA, 2012b). Of the 7.7% of emerging adults who were able to receive treatment in 2010, 563,000 sought treatment for illicit drugs, 611,000 sought treatment for alcohol, and 313,000 sought treatment for both. Of individuals age 12 years or older who needed treatment and did not receive it, approximately 341,000—or 33.3%—reported having made unsuccessful efforts to get treatment (SAMHSA, 2012c).

While the challenges to treatment access are as numerous as they are complex, inability to pay has consistently been cited as one of the most serious and intractable barriers to receiving SUD treatment. This is especially true for emerging adults, who have historically had the highest rates of uninsurance in the nation (CMS, 2016f). The population of young adults ranging from ages 18–29 has often been referred to as the "young invincibles," a term coined in the health insurance industry to refer to the common perception among this group that they are immune from sickness and injury and thus do not need to purchase health insurance. Among emerging adults who needed treatment for an SUD but did not receive it, 37.3% cited a lack of healthcare coverage as their main reason for not receiving treatment. An additional 8.2% said they had healthcare coverage, but that it did not cover treatment costs (SAMHSA, 2014b).

In 2009—just prior to the enactment of the law—only 57.2% of emerging adults aged 21–24 admitted for SUD treatment had health insurance coverage for SUD treatment (Saloner, Antwi, Maclean, & Le Cook, 2015). The majority of emerging adults with SUD are not in the workforce and, consequently, do not have access to employer-sponsored insurance (SAMHSA, 2012b). Most are male young adults without dependents, and before implementation of the ACA, did not qualify for publicly sponsored health insurance programs (SAMHSA, 2012b). In the Medicaid program's early years, SUDs were recognized as qualifying disabilities for SSI, through which enrollees would become automatically eligible to receive Medicaid coverage. However, in 1997, SUDs were formally excluded as qualifying disabilities for SSI, effectively closing the door, for nearly 20 years, on Medicaid eligibility for many individuals with an SUD who were not eligible for Medicaid through other means (Gresenz, Watkins, & Podus, 1998; Swartz, Lurigio, & Goldstein, 2000).

Variation in SUD treatment access is dependent on insurance status—more so than in other sectors of the healthcare industry (Bouchery, Harwood, Dilonardo & Vandivort-Warren, 2012). SUD treatment spending presents a clear picture of this problem, with federal, state, and local government sources, including Medicaid, accounting for 77% of SUD treatment costs before enactment of the ACA. Just 10% of non-public spending came from private insurance, and the rest came from out-of-pocket spending and other private sources (Open Society Foundations, 2010). In comparison, private insurance covers almost four times the proportion of spending on other medical care (Open Society Foundations, 2010). One of the major reasons for higher amounts of public spending are the frequent restrictions placed on SUD treatment coverage by private insurers. Several studies have suggested that Medicaid beneficiaries have greater access to specialized SUD treatment than those with private or no insurance, as the majority of state plans cover at least some SUD treatment services. In fact, individuals with public insurance such as Medicaid, Medicare, and CHAMPS/VA have been shown to have up to 90% greater odds of receiving SUD treatment when compared to those with private insurance (Bouchery et al., 2012). However, individuals on publicly funded plans such as these make up only 26% of individuals with SUD treatment disorders (70%) (Ridic, Gleason, & Ridic, 2012).

Moreover, emerging adults in some areas of the country are more likely to face challenges in accessing treatment. Historically, people of all ages living in the South, Southwest, and Great Plains regions of the country have reported lower access to SUD treatment than people living in other regions (McAuliffe, LaBrie, Woodworth, Zhang, & Dunn, 2003). Many of the states with the highest birth rates in the country are located in these regions, a phenomenon which may exacerbate this problem over time. State inequities in access to treatment may occur for numerous reasons. First, states vary in their capacity to contribute general funds to supplement federal and private funding for SUD treatment. Wealthier states and those with higher tax rates typically contribute more state funding for SUD treatment than states with fewer resources (McAuliffe et al., 2003). Some states even have limits on the use of state general funds for SUD treatment services. Second, as described earlier, Medicaid coverage for SUD treatment, while typically more comprehensive than private insurance coverage for SUD treatment, varies significantly from state to state (Grogan et al., unpublished manuscript). Third, prior to the expansion of parity requirements under the ACA, states varied with regard to parity law: Some states have legislation requiring that coverage for SUD treatment be no more restrictive than benefits for other medical and surgical services, while others do not (Rowan, McAlpine, & Blewett, 2013). Fourth, states have different sociodemographic profiles. It is well known that gender, race, ethnicity, age, and a host of other factors influence individuals' likelihood of receiving treatment.

Treatment Quality

The SUD treatment field has struggled historically with poor rates of adoption of evidence-based interventions. This is in part due to an elusive and highly debated etiological understanding of addiction, which permitted the prolonged use of treatment strategies that fail to address addiction as a chronic disease overall, and specifically among emerging adults (McLellan, McKay, Forman, Cacciola, & Kemp, 2004; McLellan & Meyers, 2004). More recently, evidence-based interventions for treatment of SUD among emerging adults have surfaced. However, the adoption of these interventions has been slow, and implementation with fidelity has been limited. As a result, the quality of treatment that patients receive varies significantly across SUD treatment programs. While many factors influence these differences in quality, issues related to financial and organizational resources and the professionalization of staff are especially important (McLellan & Meyers, 2004).

The quality of SUD treatment that people receive is in part dependent on how their treatment is financed. In comparing SUD treatment programs financed by public versus private dollars, privately financed programs (e.g., through private insurance) are more likely to offer core medical and treatment services such as assessment, counseling, medication-assisted treatment (MAT), peer support group services, and continuing care. On the other hand, publicly financed providers (e.g., receiving primarily Medicaid, block grants, and state and local funding) are more likely to also offer wraparound and supportive services that address access and retention issues, facilitate care for individuals, and can be administered on site or through referral linkages. Wraparound services include medical, mental health, HIV/AIDS, transportation, employment/education, and transportation services, among others (Ducharme, Mello, Roman, Knudsen, & Johnson, 2007). Financing is an especially significant issue for emerging adults. Many individuals do not have insurance, or they have plans that provide no or minimal coverage for SUD treatment.

The SUD treatment field employs significantly fewer staff with professional training than staff employed in other fields within the healthcare system. Of primary concern is the historical lack of credentialing, training, licensure requirements, and supervision for counselors and other providers of SUD treatment. The absence of a high-quality professional staff is extremely prevalent; among substance use treatment providers who rely on public sources for the majority of funding, fewer than half employ counselors trained at the master's degree level, a third do not have a physician, and three-quarters of program directors hold a bachelor's degree or less (Buck, 2011). Even so, the SUD treatment field has been subject to many of the same requirements as mainstream healthcare financing, despite often lacking the administrative, financial, and infrastructure support required to meet those standards (Buck, 2011). The result is increased barriers to service reimbursement and, in turn, a lack of financial coverage and treatment options for patients, especially emerging adults (Humphreys & McLellan, 2011).

For example, in order for a facility to accept Medicaid as payment for SUD treatment, many states require that a physician be involved in treatment planning and/or that counselors maintain a certain level of education and licensure, along with various other provisions that limit an agency's ability to accept these enrollees (Knudsen, Oser, Abraham, & Roman, 2012). Private insurance providers set similar standards regarding staff and administrative functioning. Thus issues with quality and professionalization of staff make it much more challenging to receive reimbursement from Medicaid and private-insurance providers for service. In addition, a smaller or less qualified staff often indicates fewer treatment options being available to patients. Evidence-based interventions involving MAT, for example, require the involvement of a qualified physician (Knudsen et al., 2012). Finally, the treatment of co-occurring disorders and general medical care has also been linked to more positive outcomes for individuals in SUD treatment, although many facilities lack the organizational capacity to employ the professionals with the training required to provide and bill for such services (Knudsen et al., 2012).

The result has been poor adoption of evidence-based intervention in SUD treatment settings. MATs, such as methadone, buprenorphine, and naltrexone for opioid use disorders, and disulfiram, acamprosate, and naltrexone for alcohol use disorders, offer one such example of an emerging and highly effective evidence-based treatment yet to become widely available to the public. For persons with alcohol use disorders, MATs are associated with fewer inpatient treatment admissions and 30% less healthcare cost than persons not receiving MATs (Baser, Chalk, Rawson, & Gastfriend, 2011). For individuals with opiate use disorders, MATs have proven to be safe, cost-effective, and capable of reducing the risk of fatal overdose by as much as 50% (Volkow, Frieden, Hyde, & Cha, 2014). Additionally, MATs have been associated with higher rates of treatment retention, improvements in social functioning, and decreases in patient criminal activity and the transmission of infectious diseases (Volkow et al., 2014). Despite the promise of these treatments, MATs are extremely underutilized—roughly one-quarter of individuals with dependence problems ever receive medication assistance, and only 8% of facilities offer this service (SAMHSA, 2012a). Emerging adults represent a large proportion of individuals with opioid-related problems and bear much of the brunt of policy coverage failures for MAT.

Finally, despite growing recognition that SUDs are a chronic condition, there is still a tendency to deliver treatment as if it were an acute disorder (McLellan, Lewis, O'Brien, & Kleber, 2000). This approach falls short in taking into consideration the importance of recovery support services, including housing, education, employment services, peer-delivered support services, and cultural and spiritual supports, among others. Moreover, the universal failure to acknowledge substance use as a highly prevalent chronic condition has led to insufficiencies not just within the specialty treatment sector but also among the many other systems in which individuals with SUDs are likely to reside. Problems with substance use are clearly prevalent and present themselves in schools, primary care practices, mental health clinics, and criminal justice settings, yet there is insufficient training, organization, and reimbursement available for screening, assessment, and referral to treatment for persons with SUD (McLellan & Meyers, 2004).

THE ACA'S IMPACT ON SUD TREATMENT FOR EMERGING ADULTS

The Affordable Care Act has dramatically expanded coverage for SUD treatment in the United States. Through the creation of state health insurance exchanges, a major expansion of the Medicaid program, and the provision to allow adult children to retain health insurance coverage through a parent's plan until they reach 26 years of age, the law has increased access to SUD treatment services for as many as 50 million individuals with current SUDs (McLellan & Woodworth, 2014). The ACA has also established a requirement that all enrollees in the newly established state health insurance exchanges and Medicaid expansion plans receive at least some health insurance benefits for treatment of SUD (Buck, 2011; Mechanic, 2012). Finally, the law also requires nearly all large health insurance plans to provide SUD treatment benefits at parity with other medical services. In addition to improving the accessibility and quality of SUD treatment in the United States, these changes have sparked a major transition in SUD treatment away from a specialty treatment system that has historically relied heavily on public grant funds and operated outside of the mainstream of healthcare and toward an insurance-financed system in which SUD treatment is increasingly offered in traditional and integrated medical settings (Andrews, Grogan, Brennan & Pollack, 2015; Humphreys & Frank, 2014; Mechanic, 2012). Arguably, no other sector of the healthcare system will be so profoundly transformed by the ACA.

Health Insurance Expansions under the ACA

As described earlier, few emerging adults with SUDs receive treatment, and inability to pay for treatment has been cited as a major impediment to access. The ACA represents a dramatic step forward in removing financial barriers to SUD treatment access by greatly expanding health insurance coverage. The law achieves this goal through three major provisions: the creation of government-sponsored, privately administered state health insurance exchanges, through which individuals can purchase private health insurance at affordable rates; a major expansion of the Medicaid program; and a provision allowing adult children to retain health insurance coverage through a parent's or custodian's plan until age 26. Since the law was enacted in 2010, the percentage of emerging adults without health insurance has been cut in half—from a historic high point of almost 30% to just 14.8% by the first quarter of 2016. By 2016, the percentage of all adults who lacked insurance decreased by 32%—a massive policy accomplishment by any measure (Gallup, 2011, 2016). Moreover, fewer emerging adults reported that cost was a barrier to receiving SUD. In 2012—2 years after implementation of the dependent coverage provision—44% of emerging adults indicated cost was a major impediment to receiving treatment, down from 54% in 2009 (Gallup, 2011).

MEDICAID EXPANSION

The ACA's expansion of Medicaid represents the largest increase in enrollment in the program's 50-year history. As it was originally enacted in 2010, the law removed categorical restrictions on Medicaid eligibility that had previously limited enrollment to parents, children, elderly persons, and disabled individuals, extending coverage to millions of the uninsured. Under the ACA, all U.S. citizens, including those with SUD, could qualify to receive Medicaid benefits if they the met the income eligibility requirement stipulating an income no greater than 138% of the FPL (Buck, 2011). Policymakers estimated that as many as 15 million uninsured adults could become eligible for Medicaid by 2014 as a result of the ACA (Kenney, Lynch, Haley & Huntress, 2012).

However, this provision was struck a major blow in June 2012 when the United States' Supreme Court deemed it unconstitutional in a case entitled *National Federation of Independent Business v. Sebelius.* The Court stated that the law's ultimatum to states to adopt the Medicaid expansion or lose all federal funding for their state Medicaid programs was unduly coercive (Kaiser Family Foundation, 2012). As a result of the decision, only 24 states and the District of Columbia adopted the Medicaid expansion at the start of implementation in January 2014. Since that time, an additional six states have opted in (Alaska, Indiana, Michigan, Montana, New Hampshire, and Pennsylvania). Nonetheless, 20 states—home to approximately 3.1 million people who meet the new federal eligibility criteria for Medicaid—remain in opposition to the expansion (Garfield, Damico, Cox, Claxton, & Levitt, 2015).

States that have expanded Medicaid are experiencing a significant infusion of new funding for SUD treatment. Estimates suggest 14% of Medicaid expansion enrollees have an SUD—a rate that is roughly 50% higher than that of the general population (Busch, Meara, Huskamp, & Barry, 2013). Because the majority of the costs for SUD treatment for this substantial population were paid for by states prior to Medicaid expansion, states that have expanded Medicaid report that they anticipate a reduction in use of their general funds to pay for SUD treatment. Reductions in costs among these states range from $7 million to as much as $190 million in 2015 alone (SAMHSA, 2014a). The majority of these states have indicated that they intend to reallocate freed-up funds toward SUD outreach and prevention (Andrews et al., 2015). Emerging adults are among the greatest beneficiaries of these changes, as childless adults, and especially young, single men, make up the largest proportion of newly eligible Medicaid enrollees in these states (Pickens, Dunn & Glebe, 2012). Moreover, among emerging adults who were uninsured in 2010, more than half—52%—are members of families with incomes under 133% of poverty and would therefore be eligible for coverage under the Medicaid expansion (Collins & Nicholson, 2010).

Conversely, many low-income emerging adults in states that have not adopted the Medicaid expansion continue to face substantial financial barriers to SUD treatment access. A large number of individuals with SUD will not receive the benefits of Medicaid expansion because of states' decisions to opt out. Of uninsured adults ages 18–64 who met criteria for an SUD in the past year, approximately 34.1% would have qualified for treatment coverage under Medicaid but lived in non-Medicaid expansion states in 2013 (SAMHSA, 2015).

Many of the states that have not adopted the expansion—located primarily in the Southeast and Great Plains regions of the country—have some of the highest proportions of low-income residents. These states would yield some of the greatest benefits by opting in to the expansion. Of special concern is the potential of the uneven expansion of Medicaid to exacerbate disparities in access to SUD treatment in the United States. Given the large number of African American and Native American residents living in states that have opted not to expand Medicaid, these populations have benefited disproportionately less from the expansion than other racial and ethnic groups. In 2012—just before the expansion of Medicaid—approximately 60% of African Americans and 70% of Native Americans lived in non-expansion states (Andrews, Guerrero, Wooten, & Legnick-Hall, 2015).

HEALTH INSURANCE EXCHANGES
In addition to Medicaid expansion, the ACA includes another major option for young adults who lack affordable health insurance coverage: state health insurance exchanges. Through the exchanges, all Americans are provided with the option to purchase comprehensive health insurance at affordable large-group rates. These insurance exchanges can be set up and regulated by state governments, though states may seek support from the federal government, or default completely to federally facilitated marketplaces. In order to broaden risk pools, some states

may enter into partnerships with other states in their region to establish these insurance exchanges. In the case of state-run exchanges, consumers apply for and enroll in coverage using platforms established by the state; in all other instances, consumers use the federal platform—healthcare.gov—to enroll. Insurance exchanges are administered by for- and non-profit private insurers through qualified health plans that meet federally outlined standards of consumer protection, including coverage of "essential health benefits" and limits on cost-sharing. The exchanges provide options for many Americans who could not afford adequate health insurance coverage prior to the ACA—the majority of whom do not have access to employer-sponsored coverage or have coverage they cannot use owing to high cost-sharing requirements. Uninsured individuals who do not enroll in the exchanges or another health insurance plan are subject to a fine equal to 2.5% of their household income or $695, whichever is higher. Currently, nearly 10 million Americans have health insurance through the exchanges.

To assist with the cost of these health insurance plans, the federal government provides subsidies, either through cost-sharing, which lowers deductibles, copayments and out-of-pocket limits, or premium tax credits. Cost-sharing subsidies are available for households with incomes between 100% and 250% of the FPL, and premium tax credits are extended up to 400% of the FPL (Collins, Gunja, Rasmussen, Doty & Beutel, 2015). All assistance is provided at scale, with those who have lower incomes receiving a greater amount of support. In 2015, 84% of Americans participating in a health insurance exchange received federal tax credits and 56% received cost-sharing subsidies to help cover costs (Collins, Gunja, Rasmussen, Doty, & Beutel, 2015).

The exchanges rely on high levels of enrollment to keep costs down. Because young adults make up a major portion of the population of uninsured Americans with few health problems, enrollment of this population is critical for a broad and diverse risk pool within the exchanges. Despite critics who argued these "young invincibles" would not likely opt in, evidence points to affordability, not invincibility, as the reasoning behind this population's lack of coverage (Collins, Rasmussen, Garber, & Doty, 2013). The exchanges offer a fitting response to this need, as 6 in 10 emerging adults now qualify for subsidies, resulting in coverage that costs $100 or less per month. Moreover, a low-income emerging adult who enrolls in the one of the exchange's moderate-cost "silver" plans will receive coverage equivalent to a highest-cost "platinum" level plan, essentially providing the best coverage at the cheapest price for any American (Collins, Gunja, Rasmussen, et al., 2015). It is no wonder, then, that more young adults have signed up for insurance through the exchanges than any other age demographic, accounting for 31% of adult enrollees in 2015 (Collins, Gunja, Doty, & Beutel, 2015). In addition, with more than 80% of the 2013 uninsured emerging adult population meeting eligibility requirements for subsidized marketplace insurance plans or Medicaid, more young adults are expected to gain coverage in the future (Collins et al., 2013). However, awareness is a major barrier to increasing enrollment; only a quarter of emerging adults said they were aware of the marketplaces in 2013, with low-income emerging adults were among the least aware.

EXTENSION OF COVERAGE FOR EMERGING ADULTS

One provision of the ACA that holds great importance for emerging adults is the allowance for children to remain on a parent's or custodian's insurance plan until age 26. All health insurance plans that offer coverage for dependents are subject to the provision. This provision, known as the dependent coverage mandate, applies regardless of many major life changes and circumstances, including living situation, marital or student status, degree of financial independence, or having a dependent of one's own. To encourage uptake of this option, the ACA allows parents to deduct the value of the cost of coverage of the adult child included on the plan from their taxable income while they remain enrolled.

The dependent coverage mandate has already made a significant impact on the uninsured young adult population. Data from the year prior to the ACA indicate that approximately 42% of emerging adults who had dependent coverage in high school lost that coverage upon graduation (Collins &Nicholson, 2010). Of those individuals, 46% remained uninsured for 2 years or longer. Four years later, when many emerging adults are graduating from 4-year colleges, these numbers jump significantly, with as many as 75% of new graduates losing coverage (Collins &Nicholson, 2010). Since the ACA was enacted, these numbers have changed dramatically. In 2013—3 years after implementation of the dependent coverage mandate—an estimated 15 million young adults aged 19–25 were enrolled in their parent's insurance plan. Of that 15 million, approximately 7.8 million would not have been eligible to enroll under their parent's plans before enactment of the ACA (Collins et al., 2013).

Despite this progress, many emerging adults remain uninsured, especially low-income emerging adults, who are at higher risk for substance use. Those individuals with incomes under 133% of FPL are the least likely emerging adults to take advantage of the dependent coverage mandate. Emerging adults are far less likely to have a parent with a health plan they can join, and report less knowledge regarding new opportunities for coverage under the ACA. Still, dependent coverage for low-income adults increased from 17% in 2011 to 26% in 2013 (Collins et al., 2013).

SUD Treatment as an Essential Health Benefit

Not only does the ACA increase the number of people with health insurance, but it also requires that more health insurance plans than ever before include SUD treatment in their scope of benefits. The ACA achieves this goal through the creation of the Essential Health Benefits (EHB), a comprehensive package of health and preventative services that must be offered by non-grandfathered individual and small-group private health insurance plans, qualified health plans (QHPs) participating in the newly established state health insurance exchanges, and the benefits plans serving the Medicaid expansion population. It is estimated that approximately 5.1 million people participating in individual or small-group health insurance plans have gained benefits to cover SUD treatment as a result of the ACA (Beronio, Glied, Po & Skopec, 2013). QHPs participating in a state health insurance exchange cannot put a lifetime limit on coverage for services in any EHB category, including SUD treatment. Undoubtedly, this a major step forward for the SUD treatment field. Not only does the inclusion of SUD treatment in the EHB package insure basic health insurance coverage for treatment of SUD, it also has great symbolic importance: With the ACA, the federal government recognizes SUD not only as a medical condition but one that should be considered a core service provided as part of any healthcare system.

Despite these important steps forward, the EHB provision leaves some important gaps in coverage. For example, the ACA does not provide a clear and consistent definition of what adequate coverage for SUD treatment is. In each state, specific EHB are defined by what is offered in the state's identified "benchmark plan," which states can select from any of the following established health insurance plans: the Federal Employees Health Benefit Plan Coverage (FEHBP Health Insurance Coverage); state Employee Health Benefit Coverage; the health maintenance organization plan that has the largest insured commercial, non-Medicaid enrollment in the state; or another Health and Human Services (HHS) Secretary–approved coverage that provides appropriate coverage (CMS, 2016c). If the state's benchmark plan does not include coverage for SUD treatment, the state must establish a minimum level of coverage. In both cases, what is required is left to the discretion of individual states, both in terms of the selection of the benchmark plan and in the establishment of benefit minimums for EHB services not included in the benchmark plan.

Moreover, there are several large insured populations whose plans are not included in the EHB requirements: traditional, non-expansion Medicaid enrollees, and individuals participating in grandfathered private health insurance plans. To put this in perspective, approximately 25% of covered workers were enrolled in a grandfathered plan in 2015, and approximately 22.7 million adults were enrolled in traditional (i.e., non-expansion programs) Medicaid in 2016 (Kaiser Family Foundation, 2015; CMS, 2016d). These plans are exempt from the requirement to cover SUD treatment, though, fortunately, the majority do provide at least some basic benefit despite the lack of a federal mandate to do so.

Extension of MHPAEA Parity Requirements

Before the ACA, SUD treatment benefits were often subjected to more stringent utilization review and limitations than other medical services. The ACA responds to this concern by requiring health insurance coverage provided through the state health insurance exchanges, Medicaid managed care, and Medicaid alternative benefit plans to comply with statutory parity requirements enacted as part of the Mental Health Parity and Addiction Equity Act (MHPAEA) (Beronio, Glied, Po, & Skopec, 2013). The MHPAEA requires that employers ensure that their limits on use of behavioral health services—including SUD treatment—are no more restrictive than that of other surgical and medical services offered by the plan

(Frank, Beronio, & Glied, 2014). Through the parity requirements, legislators have sought to eliminate discriminatory practices targeting treatment of behavioral health disorders, including SUD treatment. The requirements mandate parity across a wide range of service utilization management tools and practices, including "copays, coinsurance, and out-of-pocket maximums; limitations on services utilization, such as limits on the number of inpatient days or outpatient visits that are covered; the use of care management tools; coverage for out-of-network providers; and criteria for medical necessity determinations" (CMS, 2016b).

When passed in 2008, the MHPAEA requirements were restricted to health insurance plans for large employers (i.e., organizations that employed greater than 50 employees) that already covered SUD treatment. The ACA extended the MHPAEA statutory parity requirements to the newly established Medicaid alternative benefit plans for the expansion population, as well as QHPs participating in state health insurance exchanges. As a result of these ACA provisions, it is projected that approximately 5 million people with health insurance have gained coverage for behavioral health services as part of their plan through the ACA (Beronio, Glied, & Frank, 2014). A significant proportion of this population is already insured but is covered under health insurance plans that opted not to provide coverage for behavioral health services, including SUD treatment.

The extension of MHPAEA's statutory parity requirements to the health insurance exchanges and major segments of the Medicaid population has great potential to improve the accessibility and quality of SUD treatment in the United States. The provision holds promise to bring service provision and clinical recommendation into better alignment by treating SUD much like any other medical condition. However, it remains to be seen how this will play out in practice. Studies that have evaluated the effects of the MHPAEA on service utilization in large health insurance plans have found only a very modest impact on utilization (Busch et al., 2014). This may also turn out to be the case in state health insurance exchanges and Medicaid. Additionally, there have been a number of concerns raised about the lack of regulation of the implementation of the MHPAEA parity requirements within Medicaid and the qualified health plans (Grogan et al., unpublished manuscript). Little is known at this juncture about how well plans are (or are not) complying with these federal regulations. Moreover, the ACA does not require that Medicaid programs comply with MHPAEA requirements in non–managed care plans offered to enrollees who are not enrolled in an alternative benefit plan.

Implications for Treatment Access

As a result of the ACA, an anticipated 500,000 emerging adults are predicted to get SUD treatment in 2020—a 30% increase in treatment receipt (Ali, Teich, Woodward, & Han, 2016; SAMHSA, 2014a). SUD treatment spending is predicted to grow in tandem, from $24.3 billion in 2009 to $42.1 billion in 2020 (SAMHSA, 2014a). SUD treatment spending from public sources is predicted to increase to 71% by 2020, a rate that outpaces the spending increase projected for general healthcare spending (53%). This growth is largely attributable to expanded Medicaid eligibility and federal subsidies for enrollees in state health insurance exchanges (SAMHSA, 2014a).

However, it remains unclear whether simply extending health insurance coverage for SUD treatment will necessarily result in expanded access to treatment. As implementation of the ACA continues to unfold, there is growing concern that the nation's current SUD system lacks the capacity to respond to increasing demand for its services generated by the ACA. At present, just under half of SUD treatment providers accept Medicaid, and an even smaller percentage of programs accept private insurance (Terry-McElrath et al., 2011). While relatively little is known about the reasons for some SUD treatment programs not accepting insurance, a growing number of stakeholders have raised concerns that some— especially the many private, nonprofit SUD treatment programs that make up the "safety net" treatment system for low-income individuals—may lack the administrative and staffing capacity required to become insurance-certified providers in their states (Andrews, 2014; Andrews et al., 2015; Buck, 2011).

Indeed, some SUD treatment programs lack the capacity to participate in any insurance because they cannot meet basic insurance provider certification requirements. Such barriers to entry into the publicly funded insurance market are rare in general healthcare settings. For example, Medicaid program requirements related to medical billing and reporting require major investment in information technology among SUD treatment programs that do not already have such capabilities. In a nationally representative study of 175 SUD treatment programs, investigators found that 20% had no information technology services (including voice mail), and 50% had information technology services available only for administrative staff (McLellan & Meyers, 2004). Yet, a recent study found few states reporting that they are providing any support to SUD treatment programs to enhance information technology to meet insurance provider requirements (Andrews et al., 2015).

Additionally, SUD treatment programs that rely primarily on paraprofessionals and people in recovery may face challenges in meeting health insurance requirements stipulating involvement of medical and other certified healthcare professionals in the provision of SUD treatment. Prior research suggests that employment of such professionals is severely limited when compared with other areas of healthcare. In the study conducted by McLellan, Carise, and Kleber (2003), less than 50% of SUD treatment programs had either a physician or a nurse on staff. In a study of 3,267 facility directors, clinical directors, and program counselors working state-licensed substance abuse treatment programs, Mulvey, Hubbard, and Hayashi (2003) found that less than 50% of SUD treatment staff had a professional or other master's degree. These estimates suggest that many SUD treatment programs will need to recruit and retain professional staff who typically require higher levels of pay than paraprofessionals in order to obtain—or maintain—Medicaid certification. Yet, access to capital to make such staffing upgrades may be limited in the SUD treatment system, especially among providers reliant on public grants. Moreover, workforce shortages, recruitment, and retention of staff have been long-standing workforce challenges in the SUD treatment system (SAMHSA, 2013b).

ACA Provisions to Promote Service Integration

Historically, SUD treatment has been provided in specialized settings separate from other general and mental health services. While distinctions between the two arenas of physical and behavioral health have allowed SUD treatment facilities to maintain focus on the specialized needs of individuals with SUD, the current system has faced major challenges in addressing the needs of people with co-occurring and other chronic health conditions. Often these facilities attempt managing one primary condition (i.e., substance use) while the symptoms of other conditions (e.g., depression, anxiety, PTSD) go unaddressed. As a result, co-occurring conditions go untreated, or patients are forced to seek care from multiple physicians and/or facilities. This can lead to poor care coordination, conflicting and poorly managed treatment plans, increasingly negative treatment outcomes, and higher costs. In response to these concerns, several provisions of the ACA were designed to encourage the integration of behavioral and physical healthcare.

According to SAMHSA, integrated care is the most effective approach to providing the best outcomes for patients with multiple healthcare needs. The Agency for Healthcare Research and Quality (2013) defines behavioral health integration as

> care resulting from a practice team of primary care and behavioral health clinicians, working together with patients and families, using a systematic and cost-effective approach to provide patient-centered care for a defined population. This care may address mental health and substance abuse conditions, health behaviors (including their contribution to chronic medical illnesses), life stressors and crises, stress-related physical symptoms, and ineffective patterns of health care utilization. (p. 15)

The ACA attempts to encourage improved service integration by expanding coverage provisions for SUD screening, treatment, and prevention in general medical care settings, as well as by providing financial incentives to promote care coordination and integration within Medicaid.

The push for integrated care models under the ACA is especially relevant considering approximately two-thirds of individuals entering SUD treatment had a co-occurring mental health problem in the past year, with emerging adults at the greatest level of risk (Chan, Dennis, & Funk, 2008). In addition, it has been well established that physical and behavioral health conditions have high rates of co-occurrence (ABHW, 2015). In fact, unmet behavioral health needs are often cited as a major driver of complicating medical treatments for practitioners and have been associated with less desirable patient outcomes due to low treatment adherence and unaddressed behavioral health needs (Burnam & Watkins, 2006). For example, persons diagnosed with SUD are roughly twice as likely to suffer from mood and anxiety disorders (National Institute on Drug Abuse [NIDA], 2008). In addition, circumstances of substance use and related high-risk behaviors may put individuals at increased risk for trauma and other adverse health conditions. One study found rates of co-occurring PTSD and SUD as high as 43% among individuals in inpatient drug treatment, with higher incidences of sexual abuse, physical abuse, and rape (Meisler, 1996). Individuals are also at increased risk for a large range of physical health issues related to substance use, such as cardiomyopathy, gastritis, liver disease, and pneumonia (ABHW, 2015). Thus, providing integrated care is a key step in meeting the complex behavioral, mental, and primary healthcare needs of individuals with SUD.

In addition to improving care coordination for individuals with co-occurring conditions, health service integration has the potential to reduce several barriers to SUD treatment. First, increased integration has the potential to increase prevention, screening, assessment, and referral practices in general healthcare settings such as the emergency department and primary care, as well as within the community, through schools and other related programs with the potential to reach emerging adults. This may be especially important among emerging adults, who are less likely to have a regular source of care than persons from other age groups (McLellan & Meyers, 2004). Second, integration may help reduce the stigma associated with SUD. As it commonly occurs now, SUD treatment provided in specialty settings is cut off from general healthcare, suggesting it is somehow different than other health issues. Emerging adults may be particularly sensitive to the stigma associated with substance use treatment because of the normalization of substance use in social settings. One study, for example, found college students have some of the highest prevalence rates for SUD and also the lowest treatment rates (Blanco et al., 2008). Thus, the integration of SUD screening and treatment services within settings more commonly frequented by emerging adults could prove instrumental to increasing SUD treatment access and retention.

Care Coordination and Value-Based Purchasing Models

The ACA includes two major provisions designed to enhance care coordination and improve integration of primary care and behavioral health services. First, it establishes a new Medicaid option to establish health homes for enrollees with complex healthcare needs. Established under Section 2703 of the Affordable Care Act of 2010, the Medicaid Health Home (HH) program enables states to contract with designated healthcare providers or teams of providers to provide comprehensive, coordinated healthcare to select enrollees with chronic conditions (CMS, 2016e). The aim of health homes is to improve healthcare quality, clinical outcomes, and patient care experience, while also reducing per capita costs through cost-effective services. Health homes are required to offer a range of services, including comprehensive care management; care coordination and health promotion; transition care from inpatient to other care settings; individual and family support; referral to community and social support services; and use of health information technology to link services. To encourage take-up of the option, the ACA authorizes a 90% enhanced federal medical assistance percentage rate for the first 2 years that a state's Medicaid health home state plan amendment is in effect. At present, 19 states and the District of Columbia have implemented health homes within their Medicaid programs, for a total of 28 approved Medicaid health home models (CMS, 2016a).

Second, through the ACA-established CMS Innovation Center, two demonstration projects are testing the effectiveness of primary care medical home (PCMH) models. The Federally Qualified Health Center (FHQC) Advanced Primary Care Demonstration Project enables interdisciplinary teams working within FHQCs to provide coordinated health services to patients in their care. The Multi-Payer Advanced Primary Care Practice Demonstration is funding eight state-led initiatives that include Medicaid, as well as substantial participation by Medicare and private health insurers. The demonstration program will pay a monthly care management fee for beneficiaries receiving primary care from advanced primary care (APC) practices. The care management fee is intended to cover care coordination, improved access, patient education, and other services to support chronically ill patients. These models may hold special promise for the treatment of emerging adults, who have high rates of co-occurring mental health and substance use disorders and have less experience navigating the healthcare system than other adults.

Promoting SUD Services in Non-Specialty Healthcare Settings

In addition to the many improvements in specialized SUD treatment, the ACA improves coverage for SUD treatment services that can be provided in non-specialty medical care settings, thus providing new incentives for programs that offer SUD screening, treatment, and prevention. As of January 1, 2013, per Section 4106 of the ACA, states can receive a one percentage point increase in their federal Medicaid match rate for preventive services if they cover, without cost-sharing, all the adult preventive services recommended by the federally convened U.S. Preventive Services Task Force and Centers for Disease Control, and Prevention's Advisory Committee on Immunization Practices (Kaiser Family Foundation, 2014). These preventative services include counseling for nicotine and alcohol use, which may be of particular importance among emerging adults, especially those in college (Monaghan, 2014). In addition, the ACA requires mandatory coverage by Medicaid for tobacco cessation treatment, including both counseling and medication, for pregnant women. Finally, the ACA disallows private insurance plans that cover SUD-related preventative services to require patient cost-sharing. Taken together, these changes help to increase emerging adults' access to SUD treatment and other related services by addressing some of the barriers related to access, availability, and convenience of services.

As a consequence of these changes, SUD treatment provided outside of specialty settings is expected to increase its share of all SUD treatment from 15% to 19% from 2009 to 2020. These changes are likely to be driven by the expansion of private insurance and Medicaid coverage, the main payers for office-based treatment (SAMHSA, 2014a). Specialty SUD treatment centers are expected to reduce their market share from 42% to 37% from 2009 to 2020, given that many of these specialty providers do not currently have the capacity to accept Medicaid and insurance payment and have had a legacy of treating those without insurance through other funding sources such as block grants and state and local funding (SAMHSA, 2014a). Hospital-based SUD treatment accounted for approximately 31% of spending and is expected to remain at similar levels in 2020 (SAMHSA, 2014a).

CONCLUSION

Emerging adults are at the greatest risk of developing SUD but are least likely to receive SUD treatment. High rates of uninsurance among this population contribute to this problem; inability to pay is the most cited reason for failure to receive treatment. The ACA has paved the way toward real solutions to these problems as more emerging adults become eligible for healthcare coverage, and more insurers are required to cover SUD treatment at parity with other health services. Some major accomplishments are already evident, as uninsurance among emerging adults has fallen 14% just 1 year after implementations of the dependent coverage provision. Moreover, the expansion of Medicaid eligibility and creation of insurance marketplace exchanges have the potential to extend insurance to over 80% of emerging adults. These coverage expansions have proven instrumental in addressing SUD treatment need among emerging adults, as fewer are citing cost as a major barrier to receiving SUD treatment. However, ensuring treatment access will require an increase in treatment providers who accept public and private insurance, and better coordination and integration of health and behavioral services. The ACA holds the potential to improve integration of SUD treatment with mainstream medical care, but whether the promise of reform becomes reality remains to be seen.

The ACA has already improved the accessibility and quality of SUD treatment for emerging adults in the United States and, barring any major changes, is expected to continue to do so in the years ahead. However, many emerging adults lack awareness of their options for insurance coverage, indicating that outreach and education will also be key to continued progress. Even more critical, however, is the refusal by some state governments to expand Medicaid. With almost 30% of emerging adults living in poverty, those who live in non-expansion states will remain ineligible for Medicaid and subsidized private plans through insurance exchanges (Collins et al., 2013). Thus, improving treatment access brings continuing challenges for implementation of the ACA, including variations in SUD treatment supply, access, and quality, and the persistent sociodemographic barriers and disparities.

REFERENCES

Abraham, A. J., Knudsen, H. K., Rieckmann, T., & Roman, P. M. (2013). Disparities in access to physicians and medications for the treatment of substance use disorders between publicly and privately funded treatment programs in the United States. *Journal of Studies on Alcohol and Drugs, 74,* 258–265.

Agency for Healthcare Research and Quality. (2013). *Lexicon for Behavioral Health and Primary Care Integration* (AHRQ Publication No. AHRQ 13-IP001-EF). Rockville, MD.

Ali, M., Teich, J., Woodward, A., & Han, B. (2016). The implications of the Affordable Care Act for behavioral health services utilization. *Administration & Policy in Mental Health & Mental Health Services Research, 43*(1), 11–22.

Andrews, C. M. (2014). The relationship of state Medicaid coverage to Medicaid acceptance among substance abuse treatment providers in the United States. *Journal of Behavioral Health Services and Research, 41*(4), 460–472.

Andrews, C., Abraham, A., Grogan, C. M., Pollack, H. A., Bersamira, C., Humphreys, K., & Friedmann, P. (2015). Despite resources from the ACA, most states do little to help addiction treatment programs implement health care reform. *Health Affairs, 34*(5), 828–835.

Andrews, C., Grogan, C. M., Brennan, M., & Pollack, H. A. (2015). Lessons from Medicaid's divergent paths on mental health and addiction services. *Health Affairs, 34*(7), 1131–1138.

Andrews, C. M., Guerrero, E. G., Wooten, N. R., & Legnick-Hall, R. (2015). The Medicaid expansion gap and racial and ethnic minorities with substance use disorders. *American Journal of Public Health, 105*(S3), S452–S454.

Association for Behavioral Health and Wellness. (2015). *Healthcare integration in the era of the Affordable Care Act.* Retrieved from http://www.integration.samhsa.gov/integrated-caremodels/Healthcare_Integration_In _the_Era_of_ACA.pdf

Baser, O., Chalk, M., Rawson, R., & Gastfriend, D. R. (2011). Alcohol dependence treatments: Comprehensive healthcare costs, utilization outcomes, and pharmacotherapy persistence. *American Journal of Managed Care, 17*(8), 222–234.

Beronio, K., Glied, S., Po, R., & Skopec, L. (2013). *Affordable Care Act will expand mental health and substance use disorder benefits and parity protections for 62 million Americans.* Retrieved from http://www.integralcare.org/sites/default/files/files/Mental_health_parity_final_19Feb20151%20v5.pdf

Beronio, K., Glied, S., & Frank, R. (2014). How the Affordable Care Act and Mental Health Parity and Addiction Equity Act greatly expand coverage of behavioral health care. *Journal of Behavioral Health Services & Research, 41*(4), 410–428.

Blanco, C., Okuda, M., Wright, C., Hasin, D. S., Grant, B. F., Liu, S., & Olfson, M. (2008). Mental health of college students and their non-college-attending peers. *Archives of General Psychiatry, 65*(12), 1429–1437.

Bouchery, E. E., Harwood, H. J., Dilonardo, J., & Vandivort-Warren, R. (2012). Type of health insurance and the substance abuse treatment gap. *Journal of Substance Abuse Treatment, 42*(3), 289–300.

Buck, J. A. (2011). The looming expansion and transformation of public substance abuse treatment under the Affordable Care Act. *Health Affairs, 30*(8), 1402–1410.

Burnam, M. A., & Watkins, K. E. (2006). Substance abuse with mental health disorders: Specialized public systems and integrated care. *Health Affairs, 25*(3), 648–658.

Busch, S. H., Epstein, A. J., Harhay, M. O., Fiellin, D. A., Un, H., Leader Jr., D., & Barry, C. L. (2014). The effects of federal parity on substance use disorder treatment. *American Journal of Managed Care, 20*(1), 76–82.

Busch, S. H., Meara, E., Huskamp, H. A., & Barry, C. L. (2013). Characteristics of adults with substance use disorders expected to be eligible for Medicaid under the ACA. *Psychiatric Services, 64*(6), 520–526.

Callahan, J. J., Shepard, D. S., Beinecke, R. H., Larson, M. J., & Cavanaugh, D. (1995). Mental health/substance abuse treatment in managed care: The Massachusetts Medicaid experience. *Health Affairs, 14*(3), 173–184.

Centers for Medicare & Medicaid Services. (2005). *Medicaid at-a-glance, 2005.* Retrieved from https://www.cms.gov/Research-Statistics-Data-and-Systems/Computer-Data-and-Systems/MedicaidDataSourcesGenInfo/Downloads/maag2005.pdf

Centers for Medicare & Medicaid Services. (2016a). *Approved Medicaid health home state plan amendments.* Retrieved from https://www.medicaid.gov/state-resource-center/medicaid-state-technical-assistance/health-homes-technical-assistance/downloads/hh-map_v55.pdf

Centers for Medicare & Medicaid Services. (2016b). *Behavioral health services.* Retrieved from https://www.medicaid. gov/medicaid-chip-program-information/by-topics/benefits/mental-health-services.html

Centers for Medicare & Medicaid Services. (2016c). *Benchmark services.* Retrieved from https://www.medicaid.gov /Medicaid-CHIP-Program-Information/By-Topics/Benefits/Benchmark-Benefits.html

Centers· for Medicare & Medicaid Services. (2016d). *Medicaid & CHIP: March 2016 monthly applications, eligibility determinations and enrollment report, May 25, 2016.* Retrieved from https://www.medicaid.gov/medicaid-chip-program-information/program-information/downloads/march-2016-enrollment-report.pdf

Centers for Medicare & Medicaid Services. (2016e). *Medicaid health homes: An overview.* Retrieved from https://www.medicaid.gov/state-resource-center/medicaid-state-technical-assistance/health-homes-technical-assistance/downloads/hh-overview-fact-sheet-sep-2016.pdf

Centers for Medicare & Medicaid Services. (2016f). *Young adults and the Affordable Care Act: Protecting young adults and eliminating burdens on families and businesses.* Retrieved from https://www.cms.gov/CCIIO/Resources/Files/adult_child_fact_sheet.html

Chan, Y. F., Dennis, M. L., & Funk, R. R. (2008). Prevalence and comorbidity of major internalizing and externalizing problems among adolescents and adults presenting to substance abuse treatment. *Journal of substance abuse treatment, 34*(1), 14–24.

Chuang, E., Wells, R., & Alexander, J. A. (2011). Public managed care and services access in outpatient substance abuse treatment units. *Journal of Behavioral Health Services and Research, 38*(4), 444–463.

Collins, S. R., Gunja, M., Doty, M. M., & Beutel, S. (2015). *To enroll or not to enroll? Why many American have gained insurance under the Affordable Care Act* (Issue Brief). Retrieved from http://www.commonwealthfund.org/~/media/files/publications / issue-brief/2015/sep/1837_collins_to_enroll_not_enroll_tb.pdf

Collins, S. R., Gunja, M., Rasmussen, P. W., Doty, M. M., & Beutel, S. (2015). *Are marketplace plans affordable? Perspectives from the Commonwealth Fund Affordable Care Act Tracking Survey, March–May 2015* (Issue Brief). Retrieved from http://www.commonwealthfund.org/~/media/files/publications/issue-brief/2015/sep/1838_collins are_marketplace_plans_affordable_tb.pdf

Collins, S. R., & Nicholson, J. L. (2010). *Rite of passage: Young adults and the Affordable Care Act of 2010* (Issue Brief). Retrieved from http://www.commonwealthfund.org/~/media/Files/Publications/Issue%20Brief/2010/May/1404_Collins_rite_of_passage_2010_v3.pdf

Collins, S. R., Rasmussen, P. W., Garber, T., & Doty, M. M. (2013). *Covering young adults under the Affordable Care Act: The importance of outreach and Medicaid expansion* (Issue Brief). Retrieved from http://www.commonwealthfund.org/publications/issue-briefs/2013/aug/covering-young-adults-under-the-affordable-care-act

Coughlin, T. A., & Zuckerman, S. (2002). *States use of Medicaid maximization strategies to tap federal revenues: Program implications and consequences.* Retrieved from http://www.urban.org/research/publication/states-use-medicaid-maximization-strategies-tap-federal-revenues

Cowell, A., McCarty, D., & Woodward, A. (2003). Impact of federal substance abuse block grants on state substance abuse spending: Literature and data review. *Journal of Mental Health Policy and Economics, 6*(4), 173–180.

Deck, D. D., McFarland, B. H., Titus, J. M., Laws, K. E., & Gabriel, R. M. (2000). Access to substance abuse treatment services under the Oregon Health Plan. *Journal of the American Medical Association, 284*(16), 2093–2099.

Ducharme, L. J., Mello, H. L., Roman, P. M., Knudsen, H. K., & Johnson, A. J. (2007). Service delivery in substance abuse treatment: Reexamining "comprehensive" care. *Journal of Behavioral Health Services & Research, 34*(2), 121–136.

Ettner, S. L., Denmead, G., Dilonardo, J., Cao, H., & Belanger, A. J. (2003). The impact of managed care on substance abuse treatment patterns and outcomes of Medicaid beneficiaries: Maryland's health choice program. *Journal of Behavioral Health Services & Research, 31*(1), 41–62.

Frank, R. G., Beronio, K., & Glied, S. A. (2014). Behavioral health parity and the Affordable Care Act. *Journal of Social Work in Disability & Rehabilitation, 13*, 31–43. doi: 10.1080/1536710X.2013.870512

Frank, R. G., McGuire, T. G., Regier, D. A., Manderscheid, R., & Woodward, A. (1994). Paying for mental health and substance abuse care. *Health Affairs, 13*(1), 337–342.

Gabel, J. R., Whitmore, H., Pickreign, J. D., Levit, K. R., Coffey, R. M., & Vandivort-Warren, R. (2007). Substance abuse benefits: Still limited after all these years. *Health Affairs, 26*(4), w474–w482. doi: 10.1377/hlthaff.26.4.w474

Gallup. (2011, September). *In U.S. significantly fewer 18- to 25-year-olds uninsured.* Retrieved from http://www.gallup.com/poll/149558/Significantly-Fewer-Year-Olds-Uninsured.aspx

Gallup. (2016, April). *U.S. uninsured rate at 11.0%, lowest in eight-year trend.* Retrieved from http://www.gallup.com/poll/190484/uninsured-rate-lowest-eight-year-trend.aspx?g_source=CATEGORY_WELLBEING&g_medium=topic&g_campaign=tile

Garfield, R., Damico, G., Cox, C., Claxton, G., & Levitt, L. (October, 2015). *New estimates of eligibility for ACA coverage among the uninsured.* Retrieved from http://mediad.

publicbroadcasting.net/p/   healthnewsfl/files/201510/issue-brief-new-estimates-of-eligibility-for-aca-coverage-among-the-uninsured.pdf

Garfield, R. L., Lave, J. R., & Donohue, J. M. (2010). Health reform and the scope of benefits for mental health and substance use disorders. *Psychiatric Services*, 61(11), 1081–1086.

Gresenz, C. R., Watkins, K., & Podus, D. (1998). Supplemental security income, disability insurance, and substance abusers. *Community Mental Health Journal*, 34(4), 337–350. doi: 10.1023/A:1018779805833

Grogan, C. M., Andrews, C. M., Abraham, A. J., Pollack, H. A., Humphreys, K. N., Smith, B., & Friedmann, P. D. (2017). *State Medicaid coverage and limits for substance use disorder treatment services*. Manuscript in preparation.

Hodgkin, D., Horgan, C. M., Garnick, D. W., & Merrick, E. L. (2009). Benefit limits for behavioral health care in private health plans. *Administration and Policy in Mental Health and Mental Health Services Research*, 36(1), 15–23. doi: 10.1007/s10488-008-0196-5

Hodgkin, D., Shepard, D. S., Anthony, Y. E., & Strickler, G. K. (2004). A publicly managed Medicaid substance abuse carve-out: Effects on spending and utilization. *Administration and Policy in Mental Health and Mental Health Services Research*, 31(3), 197–217.

Humphreys, K., & Frank, R. G. (2014). The Affordable Care Act will revolutionize care for substance use disorders in the United States. *Addiction*, 109(12), 1957–1958. doi: 10.1111/add.12606

Humphreys, K., & McLellan, T. A. (2011). A policy-oriented review of strategies for improving the outcomes of services for substance use disorder patients. *Addiction*, 106(12), 2058–2066.

Institute of Medicine. (1996). Managed care. In *Pathways of addiction: Opportunities in drug abuse research* (pp. 222–249). Washington, DC: National Academies Press.

Kaiser Family Foundation. (July, 2012). *A guide to the Supreme Court's Affordable Care Act decision*. Retrieved from https://kaiserfamilyfoundation.files.wordpress.com / 2013/01/8332.pdf

Kaiser Family Foundation. (November, 2014). *Appendix A: ACA Section 4106 increase in FMAP for coverage of preventive services in Medicaid*. Retrieved from http://kff.org/report-section/coverage-of-preventive-services-for-adults-in-medicaid-appendices/

Kaiser Family Foundation. (2015). *2015 Employer Health Benefits Survey Section Thirteen: Grandfathered health plans*. Retrieved from http://kff.org/report-section/ehbs-2015-section-thirteen-grandfathered-health-plans/

Kenney, G. M., Lynch, V., Haley, J., & Huntress, M. (2012). Variation in Medicaid eligibility and participation among adults: Implications for the Affordable Care Act. *Inquiry*, 49, 231–253.

Knudsen, H. K., Oser, C. B., Abraham, A. J. & Roman, P. M. (2012). Physicians in substance abuse treatment workforce: Understanding their employment within publicly funded treatment organizations. *Journal of Substance Abuse Treatment*, 43(2), 152–160.

Lemak, C. H., & Alexander, J. A. (2001). Managed care and outpatient substance abuse treatment intensity. *Journal of Behavioral Health Services & Research*, 28(1), 12–29. doi: 10.1007/BF02287231

Levit, K. R., Kassed, C. A., Coffey, R. M., Mark, T. L., Stranges, E. M., Buck, J. A., & Vandivort-Warren, R. (2008). Future funding for mental health and substance abuse: Increasing burdens for the public sector. *Health Affairs, 27*(6), w513–w522.

Maglione, M., & Ridgely, M. S. (2006). Is conventional wisdom wrong? Coverage for substance abuse treatment under Medicaid managed care. *Journal of Substance Abuse Treatment, 30*(4), 285–290.

Mark, T. L., & Coffey, R. M. (2004). The decline in receipt of substance abuse treatment by the privately insured, 1992–2001. *Health Affairs, 23*(6), 157–162.

Mark, T. L., Coffey, R. M., King, E., Harwood, H., McKusick, D., Genuardi, J., . . . Buck, J. A. (2000). Spending on mental health and substance abuse treatment, 1987–1997. *Health Affairs, 19*(4), 108–120.

Mark, T. L., Levit, K. R., Vandivort-Warren, R., Coffey, R. M., Buck, J. A., & SAMHSA Spending Estimates Team. (2007). Trends in spending for substance abuse treatment, 1986–2003. *Health Affairs (Project Hope), 26*(4), 1118–1128.

Mark, T. L., Levit, K. R., Vandivort-Warren, R., Buck, J. A., & Coffey, R. M. (2011). Changes in US spending on mental health and substance abuse treatment, 1986–2005, and implications for policy. *Health Affairs, 30*(2), 284–292.

Mark, T. L., & Vandivort-Warren, R. (2012). Spending trends on substance abuse treatment under private employer-sponsored insurance, 2001–2009. *Drug and Alcohol Dependence, 125,* 203–207. doi: 10.1016/j.drugalcdep.2012.02.013

McAuliffe, W. E., LaBrie, R., Woodworth, R., Zhang, C., & Dunn, R. P. (2003). State substance abuse treatment gaps. *American Academy of Addiction Psychiatry, 12*(2), 101–121.

McCarty, D., & Argeriou, M. (2003). The Iowa Managed Substance Abuse Care Plan: Access, utilization, and expenditures for Medicaid recipients. *Journal of Behavioral Health Services & Research, 30*(1), 18–25.

McLellan, A. T., Carise, D., & Kleber, H. D. (2003). Can the national addiction treatment infrastructure support the public's demand for quality care? *Journal of Substance Abuse Treatment, 25*(2), 117–121.

McLellan, A. T., Lewis, D. C., O'Brien, C. P., & Kleber, H. D. (2000). Drug dependence, a chronic mental illness implication for treatment, insurance, and outcomes evaluation. *Journal of the American Medical Association, 284*(13), 1689–1695.

McLellan, A. T., McKay, J. R., Forman, R., Cacciola, J., & Kemp, J. (2004). Reconsidering the evaluation of addiction treatment: From retrospective follow-up to concurrent recovery monitoring. *Addiction, 100,* 447–458.

McLellan, A. T., & Meyers, K. (2004). Contemporary addiction treatment: A review of systems problems for adults and adolescents. *Biological Psychiatry, 56*(10), 764–770.

McLellan, A. T., & Woodworth, A. M. (2014). The Affordable Care Act and treatment for "substance use disorders:" Implication of ending segregated behavioral health care. *Journal of Substance Abuse Treatment, 46*(5), 541–545.

Mechanic, D. (2012). Seizing opportunities under the affordable care act for transforming the mental and behavioral health system. *Health Affairs, 31*(2), 376–382.

Meisler, A. W. (1996). *Trauma, PTSD, and substance abuse.* White River Junction, VT: National Center for PTSD. Retrieved from http://www.ptsd.va.gov/professional/newsletters/research-quarterly/V7N4.pdf

Monaghan, M. (2014). The Affordable Care Act and implications for young adult health. *Translational Behavioral Medicine, 4*(2), 170–174.

Mulvey, K. P., Hubbard, S., & Hayashi, S. W. (2003). A national study of the substance abuse treatment workforce. *Journal of Substance Abuse Treatment, 24*(1), 51–57.

National Association of State Alcohol and Drug Abuse Directors. (2016, February). *NASADAD fact sheet: Substance Abuse Prevention and Treatment (SAPT) block grant.* Retrieved from http://nasadad.org/2015/02/sapt-block-grant-fact-sheet-feb-2016/

National Institute on Drug Abuse. (2008). *Research Report Series: Comorbidity: Addiction and other mental illnesses* (NIH Publication Number: 10-5771). Retrieved from https://www.drugabuse.gov/sites/default/files/rrcomorbidity.pdf

Open Society Foundations. (2010). *Defining the addiction treatment gap.* Retrieved from https://www.opensocietyfoundations.org/sites/default/files/data-summary-20101123.pdf

Pickens, G., Dunn, D., & Glebe, T. (2012). *Medicaid expansion: Profiling the future Medicaid eligible population.* Retrieved from http://truvenhealth.com/portals/0/assets/HP_ 11513_ 0912_MedicaidExpansionEbook_WP_WEB.pdf

Ridic, G., Gleason, S., & Ridic, O. (2012). Comparisons of health care systems in the United States, Germany, and Canada. *Materia Socio-Medica, 24*(2), 112–120.

Rogowski, J. A. (1992). Insurance coverage for drug abuse. *Health Affairs, 11*(3), 137–148.

Rowan, K., McAlpine, D. D., & Blewett, L. A. (2013). Access and cost barriers to mental health care by insurance status, 1999–2010. *Health Affairs, 32*(10), 1723–1730.

Saloner, B., Antwi, Y. A., Maclean, J. C., & Le Cook, B. (2015). Access to health insurance and utilization of public sector substance use treatment: Evidence from the Affordable Care Act dependent coverage provision. Unpublished manuscript, Department of Economics, Temple University, Philadelphia, Pennsylvania.

Scott, J. E., Greenberg, D., & Pizarro, J. (1992). A survey of state insurance mandates covering alcohol and other drug treatment. *Journal of Mental Health Administration, 19*(1), 96–118.

Sosin, M. R. (2002). Negotiating case decisions in substance abuse managed care. *Journal of Health and Social Behavior, 43*(3), 277–295.

Stewart, M. T., & Horgan, C. M. (2011). Health services and financing of treatment. *Alcohol Research and Health, 33*(4), 389.

Substance Abuse and Mental Health Services Administration. (2009). *State inventory of Medicaid MHSUD services 2009.* Rockville, MD: Author. Retrieved from: http://store.samhsa.gov/shin/content/ /NMH05-0202/NMH05-0202.pdf.

Substance Abuse and Mental Health Services Administration. (2012a). *National Survey of Substance Abuse Treatment Services (N-SSATS): 2012.* Retrieved from http://archive.samhsa.gov /data/DASIS/NSSATS2012_Web.pdf

Substance Abuse and Mental Health Services Administration. (2012b). *Results from the 2010 National Survey on Drug Use and Health: Detailed tables.* Retrieved from http://www.samhsa.gov/data/sites/default/files/NSDUHNationalFindingsResults2010-web/2k10ResultsTables/NSDUHTables2010R/HTM/Cover.htm

Substance Abuse and Mental Health Services Administration. (2012c). Results from the 2010 National Survey on Drug Use and Health, Volume 1: Summary of national findings (HHS Publication No. SMA 11-4658). Rockville, MD: Author.

Substance Abuse and Mental Health Services Administration. (2013a). National expenditures for mental health services and substance abuse treatment, 1986–2009 (HHS Publication No. SMA-13-4740). Rockville, MD: Author.

Substance Abuse and Mental Health Services Administration. (2013b). *Report to Congress on the Nation's Substance Abuse and Mental Health Workforce Issues*. Retrieved from: http://store.samhsa.gov/shin/content/PEP13-RTC-BHWORK/PEP13-RTC-BHWORK.pdf

Substance Abuse and Mental Health Services Administration. (2014a). Projections of national expenditures for treatment of mental and substance use disorders, 2010–2020 (HHS Publication No. SMA-14-4883). Rockville, MD: Author.

Substance Abuse and Mental Health Services Administration. (2014b). *The NSDUH Report: Substance use and mental health estimates from the 2013 National Survey on Drug Use and Health: Overview of findings*. Retrieved from https://store.samhsa.gov/shin /content/NSDUH14-0904/NSDUH14-0904.pdf

Substance Abuse and Mental Health Services Administration. (2015). *The CBHSQ Report: State Participation in the Medicaid Expansion Provision of the Affordable Care Act: Implications for uninsured individuals with a behavioral health condition*. Retrieved from https://www.samhsa.gov/data/sites/default/files/report_2073/ShortReport-2073.pdf

Swartz, J. A., Lurigio, A. J., & Goldstein, P. (2000). Severe mental illness and substance use disorders among former Supplemental Security Income beneficiaries for drug addiction and alcoholism. *Archives of General Psychiatry, 57*(7), 701–707.

Terry-McElrath, Y. M., Chriqui, J. F., & McBride, D. C. (2011). Factors related to Medicaid payment acceptance at outpatient substance abuse treatment programs. *Health Services Research, 46*(2), 632–653.

United States Government Publishing Office. (2017). *Subpart L—Substance Abuse Prevention and Treatment block grant* [data file]. Retrieved from http://www.ecfr.gov/cgi-bin/text-idx?SID=924d3cbb25090735c55a29d6bca36e45&mc=true &node=sp45.1.96.l&rgn=div6#se45.1.96_1124

Volkow, N. D., Frieden, T. R., Hyde, P. S., & Cha, S. S. (2014). Medication-assisted therapies—tackling the opioid-overdose epidemic. *New England Journal of Medicine, 370*, 2063–2066.

7

Facilitators, Friends, or the Formerly Afflicted?

Integrating Peers into Emerging Adults' Substance Use Interventions

DOUGLAS C. SMITH, FRANK J. SCHWEBEL, AND MARY E. LARIMER ■

INTRODUCTION

Multiple forces converge around the idea of integrating peers in emerging adult substance use disorder (SUD) treatment and prevention models. Such forces include the desire to deliver services in the most cost-efficient manner possible, the notion that individuals from similar backgrounds may be credible intervention facilitators, the basic science findings that social networks influence emerging adults' substance use, and the political recovery advocacy movement seeking direct involvement of individuals in recovery in the design and delivery of recovery-oriented services. However, because these forces emanate from different perspectives (i.e., service delivery efficiency, social network influence, recovery advocacy) and all use the term *peer*, issues of conceptual clarity arise. This chapter reviews the literature on three different types of peer involvement for emerging adults: peer-delivered services, peer-enhanced services, and peer recovery support services.

Defining Peer Services

As noted, the term *peer* is broadly used in the field, encompassing at least three different meanings. A peer could be another emerging adult who is yet unknown to the emerging adult but tasked with delivering a peer-led intervention (i.e., facilitators). Or, peers could be the friends or drinking buddies of the emerging adult with an SUD who presents for treatment. Finally, a peer could also be an individual who formerly suffered from an SUD and is now tasked with providing paraprofessional treatment services to emerging adults.

All three types of peers could potentially be integrated into SUD prevention or intervention programs for emerging adults. For purposes of clarity, *peer-delivered* interventions are defined here as interventions facilitated by other emerging adults yet unknown to intervention participants. The defining feature of this model is that services are facilitated by other emerging adults, typically under the supervision of professionals or volunteer coordinators. *Peer-enhanced* interventions, by contrast, are professionally delivered and integrate friends who are known to the emerging adults receiving the intervention. Thus, the defining feature of this model is that there is a target client who is assessed as being in need of treatment or prevention, and the intervention includes a current friend from that targeted emerging adults' social network. In peer-enhanced models, friends are typically asked to assist the targeted emerging adults in meeting substance use or harm reduction goals. Finally, *peer recovery support* interventions are those implemented with individuals who were formerly afflicted by substance use disorders. Table 7.1 presents definitions of these three types of peers, examples of studies using such peers, and the assumptions upon which each type of peer model are based.

The remainder of this chapter reviews the rationale and empirical support for each type of peer intervention for emerging adults, concluding each section with a summary of the current state of affairs and future research recommendations. It includes both prevention and intervention studies, with emerging adults seen in a wide range of practice settings along the continuum of clinical severity.

PEERS AS FACILITATORS: PEER-DELIVERED INTERVENTIONS

Rationale

The impetus to involve peers in providing counseling or delivering interventions was likely influenced by financial and temporal limitations in reliance on professionals (Hart, 1998; Mastroleo, Turrisi, Carney, Ray, & Larimer, 2010). Potential relational and credibility advantages of involving individuals close in age and experience to the target population were also considered (Schroeder & Prentice, 1998; Sloane & Zimmer, 1993). One population providing peer counseling has been college students. In comparison to professionally trained individuals, who are in high demand and limited supply, require years of training, and generally require significant financial compensation, college-aged peers can be readily found, trained relatively quickly, and often agree to participate in exchange for course credit or supervised experience. Over the years, peer counselors have been found to be effective in dealing with academic and health problems in a college

Table 7.1. DEFINITIONS OF PEER ROLES IN EMERGING ADULT SUBSTANCE USE DISORDER INTERVENTIONS

	Who Is the Peer?	Examples	Assumptions	Benefits
Peer-delivered	Peer is the intervention *facilitator*. Individuals with shared characteristics with targeted emerging adults facilitate the intervention.	Cimini et al. (2009) compared the efficacy of peer-facilitated motivational interviewing, peer theater, and peer didactic education for students violating campus alcohol policy.	Peers are credible sources of alcohol and drug information.	Low cost
Peer-enhanced	Peer is *friend* integrated into therapist-delivered intervention. Emerging adult who is target of intervention knows the peer.	Smith et al. (2016) asked emerging adults to bring a close friend to treatment sessions and trained the friend to support the target client's substance use goals. Neighbors et al. (2012) asked close friends to participate in a Web-based personalized feedback intervention to reduce 21st birthday drinking.	Receptive to influence of individuals already in social networks. Buddy system for behavior change. Increase social support	Expand intervention effects to friends
Peer recovery support	Peer is *formerly afflicted* individual serving as facilitator or adjunct to primary treatment. Individuals who have recovered from a substance use disorder support the emerging adult.	No current examples specific to emerging adults. See Chapter 9 on recovery colleges.	Individuals with past history can share valuable experience and support.	Low-cost continuing care option

setting (Cuijpers [2002] provides a review of the literature). These findings provided additional motivation to expand peer-delivered interventions on college campuses to other problems, including SUD treatment and prevention.

Potential Mechanisms of Action

According to social learning theory, individuals learn and are influenced through a variety of group processes, including norms for behaviors, modeling of behaviors, and peer support for engagement in behaviors (Bandura, 1977, 1986). This is particularly relevant in the prevention and treatment of hazardous alcohol use, where modeling effects of peers can influence the amount of drinking (Caudill & Marlatt, 1975; Crawford & Novak, 2007; Larimer et al., 2001; Wang, Hipp, Butts, Jose, & Lakon, 2016). Peer influence has been found to be especially significant for males with a history of heavy drinking (Collins, Parks, & Marlatt, 1985; Lied & Marlatt, 1979). Larimer and colleagues (2001) were among the first to systematically investigate the effectiveness of a peer-delivered intervention for reducing hazardous alcohol use. They did this in a setting in which the role of peer influence is believed to be strong: fraternities (Soule, Barnett, & Moorhouse, 2015; Wechsler, Kuh, & Davenport, 2009).

Research on Peer Versus Professional Service Delivery

Larimer et al. (2001) developed an intervention that combined group and individual, brief motivational enhancement sessions based on the Brief Alcohol Screening and Intervention for College Students (BASICS; Dimeff, 1999; Marlatt et al., 1998), which was designed to reduce drinking and drinking-related consequences among first-year fraternity students. Fraternities were randomly assigned to receive either a motivational-enhancement intervention with feedback both about their individual alcohol use (individual component) and about the norms of the use of all members of their fraternity house (housewide component) ($n = 6$ fraternity houses) or a treatment-as-usual control condition (a 1-hour housewide didactic alcohol information presentation; $n = 6$ houses). Individual sessions included an interview about participants' drinking use, patterns, and normative perceptions; and feedback that reviewed their alcohol-related expectancies, drinking-related consequences (if any), and strategies to encourage moderation of their drinking (if they were drinking at a problematic level). Individual sessions were delivered either by five undergraduate peer interviewers (peer-delivered BASICS) or by two advanced clinical psychology graduate students, one master's level clinician, and one licensed psychologist (professional BASICS). Both groups received 8 to 12 hours of didactic training and one or two supervised interviews prior to the beginning of the study. Peers received minimal ongoing supervision commensurate to the supervision received by their professional counterparts. Housewide feedback sessions were similar to individual sessions in their approach and content but were focused on presenting aggregate house-wide drinking data and norms. Both intervention conditions (peer-delivered and professional BASICS) resulted in a decrease in total average alcohol use and a decrease in typical peak blood alcohol content (BAC). At baseline, no significant difference between peer-delivered BASICS and professional BASICS groups were found for any of the seven drinking or alcohol-related consequences measures. Significant group differences were found for typical peak BAC post-treatment, with an effect size of $d = .58$. Fraternity members in the peer-delivered BASICS condition reported significantly greater reductions in typical peak BACs than for individuals in the professional BASICS condition, with no other differences between conditions. Thus the peer-delivered intervention appeared to be at least as effective as the professionally delivered intervention across all outcomes, with some advantage for peer-delivered interventions in reducing peak BACs.

Another study compared the effectiveness of a peer- and professionally delivered multicomponent skills group (Lifestyle Management Class; LMC) designed to decrease heavy alcohol use and behavioral risks associated with drinking for college students compared to an assessment-only (wait-list control) group (Fromme & Corbin, 2004). Each LMC consisted of two manualized, 2-hour group meetings and was led by a male and female provider pair. Peer and professional LMC leaders received at least 16 hours of training. Peers facilitators were undergraduate volunteers compensated with course credit, and professionals facilitators were four doctoral students who had earned master's degrees and 2 years of treatment experience. Study participants included university-mandated ($n = 124$) and voluntary ($n = 452$) participants. Participants and an outside evaluator scored the professionally delivered LMC more positively than the peer-delivered LMC. This contrasts with prior findings (Larimer et al., 2001) that students more positively receive peer-led interventions than interventions led by professionals. The outside evaluator also viewed the professional delivery as being more adherent to the program and higher in quality. Nevertheless, statistical analyses of the data comparing peer- and professionally delivered LMCs suggest that the outcomes were quite comparable and both were superior to the control condition. There was a nonstatistically significant trend toward mandated LMC male participants having greater decreases in heavy drinking than females when receiving peer delivery; however, no statistically significant gender differences for participants were found.

Supervision and Therapist Skills

Although supervision is a tenet of peer-delivered interventions (Larimer et al., 2004), the impact of supervision on adherence, competence, and impact of peer-delivered interventions has only more recently begun to be systematically investigated. Two studies have directly and indirectly investigated the effect of continual supervision and training on peer-delivered interventions. Mastroleo and colleagues (2010) trained two peer counselor groups for 12 hours over the course of 2 days to deliver BASICS to college students. Training included a review of BASICS, the viewing of recordings of sample BASICS and motivational interviewing (MI) sessions, a review of feedback information for BASICS sessions, and a brief overview of MI. Post-training, one peer group was randomly assigned to receive 1-hour of individual and 1 hour of group supervision weekly, and the other group received no supervision. Intervention participants were randomly assigned to BASICS with ongoing peer training, BASICS without ongoing training, or a wait-list control. Both treatment groups were more effective than the control group in reducing total number of drinks per week and heavy drinking behavior, with no significant differences between peer training conditions. When comparing peer effectiveness at using MI skills (i.e., open questions, reflections; Mastroleo, Mallett, Turrisi, & Ray, 2009), the group receiving weekly supervision asked significantly fewer closed-ended questions and trended toward asking more open-ended questions and using more simple reflections. No significant difference was found between groups in use of complex reflections. The peer group that did not receive supervision displayed static or deteriorating MI skills, whereas the peer group receiving supervision showed growth in MI skills over time. This finding suggests that while both groups were more effective than the control in reducing drinking, over time, supervision may help peer counselors maintain and refine skills that help improve the quality of treatment and, ultimately, improve treatment outcomes. However, we would note that, in this study, this was not reflected in alcohol outcomes of participants receiving these interventions. More work could focus on the cost-effectiveness of peer-delivered models under various supervision strategies.

Tollison and colleagues (2008) also investigated the effectiveness of peer-delivered BASICS with an additional focus on how peer facilitators use MI strategies (questions and reflections). Peer facilitators received similar training to that described in the Mastroleo (2010) study and were approved to begin leading sessions once they demonstrated initial proficiency in MI and BASICS content. The primary investigator and clinical psychology doctoral students led weekly group supervision. To assess peer facilitator level of MI adherence and proficiency, BASICS sessions were recorded and scored using Motivational Interviewing Treatment Integrity (MITI) scales (the standardized MI scoring tool used to assess beginner level of MI proficiency; Moyers, Martin, Manuel, Hendrickson, & Miller, 2005). On average, during the clinical trial, peer facilitators were rated as having beginner proficiency on empathy (average peer facilitator score: 5.0, beginner proficiency score: 5.0), percent MI-adherent statements (peer average score: 98.7%, beginner proficiency score: 90%), and percent open questions (peer average score: 49.4%, beginner proficiency score: 50%). Peer facilitators, on average, did not meet the criteria for proficiency on MI spirit (peer average: 4.8, beginner proficiency: 5.0), ratio of reflections to questions (peer average: 0.45, beginner proficiency: 1.0), or percent of complex reflections (peer average: 35.7%, beginner proficiency: 40%). The results of the BASICS intervention indicated that type of question (i.e., open or closed) did not have a statistically significant impact on participant drinking, and a higher number of simple reflections was associated with increased drinking at 3-month follow-up assessment. However, the negative association between simple reflections and increased drinking at 3-month follow-up was mitigated by the increased use of complex reflections (such that peer counselors who used more complex reflections in addition to simple reflections demonstrated better participant outcomes than counselors relying more exclusively on simple reflections). These results suggest that continued training and supervision is important to help peer facilitators remain effective by developing their complex reflection skills.

Efficacy of Peer-Delivered Interventions

Another focus of study has been on the overall efficacy of peer-delivered BASICS for reduction of college student hazardous drinking compared to other interventions or no treatment. One study compared peer-delivered BASICS to a parent handbook intervention alone, to a parent handbook intervention combined with peer-delivered BASICS (referred to as combined treatment), and to an assessment-only control group (Turrisi et al., 2009). Incoming college freshman were recruited to participate in the study, and participants were randomly assigned to one of four conditions: (1) peer-delivered BASICS, (2) parent intervention, (3) combined treatment, or (4) control. The BASICS intervention consisted of the same components described in Larimer and colleagues' (2001) study. The parent intervention consisted of mailing a handbook to parents with information about college student drinking, methods for communicating with teens, tips for discussing with teens how to resist peer pressure, and information regarding the negative effects of alcohol on the teen body. Parents were asked to complete a questionnaire and send back the handbook with notes to ensure they reviewed the material. The combined condition included all components of the BASICS and parent intervention. Peers (18 undergraduate and 3 entry-level graduate students) were trained and instructed to introduce themselves as peers and to use inclusive language such as "we" and "us" when discussing decisions regarding alcohol use. Peers were allowed to facilitate BASICS once they demonstrated the ability to attain initial competency in MI (Miller & Rollnick, 1991; Moyers et al., 2005) and BASICS. Facilitators participated in weekly group and individual supervision led by the investigators. The combined treatment produced the best results, with significant reductions in consumption of alcohol (peak BAC, Cohen's $d = .26$) and in high-risk drinking (drinks per weekend, $d = .20$; drinks per week, $d = .16$) and fewer alcohol-related consequences ($d = .20$) at 10-month follow-up compared to the control group. The peer-delivered BASICS condition alone was associated with a reduction in weekend drinking in comparison to the parent handbook intervention alone ($d = .16$) and control ($d = .18$). Peer-delivered BASICS was also associated with a reduction of peak BAC in comparison to the control ($d = .16$), further supporting the efficacy of peer-delivered interventions. Notably, the parent handbook alone did not significantly differ from the control condition on drinking or drinking consequences.

Donohue, Allen, Maurer, Ozols, and DeStefano (2004) compared the effectiveness of a peer-delivered cognitive-behavioral skills intervention against a computerized "Alcohol 101" course designed to decrease alcohol use for college students. The skills intervention involved consideration of possible personal negative consequences from drinking and modeling how to refuse a drink. Alcohol 101 allows students to virtually experience positive and negative outcomes from drinking and receive estimated information regarding their current "BAC" at a virtual bar. Peer facilitators (12 undergraduate volunteers) were trained in the skills intervention, familiarized with the Alcohol 101 course, and received supervision (the frequency of which and type, individual or group, are not reported). Participants were randomly assigned, and both treatment groups reported reductions in number of drinks per drinking occasion ($p < .05$). Alcohol 101 participants responded more favorably to the intervention than did skills intervention participants. However, high-risk students in the peer-delivered skills intervention reduced their number of drinks and number of drinking days per month significantly more than Alcohol 101 participants. Of note, no control group was used in this study.

Cimini and colleagues (2009) compared the effectiveness of three peer-delivered brief alcohol interventions for college students (small-group MI, motivationally enhanced peer theater, and an interactive alcohol education program). The MI group focused on motivating participants to reduce alcohol consumption through evaluation of alcohol use, discussion of negative alcohol-related consequences, and reflection of values. Also, psychoeducation about alcohol use, its consequences, and college norms on alcohol use were provided in the peer-delivered MI group. Peer theater was an interactive show, delivered by student actors, playing out scenarios depicting attitudes and behaviors about alcohol use. The alcohol education program was primarily psychoeducational about the effects of alcohol, drink size, BAC, and tolerance. Also, peer facilitators guided discussions about the campus culture regarding drinking and the use of protective behavioral strategies to reduce risk when drinking. All peer facilitators for the study were initially trained in all intervention conditions before being assigned to one of them. They all received 1 hour of weekly group supervision, and MI facilitators received an extra hour of weekly individual supervision. Study participants were mandated to participate due to university alcohol policy violations. Results indicated no statistically significant pre-post effects or treatment effects. A secondary analysis found that changes in perceived norms and use of protective behavioral strategies were correlated with changes in alcohol use and alcohol-related problems regardless of condition ($p < .01$). On average, facilitators for the MI and peer theater conditions received MITI (Moyers et al., 2005) scores that were higher in global empathy and MI spirit (MI: 4.48, 4.09; theater: 4.25, 4.12) than for interactive education sessions (3.69, 3.46). However, the group differences were not statistically significant, and all MITI scores were below beginner levels of adherence (empathy and MI spirit: 5.0; Moyers et al., 2005), a limitation of this study. The researchers reported that, in exit interviews, facilitators reported not feeling comfortable in their role until after six to eight sessions, which suggests that further training and supervision might have been helpful.

Sorsdahl and colleagues (2015) compared the effectiveness of peer-delivered MI, MI plus Problem Solving Therapy (MIPST), and a psychoeducational control group for individuals admitted to an emergency department in South Africa. The MI group received a 20-minute-long brief intervention developed by the World Health Organization. The MIPST group received a five-session intervention adapted from a previous intervention tested among South Africans with psychological distress in disadvantaged communities. Sessions were approximately 1 week apart and lasted 45 to 60 minutes. During sessions, counselors and participants identified and explored problems happening in the participant's life, and the counselor taught a problem-solving therapy (PST) approach to address the problems. Participants were assigned homework to complete between sessions. The control group received a brochure providing information about the effects of substance use but no counseling. The five peer facilitators had bachelor's level education or equivalent experience and originated from the communities where the interventions occurred. Peer facilitators received an initial 18 hours of training and proficiency testing in MI from an MI-certified trainer. Over the course of the intervention, facilitators received 3 half-day MI booster sessions to ensure that skills were being applied appropriately. Peer facilitators also completed 12 hours of PST training and proficiency testing. Additionally, peer facilitators received biweekly supervision and debriefing sessions. Study participants ($N = 531$) were screened in the emergency department and invited to participate in the study if they met moderate to high-risk substance use criteria. The average age of participants was 28 years old. Results were measured using the Alcohol, Smoking and Substance Involvement Screening Test (ASSIST). All three conditions led to decreased ASSIST scores from baseline to 3-month follow-up. ASSIST scores were significantly lower in the MIPST group than in the MI and control groups ($p < .05$). No significant differences were found between the MI and control groups.

Knowns and Unknowns

Past research has suggested the use of peers as possibly being effective in delivering substance use interventions (Bandura, 1977, 1986; Caudill & Marlatt, 1975; Collins et al., 1985; Cuijpers, 2002). Larimer et al. (2001) demonstrated that peer delivery could be an innovative, efficacious, and potentially cost-effective method of delivering an intervention to reduce risky alcohol use. Furthermore, the results indicated that peers were at least as effective as professionals at intervention delivery. A subsequent analysis for a conference presentation replicated and extended the initial Larimer et al. (2001) study with 3 years of sorority data and an additional year of fraternity data (O'Leary et al., 2002). The results indicated statistically significant main effects for males and for the overall peer-delivered intervention, replicating what was found in the initial study. However, there were no main effects of intervention for females, raising the possibility that the efficacy of peer-delivered interventions may be moderated by gender.

Fromme and Corbin (2004) and Turrisi and colleagues (2009) provided additional support for the efficacy of using peer-delivered interventions to decrease hazardous alcohol use among college students. Turrisi and colleagues' results indicated that a parent intervention in tandem with a peer-delivered intervention might be particularly efficacious in reducing harmful drinking. Fromme and Corbin's results included a nonsignificant trend toward recipient-gender moderating the effectiveness of treatment. Further investigation into gender of intervention recipient as a moderator of treatment efficacy is merited.

All the peer-delivered interventions reviewed included a supervision component (individual, group, or both). While supervision is a standard part of peer-delivered intervention protocols, its effects were not directly studied until 2010, by Mastroleo et al. The investigators did not find a difference in outcome effectiveness between groups receiving or not receiving supervision. However, a statistically significant difference was found in the quality of MI skill as rated by MITI scoring; on average, the unsupervised peers demonstrated static or deteriorating MI skills whereas the supervised peers' MI skills improved. Tollison and colleagues (2008) found that better peer therapist MI skills were related to better drinking outcomes for participants, supporting the importance of supervision as a means to maintain and improve peer therapists' skills. Fromme and Corbin's (2004) results indicated that professionals are generally perceived as being more adherent to intervention material and higher in perceived intervention quality. This may be attributed to the limited training and supervision typically received by peers. Furthermore, professionals will often have much more practice with the skills and materials than the peers. A majority of the trainings were approximately 2 days or 12 hours long. MI literature has shown that 2-day training is generally insufficient for training a professional to be MI adherent, and this seems unlikely to be sufficient training for inexperienced young adults delivering interventions (Mastroleo et al., 2010; Miller & Mount, 2001). Based on study results it is clear that continued supervision is an important component of peer-delivered interventions and one that can help maintain and even improve peers' skills. More research on training of peers for intervention delivery is merited.

Further research has indicated that peer-delivered interventions can be effective in decreasing drinks per drinking occasion and that other innovative methods of delivering peer-directed interventions (e.g., peer theater) can be effective in decreasing rates of alcohol use and negative outcomes due to drinking (Cimini et al., 2009; Donohue et al., 2004; Sorsdahl et al., 2015). In sum, these findings suggest that peer-delivered interventions have a promising future in helping with the application of universal or targeted brief interventions for adolescents and young adults in a variety of domains and particularly regarding substance use. While some perceived disadvantages of peer delivery have been noted (e.g., peers are less knowledgeable or less skilled) and supervision is advisable for increased effectiveness, results indicate that an inexpensive treatment delivery method, namely peers, can be as or more effective than one using professionals.

PEERS AS FRIENDS: PEER-ENHANCED INTERVENTIONS

Rationale

As defined earlier, peer-enhanced interventions are professionally or electronically delivered interventions that include an emerging adult targeted by the SUD intervention, as well as one or more friends of that individual who are asked to attend sessions. Unlike peer facilitators in peer-delivered models, peer-enhanced interventions involve the current friends of the target client, who are asked to support this targeted emerging adult's efforts to change.

Numerous study findings support the rationale for including an individual's friends in their SUD treatment episodes. First, there appear to be numerous friends to draw upon from emerging adults' social networks, as individuals with alcohol use disorders report having approximately five friends in their current social networks, more than most other types of network members (Mowbray, Quinn, & Crawford, 2014). Because of the influence of these peers on emerging adults' drinking (Lau-Barraco, Braitman, Leonard, & Padilla, 2012), drinking reduction strategies on high-risk drinking days (Lewis et al., 2015), and readiness to change (Goodman, Peterson-Badali, & Henderson, 2011), researchers frequently propose that peer-enhanced interventions may be impactful. Third, changes in social support are associated with changes in substance use over time. For example, emerging adults in AA benefit from eliminating pro-drinking social network members, but AA attendance did not increase pro-abstinence network members (Hoeppner, Hoeppner, & Kelly, 2014). Thus, one possibility is that instead of relying on forming new pro-abstinence bonds in mutual aid societies, we could focus on alternative strategies to foster pro-abstinence behaviors among emerging adults' existing peers. Fourth, studies also show that the friends of emerging adults with heavy substance use are emotionally close, have regular contact (Lau-Barraco & Linden, 2014), and report being amenable to supporting their substance use treatment (Smith, Cleeland, Middleton, & Godley, 2013). Finally, emerging adults' friends may also reduce their substance use when placed in a helping role (Smith, Davis, Dumas, & Ureche, 2016). Given that substance use is sometimes common in emerging adults' social networks, and the low substance use treatment utilization by emerging adults, this could expand the benefits of substance use treatment to non-treatment-seeking peers.

Research Findings

CONTROLLED STUDIES

There are only a handful of randomized studies that have delivered peer-enhanced interventions to emerging adults. Lee and colleagues (2014) randomized students going on spring break trips to brief personalized feedback interventions with or without peer involvement (i.e., receiving normative feedback). A very large proportion of peers assigned to the two peer-enhanced conditions (>90%) received normative feedback on drinking electronically. Few of the interventions in this study performed better than the control condition, including the two peer-enhanced conditions (i.e., Web-based BASICS plus friend, and in-person BASICS plus friend interventions). In interpreting these findings, the authors noted that only a small percent of targeted students (35%) actually went on spring break trips with their friends and participated in the intervention. Thus, one consideration in designing peer-enhanced treatments is ensuring that selected peers are in a position to influence the targeted emerging adults' substance use. If peers do not regularly spend time with the emerging adult with the substance use problem, these peers may be ineffective at helping them reduce their use.

A second study delivered a peer-enhanced intervention to reduce college students' risky drinking-related behavior on 21st birthday celebrations. Similar to Lee and colleagues' (2014) study, peers received electronic feedback such as normative drinking feedback and suggestions on keeping their friends safe (Neighbors et al., 2012). They, too, found that a large proportion of peers (85%) across the peer-enhanced conditions completed the brief intervention. Relative to control-group participants, those in the peer-enhanced conditions had fewer drinking consequences during 21st birthday drinking events. However, drinking was similarly high across all conditions, with participants typically consuming about 10 drinks on their 21st birthdays.

Finally, one small study ($n = 28$) targeted college students mandated for violations of university alcohol policies (O'Leary-Tevyaw, Borsari, Colby, & Monti, 2007). Emerging adults received either individual-based or peer-enhanced MI. Those receiving peer-enhanced MI had larger reductions in alcohol use at 1 month compared to participants in the individual MI condition. Also, participating friends' drinking levels were similar to those of the target emerging adults, and these friends also demonstrated a reduction in heavy drinking days at follow-up.

NON-CONTROLLED STUDIES

Smith and colleagues (2016) developed and tested a peer-enhanced version of the community reinforcement approach (CRA; Meyers & Smith, 1995) with emerging adult dyads ($n = 69$) where treatment-seeking emerging adults with alcohol use disorders (i.e., identified client) nominated peers to participate in their treatment. The peer supported the identified client's efforts to reduce drinking, and the treatment focused on training peers to provide social support to clients (i.e., reinforce clients' efforts to change, participate in non-alcohol and drug-related social activities with them). Identified clients received one MI session and up to 12 CRA sessions of cognitive-behavioral therapy. Peers received one session of MI, one session in which they learned skills to support their friend, and one session in which they planned social activities. Most target clients were able to bring a peer for 97% (34/35) for research assessments, and 65.7% of peers attended one or more intervention session. Notably, peers and identified clients both reduced their binge drinking at 3-month (peer $d = .55$, identified client $d = .23$) and 6-month (peer d = .39, identified client $d = .56$) follow-up.

Knowns and Unknowns

Currently, we have very few studies on peer-enhanced treatments, so this literature is limited in several ways. First, of the four studies that do exist, two only apply to event-specific drinking (i.e., Lee et al., 2014; Neighbors et al., 2012), and only one study was implemented with individuals with bona fide substance use disorders (Smith et al., 2016) in a community setting (i.e., not college). Thus, one major gap in our knowledge is whether peer-enhanced treatments can result in better treatment outcomes for persons with substance use disorders. Second, most of these studies' findings are limited to drinking outcomes. Although Smith et al.'s (2016) study included a large proportion of marijuana-using emerging adults, this study was not controlled. In addition, there are ethical questions about integrating peers into interventions when the peers themselves may also be heavy drinkers or substance users. However, there is no current evidence that these interventions harm the targeted emerging adult, and in both studies with heavily drinking peers, peers reduced their drinking and drug use (O'Leary-Teveyaw et al., 2007; Smith et al., 2016). Finally, we know little about the mechanisms of change operating in peer-enhanced treatments. That is, we don't know if their beneficial effects for targeted emerging adults may be due to peers reducing their substance use, peers increasing their social support to the targeted emerging adult, or some other mechanism.

Despite these limitations, there are several promising findings in these early studies and areas that seem worth investigating. First, across the studies, access to peers who are willing to participate in interventions to help their friends does not appear to be a concern. Across studies, treatment receipt ranges between 66% and 90% among peers. However, we note that the protocols for peer involvement are all very brief. Peer intervention use was higher in studies that delivered one-time, online feedback to peers, but in these studies intervention effects were also small and inconsistent relative to control groups. Thus, one potential delivery format for the next generation of peer-enhanced interventions could be mobile applications that place low time demands on peers but allow for continuous contact over a longer period of time. Second, in the two studies that measured peer substance use, notable reductions in substance use were made by the peers (O'Leary-Tevyaw et al., 2007; Smith et al., 2016). However, both studies were small and need to be replicated with larger samples. Such studies could estimate whether peers make significant reductions in their use relative to peers assigned to control conditions, how durable these reductions are, and if peers' changes in substance use predict longer-term reductions in use by targeted clients. Any reductions in substance use by peers could be considered a secondary benefit for these interventions. One could argue that expanding the reach of traditional substance use treatments to non-treatment-seeking peers is in itself a positive outcome, assuming low-cost delivery methods exist and there are no harms to targeted emerging adults. Finally, there are no examples of group-based interventions for emerging adults and their friends. Such interventions have the benefit (to providers) of efficiently using staff members' time because they can treat numerous people at once.

In summary, there have been very few attempts to implement peer-enhanced treatments with emerging adults. Among those studies that have, there are some promising findings such as reduced drinking among both targeted clients and peers. They have inconsistent effects when applied to event-specific drinking, but future studies may improve upon these earlier models to make peer-enhanced treatments more impactful.

PEERS AS THE FORMERLY AFFLICTED: PEER RECOVERY SUPPORT INTERVENTIONS

Rationale

Throughout its history the SUD treatment system has long employed individuals in recovery from substance use disorders (White, 2009). The treatment system has also relied on mutual aid societies such as Alcoholics Anonymous to serve a vital role for continuing care for individuals during and after treatment. Because of the work of recovery advocacy movements such as the Faces and Voices of Recovery (http://facesandvoicesofrecovery.org/), there is renewed interest in harnessing the experience of the millions of individuals in long-term recovery into peer recover support interventions. In these interventions, individuals formerly afflicted by substance use disorders and now in stable recovery serve as volunteers, peer recovery support specialists, or recovery coaches. Peer recovery support specialists' main qualification is experiential and their role is nonclinical. Thus, they may have credibility with individuals in treatment because of their lived experiences. From the perspective of the recovery advocacy groups, in peer recovery support interventions the value of such experiential knowledge of individuals in recovery is recognized (Laudet & Humphreys, 2013).

In addition to recognizing the value of recovering individuals' lived experience, another key reason exists for implementing peer recovery support models: Peer recovery support models may help fill current shortcomings in the system of care for individuals suffering from chronic substance use problems. That is, the current treatment system has been criticized for attempting to provide only short-term acute care to individuals with a chronic health problem (Kelly & White, 2011). When viewed as chronic health problems, remission rates for substance use disorders are similar to those for other health conditions like cancer, chronic obstructive pulmonary disease, or hypertension (McLellan, Lewis, O'Brien, & Kleber, 2000). Yet our treatment capacity to provide ongoing follow-up care is spotty. Thus peer recovery support models could play a vital role in transforming the larger system of care, and it is possible that they could represent cost-effective models.

Research Findings

Two systematic reviews on peer recovery support systems exist, and both reveal a paucity of work with emerging adults (Bassuk, Hanson, Greene, Richard, &

Laudet, 2016; Reif et al., 2014). Sanders and colleagues (1998) reported delivering a peer recovery model to pregnant and postpartum emerging adult women (mean age = 29). Peer support workers were in recovery themselves, had a minimum of 1 year of sobriety, and received 3 months of training. They were supervised by an interdisciplinary team consisting of a social worker, nurse, and medical director. Emerging adults who received the peer support program were more satisfied than those who received a professionally delivered program, the effect being stronger for younger emerging adults who were under age 25. No studies reviewed in these systematic reviews, nor those included in a large white paper report on peer recovery support (Chapman, Blash, & Chan, 2015), appear to have examined emerging adults' actual substance use outcomes. In short, outside of the work on recovery colleges (see Chapter 9), which may or may not include peer recovery support workers, we know practically nothing about the outcomes of emerging adults receiving peer recovery support services.

Knowns and Unknowns

Two separate reviews point to the promise of delivering peer recovery support models with older adults, yet neither review calculated effect sizes, owing to concerns over aggregating findings across a wide array of peer recovery support models (Bassuk et al., 2016). Models have included training a peer to deliver a one-shot brief MI to individuals getting services in opioid clinics, drop-in centers employing peer recovery support workers, and peer support groups consisting of individuals in recovery from co-occurring substance use and thought disorders. It is likely that some emerging adults were included in these studies, but the average participant in these studies ranged in age from 40 to 50 years of age.

The most common model discussed in the literature for emerging adult peer support for emerging adults are collegiate recovery communities (aka recovery colleges). These models have been in existence since 1988, with the first sober student housing established at Rutgers University (Harris, Baker, & Cleveland, 2010). Programs can include sober housing, on-site 12-step meetings, courses in addictions studies, drug-free social events, and scholarship incentive programs. Although it is unclear how many of these programs employ a professional or paraprofessional staff member, Harris and colleagues (2010) note that peer mentoring by other students in recovery is included in Texas Tech University's program. The research on these programs is still in its infancy (Laudet & Humphreys, 2013). One problem with evaluating these programs is that randomization of students to a collegiate recovery college or "college as usual" is likely not feasible, so it is likely that quasiexperimental evaluations will be used. Thus, much more research is needed on these models. (For a more comprehensive discussion of collegiate recovery communities, see Chapter 9 in this volume.)

Although collegiate recovery communities represent promising peer recovery support models, they will be limited in their reach to college-bound emerging adults. Given the large pool of adolescents who enter treatment and may potentially be in recovery by the time they reach emerging adulthood (Wiebe, Cleveland, & Harris, 2010), there may be other opportunities outside of university life to deploy peer recovery support models to emerging adults. Although we do not yet have research available in this area, it is reasonable to assume that emerging adults may be more receptive to receiving peer support services from other emerging adults. For example, emerging adults attend more AA meetings when there is a higher concentration of young people attending such meetings. Thus, more research is needed on how to enlist, train, and organize emerging adults as peer support specialists for non-college-attending emerging adults with substance use disorders.

SUMMARY

Research efforts to study peer-delivered (i.e., facilitators), peer-enhanced (i.e., friends), and peer recovery support (i.e., formerly afflicted) interventions are just beginning to appear in the literature. Given the initially promising findings using emerging adults in peer-delivered models, additional research should focus on continuing to establish efficacy and completing cost-effectiveness analyses that formally quantify whether savings are achieved by using peer facilitators. Peer-enhanced models have produced mixed findings in terms of efficacy relative to controls and other active non-peer-enhanced models, but the literature is largely limited to event-specific drinking studies (i.e., spring break and 21st birthday drinking). Additional research is needed with non-college-emerging adults with bona fide substance use disorders, and studies should focus on measuring the impact of such interventions on the friends who are participating in support roles, as well as the mechanisms of chance operating in these models. Finally, peer recovery support interventions have a long history in the SUD system of care, but they have yet to be fully evaluated for emerging adults. Additional research is needed on both collegiate recovery communities and interventions that target non-college-attending emerging adults. All three types of peer interventions may represent innovative approaches to emerging adult substance use.

REFERENCES

Bandura, A. (1977). *Social learning theory.* Englewood Cliffs, NJ: Prentice Hall.

Bandura, A. (1986). *Social foundations of thought and action: A social cognitive theory.* Englewood Cliffs, NJ: Prentice-Hall.

Bassuk, E. L., Hanson, J., Greene, R. N., Richard, M., & Laudet, A. (2016). Peer-delivered recovery support services for addictions in the United States: A systematic review. *Journal of Substance Abuse Treatment, 63,* 1–9.

Caudill, B. D., & Marlatt, G. A. (1975). Modeling influences in social drinking: An experimental analogue. *Journal of Consulting and Clinical Psychology, 43*(3), 405–415. doi: 10.1037/h0076689

Chapman, S., Blash, L., & Chan, K. (2015). *The peer provider workforce in behavioral health: A landscape analysis*. San Francisco: UCSF Health Workforce Research Center on Long-Term Care.

Cimini, M. D., Martens, M. P., Larimer, M. E., Kilmer, J. R., Neighbors, C., & Monserrat, J. M. (2009). Assessing the effectiveness of peer-facilitated interventions addressing high-risk drinking among judicially mandated college students. *Journal of Studies on Alcohol and Drugs, Supplement, 16*, 57–66.

Collins, R. L., Parks, G. A., & Marlatt, G. A. (1985). Social determinants of alcohol consumption: The effects of social interaction and model status on the self-administration of alcohol. *Journal of Consulting and Clinical Psychology, 53*(2), 189–200. doi: 10.1037/0022-006X.53.2.189

Crawford, L. A., & Novak, K. B. (2007). Resisting peer pressure: Characteristics associated with other-self discrepancies in college students' levels of alcohol consumption. *Journal of Alcohol & Drug Education, 51*(1), 35–62.

Cuijpers, P. (2002). Peer-led and adult-led school drug prevention: A meta-analytic comparison. *Journal of Drug Education, 32*(2), 107–119. doi: 10.2190/LPN9-KBDC-HPVB-JPTM

Dimeff, L. A. (Ed.). (1999). *Brief Alcohol Screening and Intervention for College Students (BASICS): A harm reduction approach*. New York: Guilford Press.

Donohue, B., Allen, D. N., Maurer, A., Ozols, J., & DeStefano, G. (2004). A controlled evaluation of two prevention programs in reducing alcohol use among college students at low and high risk for alcohol related problems. *Journal of Alcohol & Drug Education, 48*(1), 13–33.

Fromme, K., & Corbin, W. (2004). Prevention of heavy drinking and associated negative consequences among mandated and voluntary college students. *Journal of Consulting and Clinical Psychology, 72*(6), 1038–1049. doi: 10.1037/0022-006X.72.6.1038

Goodman, I., Peterson-Badali, M., & Henderson, J. (2011). Understanding motivation for substance use treatment: The role of social pressure during the transition to adulthood. *Addictive Behaviors, 36*(6), 660–668.

Harris, K. S., Baker, A., & Cleveland, H. H. (2010). Collegiate recovery communities: What they are and how they support recovery. In H. H. Cleveland, K. S. Harris, & R. P. Wiebe (Eds.), *Substance abuse recovery in college* (pp. 9–22). New York: Springer.

Hart, G. J. (1998). Peer education and community based HIV prevention for homosexual men: Peer led, evidence based, or fashion driven? *Sexually Transmitted Infections, 74*(2), 87–89.

Hoeppner, B. B., Hoeppner, S. S., & Kelly, J. F. (2014). Do young people benefit from AA as much, and in the same ways, as adult aged 30+? A moderated multiple mediation analysis. *Drug and Alcohol Dependence, 143*, 181–188.

Kelly, J. F., & White, W.L. (2011). Recovery management and the future of addiction treatment and recovery in the USA. In J. F. Kelly & W. L. White (Eds.), *Addiction recovery management: Theory, research and practice*. New York: Springer.

Larimer, M. E., Cronce, J. M., Lee, C. M., Kilmer, J. R., et al. (2004). Brief intervention in college settings. *Alcohol Research and Health, 28*(2), 94.

Larimer, M. E., Turner, A. P., Anderson, B. K., Fader, J. S., Kilmer, J. R., Palmer, R. S., & Cronce, J. M. (2001). Evaluating a brief alcohol intervention with fraternities. *Journal of Studies on Alcohol, 62*(3), 370–380. doi: 10.15288/jsa.2001.62.370

Lau-Barraco, C., Braitman, A. L., Leonard, K. E., & Padilla, M. (2012). Drinking buddies and their prospective influence on alcohol outcomes: Alcohol expectancies as a mediator. *Psychology of Addictive Behaviors*, *26*(4), 747.

Lau-Barraco, C., & Linden, A. N. (2014). Drinking buddies: Who are they and when do they matter?. *Addiction research & theory*, *22*(1), 57–67.

Laudet, A. B., & Humphreys, K. (2013). Promoting recovery in an evolving policy context: What do we know and what do we need to know about recovery support services? *Journal of Substance Abuse Treatment*, *45*(1), 126–133.

Lee, C. M., Neighbors, C., Lewis, M. A., Kaysen, D., Mittmann, A., Geisner, I. M., . . . Larimer, M. E. (2014). Randomized controlled trial of a spring break intervention to reduce high-risk drinking. *Journal of Consulting and Clinical Psychology*, *82*(2), 189–201.

Lewis, M. A., Sheng, E., Geisner, I. M., Rhew, I. C., Patrick, M. E., & Lee, C. M. (2015). Friend or foe: Personal use and friends' use of protective behavioral strategies and spring break drinking. *Addictive Behaviors*, *50*, 96–101.

Lied, E. R., & Marlatt, G. (1979). Modeling as a determinant of alcohol consumption: Effect of subject sex and prior drinking history. *Addictive Behaviors*, *4*(1), 47–54. doi: 10.1016/0306-4603(79)90020-0

Marlatt, G. A., Baer, J. S., Kivlahan, D. R., Dimeff, L. A., Larimer, M. E., Quigley, L. A., . . . Williams, E. (1998). Screening and brief intervention for high-risk college student drinkers: Results from a 2-year follow-up assessment. *Journal of Consulting and Clinical Psychology*, *66*(4), 604–615. doi: 10.1037/0022-006X.66.4.604

Mastroleo, N. R., Mallett, K. A., Turrisi, R., & Ray, A. E. (2009). Psychometric properties of the Peer Proficiency Assessment (PEPA): A tool for evaluation of undergraduate peer counselors' motivational interviewing fidelity. *Addictive Behaviors*, *34*(9), 717–722. doi: 10.1016/j.addbeh.2009.04.008

Mastroleo, N. R., Turrisi, R., Carney, J. V., Ray, A. E., & Larimer, M. E. (2010). Examination of post-training supervision of peer counselors in a motivational enhancement intervention to reduce drinking in a sample of heavy drinking college students. *Journal of Substance Abuse Treatment*, *39*(3), 289–297. doi: 10.1016/j.jsat.2010.06.005

McLellan, A. T., Lewis, D. C., O'Brien, C. P., & Kleber, H. D. (2000). Drug dependence, a chronic medical illness: Implications for treatment, insurance, and outcomes evaluation. *Journal of the American Medical Association*, *284*(13), 1689–1695.

Meyers, R. J., & Smith, J. E. (1995). *Clinical guide to alcohol treatment: The community reinforcement approach.* Guilford Press: New York.

Miller, W. R., & Mount, K. A. (2001). A small study of training in motivational interviewing: Does one workshop change clinician and client behavior? *Behavioural and Cognitive Psychotherapy*, *29*(04), 457–471. doi: 10.1017/S1352465801004064

Miller, W. R., & Rollnick, S. (1991). *Motivational interviewing: Preparing people to change addictive behavior.* New York: Guilford Press.

Mowbray, O., Quinn, A., & Cranford, J. A. (2014). Social networks and alcohol use disorders: Findings from a nationally representative sample. *American Journal of Drug and Alcohol Abuse*, *40*(3), 181–186.

Moyers, T. B., Martin, T., Manuel, J. K., Hendrickson, S. M. L., & Miller, W. R. (2005). Assessing competence in the use of motivational interviewing. *Journal of Substance Abuse Treatment*, *28*(1), 19–26. doi: 10.1016/j.jsat.2004.11.001

Neighbors, C., Lee, C. M., Atkins, D. C., Lewis, M. A., Kaysen, D., Mittmann, A., . . . Larimer, M. E. (2012). A randomized controlled trial of event-specific prevention strategies for reducing problematic drinking associated with 21st birthday celebrations. *Journal of Consulting and Clinical Psychology, 80*(5), 850–862. doi: 10.1037/a0029480

O'Leary, T. A., Brown, S. A., Colby, S. M., Cronce, J. M., D'Amico, E. J., Fader, J. S., . . . Monti, P. M. (2002). Treating adolescents together or individually? Issues in adolescent substance abuse interventions. *Alcoholism: Clinical and Experimental Research, 26*(6), 890–899. doi: 10.1111/j.1530-0277.2002.tb02619.x

O'Leary-Tevyaw, T., Borsari, B., Colby, S. M., & Monti, P. M. (2007). Peer enhancement of a brief motivational intervention with mandated college students. *Psychology of Addictive Behaviors, 21*(1), 114–119. doi: 10.1037/0893-164X.21.1.114

Reid, A. E., Carey, K. B., Merrill, J. E., & Carey, M. P. (2015). Social network influences on initiation and maintenance of reduced drinking among college students. *Journal of Consulting and Clinical Psychology, 83*(1), 36–44. doi: 10.1037/a0037634

Reif, S., Braude, L., Lyman, D. R., Dougherty, R. H., Daniels, A. S., Ghose, S. S., . . . Delphin-Rittmon, M. E. (2014). Peer recovery support for individuals with substance use disorders: Assessing the evidence. *Psychiatric Services, 65, 853–861.*

Sanders, L. M., Trinh, C., Sherman, B. R., & Banks, S. M. (1998). Assessment of client satisfaction in a peer counseling substance abuse treatment program for pregnant and postpartum women. *Evaluation and Program Planning, 21*(3), 287–296.

Schroeder, C. M., & Prentice, D. A. (1998). Exposing pluralistic ignorance to reduce alcohol use among college students. *Journal of Applied Social Psychology, 28*(23), 2150–2180. doi: 10.1111/j.1559-1816.1998.tb01365.x

Sloane, B. C., & Zimmer, C. G. (1993). The power of peer health education. *Journal of American College Health, 41*(6), 241–245. doi: 10.1080/07448481.1993.9936334

Smith, D. C., Cleeland, C., Middleton, A., & Godley, M. D. (2013). Willingness and appropriateness of peers participating in emerging adults' substance misuse treatment. *Journal of Substance Abuse Treatment, 45*, 148–154. doi: 10.1016/j.jsat.2013.01.008

Smith, D. C., Davis, J. P., Dumas, T., & Ureche, D. J. (2016). Six month outcomes of a peer-enhanced community reinforcement approach for emerging adults with substance misuse: A preliminary study. *Journal of Substance Abuse Treatment, 61*, 66–73.

Sorsdahl, K., Stein, D. J., Corrigall, J., Cuijpers, P., Smits, N., Naledi, T., & Myers, B. (2015). The efficacy of a blended motivational interviewing and problem solving therapy intervention to reduce substance use among patients presenting for emergency services in South Africa: A randomized controlled trial. *Substance Abuse Treatment, Prevention, and Policy, 10*(1), 46. doi: 10.1186/s13011-015-0042-1

Soule, E. K., Barnett, T. E., & Moorhouse, M. D. (2015). Protective behavioral strategies and negative alcohol-related consequences among US college fraternity and sorority members. *Journal of Substance Use, 20*(1), 16–21. doi: 10.3109/14659891.2013.858783

Tollison, S. J., Lee, C. M., Neighbors, C., Neil, T. A., Olson, N. D., & Larimer, M. E. (2008). Questions and reflections: the use of motivational interviewing microskills in a peer-led brief alcohol intervention for college students. *Behavior Therapy, 39*(2), 183–194.

Turrisi, R., Larimer, M. E., Mallett, K. A., Kilmer, J. R., Ray, A. E., Mastroleo, N. R., . . . Montoya, H. (2009). A randomized clinical trial evaluating a combined alcohol intervention for high-risk college students. *Journal of Studies on Alcohol and Drugs*, *70*(4), 555–567.

Wang, C., Hipp, J. R., Butts, C. T., Jose, R., & Lakon, C. M. (2016). Coevolution of adolescent friendship networks and smoking and drinking behaviors with consideration of parental influence. *Psychology of Addictive Behaviors*, *30*(3), 312–324. doi: 10.1037/adb0000163

Wechsler, H., Kuh, G., & Davenport, A. E. (2009). Fraternities, sororities and binge drinking: Results from a national study of American colleges. *Journal of Student Affairs Research and Practice*, *46*(3), 763–784. doi: 10.2202/1949-6605.5017

White, W. (2009). Peer-based addiction recovery support: History, theory, practice, and scientific evaluation. Chicago, IL: Great Lakes Addiction Technology Transfer Center and Philadelphia Department of Behavioral Health and Mental Retardation Services. Available at http://www.naadac.org/assets/1959/whitew2009_peer-based_addiction_recovery_support.pdf

Wiebe, R. P., Cleveland, H. H., & Harris, K. S. (2010). The need for college recovery services. In *Substance Abuse Recovery in College* (pp. 1–8). New York: Springer.

8

Emerging Adults, Mutual-Help Organizations, and Addiction Recovery

What Does the Science Tell Us?

BRANDON G. BERGMAN, JOHN F. KELLY,
NILOFAR FALLAH-SOHY, AND SARAH MAKHANI ■

INTRODUCTION

Individuals in the stage of the life course between adolescence and established adulthood, a period that has been coined emerging adulthood (Arnett, 2015; Arnett, Žukauskienė, & Sugimura, 2014), often face critical life challenges, such as leaving home, finding a romantic partner, and cultivating a vocation or career. These new experiences typically occur at the same time as such individuals gain more freedom and decision-making autonomy than ever before, while also remaining vulnerable to some of the difficulties with impulse control and planning that are typical of adolescents (Wilens & Rosenbaum, 2013). Thus, failure to meet these challenges and adjust successfully to these transitions can result in life-impacting problems. Given that emerging adults (ages 18 to 29[1]) are likely to socialize in networks that introduce and reinforce alcohol and other drug use (Borsari & Carey, 2001; Cook, Bauermeister, Gordon-Messer, & Zimmerman, 2013; Stoddard, Bauermeister, Gordon-Messer, Johns, & Zimmerman, 2012), it

---

1. Although it is a developmental stage of the life course, not an age range per se, ages 18 to 29 typically encompass the achievement of major emerging adult milestones for most individuals (Arnett, 2015; Arnett et al., 2014). In this chapter, we use the term *emerging adulthood* to represent this age range and specify other age ranges (e.g., 18–24 years) as appropriate.

follows that the specific risk for substance use disorder (SUD) is higher among emerging adults than any other age group. For example, nationally representative epidemiological data suggest that emerging adults' rates of current alcohol (27%) and other drug use disorder (8%) are two to three times greater than those of 30- to 44-year-olds and 45- to 64-year-olds (Grant et al., 2015, 2016), and three times greater than rates for adolescents (Substance Abuse and Mental Health Services Administration [SAMHSA], 2014a).

The Value of Mutual-Help Organizations

Participation in SUD treatment, on average, is associated with enhanced absti- nence and reduced harm for adults more generally (Miller & Wilbourne, 2002; Prendergast, Podus, Chang, & Urada, 2002; Weisner, Matzger, & Kaskutas, 2003); however, resumption of use is common after an acute episode of abstinence- based treatment. Studies have shown only 20%–30% of treatment-seekers remain abstinent during the first post-treatment year (Hunt, Barnett, & Branch, 1971; Witkiewitz & Masyn, 2008). As such, ongoing recovery support services that can help individuals to maintain progress accrued during treatment or to interrupt any substance-using behavior before it results in full SUD reinstatement are critical elements of a comprehensive recovery plan (Kelly & White, 2011). These recovery management activities may be professional (Dennis, Scott, & Funk, 2003; Godley et al., 2014; McKay, 2010) or nonprofessional community-based services.

The most commonly sought of all recovery management options—both pro- fessional and nonprofessional—are 12-step and other mutual-help organizations (MHOs), such as Alcoholics Anonymous (AA), Narcotics Anonymous (NA), and SMART Recovery (Grant et al., 2015, 2016). MHOs are free resources that are often widely available in most U.S. communities and many other English- speaking countries as well. AA and NA operate in 170 and 132 countries around the world, respectively. MHOs have been defined as support networks of indi- viduals with a shared goal of SUD abstinence and related health benefits (e.g., quality of life; Humphreys, 2004). MHOs may vary in terms of their recovery philosophy (e.g., 12-step and cognitive-behavioral) or focus (i.e., targeting spe- cific substances or catering to specific populations). Essentially beginning with their inception in the 1930s, MHOs, and 12-step MHOs (TSMHOs) in partic- ular, have played a major role in the de facto SUD healthcare system in North America and other industrialized regions (Makela et al., 1996). Only during the past 30 years, however, has research demonstrated that TSMHOs can provide important relapse prevention and recovery benefits for adults (Humphreys et al., 2004; Kaskutas, 2009; Kelly & Yeterian, 2012; Moos, 2008) as well as adolescents (Kelly & Myers, 2007). Despite methodological limitations of some earlier stud- ies (Emrick, Tonigan, Montgomery, & Little, 1993; Tonigan, Toscova, & Miller, 1996), during the past 10–15 years increased scientific rigor and sophisticated analytical approaches have increased confidence in the recovery-related benefits of TSMHO participation, particularly for AA (Humphreys, Blodgett, & Wagner,

2014; Magura, McKean, Kosten, & Tonigan, 2013; Ye & Kaskutas, 2009). Indeed, systematic referral to TSMHOs is considered by many to be part of an overall comprehensive evidence-based approach to SUD treatment, and strategies to engage patients with TSMHOs are included in most clinical practice guidelines for treating SUD (American Psychiatric Association, 2010).

Emerging Adulthood: A Gap in the Study of Mutual-Help Organizations

Until recently, almost nothing was known about TSMHO participation and derived benefit among emerging adults with SUD. This gap is important because, as mentioned earlier, these individuals have unique biopsychosocial profiles relative to their older counterparts. Moreover, emerging adults also constitute one-third of addiction treatment patients in countries like the United States (SAMHSA, 2014b) but may be even more susceptible than older adults to relapse following acute stabilization or a short-term treatment episode (Bergman, Kelly, Nargiso, & McKowen, 2016). Research has shown that destabilizing the course of SUD as early as possible increases the likelihood of a shorter addiction career (i.e., the time between SUD onset and achieving sustained remission; Dennis, Scott, Funk, & Foss, 2005; Evans, Li, Grella, Brecht, & Hser, 2013) and thus reduced substance-related harm to the individual and to society at large. Thus, it is crucial to know what role TSMHOs should (or should not) play in an evidence-based recovery management approach specifically for individuals in this age group.

This chapter reviews the research examining emerging adult participation in, and benefits derived from, MHOs, including but not limited to TSMHOs. As secondary goals, we also outline factors that might explain their TSMHO-derived benefits in helping prevent substance use and relapse (i.e., mediators) as well as factors that may influence the degree of derived gains (i.e., moderators). Relevant empirical research in the area is organized around the following four research questions, with attention paid in each section to differences between emerging adults and older adults if they have been tested:

1) To what extent do emerging adults *participate* in MHOs?
2) To what degree do emerging adults *benefit* from participation in MHOs?
3) What are the *mechanisms* through which MHO participation promotes better outcomes (i.e., mediators) for emerging adults?
4) What are the factors that influence emerging adults' MHO participation and participation-related benefit (i.e., moderators)?

Last, we will discuss the implications of these findings regarding emerging adults' recovery processes and factors that might help them achieve recovery from SUD. We will also highlight key lingering empirical questions for clinicians and clinical researchers interested in MHO recovery during this stage of the life course.

Before reviewing emerging adults' participation in MHOs, it is important first to highlight a terminology distinction. As the sophistication of TSMHO research improved, researchers began to investigate participation beyond whether an individual simply attended a meeting (Cloud, Ziegler, & Blondell, 2004). These activities include, but are not limited to, completing work on the 12 steps of a TSMHO program (the purported therapeutic program of emotional, social, and spiritual recovery), having a sponsor (a recovery mentor often with more time in recovery who guides an individual through the steps and typically provides ongoing recovery support), and socializing with other members outside of meetings. Compared to attendance alone, such active TSMHO involvement is virtually always a stronger predictor of positive SUD outcomes even though it may be operationalized in different ways (Cloud et al., 2004; Montgomery, Miller, & Tonigan, 1995; Weiss et al., 2005). Throughout this chapter, we refer to these recovery activities and behaviors specifically as "active involvement." We use *participation* as an overarching term that encompasses both attendance and active involvement.

1. TO WHAT EXTENT DO EMERGING ADULTS PARTICIPATE IN MHOS?

In one of only few studies that expressly recruited emerging adults for a study of their TSMHO participation, our research group (Kelly, Stout, & Slaymaker, 2013; Kelly, Urbanoski, Hoeppner, & Slaymaker, 2012) recruited over 300 18–24 years old individuals (*M* age = 20 years) during their stay at a residential SUD treatment program in the mid-Western United States that was specifically geared to the care of adolescent and emerging adult patients. Participants were followed up to 1 year post-discharge, with assessments conducted at 1, 3, 6, and 12 months (84%, 82%, 72%, 71% follow-up rates, respectively). The proportion who attended TSMHOs increased dramatically post-treatment, rising from less than 40% at baseline (pre-treatment) to 90% at 3-month follow-up, decreasing only slightly at the 6- and 12-month follow-ups (Figure 8.1). Similarly, mean percent days attending a meeting rose from 10% at baseline to 45% at 3-month follow-up, also attenuating somewhat by 6- and 12-month follow-ups. Active involvement was measured by an index which captured whether or not an individual engaged in each of eight activities during a follow-up period. Similar to attendance, patients' active involvement also rose sharply post-treatment—from 1.5 at baseline to 5.7 at 3-month follow-up, remaining fairly stable at 6- and 12-month follow-ups.

The most commonly reported activities (apart from attendance) across all follow-ups were (a) considering oneself a TSMHO member (72% to 83%), (b) verbal participation at meetings (75% to 83%), and (c) socializing with non-sponsor TSMHO members outside meetings (72% to 79%). While completing step work was a common activity at 3-month follow-up (81%), participation in this activity dropped off at the 6- and 12-month follow-ups (69% and 66%, respectively).

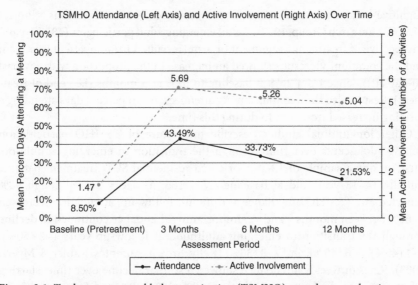

Figure 8.1 Twelve-step mutual help organization (TSMHO) attendance and active involvement over a 12-month follow-up period.
SOURCE OF DATA: Kelly, J. F., Stout, R. L., & Slaymaker, V. (2013). Emerging adults' treatment outcomes in relation to 12-step mutual-help attendance and involvement. *Drug and Alcohol Dependence, 129*(1-2), 151–157. doi:10.1016/j.drugalcdep.2012.10.005

In addition to our study designed specifically to examine emerging adults' TSMHO participation, there have been several important secondary data analyses that draw an emerging adult subsample from a larger sample of adults with SUD and other hazardous substance use. In one such study, Delucchi, Matzger, and Weisner (2008) conducted a secondary data analysis of 265 emerging adults (18–25 years) from a larger sample of adults with either alcohol use disorder (dependence from the fourth edition of the *Diagnostic and Statistical Manual of Mental Disorders* [DSM-IV], American Psychiatric Association, 2000) or "problem drinking" (meeting two of three harmful drinking criteria), who may have been recruited either from treatment settings (outpatient and inpatient) or the community. At baseline, 30% of the problem drinkers had been to AA, while 51% of those with alcohol dependence had been to AA, a statistically significant difference. Although participants were followed up for 7 years (and we present results of MHO benefit analyses later), only baseline attendance was reported.

In another study including 98 emerging adults (18–25 years) with alcohol use disorder receiving outpatient SUD treatment, 68% reported lifetime meeting attendance at baseline and 36% considered themselves a member (Mason & Luckey, 2003). Weekly or greater 30-day attendance rose sharply from 26% at baseline to 51% at 3 months but declined essentially to baseline levels by 12-month follow-up (29%).

Finally, our group (Hoeppner, Hoeppner, & Kelly, 2014) also examined AA participation among emerging adults in Project MATCH, a multi-site randomized controlled trial investigating the effects of manualized 12-step facilitation, cognitive-behavioral, and motivational enhancement interventions (Project MATCH Research Group, 1997). For all emerging adult participants (18–29 years) irrespective of treatment assignment or arm (recruited from inpatient treatment and the community), results showed an increase in the proportion with any past 90-day attendance from 26% at baseline to 52% at 3 months (i.e., end of treatment). Results also showed that, among attendees, mean percent days attending a meeting increased from 3 to 15 during this time.

Other longitudinal studies describe the nature of TSMHO participation among adolescents over time through the transition to emerging adulthood. First, among a sample of 12-step-oriented residential SUD treatment patients initially 14–18 years old at baseline ($N = 166$; M age $= 16$), although 90% reported any TSMHO attendance at 6-month follow-up, attendance decreased to 60% between months 7 and 12. Importantly, attendance continued to decline through the transition to emerging adulthood at follow-up years 1–2 (50%), 3–4 (45%), 5–6 (40%), and 7–8 (30%) (Kelly, Brown, Abrantes, Kahler, & Myers, 2008). Rates of weekly attendance showed a similar decline over time, starting off at 65%, but dropping to 35%, then 30%, 15%, 10% and 5%, respectively. Second, among SUD outpatients who were age 13–18 years at baseline enrolled in abstinence-based treatment where staff encouraged regular TSMHO attendance as part of a continuum of care (i.e., intensive outpatient program followed by relapse prevention and continuing care; $N = 391$), 20% lifetime attendance at baseline increased to 42% with 10+ meetings in the past 6 months at 1-year follow-up. As in Kelly, Brown, et al.'s (2008) study, however, attendance declined through the transition to emerging adulthood, including 12% with 10+ meetings at 3-year, 10% at 5-year, and 7% at 7-year follow-ups (Chi, Campbell, Sterling, & Weisner, 2012; Chi, Kaskutas, Sterling, Campbell, & Weisner, 2009). A similar pattern emerged for active TSMHO involvement, where rates of considering oneself a member, calling other members for help, and having a sponsor, for example, decreased by half from the 3-year to the 7-year follow-up. In addition, this study also highlighted three long-term trajectories of TSMHO participation, beginning in adolescence and continuing through emerging adulthood: (1) minimal or no attendance (60%); (2) attendance during the first year after treatment entry that drops off quickly thereafter (25%); and (3) attendance during the first year that drops off more gradually over several years (15%). Taken together, these data suggest sharp increases in adolescent TSMHO participation after engaging in SUD treatment where attendance is encouraged or facilitated, but participation declines markedly with the transition to emerging adulthood, with only 5%–7% attending regularly (e.g., weekly) several years after initially entering treatment.

In a descriptive study of a collegiate SUD treatment program (Bennett, McCrady, Keller, & Paulus, 1996) ($N = 78$; 17–34 years; M age $= 22$), among the 42 students who were followed up at 6 months, 69% reported weekly AA attendance, and 76% had a sponsor. The unique program consisted of inpatient and/or outpatient SUD treatment that was integrated with the students' college curriculum, while also offering substance-free housing and encouraging MHO participation.

Finally, in a large study, 564 young adult patients (18–39 years old) were examined within a larger sample of adults attending a health maintenance organization–covered outpatient SUD treatment program that encouraged TSMHO attendance off-site. At 5-year follow-up, 34% of these young adults reported attending a meeting in the past year, and attendees went to 89 meetings, on average, corresponding with 24% days attending a meeting (Satre, Chi, Mertens, & Weisner, 2012; Satre, Mertens, Arean, & Weisner, 2004). Using the AA Affiliation scale (Humphreys, Kaskutas, & Weisner, 1998) to measure active involvement across all TSMHO groups (i.e., not just AA), participants endorsed three out of nine activities on average, with one-half reporting lifetime identification as a TSMHO member and 47% having called a TSMHO member for help.

Comparison to Older Adults

Emerging adults with SUD may have less clinical severity than older adults, on average (Hoeppner et al., 2014). Clinical severity and, by association, more substance-related consequences are robust predictors of affiliating with recovery support services and TSMHOs in particular (Connors, Tonigan, & Miller, 2001; Morgenstern, Labouvie, McCrady, Kahler, & Frey, 1997; Rosenstock, 1990; Tonigan et al., 1996). Simply put, people who are suffering more tend to take more action to attempt to alleviate that suffering; TSMHO participation is one such strategy. Thus it follows that emerging adults may have lower rates of TSMHO participation than older adults. In the Project MATCH sample, Hoeppner et al. (2014) found emerging adults (18–29 years) and older adults (30+ years) had similar proportions of any past-90-day AA attendance at baseline, though among attendees, older adults attended twice as frequently. At 3-month follow-up (i.e., post-treatment), 52% of emerging adults reported AA attendance in the past 90 days, significantly lower than the 64% of older adults. Again, among attendees, older adults went twice as often. In the Mason and Luckey (2003) sample, descriptive comparisons showed that emerging adults (18–25 years) and older adults had similar rates of 30-day attendance at treatment entry, but lower rates of weekly attendance at 3-month (51% vs. 65%) and 12-month follow-ups (29% vs. 50%). Using a broader categorization of young adulthood as 18–39 years, Satre et al. (2004, 2012) found that young adults and older adults attended a similar number of past-year meetings at several time points across 9 years of follow-ups and had similar levels of active involvement measured by the AA Affiliation Scale at 5-year follow-up.

Summary

Overall, emerging adults demonstrate patterns of TSMHO participation consistent with prior known positive associations between SUD severity and participation among adults (Connors et al., 2001; Morgenstern et al., 1997; Tonigan et al.,

1996). For example, emerging adults who attend inpatient or residential programs appear to participate in TSMHOs during and after treatment to a greater degree than those attending outpatient programs. Similarly, emerging adults on the whole appear to participate in TSMHOs to a lesser degree than their typically more severe older adult counterparts (Hoeppner et al., 2014; Mason & Luckey, 2003). In addition, as adolescent patients transition to emerging adulthood and move further in time from an index treatment episode, their initially high TSMHO attendance seems to decline precipitously. One general point is that participants tended to be recruited from programs that, at a minimum, encouraged TSMHO participation, though not in all cases (Hoeppner et al., 2014). Whether programs with staff who do not encourage TSMHO participation would generate participation to this degree among its emerging adult patients remains unclear. Also, noticeably absent from this body of literature are studies on non-12-step MHOs, such as SMART Recovery or Secular Organization for Sobriety (Humphreys, 2004; Kelly & White, 2012).

2. TO WHAT DEGREE DO EMERGING ADULTS BENEFIT FROM PARTICIPATION IN MHOS?

As just highlighted, participation can be broken down into attendance and active involvement. We organize this section according to tests of benefit derived from each of these two modalities of TSMHO participation. For a summary of these tests of TSMHO benefit, see Table 8.1.

Attendance

In our study of emerging adults in residential treatment (Kelly et al., 2013), participants derived both greater abstinence and heavy drinking–related reductions in relation to TSMHO attendance across the first post-treatment year (though the heavy-drinking effect had an observed significance level of .06). Analyses were time-lagged (e.g., 3-month attendance associated with 6-month abstinence) and controlled for several covariates associated with outcomes (e.g., commitment to sobriety at treatment entry) and missing a follow-up (e.g., level of education). Controlling for covariates like this is a common strategy to isolate the effect of TSMHO participation on outcomes, thereby reducing the likelihood of a spurious effect. Similarly, in the Project MATCH sample of emerging adults with alcohol use disorders, participants' AA attendance at 3 months was associated with both abstinence and fewer drinks per drinking day at 15 months (Hoeppner et al., 2014).

These shorter-term (i.e., 1-year) positive effects of TSMHO attendance may extend to longer-term follow-ups as well. Measured dichotomously (yes/no), in Delucchi, Matzger, and Weisner's (2008) study, AA attendance was a significant predictor of both drinking volume and binge drinking in the year leading up to

Table 8.1. OVERVIEW OF EFFECTS OF TSMHO PARTICIPATION (ATTENDANCE AND ACTIVE INVOLVEMENT)
ON ALCOHOL AND OTHER DRUG USE

First Authors (Year)	TSMHO Fellowship	Age at Baseline (Years)	Setting	Last Follow-up (Years)	Modality	Measure	Benefit?
Delucchi (2008)	AA	18–25	I/O/C	7	Att	Yes/No	Y
Kelly, Brown (2008)	AA/NA	14–18	I	8	Att	Number	Y
Chi (2009, 2012)	All	13–18	O	7	Att	10+ (Yes/No)	Y
					Inv	3 + Activities from AA affiliation Scale (Yes/No)	Y
Kelly (2013)	All	18–24	I	1	Att	% Days	Y
					Inv	MMAS	Y*
Hoeppner (2014)	AA	18–29	O	1.25	Att	% Days	Y

NOTES: AA, Alcoholics Anonymous; Att, attendance; C, community; I, inpatient/residential; Inv, active involvement; MMAS, Multidimensional Mutual Help Activity Scale (Kelly et al., 2011); NA, Narcotics Anonymous; O, outpatient; TSMHO, 12-step mutual-help organization.
*Effect of active involvement on alcohol and other drug use is stronger than effect of attendance.

the 1-year, 3-year, 5-year, and 7-year follow-ups. This effect was independent of a host of demographic (e.g., ethnicity), clinical (e.g., baseline dependence symptoms and formal treatment attendance), and social factors (e.g., substance users in the social network). In Kelly, Brown, et al.'s (2008) study, greater attendance during the first 6 months post-discharge from inpatient care was associated with significantly better substance use outcomes up through 6 years. Across the entire 8-year follow-up (i.e., through the transition to emerging adulthood), each TSMHO meeting attended was prospectively and uniquely associated with an extra 2 days of abstinence in the next assessment period. The group-based trajectory approach in Chi et al.'s (2012) study was also suggestive of TSMHO benefit for those whose attendance gradually declined over time from adolescence through the transition to emerging adulthood. These more consistent attendees had 2 to 2.5 times greater odds of abstinence at 3-, 5-, and 7-year follow-ups compared to those with low/no attendance.

Active Involvement

Fewer studies have investigated the effects of active TSMHO involvement compared to attendance. Among the key exceptions, we showed that emerging adults continued to derive benefit from attendance when active involvement was considered in the same model (Kelly et al., 2013). Like studies examining mainly older adults (e.g., Weiss et al., 2005), the effect of active involvement on both abstinence and heavy drinking was stronger than attendance. Interestingly, the active involvement effect on abstinence strengthened over the post-treatment year, while the attendance effect weakened. When the effects of TSMHO activities were explored one at a time, considering oneself a TSMHO member and sharing at meetings were the strongest predictors of increased abstinence, while spending time with members outside meetings and step work were the strongest predictors of reduced heavy drinking. In addition, the significant beneficial effect of active involvement on abstinence persisted even after taking post-treatment professional continuing care services into account in the model (e.g., residing in a sober living environment). Each additional TSMHO activity during a follow-up period (1, 3, 6, or 12 months post-treatment) increased the odds of abstinence in that same time period by 25% (Bergman, Hoeppner, Nelson, Slaymaker, & Kelly, 2015). We have also found that having a sponsor and contact with one's sponsor are associated with abstinence during the same time period (Kelly, Greene, & Bergman, 2016). One particularly novel finding in that study was that the *quality of the relationship* between the TSMHO participant and his or her sponsor, measured by an assessment of "sponsor alliance" adapted from a well-validated measure of the professional therapeutic "working alliance" (Horvath & Greenberg, 1989), was uniquely related to abstinence. "Sponsor alliance" was an even stronger predictor of abstinence than whether or not one had contact with one's sponsor.

Comparison to Older Adults

Among the few studies to compare emerging adults and older adults on benefit derived from TSMHO participation, our group found that despite emerging
adults' lower rates of participation, they and older adults both derive significant
and similar abstinence-related benefit from AA attendance (Hoeppner et al.,
2014). However, older adults derived more AA-related benefit for reduced drinking intensity (drinks per drinking day) than did emerging adults.

Summary

Like older adults, emerging adults also appear to benefit from both TSMHO
attendance and active involvement. While more studies of active involvement are
needed, available data suggest, also like older adults, that these activities are likely
to have a greater impact on abstinence compared to attendance alone. Given the
growing body of literature on the salutary effects of having a sponsor among adults
(Tonigan & Rice, 2010; Zemore, Subbaraman, & Tonigan, 2013), early data on
the importance of this core TSMHO relationship among emerging adults (Kelly
et al., 2016) suggest it merits further attention. Finally, studies that follow individuals from adolescence through emerging adulthood highlight the importance
of ongoing attendance across this developmental transition. These data are consistent with a recovery management approach to the treatment of SUD in youth
where an initial treatment episode is simply the first step to a longer-term recovery plan (Godley, Godley, Dennis, Funk, & Passetti, 2007; Godley et al., 2010;
Kelly & White, 2011).

3. WHAT ARE THE MECHANISMS THROUGH WHICH MHO
PARTICIPATION PROMOTES BETTER OUTCOMES?

The crux of the secondary analyses by Hoeppner et al. (2014) was an examination of the mechanisms through which emerging adults derive benefit from
AA attendance and whether they differ from those for older adults (also see
later section "Comparison to Older Adults"). The study used a multiple mediation framework to examine 9-month mediators of the relationship between
3-month attendance and 15-month abstinence/drinking intensity for both
emerging adults and older adults, including self-efficacy to handle negative
affect, self-efficacy to handle risky social situations, increased religiosity/spir-
ituality, decreased depression, and increased pro-abstainers and decreased
pro-drinkers in one's social network. Pro-abstainers were individuals who
encouraged abstinence and/or discouraged drinking from the participant's perspective; pro-drinkers encouraged drinking and/or discouraged abstinence. For
emerging adults, only increased self-efficacy to handle risky social situations

and decreased pro-drinkers in the network were significant mediators of the AA effect on abstinence. On the whole, all mediators accounted for 36% of the attendance-abstinence effect. The results for the drinking intensity model were similar, though the mediators accounted only for 22% of the attendance-drinking intensity effect.

We also investigated whether changes in social network members, characterized by their own substance use as either high risk (e.g., "regular user," "possible abuser," abuser") or low risk (e.g., "infrequent user" or "abstainer"), mediated the effects of TSMHO attendance on substance use outcomes in our clinical sample of 18–24 years old emerging adults (Kelly, Stout, Greene, & Slaymaker, 2014). Results showed that increasing the number of low-risk friends and decreasing the number of high-risk friends from baseline to 6-month follow-up were strongly associated with more abstinence and less heavy drinking; however, AA attendance was *not* associated with these network changes.

In contrast, in Chi et al.'s (2009) study of adolescents through the transition to emerging adulthood, the authors found that adding the number of family members and friends who supported participants' abstinence (as well as religious service attendance) to a model testing the effect of TSMHO attendance on 30-day alcohol abstinence at 3 years reduced the effect of abstinence by more than 40%. This type of relationship between attendance, social support, and abstinence may suggest mediation. It is important to note that these models were not time-lagged, which is required to show mediation (e.g., the outcome is preceded in time by the mediator, which is preceded in time by the predictor). In fact, time-lagged effects of TSMHO attendance at 1 year on 3-year outcomes were nonsignificant, suggesting social network changes may not have been a true mediator of TSMHO effectiveness in this study either.

In addition to these more commonly tested mechanisms of TSMHO recovery, Blonigen, Timko, Finney, Moos, and Moos (2011) tested whether reduced impulsivity explained AA benefit among emerging adults (18–25 years) with alcohol use disorder and no previous SUD treatment recruited from a detoxification program or an SUD information and referral center. While reduced impulsivity has been studied comparatively less often than other TSMHO mechanisms (e.g., enhanced self-efficacy), it may be an appropriate target for investigation given its overlap with advice often heard in TSMHO meetings (e.g., "play the tape all the way through," meaning it is important to think through potential consequences of a decision before taking action). As Blonigen et al. hypothesized, decreased impulsivity did explain the effect of AA attendance on each of several outcomes: (1) reduced drinking consequences, (2) increased self-efficacy to resist drinking, (3) decreased emotional discharge coping (i.e., tension reduction–focused coping with the aim of avoiding the feeling), and (4) increased general social support in the same year. These mediation models adjusted for drinking changes, which suggests that the explanatory effect of reduced impulsivity is not accounted for simply by the impact of decreased

drinking on improved behavioral control (i.e., reduced impulsivity). It is important to note that although these results highlight reduced impulsivity as a potentially fruitful mechanism of emerging adults' TSMHO benefit worthy of further
investigation, the effects were not time-lagged as in Chi et al.'s (2009) study. The
limitations of mediation analyses that are not time-lagged such as these were
described earlier.

Comparison to Older Adults

Hoeppner et al. (2014) found that emerging adults were less likely than older
adults to increase their pro-abstinence networks via AA attendance. They were
also less likely to experience improved drinking outcomes through enhanced
self-efficacy to handle risky social situations and spirituality/religiosity. See
Figure 8.2 for differences between emerging adults and older adults in the
amount of variance of the AA effect on abstinence/drinking intensity for each
tested mechanism of behavior change. Importantly, 51% of older adults' AA
abstinence effect was explained by the full set of mediators (network changes,
negative affect and risky social situation self-efficacy, depression, and religios-
ity/spirituality) compared to just 36% for emerging adults. This difference was
even more pronounced for AA's effect on drinking intensity, accounting for 76%
of the effect in older adults, but only 22% in emerging adults. This finding suggests the model that explains AA benefit among adults may not fit as well for
emerging adults.

Regarding impulsivity, while this factor explained significant proportions of
the effect of AA attendance on positive outcomes for emerging adults, this was
not the case for older adults 44 years and older (Blonigen et al., 2011). As such,
reduced impulsivity may be an AA mechanism specific to the life stage of emerging adulthood.

Summary

TSMHO participation may help emerging adults to reduce *risky* substance-
using social network members, but it may not provide a forum to add *recovery-
supportive* social network members. The older age composition of TSMHOs, and
AA and NA in particular, with average ages of 48 and 43 years old, respectively
(Alcoholics Anonymous, 2012; Narcotics Anonymous World Services, 2016),
may limit the degree to which emerging adults can relate to other members and
their enthusiasm to develop relationships with such individuals. Although models
of AA recovery for adults more generally may not fit as well for emerging adults,
more recently delineated AA mechanisms, such as impulsivity, may further illu-
minate the TSMHO recovery experience during this life stage.

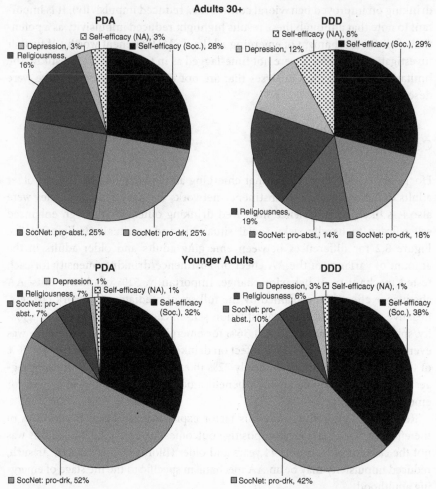

Figure 8.2 Differences between emerging adults (Younger Adults) and older adults (Adults 30+) on amount of variance in effect between AA and percent days abstinent (PDA) or drinks per drinking day (DDD) explained by each mechanism of behavior change: self efficacy to cope with negative affect (NA); self-efficacy to cope with risky social situations (Soc.); reduced pro-drinkers in one's social network (SocNet: pro-drk); increased pro-abstainers in one's social network (SocNet: pro-abst); increased religiosity/spirituality (religiousness); and decreased depression.

SOURCE OF DATA: Hoeppner, B. B., Hoeppner, S. S., & Kelly, J. F. (2014). Do young people benefit from AA as much, and in the same ways, as adult aged 30+? A moderated multiple mediation analysis. *Drug and Alcohol Dependence, 143,* 181–188. doi:10.1016/j.drugalcdep.2014.07.023

4. WHAT ARE THE FACTORS THAT INFLUENCE EMERGING ADULTS' PARTICIPATION AND PARTICIPATION-RELATED BENEFIT (MODERATORS)?

Studies highlighting moderators of MHO participation and benefit are organized next as a function of individual characteristics, meeting characteristics, and

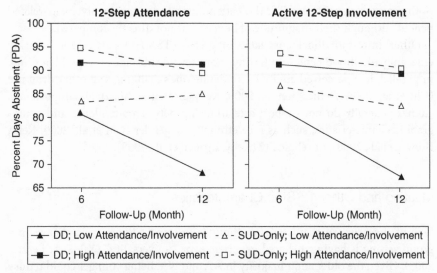

Figure 8.3 Percent days abstinent (PDA) for participants with co-occurring disorder, called dual diagnosis (DD), and those with substance use disorder only (SUD-only) as a function of median split TSMHO attendance (left) and active involvement (right). DD participants with high levels of attendance and involvement had outcomes similar to their high-attending SUD-only counterparts. DD participants with low levels of attendance and involvement had the poorest outcomes among all four groups.
SOURCE: Bergman, B. G., Greene, M. C., Hoeppner, B. B., Slaymaker, V., & Kelly, J. F. (2014). Psychiatric comorbidity and 12-step participation: A longitudinal investigation of treated young adults. *Alcoholism: Clinical and Experimental Research, 38*(2), 501–510. doi:10.1111/acer.12249. Reprinted with permission from John Wiley & Sons.

qualitative studies. The latter group of studies helps complement the primarily quantitative body of work in the area.

Individual Characteristics

Using the Kelly et al. sample of emerging adults (2013), we showed that participants with co-occurring mood and anxiety disorders (47% of the sample; determined by structured clinical interview) had similar rates of TSMHO attendance and active involvement across the post-treatment year (Bergman, Greene, Hoeppner, Slaymaker, & Kelly, 2014). Interestingly, as illustrated in Figure 8.3, despite poorer abstinence rates at 6- and 12-month follow-ups overall, the individuals with co-occurring disorders who had high active involvement (five or more activities out of eight) had abstinence rates similar to those of their SUD-only peers. As such, emerging adults with mild to moderate co-occurring disorders may benefit more from higher levels of active involvement. Chi, Sterling, Campbell, and Weisner (2013) found that adolescents with a co-occurring disorder as determined by clinical chart review (55% of the sample, including major depressive, conduct, attention-deficit hyperactivity, anxiety, psychotic, personality, and eating disorders) were *more* likely to attend 10+ meetings and to engage in 3+ activities at 1- and 3-year follow-ups (but not 5- and 7-year follow-ups).

Both groups demonstrated TSMHO attendance and active involvement-related benefit, although their magnitude of benefit was not directly compared.

Other intra-individual correlates of greater TSMHO participation during emerging adulthood center on having more severe substance use problems and, in parallel, less perceived ability to moderate one's drinking and other drug use (Chi et al., 2009; Delucchi et al., 2008; Kelly, Brown, et al., 2008). Importantly, studies generally do not support a relationship between attendance and demographic characteristics, such as race/ethnicity or gender (Chi et al., 2009; Kelly, Brown, et al., 2008), or religiosity (Kelly, Brown, et al., 2008).

Meeting and Other 12-Step Characteristics

One of the primary characteristics thought to impact therapeutic change in a group setting is having a shared experience, or "universality" (Yalom & Leszcz, 2005). Given the older adult majority in AA and NA, being younger could reduce this emotional connection for emerging adults and influence rates of participation and benefit. Measured by a categorical variable assessing the proportion of individuals present at meetings attended most often that were "about your age," attending meetings with similarly aged individuals was associated with better abstinence rates, particularly for individuals who were perhaps "on the fence" about AA/NA, attending fewer meetings overall (Labbe, Greene, Bergman, Hoeppner, & Kelly, 2013). The importance of this finding is magnified because one-third to one-half of participants reported *none* of the members were about their age. However, those who continued to attend meetings with similarly aged peers had *worse* outcomes than those who attended meetings with older individuals by 12-month follow-up. A very similar dynamic pattern of relationships between meeting age composition and better outcomes was also found in a younger adolescent sample (Kelly, Myers, & Brown, 2005).

For patients whose primary substance is a drug (i.e., other than alcohol) the explicit alcohol focus in AA compared with the broader drug/substance focus in NA (Alcoholics Anonymous, 1981, 2001; Narcotics Anonymous, 1993, 2008) could also reduce the therapeutic benefits of connecting with individuals around a shared, universal experience. Contrary to this hypothesis, however, our study did *not* show a matching effect for those emerging adults reporting a primary substance other than alcohol (e.g., opioids, stimulants, marijuana—referred to as "primary drug patients"; Kelly, Greene, & Bergman, 2014). Specifically, for these primary drug patients, a variable coding whether or not they attended more AA than NA in the first 3 months after treatment discharge did *not* predict subsequent participation in, and benefit derived from, TSMHOs at 6- and 12-month follow-ups. While primary opioid and primary stimulant patients were more likely to attend NA than primary alcohol patients, all groups attended a similar number of AA meetings (~80% of total TSMHO meetings), on average, across the post-treatment year. Potential explanations for these findings include (a) the common co-occurrence of alcohol and other drug use disorders (i.e., 62%–80% of these "primary drug" patients also met lifetime criteria for an alcohol use disorder) and (b) the conceptualization of their difficulties as "addiction" more generally, rather than addiction to any particular substance or group of substances. Both of these factors could help facilitate therapeutic processes of universality and cohesiveness (Yalom & Leszcz, 2005) among group members.

Finally, we have shown that having a sponsor, contact with one's sponsor, and the relationship between sponsor and sponsee ("sponsor alliance") are related to TSMHO attendance and active involvement (with the sponsor variables removed) during the same time period over the post-treatment year (Kelly et al., 2016). Because these behaviors were measured during the same time period, however, whether a positive sponsor experience is part of a general pattern of positive engagement in and attitudes toward TSMHOs or helps facilitate ongoing TSMHO participation should be disentangled in future studies.

Qualitative Studies

Also using the Kelly et al. (2013) sample, our group coded participants' responses to several open-ended questions regarding 12-step participation (Figure 8.4; Labbe, Slaymaker, & Kelly, 2014). Helpful aspects of meetings were coded on the basis of Yalom's group therapeutic factors (Yalom & Leszcz, 2005). As shown in Figure 8.4, results showed participants' responses were most often consistent with factors relating to universality/cohesion (43%) and installation of hope (24%). On the other hand, meeting structure (25%) and having to motivate oneself to attend (15%) were most commonly reported as aspects they disliked, while logistical barriers (30%) and low recovery motivation (22%) were the most frequently cited reasons for discontinued attendance. Having the perception that one did not have a substance use problem or need treatment was the most frequently cited reason for never attending (41%). This pattern of results was consistent with a similar systematic qualitative study with adolescents (Kelly, Myers, & Rodolico, 2008).

Among a nonclinical sample recruited from a small liberal arts college and the surrounding community, interviews with 26 emerging adults (18–28 years old) who attended at least one AA or NA meeting (Kingston, Knight, Williams, & Gordon, 2015) showed that many of the participants viewed TSMHOs favorably. However, those who had unfavorable attitudes were opposed to the concepts of powerlessness and reliance on a higher power in the TSMHO literature, as well as the slogans.

Comparison to Older Adults

To date, no studies have directly compared emerging adults and older adults on factors that influence participation in and benefit from MHOs.

What Young Adults Found *Most Helpful* about Attending 12-Step Meetings[a]		What Young Adults *Liked Least* about Attending 12-Step Meetings	
• Universality/Cohesiveness	42.9%	• Structure of Meetings	24.9%
• Instillation of Hope	23.5%	• Motivation and Interest	14.9%
• Altruism	12.6%	• Other Group Members	14.4%
• Other	11.6%	• Age Differences	10.4%
• Catharsis	9.6%	• Logistical Barriers	8.5%
		• Other	7.5%
		• Nothing	7.0%
		• 12-Step Specific Content	7.0%
		• Social Anxiety	5.5%
		• Unhelpful	1.0%

Responses to open-ended questions regarding young adults' 12-step attendance

Reasons Why Young Adults *Discontinued* 12-Step Attendance		Reasons Why Young Adults *Never Attended* 12-Step Meetings	
• Logistical Barriers	29.9%	• No Perceived Need or Problem	41.0%
• Not a Priority/Lack of Motivation	22.4%	• Other	18.8%
• Relapse/Not Intent on Sobriety	20.9%	• Lack of Knowledge	15.3%
• Unhelpful	7.5%	• Lack of Interest	15.3%
• Other Group Members	7.5%	• Perceived Inability to Relate to Other Members	5.6%
• Other	6.0%	• 12-Step Specific Factors	4.2%
• In Jail	3.0%		
• Age Differences	3.0%		

Figure 8.4 Categories of qualitative responses to open-ended interview questions.
[a]Participant responses to this question were coded on the basis of how well they fit within Yalom's group therapeutic factors (Yalom & Leszcz, 2005).
NOTE: Adapted and compiled from figures and tables in Labbe, A. K., Slaymaker, V., & Kelly, J. F. (2014). Toward enhancing 12-step facilitation among young people: A systematic qualitative investigation of young adults' 12-step experiences. *Substance Abuse, 35*(4), 399–407. doi:10.1080/08897077.2014.950001.

Summary

Like older adults (Ouimette et al., 2001; Timko, Cronkite, McKellar, Zemore, & Moos, 2013), emerging adults with a mild to moderate co-occurring psychiatric disorder (i.e., nonpsychotic) may attend as much or more than their SUD-only counterparts. These emerging adult data are also consistent with findings in large, naturalistic adolescent SUD treatment studies (Grella, Hser, Joshi, & Rounds-Bryant, 2001). However, the influence of chronic major depressive disorder and psychotic disorders, which may negatively impact one's ability to engage with the social milieu (Bogenschutz & Akin, 2000; Kelly, McKellar, & Moos, 2003), have not yet been examined. Finally, engaging with meetings that have high proportions of other emerging adults and finding a compatible sponsor early in a treatment/recovery episode may promote subsequent recovery benefit. Taken together, these data suggest it may be helpful for emerging adults to engage with young adult–specific meetings initially and to branch out to meetings with older, perhaps more experienced individuals who could serve as recovery mentors over time. Clinical interventions may be needed to facilitate these TSMHO activities among emerging adults and to help them explore their opposition to TSMHO terminology and concepts, in the context of any perceived social advantages of the MHO milieu.

SUMMARY, CLINICAL IMPLICATIONS, AND FUTURE RESEARCH DIRECTIONS

The quantity and quality of the empirical research on TSMHOs and clinical treatments that facilitate TSMHO participation (e.g., 12-step facilitation; TSF) have increased substantially during the past 25 years. This body of literature now reveals that AA in particular and TSF approaches are effective and cost-effective recovery support services (Humphreys & Moos, 2001, 2007; Humphreys et al., 2004; Kelly & Yeterian, 2012; Mundt, Parthasarathy, Chi, Sterling, & Campbell, 2012). Furthermore, dozens of studies have found that AA mobilizes the same kinds of therapeutic changes that are mobilized by professional treatments (Kelly, 2017; Kelly, Hoeppner, Stout, & Pagano, 2012; Kelly, Magill, & Stout, 2009) yet can do this for free over the long term in the communities in which people live. In addition, individuals may use AA differently to derive benefit, depending on their age (Hoeppner et al., 2014), gender (Kelly & Hoeppner, 2013), and level of SUD severity (Kelly, Hoeppner, et al., 2012). The widespread availability and, in parallel, ease of accessibility of AA and other TSMHOs suggest that these organizations serve a valuable role as adaptive and flexible community-based recovery support services (Kelly, 2017; Kelly & Yeterian, 2008). That said, despite being an almost universal treatment referral and continuing care recommendation for young people (Drug Strategies, 2003; Kelly, Yeterian, & Myers, 2008; Knudsen, Ducharme, Roman, & Johnson, 2008), relatively little research has been conducted specifically on emerging adults. While based on a limited number of studies to date, this review suggests emerging adults benefit from TSMHO participation as much as older adults. Also like older adults, having a sponsor may be an especially valuable TSMHO activity in terms of increased abstinence. Our review identified six broad gaps in the clinical literature on their MHO participation, which may be addressed by future research as outlined next.

First, most of the evidence for TSMHO participation and benefit among emerging adults comes from more severe clinical inpatient or residential treatment samples that strongly encouraged and facilitated TSMHO participation both during and following treatment. As such, future research should attempt to replicate these findings in outpatient samples.

Second, TSFs have not yet been tested specifically for emerging adults. Future research should help determine whether TSF interventions need to be developed that expressly target individuals in this life stage or whether straightforward implementation of existing TSFs already found to be efficacious for older adults (Kaskutas, Subbaraman, Withrodt, & Zemore, 2009; Litt, Kadden,

Kabela-Cormier, & Petry, 2009; Project MATCH Research Group, 1997) can be used with minimal modification. If emerging adult–specific TSF is needed, several factors from existing research should be considered: (1) treatments may emphasize facilitating attendance at young adult–specific TSMHO meetings early on and branching out to general meetings to connect with recovery mentors near the end of the intervention; (2) treatments may target emerging adults' motivation to meet people with similar experiences to whom they can relate and with whom they might share a personal bond; and (3) like TSFs designed for adults more generally, they may also help emerging adults explore attitudes regarding powerlessness and higher power concepts present in the TSMHO cultural ethos.

Third, research on non-12-step MHOs, such as SMART Recovery, is notably absent from the scientific literature on emerging adults' MHO participation. This research gap is not unique to these invidiuals. Data on whether non-12-step options are an evidence-based community resource for individuals with SUD of all ages is needed to "broaden the base" of MHO research (Kelly & White, 2012). However, these data may be particularly relevant for emerging adults, as younger individuals tend to have lower levels of spirituality (Brown, Chen, Gehlert, & Piedmont, 2013). Thus, the spiritual terminology present in TSMHO meetings and core readings could be a barrier to TSMHO attendance for emerging adults. Future research might inform the degree to which they participate in and benefit from non-12-step MHOs and whether this differs from TSMHOs.

The fourth gap in the literature is related to the prominence of emerging adults with opioid use disorder in SUD treatment. Specifically, the Treatment Episode Data Set (SAMHSA, 2014b) shows that 40%–45% of emerging adults will present to SUD treatment with heroin or another opioid as their primary substance. Although not specific to emerging adults, a common concern regarding abstinence-based TSMHO participation and clinical referrals to them centers on opioid-addicted individuals who are taking agonist therapies such as buprenorphine/naloxone (known by its brand name Suboxone) or methadone. An important distinction between taking these opioid agonist medications and opioid use underlying the disorder for which individuals are seeking treatment, is that the medications are longer-acting, with pharmacological ceiling effects to dampen any euphoric experience. Despite a substantial body of scientific literature supporting the abstinence-related and other health benefits of these empirically supported medicines (Hser et al., 2016; Mattick, Breen, Kimber, & Davoli, 2014; Weiss et al., 2015), patients on opioid agonist medications can encounter resistance and stigma in recovery. Individuals taking agonist medication may be viewed by TSMHO members as "not in recovery," or "substituting one drug for another." This may be particularly true in groups like NA, where individuals are not permitted to fully engage with the organization while on these medications (Narcotics Anonymous World Services, 1996, 2007). Very little research has been conducted on this issue to date, although a recent study reported a therapeutic benefit and synergy among these different recovery approaches (i.e., opioid agonist medication-and abstinence-focused TSMHO participation) (Monico et al., 2015). Given this prevalence of primary opioid, emerging adult patients in SUD treatment settings and the precipitous increase of opioid overdoses especially in this age group (NIDA/SAMHSA Blending Initiative, 2012), further research is very much needed to help determine whether and how these professional and pharmacological and community-based resources might best be combined for maximum recovery benefit.

Fifth, more work needs to be done on similarities and differences between models of emerging adult and older adult MHO recovery. To date, research suggests that models of how MHO participation works for older adults may not be as well suited for emerging adults (Bergman, Kelly, Nargiso, et al., 2016; Hoeppner et al., 2014). Future research in the area may benefit from including relatively novel constructs like impulsivity (Blonigen et al., 2011). Related to social network changes, future work might also test whether emerging adults do, in fact, add recovery-supportive individuals to their social networks via TSMHOs if they attend primarily young adult–focused meetings.

Finally, the proliferation of online social network sites, such as Facebook and Instagram, have spawned a wave of digital communities that cater to individuals in or seeking recovery from SUD. For example, InTheRooms.com combines the functionality of social network sites with the recovery resources and recovery-supportive individuals present in TSMHOs (Bergman, Kelly, Cristello, Sylvia, & Kelly, 2016). To date, however, little is known empirically about these modern social-recovery resources. Particularly given how prominent social network sites are in the day-to-day experiences of emerging adults (Perrin, 2015), the clinical and public health utilities of these recovery-specific social network sites for emerging adults will be important to investigate. For more information on the role of social network sites and other innovations in SUD prevention and treatment among emerging adults, see Chapter 12 in this volume.

In conclusion, research has shown that emerging adults face several challenges in their recovery from SUD, many of which are related to the saturation of their social networks with drinkers and drug users and a lower availability of recovery-supportive peers and environments (Bergman, Kelly, Nargiso, et al., 2016). MHOs could provide a rich milieu of socially derived recovery support. While emerging adults benefit from TSMHO participation, clinical interventions may be needed to increase their levels of participation, which lags behind that of older adults. Overall, poorer fits of older adult MHO models suggest novel and innovative constructs and platforms may enhance our understanding of emerging adult experiences in MHOs. As clinical research increasingly targets and illuminates MHO-related recovery during this life stage, clinicians may be better positioned to help their emerging adult patients benefit from these widely accessible, community-based recovery support services.

REFERENCES

Alcoholics Anonymous. (1981). *Twelve steps and twelve traditions.* New York: Alcoholics Anonymous World Services.

Alcoholics Anonymous. (2001). *Alcoholics Anonymous: The story of how many thousands of men and women have recovered from alcoholism* (4th ed.). New York: Alcoholics Anonymous World Services.

Alcoholics Anonymous. (2012). *2011 membership survey.* New York: Alcoholics Anonymous World Services.

American Psychiatric Association (2000). *Diagnostic and Statistical Manual of Mental Disorders,* fourth edition. Washington, DC: Author.

American Psychiatric Association. (2010). *Practice guidelines for the treatment of patients with substance use disorders, second edition.* Retrieved from http://psychiatryonline. org/pb/assets/raw/sitewide/practice_guidelines/guidelines/substanceuse.pdf

Arnett, J. J. (2015). *Emerging adulthood: The winding road from the late teens through the twenties* (2nd ed.). New York: Oxford University Press.

Arnett, J. J., Žukauskienė, R., & Sugimura, K. (2014). The new life stage of emerging adulthood at ages 18–29 years: Implications for mental health. *Lancet Psychiatry, 1*(7), 569–576. doi: 10.1016/s2215-0366(14)00080-7

Bennett, M. E., McCrady, B. S., Keller, D. S., & Paulus, M. D. (1996). An intensive program for collegiate substance abusers: Progress six months after treatment entry. *Journal of Substance Abuse Treatment, 13*(3), 219–225. doi: 10.1016/S0740-5472(96)00045-1

Bergman, B. G., Greene, M. C., Hoeppner, B. B., Slaymaker, V., & Kelly, J. F. (2014). Psychiatric comorbidity and 12-step participation: A longitudinal investigation of treated young adults. *Alcoholism: Clinical and Experimental Research, 38*(2), 501–510. doi: 10.1111/acer.12249

Bergman, B. G., Hoeppner, B. B., Nelson, L. M., Slaymaker, V., & Kelly, J. F. (2015). The effects of continuing care on emerging adult outcomes following residential addiction treatment. *Drug and Alcohol Dependence, 153,* 207–214. doi: 10.1016/ j.drugalcdep.2015.05.017

Bergman, B. G., Kelly, J. F., Cristello, J. V., Sylvia, E. J., & Kelly, N. W. (2016). Social network sites: A "new wave" of electronic health research in emerging adult substance use disorder treatment and recovery? *The Addictions Newsletter,* Summer 2016.

Bergman, B. G., Kelly, J. F., Nargiso, J., & McKowen, J. (2016). "The age of feeling in-between": Addressing challenges in the treatment of emerging adults with substance use disorders. *Cognitive and Behavioral Practice, 23,* 270–288. doi: 10.1016/ j.cbpra.2015.09.008

Bergman, B. G., Kelly, N. W., Hoeppner, B. B., Vilsaint, C. L., & Kelly, J. F. (in press). Digital recovery management: Characterizing recovery-specific social network site participation and perceived benefit. *Psychology of Addictive Behaviors.* doi: 10.1037/ adb0000255

Blonigen, D. M., Timko, C., Finney, J. W., Moos, B. S., & Moos, R. H. (2011). Alcoholics Anonymous attendance, decreases in impulsivity and drinking and psychosocial outcomes over 16 years: Moderated-mediation from a developmental perspective. *Addiction, 106*(12), 2167–2177. doi: 10.1111/j.1360-0443.2011.03522.x

Bogenschutz, M. P., & Akin, S. J. (2000). 12-step participation and attitudes toward 12-step meetings in dual diagnosis patients. *Alcoholism Treatment Quarterly, 18*(4), 31–45. doi: 10.1300/J020v18n04_03

Borsari, B., & Carey, K. B. (2001). Peer influences on college drinking: A review of the research. *Journal of Substance Abuse, 13*(4), 391–424. doi: 10.1016/ S0899-3289(01)00098-0

Brown, I. T., Chen, T., Gehlert, N. C., & Piedmont, R. L. (2013). Age and gender effects on the Assessment of Spirituality and Religious Sentiments (ASPIRES) scale: A cross-sectional analysis. *Psychology of Religion and Spirituality*, 5(2), 90–98. doi: 10.1037/a0030137

Chi, F. W., Campbell, C. I., Sterling, S., & Weisner, C. (2012). Twelve-step attendance trajectories over 7 years among adolescents entering substance use treatment in an integrated health plan. *Addiction*, 107(5), 933–942. doi: 10.1111/j.1360-0443.2011.03758.x

Chi, F. W., Kaskutas, L. A., Sterling, S., Campbell, C. I., & Weisner, C. (2009). Twelve-step affiliation and 3-year substance use outcomes among adolescents: Social support and religious service attendance as potential mediators. *Addiction*, 104(6), 927–939. doi: 10.1111/j.1360-0443.2009.02524.x

Chi, F. W., Sterling, S., Campbell, C. I., & Weisner, C. (2013). Twelve-step participation and outcomes over seven years among adolescent substance use patients with and without psychiatric comorbidity. *Substance Abuse*, 34(1), 33–42.

Cloud, R. N., Ziegler, C. H., & Blondell, R. D. (2004). What is Alcoholics Anonymous Affiliation? *Substance Use and Misuse*, 39(7), 1117–1136. doi: 10.1081/JA-120038032

Connors, G. J., Tonigan, J. S., & Miller, W. R. (2001). A longitudinal model of intake symptomatology, AA participation and outcome: Retrospective study of the Project MATCH outpatient and aftercare samples. *Journal of Studies on Alcohol*, 62, 817–825.

Cook, S. H., Bauermeister, J. A., Gordon-Messer, D., & Zimmerman, M. A. (2013). Online network influences on emerging adults' alcohol and drug use. *Journal of Youth and Adolescence*, 42(11), 1674–1686. doi: 10.1007/s10964-012-9869-1

Delucchi, K. L., Matzger, H., & Weisner, C. (2008). Alcohol in emerging adulthood: 7-year study of problem and dependent drinkers. *Addictive Behaviors*, 33(1), 134–142. doi: 10.1016/j.addbeh.2007.04.027

Dennis, M., Scott, C. K., & Funk, R. (2003). An experimental evaluation of recovery management checkups (RMC) for people with chronic substance use disorders. *Evaluation and Program Planning*, 26, 339–352.

Dennis, M. L., Scott, C. K., Funk, R., & Foss, M. A. (2005). The duration and correlates of addiction and treatment careers. *Journal of Substance Abuse Treatment*, 28(Suppl1), S51–S62. doi: 10.1016/j.jsat.2004.10.013

Drug Strategies. (2003). *Treating teens: A guide to adolescent programs*. Washington, DC: Author.

Emrick, C. D., Tonigan, J. S., Montgomery, H., & Little, L. (1993). Alcoholics Anonymous: What is currently known? In B. S. McCrady & W. R. Miller (Eds.), *Research on Alcoholics Anonymous: Opportunities and alternatives* (pp. 41–76). Piscataway, NJ: Rutgers Center of Alcohol Studies.

Evans, E., Li, L., Grella, C., Brecht, M. L., & Hser, Y. I. (2013). Developmental timing of first drug treatment and 10-year patterns of drug use. *Journal of Substance Abuse Treatment*, 44(3), 271–279. doi: 10.1016/j.jsat.2012.07.012

Godley, M., Godley, S., Dennis, M., Funk, R., & Passetti, L. (2007). The effect of assertive continuing care on continuing care linkage, adherence and abstinence following residential treatment for adolescents with substance use disorders. *Addiction*, 102(1), 81–93.

Godley, M. D., Godley, S. H., Dennis, M. L., Funk, R. R., Passetti, L. L., & Petry, N. M. (2014). A randomized trial of assertive continuing care and contingency management for adolescents with substance use disorders. *Journal of Consulting and Clinical Psychology, 82*(1), 40–51. doi: 10.1037/a0035264

Godley, S. H., Garner, B. R., Passetti, L. L., Funk, R. R., Dennis, M. L., & Godley, M. D. (2010). Adolescent outpatient treatment and continuing care: Main findings from a randomized clinical trial. *Drug and Alcohol Dependence, 110*(1–2), 44–54. doi: 10.1016/j.drugalcdep.2010.02.003

Grant, B. F., Goldstein, R. B., Saha, T. D., Chou, S. P., Jung, J., Zhang, H., . . . Hasin, D. S. (2015). Epidemiology of DSM-5 alcohol use disorder: Results from the National Epidemiologic Survey on Alcohol and Related Conditions III. *JAMA Psychiatry.* doi: 10.1001/jamapsychiatry.2015.0584

Grant, B. F., Saha, T. D., Ruan, W. J., Goldstein, R. B., Chou, S. P., Jung, J., . . . Hasin, D. S. (2016). Epidemiology of DSM-5 drug use disorder: Results from the National Epidemiologic Survey on Alcohol and Related Conditions-III. *JAMA Psychiatry, 73*(1), 39–47. doi: 10.1001/jamapsychiatry.2015.2132

Grella, C. E., Hser, Y.-I., Joshi, V., & Rounds-Bryant, J. (2001). Drug treatment outcomes for adolescents with comorbid mental and substance use disorders. *Journal of Nervous and Mental Disease, 189*(6), 384–392. doi: 10.1097/00005053-200106000-00006

Hoeppner, B. B., Hoeppner, S. S., & Kelly, J. F. (2014). Do young people benefit from AA as much, and in the same ways, as adult aged 30 + ? A moderated multiple mediation analysis. *Drug and Alcohol Dependence, 143*, 181–188. doi: 10.1016/j.drugalcdep.2014.07.023

Horvath, A. O., & Greenberg, L. S. (1989). Development and validation of the Working Alliance Inventory. *Journal of Counseling Psychology, 36*, 223–233.

Hser, Y. I., Evans, E., Huang, D., Weiss, R., Saxon, A., Carroll, K. M., . . . Ling, W. (2016). Long-term outcomes after randomization to buprenorphine/naloxone versus methadone in a multi-site trial. *Addiction, 111*(4), 695–705. doi: 10.1111/add.13238

Humphreys, K. (2004). *Circles of recovery: Self-help organizations for addictions.* Cambridge, UK: Cambridge University Press.

Humphreys, K., Blodgett, J. C., & Wagner, T. H. (2014). Estimating the efficacy of Alcoholics Anonymous without self-selection bias: An instrumental variables reanalysis of randomized clinical trials. *Alcoholism: Clinical and Experimental Research, 38*(11), 2688–2694. doi: 10.1111/acer.12557

Humphreys, K., Kaskutas, L. A., & Weisner, C. (1998). The Alcoholics Anonymous Affiliation Scale: Development, reliability, and norms for diverse treated and untreated populations. *Alcoholism: Clinical and Experimental Research, 22*(5), 974–978. doi: 10.1111/j.1530-0277.1998.tb03691.x

Humphreys, K., & Moos, R. (2001). Can encouraging substance abuse patients to participate in self-help groups reduce demand for health care? A quasi-experimental study. *Alcoholism: Clinical and Experimental Research, 25*(5), 711–716.

Humphreys, K., & Moos, R. H. (2007). Encouraging posttreatment self-help group involvement to reduce demand for continuing care services: Two-year clinical and utilization outcomes. *Alcoholism: Clinical and Experimental Research, 31*(1), 64–68. doi: 10.1111/j.1530-0277.2006.00273.x

Humphreys, K., Wing, S., McCarty, D., Chappel, J., Gallant, L., Haberle, B., . . . Weiss, R. (2004). Self-help organizations for alcohol and drug problems: Toward evidence-based practice and policy. *Journal of Substance Abuse Treatment, 26*, 151–158. doi: 10.1016/S0740-5472(03)00212-5

Hunt, W. A., Barnett, L. W., & Branch, L. G. (1971). Relapse rates in addiction programs. *Journal of Clinical Psychology*, *27*(4), 455–456.

Kaskutas, L. A. (2009). Alcoholics Anonymous effectiveness: Faith meets science. *Journal of Addictive Diseases*, *28*(2), 145–157.

Kaskutas, L. A., Subbaraman, M. S., Withrodt, J., & Zemore, S. E. (2009). Effectiveness of making Alcoholics Anonymous easier: A group format 12-step facilitation approach. *Journal of Substance Abuse Treatment*, *37*, 228–239. doi: 10.1016/j.jsat.2009.01.004

Kelly, J. F. (2017). Is Alcoholics Anonymous religious, spiritual, neither? Findings from 25 years of mechanisms of behavior change research. *Addiction*, *112*(6), 929–936. doi: 10.1111/add.13590

Kelly, J. F., Brown, S. A., Abrantes, A., Kahler, C. W., & Myers, M. (2008). Social recovery model: An 8-year investigation of adolescent 12-step group involvement following inpatient treatment. *Alcoholism: Clinical and Experimental Research*, *32*, 1468–1478. doi: 10.1111/j.1530-0277.2008.00712.x

Kelly, J. F., Greene, M. C., & Bergman, B. G. (2014). Do drug-dependent patients attending Alcoholics Anonymous rather than Narcotics Anonymous do as well? A prospective, lagged, matching analysis. *Alcohol and Alcoholism*, *49*(6), 645–653. doi: 10.1093/alcalc/agu066

Kelly, J. F., Greene, M. C., & Bergman, B. G. (2016). Recovery benefits of the "therapeutic alliance" among 12-step mutual-help organization attendees and their sponsors. *Drug and Alcohol Dependence*, *162*, 64–71. doi: 10.1016/j.drugalcdep.2016.02.028

Kelly, J. F., & Hoeppner, B. B. (2013). Does Alcoholics Anonymous work differently for men and women? A moderated multiple-mediation analysis in a large clinical sample. *Drug and Alcohol Dependence*, *130*(1-3), 186–193. doi: 10.1016/j.drugalcdep.2012.11.005

Kelly, J. F., Hoeppner, B., Stout, R. L., & Pagano, M. (2012). Determining the relative importance of the mechanisms of behavior change within Alcoholics Anonymous: A multiple mediator analysis. *Addiction*, *107*(2), 289–299. doi: 10.1111/j.1360-0443.2011.03593.x

Kelly, J. F., Magill, M., & Stout, R. L. (2009). How do people recover from alcohol dependence? A systematic review of the research on mechanisms of behavior change in Alcoholics Anonymous. *Addiction Research & Theory*, *17*(3), 236–259. doi: 10.1080/16066350902770458

Kelly, J. F., McKellar, J. D., & Moos, R. (2003). Major depression in patients with substance use disorders: Relationship to 12-Step self-help involvement and substance use outcomes. *Addiction*, *98*(4), 499–508. doi: 10.1046/j.1360-0443.2003.t01-1-00294.x

Kelly, J. F., & Myers, M. G. (2007). Adolescents' participation in Alcoholics Anonymous and Narcotics Anonymous: Review, implications and future directions. *Journal of Psychoactive Drugs*, *39*(3), 259–269. doi: 10.1080/02791072.2007.10400612

Kelly, J. F., Myers, M. G., & Brown, S. A. (2005). The effects of age composition of 12-step groups on adolescent 12-step participation and substance use outcome. *Journal of Child & Adolescent Substance Abuse*, *15*(1), 63–72. doi: 10.1300/J029v15n01_05

Kelly, J. F., Myers, M. G., & Rodolico, J. (2008). What do adolescents exposed to Alcoholics Anonymous think about 12-step groups? *Substance Abuse*, *29*(2), 53–62. doi: 10.1080/08897070802093122

Kelly, J. F., Stout, R. L., Greene, M. C., & Slaymaker, V. (2014). Young adults, social networks, and addiction recovery: Post-treatment changes in social ties and their role as a mediator of 12-step participation. *PLoS ONE, 9*(6), e100121. doi: 10.1371/journal.pone.0100121

Kelly, J. F., Stout, R. L., & Slaymaker, V. (2013). Emerging adults' treatment outcomes in relation to 12-step mutual-help attendance and involvement. *Drug and Alcohol Dependence, 129*(1-2), 151–157. doi: 10.1016/j.drugalcdep.2012.10.005

Kelly, J. F., Urbanoski, K. A., Hoeppner, B. B., & Slaymaker, V. (2011). Facilitating comprehensive assessment of 12-step experiences: A Multidimensional Measure of Mutual-Help Activity. *Alcoholism Treatment Quarterly, 29*(3), 181–203. doi: 10.1080/07347324.2011.586280

Kelly, J. F., Urbanoski, K. A., Hoeppner, B. B., & Slaymaker, V. (2012). "Ready, willing, and (not) able" to change: Young adults' response to residential treatment. *Drug and Alcohol Dependence, 121*(3), 224–230. doi: 10.1016/j.drugalcdep.2011.09.003

Kelly, J. F., & White, W. L. (2011). Recovery management and the future of addiction treatment and recovery in the USA. In J. F. Kelly, & W. L. White (Eds.), *Addiction recovery management: Theory, research and practice.* (pp. 303–316). Totowa, NJ: Humana Press.

Kelly, J. F., & White, W. L. (2012). Broadening the base of addiction mutual-help organizations. *Journal of Groups in Addiction & Recovery, 7*(2-4), 82–101. doi: 10.1080/1556035X.2012.705646

Kelly, J. F., & Yeterian, J. D. (2008). Mutual-help groups. In W. T. O'Donohue & N. A. Cummings (Eds.), *Evidence-based adjunctive treatments* (pp. 61–105). San Diego: Academic Press.

Kelly, J. F., & Yeterian, J. D. (2012). Empirical awakening: The new science on mutual help and implications for cost containment under health care reform. *Substance Abuse, 33*, 85–91. doi: 10.1080/08897077.2011.634965

Kelly, J. F., Yeterian, J. D., & Myers, M. G. (2008). Treatment staff referrals, participation expectations, and perceived benefits and barriers to adolescent involvement in twelve-step groups. *Alcoholism Treatment Quarterly, 26*(4), 427–449. doi: 10.1080/07347320802347053

Kingston, S., Knight, E., Williams, J., & Gordon, H. (2015). How do young adults view 12-step programs? A qualitative study. *Journal of Addictive Diseases, 34*(4), 311–322. doi: 10.1080/10550887.2015.1074506

Knudsen, H. K., Ducharme, L. J., Roman, P. M., & Johnson, J. A. (2008). *Service delivery and use of evidence-based treatment practices in adolescent substance abuse treatment settings.* Retrieved from http://ntcs.uga.edu/reports/Adolescent%20Study%20Summary%20Report

Labbe, A. K., Greene, C., Bergman, B. G., Hoeppner, B., & Kelly, J. F. (2013). The importance of age composition of 12-step meetings as a moderating factor in the relation between young adults' 12-step participation and abstinence. *Drug and Alcohol Dependence, 133*(2), 541–547. doi: 10.1016/j.drugalcdep.2013.07.021

Labbe, A. K., Slaymaker, V., & Kelly, J. F. (2014). Toward enhancing 12-step facilitation among young people: A systematic qualitative investigation of young adults' 12-step experiences. *Substance Abuse, 35*(4), 399–407. doi: 10.1080/08897077.2014.950001

Litt, M. D., Kadden, R. M., Kabela-Cormier, E., & Petry, N. M. (2009). Changing network support for drinking: Network support project 2-year follow-up. *Journal of Consulting and Clinical Psychology, 77*(2), 229–242. doi: 10.1037/a0015252

Magura, S., McKean, J., Kosten, S., & Tonigan, J. S. (2013). A novel application of propensity score matching to estimate Alcoholics Anonymous' effect on drinking outcomes. *Drug and Alcohol Dependence, 129*(1-2), 54–59. doi: 10.1016/j.drugalcdep.2012.09.011

Makela, K., Arminen, I., Bloomfield, K., Eisenbach-Stangl, I., Bergmark, K. H., Kurube, N., . . . Zielinski, A. (1996). *Alcoholics Anonymous as a mutual-help movement: A study in eight societies.* Madison, WI: University of Wisconsin Press.

Mason, M. J., & Luckey, B. (2003). Young adults in alcohol-other drug treatment: An understudied population. *Alcoholism Treatment Quarterly, 21*(1), 17–32. doi: 10.1300/J020v21n01_02

Mattick, R. P., Breen, C., Kimber, J., & Davoli, M. (2014). Buprenorphine maintenance versus placebo or methadone maintenance for opioid dependence. *Cochrane Database of Systematic Reviews, 2,* Cd002207. doi: 10.1002/14651858.CD002207.pub4

McKay, J. R. (2010). *Treating substance use disorders with adaptive continuing care.* Washington DC: American Psychological Association.

Miller, W. R., & Wilbourne, P. L. (2002). Mesa Grande: A methodological analysis of clinical trials of treatments for alcohol use disorders. *Addiction, 97*(3), 265–277. doi: 019 [pii]

Monico, L. B., Gryczynski, J., Mitchell, S. G., Schwartz, R. P., O'Grady, K. E., & Jaffe, J. H. (2015). Buprenorphine treatment and 12-step meeting attendance: Conflicts, compatibilities, and patient outcomes. *Journal of Substance Abuse Treatment, 57,* 89–95. doi: 10.1016/j.jsat.2015.05.005

Montgomery, H. A., Miller, W. R., & Tonigan, J. S. (1995). Does Alcoholics Anonymous involvement predict treatment outcome? *Journal of Substance Abuse Treatment, 12*(4), 241–246. doi: 10.1016/0740-5472(95)00018-z

Moos, R. H. (2008). How and why twelve-step self-help groups are effective. In M. Galanter & L. A. Kaskutas (Eds.), *Research on Alcoholics Anonymous and spirituality in addiction recovery. Recent developments in alcoholism* (pp. 393–412). New York: Springer Science + Business Media.

Morgenstern, J., Labouvie, E., McCrady, B. S., Kahler, C. W., & Frey, R. M. (1997). Affiliation with Alcoholics Anonymous after treatment: A study of its therapeutic effects and mechanisms of action. *Journal of Consulting and Clinical Psychology, 65*(5), 768–779.

Mundt, M. P., Parthasarathy, S., Chi, F. W., Sterling, S., & Campbell, C. I. (2012). 12-step participation reduces medical use costs among adolescents with a history of alcohol and other drug treatment. *Drug and Alcohol Dependence, 126*(1-2), 124–130. doi: 10.1016/j.drugalcdep.2012.05.002

Narcotics Anonymous. (1993). *It works: How and why: The twelve steps and twelve traditions of Narcotics Anonymous.* Chatsworth, CA: Narcotics Anonymous World Services.

Narcotics Anonymous. (2008). *Narcotics Anonymous* (6th ed.). Chatsworth, CA: Narcotics Anonymous World Services.

Narcotics Anonymous World Services. (1996). *Bulletin #29: Regarding methadone and other drug replacement programs.* Retrieved from https://www.na.org/?ID=bulletins-bull29

Narcotics Anonymous World Services. (2007). *NA groups & medication.* Retrieved from https://www.na.org/admin/include/spaw2/uploads/pdf/servicemat/Dec2011_NA_Groups_and_Medication.pdf

Narcotics Anonymous World Services. (2016). Narcotics Anonymous 2015 membership survey.

NIDA/SAMHSA Blending Initiative. (2012). *Buprenorphine treatment for young adults.* Retrieved from http://www.drugabuse.gov/sites/default/files/files/BupTx_YngAdlts_Factsheet.pdf

Ouimette, P., Humphreys, K., Moos, R. H., Finney, J. W., Cronkite, R., & Federman, B. (2001). Self-help group participation among substance use disorder patients with posttraumatic stress disorder. *Journal of Substance Abuse Treatment, 20,* 25–32. doi: 10.1016/S0740-5472(00)00150-1

Perrin, A. (2015). *Social networking usage: 2005–2015.* Retrieved from http://www.pewinternet.org/2015/10/08/2015/Social-Networking-Usage-2005-2015/

Prendergast, M. L., Podus, D., Chang, E., & Urada, D. (2002). The effectiveness of drug abuse treatment: A meta-analysis of comparison group studies. *Drug and Alcohol Dependence, 67*(1), 53–72. doi: 10.1016/s0376-8716(02)00014-5

Project MATCH Research Group. (1997). Matching Alcoholism Treatments to Client Heterogeneity: Project MATCH posttreatment drinking outcomes. *Journal of Studies on Alcohol, 58*(1), 7–29. doi: 10.1046/j.1360-0443.1997.9212167110.x

Rosenstock, I. M. (1990). The health belief model: Explaining health behavior through expectancies. In K. Glanz, F. M. Lewis, & B. K. Rimer (Eds.), *Health behavior and health education: Theory, research, and practice* (pp. 39–62). San Francisco: Jossey-Bass.

Satre, D. D., Chi, F. W., Mertens, J. R., & Weisner, C. M. (2012). Effects of age and life transitions on alcohol and drug treatment outcome over nine years. *Journal of Studies on Alcohol and Drugs, 73*(3), 459–468.

Satre, D. D., Mertens, J. R., Arean, P. A., & Weisner, C. (2004). Five-year alcohol and drug treatment outcomes of older adults versus middle-aged and younger adults in a managed care program. *Addiction, 99*(10), 1286–1297. doi: 10.1111/j.1360-0443.2004.00831.x

Stoddard, S. A., Bauermeister, J. A., Gordon-Messer, D., Johns, M., & Zimmerman, M. A. (2012). Permissive norms and young adults' alcohol and marijuana use: The role of online communities. *Journal of Studies on Alcohol and Drugs, 73*(6), 968–975.

Substance Abuse and Mental Health Services Administration (SAMHSA). (2014a). *Results from the 2013 National Survey on Drug Use and Health: Summary of National Findings.* NSDUH Series H-48, HHS Publication No. (SMA) 14–4863. Rockville, MD: Author.

Substance Abuse and Mental Health Services Administration (SAMHSA). (2014b). *Treatment Episode Data Set (TEDS). 2002-2012. National Admissions to Substance Abuse Treatment Services.* BHSIS Series: S-71, HHS Publication No. (SMA) 14–4850. Rockville, MD: Author.

Timko, C., Cronkite, R. C., McKellar, J., Zemore, S., & Moos, R. H. (2013). Dually diagnosed patients' benefits of mutual-help groups and the role of social anxiety. *Journal of Substance Abuse Treatment, 44,* 216–223. doi: 10.1016/j.jsat.2012.05.007

Tonigan, J. S., & Rice, S. L. (2010). Is it beneficial to have an alcoholics anonymous sponsor? *Psychology of Addictive Behaviors, 24*(3), 397–403. doi: 10.1037/a0019013

Tonigan, J. S., Toscova, R., & Miller, W. R. (1996). Meta-analysis of the literature on Alcoholics Anonymous: Sample and study characteristics moderate findings. *Journal of the Study of Alcoholism, 57,* 65–72.

Weisner, C., Matzger, H., & Kaskutas, L. A. (2003). How important is treatment? One-year outcomes of treated and untreated alcohol-dependent individuals. *Addiction*, *98*(7), 901–911.

Weiss, R. D., Griffin, M. L., Gallop, R. J., Najavits, L. M., Frank, A., Crits-Christoph, P., . . . Luborsky, L. (2005). The effect of 12-step self-help group attendance and participation on drug use outcomes among cocaine-dependent patients. *Drug and Alcohol Dependence*, *77*, 177–184. doi: 10.1016/j.drugalcdep.2004.08.012

Weiss, R. D., Potter, J. S., Griffin, M. L., Provost, S. E., Fitzmaurice, G. M., McDermott, K. A., . . . Carroll, K. M. (2015). Long-term outcomes from the National Drug Abuse Treatment Clinical Trials Network Prescription Opioid Addiction Treatment Study. *Drug and Alcohol Dependence*, *150*, 112–119. doi: 10.1016/j.drugalcdep.2015.02.030

Wilens, T. E., & Rosenbaum, J. F. (2013). Transitional aged youth: A new frontier in child and adolescent psychiatry. *Journal of the American Academy of Child and Adolescent Psychiatry*, *52*(9), 887–890. doi: 10.1016/j.jaac.2013.04.020

Witkiewitz, K., & Masyn, K. E. (2008). Drinking trajectories following an initial lapse. *Psychology of Addictive Behaviors*, *22*(2), 157–167. doi: 10.1037/0893-164X.22.2.157

Yalom, I. D., & Leszcz, M. (2005). *The theory and practice of group psychotherapy* (5th ed.). New York: Basic Books.

Ye, Y., & Kaskutas, L. A. (2009). Using propensity scores to adjust for selection bias when assessing the effectiveness of Alcoholics Anonymous in observational studies. *Drug and Alcohol Dependence*, *104*, 56–64. doi: 10.1016/j.drugalcdep.2009.03.018

Zemore, S. E., Subbaraman, M., & Tonigan, J. S. (2013). Involvement in 12-step activities and treatment outcomes. *Substance Abuse*, *34*(1), 60–69. doi: 10.1080/08897077.2012.691452

9

Collegiate Recovery Programs
for Emerging Adults

SIERRA CASTEDO AND LORI HOLLERAN STEIKER ■

INTRODUCTION

College campuses have long been associated with excessive substance use, often for the first time in a student's life. For students seeking to maintain recovery from a substance use disorder (SUD), entering a cultural milieu where alcohol and other drug consumption is the norm can force a choice between recovery protection and pursuing a higher education. For students who recognize their own problematic substance use and wish to make a change, there may be no examples of a recovery lifestyle, no recognition that college-aged students can and do find recovery at a young age, and no entry point into a community of recovery readily accessible on or near campus. Enter collegiate recovery programs: *refugia* of recovery embedded in a college or university campus.

Collegiate recovery programs (CRPs) offer support to college students in recovery from SUD. That support is centered around a community of students in recovery from SUD, recovery-supportive programming, and a space on campus where recovery is actively celebrated and normalized. While there is significant variation in CRP models, all center around a core community of support. The earliest CRPs date back almost 40 years, and the field remained small until just recently. The rapid proliferation of programs across the United States has led to a diversity of CRP models and practices that has not yet been well catalogued (Laudet, Harris, Kimball, Winters, & Moberg, 2014; Laudet, Harris, Winters, Moberg, & Kimball, 2014).

This chapter discusses the history of CRPs across the country and the current state of research on CRPs. The chapter concludes with a description of the program at the University of Texas at Austin's Center for Students in Recovery.

COLLEGIATE RECOVERY PROGRAM STANDARDS

Four essential ingredients of CRPs were agreed on in a town hall meeting at the national conference of the Association of Recovery in Higher Education (ARHE) in 2015: (1) a community of students in recovery, (2) recovery-supportive programming, (3) a dedicated space, and (4) staff. Three additional criteria, together with the four essential ingredients, form the standards and recommendations set by the ARHE (Association of Recovery in Higher Education, 2016).

Of the four essential ingredients of a CRP, the community of students in recovery from addiction is of primary importance. Communities vary greatly in size, with nascent or emerging programs counting only a handful of students, and more established programs counting well over 50 active participants (Transforming Youth Recovery, 2015). Age composition varies among programs, with a mean age of 26 for CRP students nationally. Augsburg College's StepUP program caters specifically to individuals ages 17 to 26 (Laudet, Harris, Kimball, Winters, & Moberg, 2015; StepUP Program, 2016). Community composition also varies somewhat by primary addiction, although most students (85.8%) are in recovery from substance use disorder. Other primary addictions include eating disorders (2.9%), sex addiction (1.3%), self-harm (1.2%), and gambling (0.01%) (Jones, Eisenhart, Charles, & Walker, 2016). Some programs welcome students recovering from a primary mental health diagnosis not involving a behavioral or substance addiction; currently, no data are available on the rates at which these students participate in CRPs.

Recovery-supportive programming forms another pillar of CRPs, with significant variation between programs. Most programs host weekly peer support group meetings aligning with existing mutual-aid pathways, including 12-step meetings, SMART, or a style unique to the CRP. Many programs offer a variety of sober social activities, service opportunities, and personal or professional development activities. Some programs incorporate a seminar taught by CRP staff for academic credit available to the CRP students (Casiraghi & Mulsow, 2010). About 40% of CRPs include a clinical, counseling component (Transforming Youth Recovery, 2015).

Space and staff are two CRP ingredients that frequently prove more challenging to secure, especially in the early stages of CRP development. Only about 28% of collegiate recovery programs and efforts (CRP/Es; programs in the earliest stages of development, which may not yet be formally recognized) had a dedicated space, with the remaining CRP/Es using consistently available space shared with other organizations (43%) or inconsistently available space (24%) or having no access to space (5%) (Transforming Youth Recovery, 2015). Residential housing for students in recovery was available at 18% of CRP/Es surveyed (Transforming Youth Recovery, 2015). A more recent survey of CRPs with formal recognition and membership in ARHE indicates that the majority of established programs have a dedicated space (68%), but a significant minority still do not, in spite of formal recognition and national participation (32%) (Jones et al., 2016). While space is an important facet of moving a CRP toward maturity and sustainability, dedicated space is not considered critical to starting a CRP, thus many nascent programs begin before space is secured (Transforming Youth Recovery, 2015). Similarly, dedicated staff are an important component of sustainability for a program, but only 55.6% of the formally recognized, established CRPs employ at least one full-time employee (Jones et al., 2016).

In addition to these core elements of CRPs are three more standards. While one may seem obvious—CRPs are housed within an institution of higher education that confers academic degrees (Association of Recovery in Higher Education, 2016)—the rapid growth of the field in recent years has proven this standard to be a necessary addition. If 16.3% of emerging adults met the criteria for an SUD in 2014 (Substance Abuse and Mental Health Services Administration [SAMHSA], 2015), and an unknown percentage of those young adults entered into recovery, then even the most generous estimate of CRPs,145 collegiate recovery programs or efforts (Transforming Youth Recovery, 2015), likely falls short of the need. Institutions of higher education may move slowly when implementing new programs, thus programs featuring elements of CRPs but unaffiliated with universities and belonging to the private sector have arisen to fill some of that need. If these CRP-like entities operate on a for-profit business model, they are also not in line with the ARHE standard "CRPs are non-profit entities." While private-sector entities can complement the work of CRPs, the anti-stigma message delivered by CRPs that are fully embedded in and embraced by college campuses cannot be understated.

The final standard calls for an abstinence-based approach as the gold standard of the field (Association of Recovery in Higher Education, 2016). With the rise in secondary prevention programs like BASICS on college campuses, along with services provided at traditional counseling centers and health promotions programs, support for moderate or low-risk substance use is already found on many campuses. In contrast, a relatively tiny proportion of college campuses have CRPs in which abstinence from substances is actively celebrated and supported. The promotion of sobriety as a valid way to enjoy a college experience is an important part of the work that CRPs do. Nonetheless, many CRPs welcome and fully integrate students in recovery from eating disorders and mental health conditions who may not need to abstain from substances. Some CRPs, including the CRP at the University of North Texas in Denton, Texas, are experimenting with the partial integration of students for whom moderation is the goal rather than total abstinence. The University of North Texas's model involves a tiered system of participation, with harm reduction–oriented students participating at a different tier than that for students practicing abstinence.

Given the rapid growth of CRPs in recent years, there is considerable variation in how CRPs meet these standards; the full scope of that variation is still being explored (Laudet, Harris, Winters, et al., 2014). Table 9.1 presents several key dimensions on which CRPs vary.

Table 9.1 Key Variables and Range of Variation Between Collegiate Recovery Programs (CRPs)

Variable	Explanation	Range of Variation
Admission	Formal application and admissions process may or may not be required. Admissions criteria vary. Admission to the CRP may influence admission to the college or university.	Admissions criteria range from none ("open-door policy" at University of Texas at Austin) to a formal application process requiring 1 year of sobriety, references, interviews, and advocacy for admission to the university (Texas Tech University). Some programs also have suggested age ranges (Augsburg College's StepUP program serves ages 17–26, though students outside this range may apply).
Housing	College or university housing for students in recovery associated with the CRP	As of 2015, 18% of CRPs offered housing. Housing may be located on campus (residence hall) or off-campus in a university-owned house (Rutgers University) or other building. It may comprise an entire residence hall (Augsburg's StepUP) or a portion (University of Texas at Austin).
Scholarships	Financial assistance in the form of scholarships	Scholarship amounts vary within and between programs, based on variables including service hours (both within and outside of the CRP), academic performance or improvement, financial need, and dedication to recovery. Range is from no scholarship dollars to several thousand dollars per semester.
Counseling	Some CRPs include access to counseling services within the CRP, case management services, and other clinical components. Others are nonclinical, emphasizing peer support.	CRPs range from entirely nonclinical, peer support–based models (University of Texas at Austin) to programs that require regular meetings with a counselor (StepUP). Many fall in between, with emphasis on peer support, sober socializing, and building community, while including access to counseling or case management (University of North Texas).
Space	The space used by the CRP for its daily operations	Access to space ranges from a dedicated space for CRP use only to no consistently available space (e.g. classrooms reserved week to week). Variation exists within dedicated space types, from regular 9–5 hours to 24/7, keycard access for CRP members (Oregon State University).

HISTORY OF COLLEGIATE RECOVERY PROGRAMS

The first collegiate recovery program was established in 1977, at Brown University, by Classics professor and Associate Dean Bruce Donovan. CRPs were then developed at Rutgers University, in 1983, and at Texas Tech University, in 1986 (Finch, 2008). What followed was a long period of relatively slow growth; that is, from the late 1980s to the early 2000s, fewer than 10 CRPs were established on college campuses (Laudet, Harris, Kimball, et al., 2014).

Early adopters in the 1990s and early 2000s still in operation today include Augsburg College's StepUP program (1997), Case Western Reserve University's program (2004), the program at Loyola College in Maryland (2004), and the Center for Students in Recovery at the University of Texas at Austin (2004) (Association of Recovery in Higher Education, 2015). In 2005, Texas Tech University released a comprehensive curriculum funded by SAMHSA to promote the replication of their model and proliferation of "collegiate recovery communities"—CRPs that follow the Texas Tech model—across the country (Harris, Baker, & Thompson, 2005). This curriculum and mentorship of fledgling programs, along with a growing body of evidence for CRP efficacy and support from federal agencies, including the Office of National Drug Control Policy (2010) and the Department of Education (2011), led to a growth spurt in the number of CRPs, bringing the total number to over 20 programs by 2010.

In 2012, the University of Texas System Board of Regents voted to fund the expansion of collegiate recovery programs to each of its academic institutions, with the Center for Students in Recovery (CSR) acting as a guide and mentor to the new CRPs (University of Texas System Office of Media Relations, 2012). This funding was extended and expanded in 2015 and included initiatives aimed at secondary prevention, primary prevention, and bystander intervention (University of Texas System Office of Media Relations, 2015). Other statewide initiatives soon followed, with the governor of North Carolina funding CRPs across that state in 2014 (Moon, 2014), and the Arizona governor bringing CRPs to three schools in that state, in 2015 (Governor's Office for Youth, Faith and Family, 2015).

In 2013, the Stacie Mathewson Foundation created the non-profit Transforming Youth Recovery, which undertook an initiative to provide $10,000 seed grants to 100 schools for the establishment of CRPs. These grantees, called collegiate recovery efforts by Transforming Youth Recovery, contributed to the exponential growth in the number of CRP/Es from 2013 to the most recent count in 2015. As of 2015, 145 CRP/Es were in existence, representing a 1,712.5% change since 2004 (Transforming Youth Recovery, 2015). As part of these growth efforts, Transforming Youth Recovery conducts annual surveys of grantees, identifying and refining assets that are critical to starting a new collegiate recovery effort and essential to serving students and sustaining programs, along with additional assets that are helpful to serving students (Transforming Youth Recovery, 2015). The reports generated from these surveys are described in greater detail later in this chapter.

Statewide initiatives in confluence with Transforming Youth Recovery's seed grant program built upon the solid foundation laid by earlier replication efforts led by Texas Tech and SAMHSA. This catalyzed the exponential growth of CRPs in recent years. With CRP/Es at just over 3% of the 4,706 degree-granting institutions of higher education in the United States, recovery support on college campuses is still a relatively rare resource (National Center for Education Statistics, 2016). Two primary resources exist to locate colleges and universities with CRPs: the Association of Recovery in Higher Education Collegiate Recovery Program Members list, available at http://collegiaterecovery.org/programs, and the Transforming Youth Recovery Collegiate Recovery Asset Map, available at https://collegiaterecovery.capacitype.com/map. A third resource, Recovery Campus magazine's Directory of Collegiate Recovery Programs, is being published in 2017.

COLLEGIATE RECOVERY RESEARCH

Introduction

Research on a variety of recovery supports is currently receiving greater attention, including the emerging complementary field of peer-delivered recovery support services (Bassuk, Hanson, Greene, Richard, & Laudet, 2016). Greater research on young people accessing recovery supports is also under way (Kelly, Stout, & Slaymaker, 2013). Almost as long as CRPs have existed there has been research on young people participating in CRPs, but few studies have examined the programs themselves or examined data across multiple institutions. This is likely because too few CRPs were in existence, and to make matters worse, existing programs had insufficient data-collection infrastructure.

This section provides an overview of the available research on CRPs and identifies gaps in the literature. Much of the earliest literature published about CRPs was descriptive, usually evaluating a single aspect of a single CRP. There are also descriptions and evaluations of CRP students, although these, too, tend to focus only on a single CRP. Before the rapid growth of CRPs facilitated by the Transforming Youth Recovery grant initiative there were early attempts to look across institutions at multiple CRPs. Since 2014, large-scale, multi-institutional data collection, analysis, and publications have occurred on a scale not previously accomplished.

Previous reviews of collegiate recovery literature identified needed research (Laudet, Harris, Kimball, et al., 2014; Watson, 2014), with multiple efforts now under way to close some of these gaps (Jones et al., 2016; Laudet et al., 2015; Transforming Youth Recovery, 2015). The collegiate recovery field's rapid growth in recent years provides greater urgency to fill these research gaps, particularly as it relates to establishing best practices, understanding those best practices in light of particular campus cultural variables, and understanding and defining the variety of CRP models.

Early Research: The Descriptive Era

Much of what can be called the descriptive era of CRP research was driven by the desire to disseminate a novel, much-needed concept to professionals across as many fields as possible, including social workers (Grahovac, Holleran Steiker, Sammons, & Millichamp, 2011), substance use disorder clinicians (Cleveland, Harris, Baker, Herbert, & Dean, 2007), student affairs and other higher education professionals (Harris et al., 2005; Perron et al., 2011), and non-academic professionals (Sullivan Moore, 2012). The early goal of this descriptive work was to encourage institutions to adopt CRPs and raise awareness of CRPs.

These descriptions were rarely ever solely descriptions and usually presented some data that would be useful for supporting the creation of a CRP at the reader's home institution. For example, Botzet, Winters, and Fahnhorst (2008) described Augsburg College's StepUP program through the results of a modified Global Appraisal for Individual Needs (GAIN) (Dennis, 1998) survey of 83 current and former StepUP program students. The highly favorable results of this study offered strong supporting evidence in favor of establishing a new collegiate recovery program at an institution. Similarly, evaluations and analyses of Texas Tech University's collegiate recovery community (CRC) provided both a model for replication and evidence of the model's positive impact on student outcomes. Bell and colleagues (2009) conducted a qualitative feedback survey of 15 first-year Texas Tech University CRC students multiple times throughout their first year, demonstrating that the support provided by the CRC is essential for many students in recovery. Casiraghi and Mulsow (2010) evaluated a single component of the Texas Tech CRC by focusing specifically on their program's seminars for academic credit. They explored whether an academic component to a CRP was valuable programmatically and to the students (Casiraghi & Mulsow, 2010). Wiebe, Cleveland, and Dean (2010) and Cleveland, Wiebe and Wiersma (2010) focused on how Texas Tech students involved with the CRC were able to avoid relapse and temptation in the college environment. Rutgers University's model of a CRP built around a campus recovery house provides important evidence in support of recovery-supportive housing efforts on campus as a way to complete the continuum of care (Laitman, Kachur-Karavites, & Stewart, 2014).

Several of these early research initiatives also focused on CRP student demographics and life histories, though only within a single CRP population. Cleveland and Groenendyk (2010) examined the daily lives of students involved in the Texas Tech CRC, including the frequency and type of social interactions that formed the "substrate of abstinence support" (p. 78). Cleveland, Baker, and Dean (2010) surveyed 52 active members of the Texas Tech CRC over 11 months, gathering data on treatment episode history, drugs of choice, substance use history, family dynamics, religiosity, 12-step participation, living situation, and basic demographics. While focusing only on a single CRP population, this study laid important groundwork for the national CRP student snapshot conducted by Laudet and colleagues (2015) several years later.

Early Multi-Institutional Research

Early forays into multi-institutional research on CRPs included multiple efforts to collate the body of research on CRPs into literature reviews. Smock, Baker, Harris, and D'Sauza (2011) offer a review from the perspective of social support in collegiate recovery communities, focusing primarily on reviewing the body of literature from Texas Tech's CRC researchers but including other resources as well. Importantly, Smock and colleagues called for CRPs to be considered an evidence-based practice, given the existing data, and to be added to the National Registry of Evidence-Based Programs and Practices (NREPP), which at the time did not include recovery supportive programs in its repository (Smock et al., 2011). As discussed later in the Methodological Considerations section, many of these studies do not meet the standards of NREPP inclusion, as they are not randomized or rigorous quasiexperiments. A broader multi-institutional literature review examined the benefits of recovery-supportive housing on three campuses: Rutgers University, Texas Tech University, and Augsburg College (Watson, 2014).

A significant acknowledgment of diversity within CRP models came from Perron and colleagues (2011), who divided program models into a formal, top-down approach to supporting students and a bottom-up, student-driven approach to support students in recovery. Formal program models included those programs that were well established in 2011: Rutgers University, Augsburg College's StepUP program, and Texas Tech University's CRC (Perron et al., 2011). The informal model described was the University of Michigan student organization Students for Recovery (SFR) (Perron et al., 2011; Perron, Grahovac, & Parrish, 2010). SFR was the primary actor galvanizing the community of students in recovery, organizing campus-based 12-step meetings and educating the campus and community about addiction and recovery. Today, numerous CRPs combine both approaches, with a formal CRP and student organization branch operating in unison.

A greater acknowledgment of multiple models in the collegiate recovery movement came from the first nationwide survey of CRPs (Laudet, Harris, Winters, et al., 2014). Laudet and colleagues (2014) recommended that, because CRPs begin organically and are embedded within a unique campus culture, variations in programs must be accounted for before any model is evaluated. In a separate paper, Laudet and colleagues (2014) reviewed the current state of knowledge about CRPs nationally and identified key areas where research is needed, including systematic evaluation and documentation of CRPs and CRP models. The authors also identified the collection of demographic information and addiction recovery history from CRP students, as well as documentation of the diversity of CRP programs as research priorities, gaps that the authors filled in an NIH-funded study described in the next section (Laudet, Harris, Kimball, et al., 2014).

Multi-Institutional Research after Rapid Growth of CRP Field

Several of the research gaps identified by Laudet, Harris, Winters, Moberg and Kimball (2014) were subsequently addressed in their large-scale survey of CRP students (Laudet et al., 2015). The survey was administered in 2012 to 600 students participating in 29 collegiate recovery programs in 19 states, with an 81% response rate for 486 respondents (Laudet et al., 2015). The survey included demographic and life history information similar to that collected by Cleveland et al. (2010) within Texas Tech's CRC. From this national reference data of CRP students, several growth edges have been identified. First, CRP demographics are not reflective of the gender, racial, and ethnic makeup of university campuses nationwide, skewing more heavily white and male than the general campus population. This has led to the formation of an informal work group within the Association of Recovery in Higher Education to improve diversity and inclusion. Laudet and colleagues' follow-up publication of the survey data revealed students' motivations for joining CRPs (Laudet, Harris, Kimball, Winters, & Moberg, 2016). The three primary reasons that students joined CRPs were (1) ready access to a recovery-supportive peer network, (2) a desire to "do college sober" and have a genuine college experience free from substance use, and, less prominently, (3) to give back and be of service while in college (Laudet et al., 2016). Two-thirds of CRP students' enrollment decisions were based on CRP availability and structure, with 72% of that subset stating that they would not have attended college without a CRP present (Laudet et al., 2016).

Transforming Youth Recovery's annual surveys of grantees have also resulted in two reports compiling data about collegiate recovery programs and efforts across the nation (Transforming Youth Recovery, 2014, 2015). The 2014 report focused primarily on two areas: the 38 assets and a network examination (Transforming Youth Recovery, 2014). Transforming Youth Recovery's 38 assets are divided into three main categories: (1) assets that are critical to start a program and begin serving students in recovery; (2) assets that are essential to longer-term support of students but are not critical to start a program; and (3) additional assets that are helpful but are neither critical to start a program nor essential to long-term success (Transforming Youth Recovery, 2014). Assets may be individuals, associations, or institutions, and there is much overlap between the assets considered critical to start a CRP and the standards set by the ARHE, including space, staff, a community of students, and mutual-aid support groups. The network examination component of the 2014 report was intended to help CRP/Es expand their reach by better understanding existing communities and to help identify gaps in existing networks (Transforming Youth Recovery, 2014). The survey also examined staffing, program model (clinical, peer-based, or social-based), average number and range of engaged students at each stage of program development, and the ratio of the number of students invited to participate in the CRP to the number of students engaged (Transforming Youth Recovery, 2014). In this latter metric, more established CRPs had higher engagement ratios (one engagement for every two invitations) than those of programs in earlier stages of development (one engagement for every three to five invitations) (Transforming Youth Recovery, 2014). Programs with dedicated space also had the highest engagement ratios, further supporting the importance of a dedicated space as an asset critical to starting a CRP (Transforming Youth Recovery, 2014). The 2015 Transforming Youth Recovery report also examined assets and networks (named "connections" in this report) and added CRP/E compositions and practices (Transforming Youth Recovery, 2015). "Compositions" refer to staffing, use of space, presence/absence of a residential housing component, and model archetype (clinical, peer-based, social-based) (Transforming Youth Recovery, 2015). "Practices" refer to ongoing recovery programming, activities, and support services for students in recovery (Transforming Youth Recovery, 2015).

More efforts to gather national data on CRPs are under way. Results from a survey of the 54 ARHE institutional members in 2015 were presented at the 2016 ARHE national conference, with a publication soon to follow (Jones et al., 2016). The ARHE member survey captures data from the most established programs, including the longest running programs dating from the 1980s and 1990s (Jones et al., 2016). This survey captures important benchmarking data regarding CRP staffing, finances, and students served, which is of great importance to emerging programs seeking to become more established within their home institutions. A major literature review and literature database creation project is currently under way, spearheaded by ARHE's Research Committee. A national baseline data collection tool is also in development by the ARHE Research Committee.

Methodological Considerations

MEASUREMENT INSTRUMENTS

In order to choose an appropriate instrument to measure the impact of one or more CRPs, one must first determine how recovery is defined. Is relapse a failure? Most of the "wildly successful" CRPs have a mean relapse rate of 8% (Laudet et al., 2015), but is that a reasonable way to measure a student's success? Or does it encourage hiding relapse? Or does it deny the potentially positive impact of someone "testing the waters" and coming to a more definitive sense of self as a person with an SUD and a person now in recovery? Among national recovery organizations, including Faces and Voices of Recovery, there is a push to shift the language from "relapse" to more neutral language reflective of stage of change, including "resumption of use," "recurrence," or "partial remission" (White & Ali, 2010). The "relapse = failure" paradigm has long been called into question, particularly in light of a growing acknowledgment of SUD as a chronic illness requiring long-term care (McLellan, Lewis, O'Brien, & Kleber, 2000).

Presently, there are no standardized measures used at CRPs but, given the focus on methodological issues within ARHE, the development of a standard data collection instrument may ease this problem. CRPs are using the growing national evidence base, which is shifting from simply demographic information and oversimplified measurement of "sobriety" (often without consideration of the role of resumption in use for movement along the stage of change and readiness continuum) to more recovery-centered instruments such as the Assessment of Recovery Capital (ARC) (Groshkova, Best, & White, 2013) and quality of life (QOL) measures (WHOQOL Group, 1998). "Recovery capital" is the sum of the resources an individual can draw on to initiate and sustain recovery from substance use problems, a concept not well measured by usual problem-based assessments of treatment outcomes (Groshkova et al., 2013). The Recovery Capital measurement instrument has been validated for this population; it was found to be a stable measure substantially related to other similar measures and to duration of recovery, suggesting it might aid recovery-oriented assessment of treatment services and of an individual's progress and needs. However, it will be important to test whether the measure can predict later recovery, and rather than assessing an underlying ability to recover, it seems partly to measure recovery itself (Groshkova et al., 2013). The World Health Organization Quality of Life instrument measures a number of domains relevant to recovery: Overall Quality of Life and General Health, Physical Health (e.g., energy, fatigue, pain, discomfort, sleep, and rest), Psychological (body image, appearance, feelings, self-esteem, thinking, learning, memory, and concentration), Independence (e.g., activities of daily living, substance dependence, work capacity), Social Relationships (e.g., social support, family, friends, sexual activity, financial resources, safety/security, healthcare, quality of home environment, opportunities for acquiring new skills and information, recreation and leisure and physical environment, transportation), and Spiritual/Religious (e.g., personal beliefs).

The next subsection addresses the most challenging part of researching CRPs: the extensive range of services, populations served, settings, environmental aspects, and administrative departments.

VARIABLES RELATED TO DIVERSE CRP CHARACTERISTICS

The research of Alexandre Laudet and colleagues (2015) has established that, while there are some common characteristics of CRPs, the models vary drastically from one campus to another. Specific aspects of CRPs, such as residential versus club locale, small versus large, varied definitions of recovery, and voluntary versus obligatory aspects of programs, lead us to warn the reader not to compare "apples and baseballs." Laudet et al. (2015) note that, "unlike treatment programs that collect patient history upon admission to guide services, CRPs do not." While five CRPs have operated for 10 years or longer and some serve up to 80 students, two-thirds emerged in the past decade, and over half serve fewer than 10 students (Laudet et al., 2015). Clearly, the students at one CRP are unlikely to represent the breadth of experiences and issues that a cumulative study of all the varied CRPS can yield. It is for this reason that we recommend that unified efforts through the Association of Recovery in Higher Education and invested groups such as the National Development Research Institute (NDRI) continue in order to research the phenomenon rather than having each campus research "collegiate recovery students." The most critical point is that findings of small campus studies can and ought not be generalized to the larger population of college recovery students nationwide. Missions of varied CRPs may differ. Staffing and administrations vary as well—is the CRP student-run or student-organization based? Is it housed in a mental health center or department or is it freestanding? Is it under the auspices of student affairs, and, if so, how does the administration of the university see the CRP?

Also, multi-tiered systems exist (everything from "open-door" programs without membership requirement to those with some stipulations to entry due to related scholarship or housing). Those with stringent entry requirements may appear to have better outcomes from a 'length of sobriety" standpoint, but they ought not be compared with those that aim to extend participation to individuals in the earliest stages of recovery or who have not yet entered into recovery.

SAMPLES AND POPULATION

In terms of sample size, CRP programs range from a few students to hundreds. Presently, there are only six schools with 50 or more students in their core participation group. Even among established CRPs the mean size is 24, and among all ARHE members, mean student group size is 22 (Jones et al., 2016; Transforming Youth Recovery, 2015). The median is only 15 (Jones et al., 2016).

As implied earlier, inclusion/exclusion criteria vary from CRP to CRP. For example, Texas Tech's CRP has a requirement of 1 year of recovery for membership, while the University of Texas at Austin has no requirements or even membership lists. Inclusion of women, minorities, and children/youth have unique human subjects protections implications, but the diversity of a CRP may be limited by the diversity of the campus, stigma attached to recognition of substance use disorders, and willingness to associate with other people in need of CRPs.

HUMAN SUBJECTS ISSUES AND OTHER LIMITATIONS

Given the multiple vulnerabilities of emerging adults on college campuses, care must be given to protection of human subjects from the standpoint of their minor status (in some cases), drug use, and potentially incriminating data. Because students come to CRPs in the midst of crisis, researchers must be thoughtful and cautious to consider not only that consent forms and surveys can lead to research fatigue but also that if a young person gets turned off from CRP involvement by the presence of research, this could be life threatening. It cannot be denied that research impacts the culture of CRPs, especially in areas with high stigma and where traditionalist approaches to 12-step programs exist (i.e., conflict with fundamentalist interpretations of anonymity).

The question of who does the research can be complicated. Outside researchers clearly have more objectivity, but the students at the CRP may not trust them as they would their staff or peers. Many CRPs operate with limited staff and budget (Laudet, Harris, Winters, et al., 2014) and lack the resources to collect student information. Research presently is often being conducted by CRP staff who are typically close with the students and also may have power over scholarship money, housing, and hiring. Perhaps the best compromise is to have the research done by a faculty liaison whom the students know and trust, but who does not have regular contact with them. Researchers should give thought to whether it is advantageous or problematic to survey or investigate the students directly or via the directors/staff.

Social behavioral research, as in many vulnerable settings, cannot use a control group, for ethical reasons. In addition, researchers would not be smart to compare individuals with alcohol drug issues who opt out because they may be vastly different from those that choose to affiliate with a CRP. Another limitation of the research is that most CRPs have "rolling admissions" that change the demographics and data readily. Attrition can be a serious limitation: CRPs with open doors allow for sporadic attendance, and people can come and go before feeling comfortable making a strong commitment to the CRP. For example, the CRP at the University of Texas at Austin (Center for Students in Recovery) had a student who engaged briefly their freshman year and then touched base and made a second and third foray into recovery their sophomore and junior years. In the final semester of senior year, the student entered fully into recovery and has been in recovery since April 2014. These issues, combined with staffing changes, graduation of student leaders, and university climate changes (incidences on campus, such as overdose deaths of students or other drug/alcohol-related issues) all have the potential to influence research findings. History has power in these settings. The most recent and potent example is that at Texas A&M, where a student overdose and related arrests have impacted students' willingness to identify as an addicted person.

Collegiate recovery programs often involve students who may be recovering from a variety of substance disorders, mental health challenges, and process disorders. Eating disorders, Internet addiction, and binge drinking are all issues that are relevant to CRPs but may require unique programming and group open-mindedness, not to mention qualitative or quasiexperimental research mechanisms.

Growth Areas

Research has been identified as a major growth area for the field of collegiate recovery. At present, few faculty have positions exclusively dedicated to the study of recovery. Funding streams are limited. CRP staff typically do not hold faculty positions and are instead dedicated to the daily functioning of the space and providing services to students.

While CRPs are spreading across the country, several underserved areas have been identified as growth areas for the field: community colleges, historically Black colleges and universities (HBCUs), tribal colleges, rural campuses, and underserved populations on campuses with existing CRPs. Alignment with the goals of mental health recovery supports on campus is also a growth area for the collegiate recovery field. In July 2016, SAMHSA convened the National Summit on Recovery Support in Collegiate Environments, bringing together leaders from the collegiate recovery field, HBCUs, community colleges, tribal colleges, collegiate mental health, and student leaders belonging to underserved populations. The intent was to "identify and advance (a) best practices in supporting students in collegiate environments, (b) strategies to align recovery support programs with other campus-based health and social services, and (c) opportunities for new and existing collegiate recovery support programs to build capacity and infrastructure" (SAMHSA, 2016, p. 2). In addition to the support from SAMHSA, the Association of Recovery in Higher Education has an informal working group dedicated to diversity and inclusion in CRPs.

THE CENTER FOR STUDENTS IN RECOVERY AT THE UNIVERSITY OF TEXAS AT AUSTIN

The Center for Students in Recovery (CSR) at the University of Texas (UT) at Austin was established in 2004 to serve a handful of students in recovery. In its 12-year history, CSR has undergone significant shifts while maintaining its core mission: to provide a supportive community where students in recovery and in hope of recovery can achieve academic success while enjoying a genuine college experience free from alcohol and other drugs. One major shift was the formalization of CSR as a stand-alone program within the Division of Student Affairs, in 2013. While maintaining close ties and a clear bridge to clinical resources on campus, CSR is strictly nonclinical in nature. This emphasis on peer support provides an entry point for students who view clinical resources with trepidation, in addition to being the appropriate level of care for students in well-established recovery. Throughout its history, it has been CSR's goal to meet students "where they are" in the stages of change (Holleran Steiker, 2016).

As mentioned earlier, CRP models vary significantly based on the campus culture in which they were formed. CSR's model differs from many in that it is entirely open door with no formal membership or entry requirements. Participation is completely voluntary. Students with multiple years of long-term recovery are welcome, as are students not yet in recovery. Additionally, students enrolled at other higher education institutions, or people considering pursuing a higher education but not yet enrolled, are also welcome to participate fully. A major contributing factor to this policy of inclusion is the large, vibrant, and young recovery community off-campus, including some who attend the local community college while seeking to transfer to the University of Texas.

A useful way to conceptualize the variation across CRPs is to describe how a program meets the standards and recommendations set by the Association of Recovery in Higher Education described earlier in this chapter, with particular emphasis on community, space, staff, and recovery-supportive programming. These four pillars will be discussed next. The additional three standards are straightforward. CSR's mission includes helping students "achieve academic success while enjoying a genuine college experience free from alcohol and other drugs," maintaining abstinence-based recovery as a core principle. As a standalone program within the Division of Student Affairs at the University of Texas at Austin, CSR functions as a student service and resource center within a larger non-profit institution.

Community

The community of students in recovery at CSR varies widely in terms of academic status, recovery time and type, age, background, and life experiences. As described earlier, CSR's open-door policy results in a community whose recovery time ranges from 0 days to 10 or more years. Students can be categorized into three broad categories: nontraditional students in established, long-term recovery pursuing an education after a significant absence from the educational setting; traditional undergraduate and graduate students new to recovery, remaining in school or returning after a brief hiatus for inpatient treatment or other care; and recovery high school students entering college as traditional first-year students. Throughout its history, CSR has had high participation from nontraditional students in established recovery, thanks to the large, vibrant recovery community surrounding the UT Austin campus, and thanks to staff who have actively participated in that community. As CSR grew in visibility as a campus resource, the second group, consisting of traditional students new to recovery, began to make up a significant portion of the students participating in CSR. This provided an excellent opportunity for students in more established recovery to mentor, sponsor, and support those students with less recovery time. Few students from recovery high schools have participated in CSR because UT Austin has lacked targeted recovery-supportive housing options on campus. With the opening of a recovery-friendly living learning community in the fall of 2017, CSR hopes to encourage more recovery high school graduates to attend UT Austin. CSR also has extensive interactions, including a mentorship program, with the UT Charter School University High School (UHS), Austin's only recovery high school. Thanks to its proximity to CSR, UHS students attend peer support meetings at CSR and interact regularly with CSR students and staff. CSR also held its first annual college informational session in 2016 for high school students enrolled at three recovery high schools (UHS, Archway Academy and Cates Academy), one adolescent treatment center (Phoenix House), and an alternative peer group (Teen and Family Services—Austin) as part of an ongoing effort to build bridges to CRPs for students graduating from recovery high schools.

Recovery Programming

CSR's recovery supportive programming falls into four categories: peer support group meetings, sober social activities, service opportunities, and educational programming. Peer support group meetings occur on a weekly basis. Currently, seven peer support group meetings are held 5 days per week, although this number fluctuates each semester as students graduate, schedules change, and student preferences shift. Two weekly meetings—the CSR group activity and Campus Open Recovery on Tuesday night—have remained at the same time and day for years in order to provide a backbone of consistency, while other meetings may be more flexible. Three Alcoholics Anonymous meetings—one open, one for men, and one for women—are held in the CSR space each week. Two meetings are 12-step based but welcome those recovering from any condition. One of these 12-step all-addictions meetings is called Yoga for Recovery and features 45 minutes of yoga followed by 45 minutes of a standard 12-step discussion meeting format. Certified yoga instructors who are also in 12-step recovery teach the yoga portion and lead the peer support meeting. There are two non-12-step meetings held in the space: Nourish, an eating disorder recovery support group, and the CSR group activity. Nourish is welcoming to students in recovery from any variety of eating disorder and is inclusive of any kind of recovery pathway. The meeting is peer-led, but the meeting anchor receives guidance and support from the CSR staff and the university's Mindful Eating program staff. The CSR group activity varies in content and format each week. Examples of past group activities include mural painting, accountability groups, guest expert speakers, meditation workshops, and scavenger hunts.

The educational programming at CSR includes some sessions of the CSR group activity but also includes the Seminar on Addiction and Recovery (SOAR). SOAR is a monthly speaker-series featuring an expert on addiction and/or recovery. Speaker topics range from overdose prevention and naloxone training to immune signaling in alcohol dependence. SOAR lectures are open to the public and intended to educate both CSR students and the campus at large. SOAR lectures also give students who may have qualms about making an initial visit to CSR a low-stakes opportunity to visit the space. CSR staff members provide educational programming for classes, student organizations, and professional groups intended to lower stigma around students in recovery and provide information about CSR and CRPs in general. Presentations geared toward students provide basic information about how to be an ally to other students in recovery or to a peer actively struggling with SUD. This is intended to empower students to help get a peer in need connected to resources that will help the student find recovery.

Sober social activities include organized events planned and implemented by CSR staff as well as peer-organized and led activities. Past events have included sober tailgates, sober dance parties, bowling, and ugly holiday sweater parties. Sober social activities organized by students include game nights, pumpkin carving, and trail running groups. CSR staff also organize camping trips and retreats for students, usually in conjunction with one or more other CRPs' students.

Collaboration with other CRPs, with recovery high schools, and with other facets of the larger recovery community is a recurring theme in CRP sober social activities, as this integration with a larger recovery community provides more opportunities for students to find sober social supports.

Space and Staff

At its founding CSR did not have dedicated space outside of the founding director's office. Meetings and programming were held in borrowed classrooms throughout campus, which could lead to confusion and students missing meetings because they became lost or did not have the correct room location. Dedicated space for CSR was secured in 2009 and, because it was a former boiler room, required an extensive remodel before move-in. This dedicated location was in the basement of the School of Social Work at the far southern edge of campus. The dedicated location served CSR well, allowing for greater community-building activities, as students could now use the space to study or socialize with fellow students in recovery outside of a scheduled support group meeting. In 2014, CSR moved to a more central and symbolically important campus location: the Darryl K. Royal Texas Memorial Football Stadium. With football as the most visible athletic event and perhaps the most visible campus event overall, CSR's current location further communicates to the on- and off-campus community that students in recovery are a valued part of campus. The larger space also allows for a separate study room and small library of recovery literature to provide a quiet and recovery-supportive space for students in recovery to work. The larger meeting room enables a greater range of programming, including SOAR and the hybrid yoga/12-step meeting, neither of which would be feasible in CSR's previous location.

Student assistants—part-time undergraduate or graduate student workers paid hourly—are hired from within the community of students in recovery to help keep the space open for students wishing to use CSR as a safe space during the school day. The staff was further expanded with the hiring of a second full-time position to complement the duties of the director: a program coordinator. The program coordinator oversees the CSR group activity, CSR-led sober social activities, coordinated service opportunities, and educational programming. The program coordinator also works with students who wish to form new peer-led groups or change existing programming. Currently, the program coordinator is responsible for outreach to campus partners, including student organizations, other campus services, professors, and committees, in addition to the programming already described. The director serves as the primary off-campus liaison, including fundraising, and representing CSR at the national, state, and local levels. The director oversees CSR financials, staffing, and other administrative issues. Additionally, the director makes decisions about scholarships, including evaluating applicants, distributing scholarship funds, and raising funds for scholarships. The CSR Council is also coordinated and facilitated by the CSR director. The council is a volunteer body that serves to brainstorm ideas for CSR programming, outreach, and development activities and tackle specific tasks. The Council consists of students, alumni, UT staff and faculty, and off-campus community supporters. CSR also employs a graduate assistant to take on specific projects. Currently, the CSR graduate assistant works with the CSR director and the staff of University High School (UHS) to coordinate the mentorship program matching CSR students to UHS students in recovery. This mentorship program is intended to build a bridge to college for recovery high school juniors and seniors.

Impact at University of Texas at Austin and Beyond

In the 2015–2016 academic year, CSR had personal interactions with 2,694 members of the campus community, primarily students. These personal interactions include the core CSR participants: a fluctuating group of students and prospective students who regularly attend meetings at CSR, participate in CSR programming, and form the foundation of the community of support, which numbered 50 that year. Peripheral participants are a group of students who are engaged with CSR, but to a lesser degree: these students engage with CSR at least once per semester, but that engagement may be via event attendance only, or only participating in service opportunities. Peripheral participants are typically students in established recovery who have transitioned into a stage of school or work that prevents them from interacting more regularly with CSR but who keep active ties at least once per semester. This group numbered 220 in 2015–2106. The number of event or other programming attendees, plus students that reached out for help but did not engage with CSR long term, totaled 1,072. Finally, over 1,300 students were engaged in class and student organization presentations in 2015–2016.

These in-class and student organization presentations are an essential way that CSR helps normalize recovery on campus and empowers students to respond when their peers ask for help. Each presentation includes education about CSR as a resource, CRPs generally, addiction recovery basics, and a brief recovery ally training. The recovery ally training follows the outline in Figure 9.1.

Combatting stigma is an important part of CSR's work, which is facilitated greatly by in-class presentations. Stigma influences not only how the general population views addiction but also how healthcare professionals treat their patients (Kelly & Westerhoff, 2010). With UT Austin training nurses, social workers, counselors, pharmacists, and physicians, this early exposure to stigma-combatting efforts is essential. The effects of public service announcements and health promotion campaigns are known to be temporary but have greater success when coupled with on-the-ground efforts like those undertaken at CSR (Noar, 2006; Noar, Palmgreen, Chabot, Dobransky, & Zimmerman, 2009; Snyder et al., 2004; Wakefield, Loken, & Hornik, 2010). When these on-the-ground efforts include in-person interactions with the perceived out-group (people in recovery from SUD), accomplished at CSR by having a student in recovery share their story during an in-class presentation, the ameliorative effects are lasting and significant (Broockman & Kalla, 2016). College is a transformative time for many students,

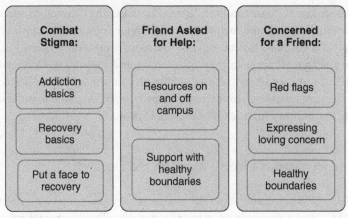

Figure 9.1. Brief recovery ally training outline used by the Center for Students in Recovery at the University of Texas at Austin, during classroom and student organization presentations.

and CSR seeks to include shifting attitudes toward people in recovery from SUD among those transformations.

CSR's efforts have been expanded to each UT System academic institution in an initiative that began in 2012. The 2015–2016 academic year impacts of these programs totaled 8,685 campus community members across the eight UT System academic campuses. While this number does not represent a majority of UT System campus constituents, it represents a tremendous improvement over the total lack of targeted addiction recovery efforts that characterized the landscape before the initiative.

The impact of CSR extends far beyond campus. In November 2014, CSR staff helped form the Recovery Oriented Community Collaborative with recovery community organizations and other recovery resources in Austin, Texas. This model of local collaboration is being replicated across the state by RecoveryPeople, a SAMHSA-funded initiative based in Austin. CSR also actively collaborates with other CRPs in the state, including an effort to bring the national conference for the Association of Recovery in Higher Education to Houston, Texas, in 2018 with the CRP at the University of Houston.

CSR actively participates at the national level as well. Transforming Youth Recovery frequently uses CSR staff expertise to guide and mentor emerging CRPs and develop best practices for the field. CSR actively participates with the Association of Recovery in Higher Education to further the collegiate recovery movement. The Association of Recovery Schools, the national organization for recovery high schools, held its 2016 conference in conjunction with CSR and University High School. Further, CSR has gained national media attention and recognition with features in *The Huffington Post* and on National Public Radio in 2015, and with an American College Health Association Best Practices in College Health Award, in 2012 (American College Health Association, n.d.; Goodwyn, 2015; Kingkade, 2015).

CONCLUSION

The interdisciplinary and interinstitutional collaboration that the Center for Students in Recovery at the University of Texas at Austin employs is characteristic of the collegiate recovery movement. CRPs and the national organizations that serve them represent a tremendous opportunity for extensive collaboration with treatment centers, private practice clinicians, and other on- and off-campus resources. As the growth of the collegiate recovery movement across the country continues, those already serving collegiate populations with substance use disorders can play a major role in supporting that growth. Faculty, staff, alumni, and parents of children enrolled at institutions of higher education can advocate for the creation of a CRP at that institution and can lend support, belonging, and an influential voice to the students who wish to access that resource. These advocates—whether they are attached to a university or serve the off-campus community—are critical components of any collegiate recovery effort (Transforming Youth Recovery, 2015). As a recent report suggests, collegiate recovery programs are a "win-win proposition" for college students, institutions of higher education, and the communities in which they are embedded (Bugbee, Caldeira, Soong, Vincent, & Arria, 2016).

REFERENCES

American College Health Association. (n.d.). *Award recipients*. Retrieved September 30, 2016, from http://www.acha.org/ACHA/About/Award_Recipients.aspx#bp

Association of Recovery in Higher Education. (2015). *The collegiate recovery movement: A history*. Retrieved from http://collegiaterecovery.org/the-collegiate-recovery-movement-a-history/

Association of Recovery in Higher Education. (2016). *Standards and recommendations*. Retrieved from http://collegiaterecovery.org/standards-and-recomendations/

Bassuk, E. L., Hanson, J., Greene, R. N., Richard, M., & Laudet, A. B. (2016). Peer-delivered recovery support services for addictions in the United States: A systematic review. *Journal of Substance Abuse Treatment, 63*, 1–9. doi: 10.1016/j.jsat.2016.01.003

Bell, N. J., Kanitkar, K., Kerksiek, K. A., Watson, W., Das, A., Kostina-Ritchey, E., . . . Harris, K. (2009). "It has made college possible for me": Feedback on the impact of a university-based center for students in recovery. *Journal of American College Health, 57*(6), 650–658. doi: 10.3200/JACH.57.6.650-658

Botzet, A. M., Winters, K., & Fahnhorst, T. (2008). An exploratory assessment of a college substance abuse recovery program: Augsburg College's StepUP Program. *Journal of Groups in Addiction & Recovery, 2*(2-4), 257–270. doi: 10.1080/15560350802081173

Broockman, D., & Kalla, J. (2016). Durably reducing transphobia: A field experiment on door-to-door canvassing. *Science, 352*(6282), 220–224. doi: 10.1126/science.aad9713

Bugbee, B. A., Caldeira, K. M., Soong, A. M., Vincent, K. B., & Arria, A. M. (2016). *Collegiate recovery programs: A win-win proposition for students and colleges*. College Park, MD: Center on Young Adult Health and Development. Retrieved from http://www.cls.umd.edu/docs/CRP.pdf

Casiraghi, A. M., & Mulsow, M. (2010). Building support for recovery into an academic curriculum: Student reflections on the value of staff run seminars. In H. H. Cleveland, K. S. Harris, & R. P. Wiebe (Eds.), *Substance abuse recovery in college* (pp. 113–143). New York: Springer US.

Cleveland, H. H., Baker, A., & Dean, L. R. (2010). Characteristics of collegiate recovery community members. In H. H. Cleveland, K. S. Harris, & R. P. Wiebe (Eds.), *Substance abuse recovery in college* (pp. 37–56). New York: Springer US.

Cleveland, H. H., & Groenendyk, A. (2010). Daily lives of young adult members of a collegiate recovery community. In H. H. Cleveland, K. S. Harris, & R. P. Wiebe (Eds.), *Substance abuse recovery in college* (pp. 77–95). New York: Springer US.

Cleveland, H. H., Wiebe, R. P., & Wiersma, J. D. (2010). How Membership in the Collegiate Recovery Community Maximizes Social Support for Abstinence and Reduces Risk of Relapse. In H. H. Cleveland, K. S. Harris, & R. P. Wiebe (Eds.), *Substance Abuse Recovery in College* (pp. 97–111). Springer US.

Cleveland, H. H., Harris, K. S., Baker, A. K., Herbert, R., & Dean, L. R. (2007). Characteristics of a collegiate recovery community: Maintaining recovery in an abstinence-hostile environment. *Journal of Substance Abuse Treatment, 33*(1), 13–23. doi: 10.1016/j.jsat.2006.11.005

Dennis, M. L. (1998). *Global Appraisal of Individual Needs (GAIN) manual: Administration, scoring, and interpretation.* Bloomington, IL: Lighthouse Publications.

Finch, A. J. (2008). Rationale for including recovery as part of the educational agenda. *Journal of Groups in Addiction & Recovery, 2*(2-4), 1–15. doi: 10.1080/15560350802080704

Goodwyn, W. (2015). Amid rising concern about addiction, universities focus on recovery.

Governor's Office for Youth, Faith and Family. (2015). *Collegiate recovery.* Retrieved September 16, 2016, from http://substanceabuse.az.gov/substance-abuse/collegiate-recovery-0

Grahovac, I., Holleran Steiker, L., Sammons, K., & Millichamp, K. (2011). University centers for students in recovery. *Journal of Social Work Practice in the Addictions, 11*(3), 290–294. doi: 10.1080/1533256X.2011.593990

Groshkova, T., Best, D., & White, W. (2013). The assessment of recovery capital: Properties and psychometrics of a measure of addiction recovery strengths. *Drug and Alcohol Review, 32*(2), 187–194. doi: 10.1111/j.1465-3362.2012.00489.x

Harris, K., Baker, A., & Thompson, A. (2005). *Making an opportunity on your campus: A comprehensive curriculum for designing collegiate recovery communities.* Lubbock: Center for the Study of Addiction and Recovery, Texas Tech University.

Holleran Steiker, L. (2016). *Youth and substance use: Prevention, intervention, and recovery.* New York: Oxford University Press.

Jones, J. A., Eisenhart, E., Charles, B., & Walker, N. (2016, April). *Results of the 2015 National Collegiate Recovery Programs Profiles Study.* Presented at the Association of Recovery in Higher Education 7th Annual Conference, Atlanta, GA.

Kelly, J. F., Stout, R. L., & Slaymaker, V. (2013). Emerging adults' treatment outcomes in relation to 12-step mutual-help attendance and active involvement. *Drug and Alcohol Dependence, 129*(1-2), 151–157. doi: 10.1016/j.drugalcdep.2012.10.005

Kelly, J. F., & Westerhoff, C. M. (2010). Does it matter how we refer to individuals with substance-related conditions? A randomized study of two commonly used terms. *International Journal of Drug Policy*, *21*(3), 202–207. doi: 10.1016/ j.drugpo.2009.10.010

Kingkade, T. (2015, May 28). *How Texas college students are using yoga and tailgating to stay sober*. Retrieved from http://www.huffingtonpost.com/2015/05/27/college-programs-drug-addicts_n_7343310.html

Laudet, A. B., Harris, K., Kimball, T., Winters, K. C., & Moberg, D. P. (2014). Collegiate recovery communities programs: What do we know and what do we need to know? *Journal of Social Work Practice in the Addictions*, *14*(1), 84–100. doi: 10.1080/1533256X.2014.872015

Laudet, A. B., Harris, K., Kimball, T., Winters, K. C., & Moberg, D. P. (2015). Characteristics of students participating in collegiate recovery programs: A national survey. *Journal of Substance Abuse Treatment*, *51*, 38–46. doi: 10.1016/j.jsat.2014.11.004

Laudet, A. B., Harris, K., Kimball, T., Winters, K. C., & Moberg, D. P. (2016). In college and in recovery: Reasons for joining a collegiate recovery program. *Journal of American College Health*. *64*(3), 238–246. doi: 10.1080/07448481.2015.1117464

Laudet, A. B., Harris, K., Winters, K., Moberg, D., & Kimball, T. (2014). Nationwide survey of collegiate recovery programs: Is there a single model? *Drug & Alcohol Dependence*, *140*, e117. doi: 10.1016/j.drugalcdep.2014.02.335

Laitman, L., Kachur-Karavites, B., & Stewart, L. P. (2014). Building, engaging, and sustaining a continuum of care from harm reduction to recovery support: The Rutgers Alcohol and Other Drug Assistance Program. *Journal of Social Work Practice in the Addictions*, *14*(1), 64–83.

McLellan, A. T., Lewis, D. C., O'Brien, C. P., & Kleber, H. D. (2000). Drug dependence, a chronic medical illness. *Journal of the American Medical Association*, *284*(13), 1689–1695.

Moon, J. (2014). Governor provides funding for programs aimed at student recovery. Inside UNC Charlotte. Retrieved September 16, 2016, from http://inside.uncc.edu/news-features/2014-06-11/governor-provides-funding-programs-aimed-student-recovery

Moore, A. S. (2012, January 22). A bridge to recovery on campus. *The New York Times*, p. ED14.

National Center for Education Statistics. (2016). *Digest of Education Statistics, 2014*. Washington, DC: U.S. Department of Education.

Noar, S. M. (2006). A 10-year retrospective of research in health mass media campaigns: Where do we go from here? *Journal of Health Communication*, *11*(1), 21–42. doi: 10.1080/10810730500461059

Noar, S. M., Palmgreen, P., Chabot, M., Dobransky, N., & Zimmerman, R. S. (2009). A 10-year systematic review of HIV/AIDS mass communication campaigns: Have we made progress? *Journal of Health Communication*, *14*(1), 15–42. doi: 10.1080/ 10810730802592239

Office of National Drug Control Policy. (2010). *National Drug Control Strategy*. Washington, DC: Author.

Perron, B. E., Grahovac, I. D., Uppal, J. S., Granillo, T. M., Shutter, J., & Porter, C. A. (2011). Supporting students in recovery on college campuses: Opportunities for student affairs professionals. *Journal of Student Affairs Research and Practice*, *48*(1), 47–64. doi: 10.2202/1949-6605.6226

Perron, B. E., Grahovac, I. D., & Parrish, D. (2010). Students for recovery: A novel way to support students on campus. *Psychiatric Services*, *61*(6), 633–633. doi: 10.1176/appi. ps.61.6.633

Smock, S. A., Baker, A. K., Harris, K. S., & D'Sauza, C. (2011). The role of social support in collegiate recovery communities: A review of the literature. *Alcoholism Treatment Quarterly, 29*(1), 35–44.

Snyder, L. B., Hamilton, M. A., Mitchell, E. W., Kiwanuka-Tondo, J., Fleming-Milici, F., & Proctor, D. (2004). A meta-analysis of the effect of mediated health communication campaigns on behavior change in the United States. *Journal of Health Communication, 9*(Suppl), 71–96. doi: 10.1080/10810730490271548

StepUP Program. (2016). *Frequently asked questions.* Retrieved from http://www.augsburg.edu/stepup/frequently-asked-questions/

Substance Abuse and Mental Health Services Administration (SMAHSA). (2015). *Behavioral Health Barometer: United States, 2015* (No. HHS Publication No. SMA-16-Baro-2015). Rockville, MD: Author. Retrieved from http://store.samhsa.gov/product/Behavioral-Health-Barometer-2015/All-New-Products/SMA16-BARO-2015

Substance Abuse and Mental Health Services Administration (SAMHSA). (2016). SAMHSA's National Summit on Recovery Support in the Collegiate Environment: Agenda. Rockville, MD: Author.

Transforming Youth Recovery. (2014). *2014 Collegiate Recovery Asset Survey Report* (No. 1). Reno, NV: Author. Retrieved from http://www.transformingyouthrecovery.org/sites/default/files/resource/2014%20Collegiate%20Recovery%20Asset%20Survey%20Report_TYR%208-11-14.pdf

Transforming Youth Recovery. (2015). *Collegiate Recovery Asset Survey: 2015 Monitor.* Reno, NV: Author.

University of Texas System Office of Media Relations. (2012). *Regents expand Collegiate Student Recovery Program to all UT academic institutions.* Retrieved September 16, 2016, from http://www.utsystem.edu/news/2012/11/15/regents-expand-collegiate-student-recovery-program-all-ut-academic-institutions

University of Texas System Office of Media Relations. (2015). *Regents position UT System to serve as national model for alcohol prevention and education programs.* Retrieved September 16, 2016, from http://www.utsystem.edu/news/2015/02/12/regents-position-ut-system-serve-national-model-alcohol-prevention-and-education-pro

Wakefield, M. A., Loken, B., & Hornik, R. C. (2010). Use of mass media campaigns to change health behaviour. *Lancet, 376*(9748), 1261–1271. doi: 10.1016/S0140-6736(10)60809-4

Watson, J. (2014). How does a campus recovery house impact its students and its host institution? *Journal of Social Work Practice in the Addictions, 14*(1), 101–112.

White, W., & Ali, S. (2010). Lapse and relapse: Is it time for a new language?

WHOQOL Group. (1998). Development of the World Health Organization WHOQOL-BREF quality of life assessment. The WHOQOL Group. *Psychological Medicine, 28*(3), 551–558.

Wiebe, R. P., Cleveland, H. H., & Dean, L. R. (2010). Maintaining abstinence in college: Temptations and tactics. In H. H. Cleveland, K. S. Harris, & R. P. Wiebe (Eds.), *Substance abuse recovery in college* (pp. 57–75). New York: Springer US.

10

The Potential for Delivering Substance Use Disorder Treatments to Emerging Adults in Child Welfare Settings

JUDY HAVLICEK AND JORDAN BRACISZEWSKI ■

More than 26,000 youth exit foster care to emancipation each year in the United States (U.S. Department of Health and Human Services [DHHS], 2015). Placed into foster care due to abuse and neglect and then never permanently reunified with their families of origin or placed with alternative long-term families, these young people are "on their own" to make the transition to adulthood (Barth, 1990). After leaving child welfare systems, foster youth may be at an elevated risk of substance use disorders in adulthood (Braciszewski & Stout, 2012; Havlicek, Garcia, & Smith, 2012). Poor prospects in emerging adulthood, including low educational attainment, unemployment, early pregnancy, homelessness, and criminal justice system involvement (Barth, 1990; Courtney & Dworsky, 2006; Courtney et al., 2007; Dworsky, 2005; Dworsky, Napolitano, & Courtney, 2013; Keller, Salazar, & Courtney, 2010; McMillen et al., 2005; Pecora, Studies, & Casey Family Programs, 2005; Pecora et al., 2006; Reilly, 2003), may further exacerbate substance use in adulthood.

Despite foster youths' elevated risk for substance use disorders, many experience challenges to accessing substance use disorder (SUD) treatment during and after foster care. In a recent panel study that is following foster youth in California as they make the transition to adulthood, less than half of those with self-reported substance use problems at ages 17 and 18 reported attending an SUD treatment program in the past year (Courtney & Charles, 2015). While the attendance rate surpasses that of the normative population (i.e., ~10%; Substance Abuse and

Mental Health Services Administration [SAMHSA], 2014), foster youth already reside within a system of care. Thus, connection to behavioral health services, in theory, should be optimal. Increasing this rate is important, as studies find that the receipt of SUD treatment declines over time (Courtney, Dworsky, Cusick, Keller, & Havlicek, 2005; Courtney et al., 2007; Courtney, Dworsky, Lee, Raap, & Hall, 2010). This suggests that there may be obstacles to accessing treatment services, including some specific to this vulnerable population (McMillen et al., 2004; McMillen & Raghavan, 2009; Sakai et al., 2014).

Although young people who age out of foster care represent a small proportion of all youth in child welfare systems in the United States, federal policy has signaled a commitment to improving preparation of foster youth for adulthood (Courtney, 2009). In this chapter, we explore the potential for delivering SUD treatments to emerging adults in the context of federal policy which has expanded over the past three decades to better support the transition foster youth make to adulthood. First, we provide background information on aging-out foster youth and review what is known about alcohol and substance use disorders and associated treatment. We also discuss potential barriers to treatment engagement. Then, we offer considerations for developing programs that address population-specific needs. Our review of substance use and aging-out foster youth comes at a time when the transition to adulthood is increasingly considered an important developmental period to target interventions aimed at promoting positive health behaviors (Schulenberg, Sameroff, & Cicchetti, 2004; White & Jackson, 2004).

FOSTER YOUTH EXITING CHILD WELFARE SYSTEMS THROUGH EMANCIPATION

In 2014, there were 141,181 adolescents between the ages of 12 and 20 placed in child welfare systems across the United States (U.S. DHHS, 2015). This age group represents over one-third (33%) of all children and youth placed in child welfare systems in the United States. At the age of 18, approximately 10% of youth "age out" of child welfare systems and make the transition to adulthood. Though reflecting an "extreme" case of all youth placed into foster care (Havlicek, 2010), these young people represent one of the most socially isolated and disconnected groups of young adults in the United States. At age 24, for example, rates of employment are lower than for peers in the general population (Hook & Courtney, 2011) and worsen over time (Stewart, Kum, Barth, & Duncan, 2014). By age 26, over two-thirds of former foster males (68%) and more than one-third of females (42%) are incarcerated as adults (Courtney et al., 2011; Cusick, Havlicek, & Courtney, 2012), and between one-third (31%) and just under one-half (46%) are homeless at least once (Dworsky et al., 2013). In spite of an increased federal commitment to improving outcomes in the transition to adulthood, our current understanding of how to promote positive pathways to adulthood remains underdeveloped (Courtney, Zinn, Koralek, & Bess, 2011; Montgomery, Donkoh, & Underhill, 2006; U.S. DHHS, 2008a, 2008b).

One barrier to making the transition to adulthood may have to do with an elevated risk for alcohol and substance use problems, both previous to and concurrent with this developmental period. The transition to adulthood is a time when young people obtain the education and training needed for future careers (Arnett, 2005). Young people who enter this developmental period while misusing alcohol or drugs may be more likely to experience negative outcomes, including academic and vocational failure, violence and/or other crime, unwanted pregnancies, and sexually transmitted diseases (Hingson, Heeren, Winter, & Wechsler, 2005; Perkins, 2002). For foster youth making the transition to adulthood, evidence suggests they experience serious forms of adversity prior to foster care entry (Havlicek, 2014); approximately half report having family members with a history of drug and/or alcohol problems (Courtney, Terao, & Bost, 2004; Courtney, Charles, Okpych, Napalitano, & Halsted, 2014), and a non-trivial proportion experience maltreatment during foster care (Courtney, Piliavin, Grogan-Kaylor, & Nesmith, 2001; Havlicek & Courtney, 2015; Pecora et al., 2005), all of which point to multiple risks that may contribute to and/or compound substance use and mental health disorders in adulthood.

The extent to which foster youth have serious problems associated with the use of alcohol and other substances, however, is poorly understood. In part, substance use problems among foster youth have received limited attention in the child welfare research (Braciszewski & Stout, 2012; Havlicek et al., 2012; Keller et al., 2010). Only recently have panel studies included a standardized instrument for making accurate clinical diagnoses. These instruments have varied across studies, making it somewhat of a challenge to synthesize study findings (Havlicek, McMillen, Fedoravicius, McNelly, & Robinson, 2012). Few of these studies report details about the age of onset, severity, or co-occurrence of substance use disorders with other mental health disorders that may be critical to understanding service needs (Havlicek et al., 2012). Information about substance use quantity and frequency over time (as opposed to clinical diagnoses) is even more rare (Braciszewski & Stout, 2012).

While a relatively clear picture of alcohol use among aging-out foster youth has emerged, questions remain about the extent to which drug use is a significantly larger problem. For instance, Keller et al. (2010) reported a lifetime prevalence rate of alcohol abuse or dependence (14%) that is similar to the rate observed in a national probability study of 17- and 18-years-olds in the general population (14.5%; Merikangas et al., 2010). A more recent study of 17- to 18-year-old foster youth making the transition to adulthood in California was in line with these two studies (12.4%; Courtney & Charles, 2015). With respect to (non-alcohol) substance use disorders, Keller and colleagues found a lifetime prevalence rate that is substantially lower (6.3%) than the rate observed in the general population (16.3%; Merikangas et al., 2010). However, Keller et al. (2010) note that programming errors resulted in 338 youth not being asked follow-up questions about drug use. They, therefore, report weighted estimates based on their attempts to recontact these individuals, which ranged from 7.0% to 20.2% and was closer to rates reported by Courtney and Charles (2015) (21.3%).

Though prevalence rates of alcohol and/or substance abuse and dependence tend to be relatively similar to those for the general population of transition-aged adults, evidence suggests that peak rates may increase over time and happen later for emerging adults in child welfare systems, a time when prevalence is declining for general-population emerging adults (Braciszewski & Stout, 2012; Havlicek et al., 2012). In the largest panel study to date, which followed foster youth from ages 17–18 to age 26 in three Midwestern states, the past-year rate of alcohol abuse/dependence and drug abuse/dependence at age 19 was 10.6% and 12.5%, respectively, and at age 21, 14.2% and 5.6%, respectively (Courtney et al., 2005). At age 26, the past-year rate of alcohol abuse/dependence was 29% and other drug abuse/dependence was 43% (Courtney et al., 2011). These findings support the results from another panel study of foster youth in Missouri, which followed foster youth from ages 17 to 19. Study findings indicate that self-reported use of alcohol and marijuana increased over the course of the study (Narendorf & McMillen, 2010).

Exiting foster care early (i.e., before the age of legal emancipation) is associated with steeper increases in self-reported substance use (Courtney et al., 2005; Narendorf & McMillen, 2010). In fact, lifetime rates of alcohol and substance abuse and/or dependence diagnoses tend to be significantly higher among young people discharged from foster care. These elevations seem to arise from recent (post-exit) elevations in alcohol and drug use rather than from a pre-existing condition (Braciszewski & Stout, 2012; Courtney & Dworsky, 2006; Courtney et al., 2005). Such new diagnoses are highly prevalent. For instance, new diagnoses of alcohol and substance abuse were noted among 11% and 13% of 19-year old participants who were no longer in care (Courtney et al., 2005). Although national survey comparisons are limited by panel data, new past-year diagnoses among 18- and 19-year-olds in the general population vary between 1% and 2% (Substance Abuse and Mental Health Services Administration [SAMHSA], 2014). These findings underscore the need to screen for, prevent, and address substance use problems during critical periods of the transition to adulthood.

CRITICAL PERIODS, ENTRY INTO FOSTER CARE, AND PLACEMENTS

Other critical periods for substance use problems may be at entry into foster care and throughout child welfare system involvement. In a study of foster youth between the ages of 17 and 18 in three states, Keller et al. (2010) find that two-thirds of all alcohol-related diagnoses (69%) had an onset after entry into child welfare, whereas only about one-fifth (19%) had onset prior to entry. Part of the reason may have to do with child maltreatment and symptoms of trauma. In this study, the mean age of onset of posttraumatic stress disorder (PTSD) (11 years, on average) was earlier than for alcohol use diagnoses (14 years, on average) and substance use diagnoses (14 years, on average), which adds support for the need to implement routine screening and assessment of behavioral health needs at entry and at regular periods following involvement with the child welfare system. One persistent challenge to implementing routine screening of alcohol and substance use disorders is that mental health screening and assessments are inconsistent across states, and even if screened, most states may also face a scarcity of behavioral health services, such as substance use treatment (McCarthy, Van Buren, & Irvine, 2007), to address identified needs.

Several studies suggest certain types of placements in the child welfare system may warrant close monitoring of substance use and perhaps offer opportunities for education and awareness of substance use. For instance, in one study, youth in kinship care were least likely to meet a diagnosis for substance use disorders, whereas youth living in independent living were more likely to meet criteria for an alcohol disorder (Keller et al., 2010). This finding is consistent with other research that shows that residing in an independent living program may be associated with increased rates of substance use disorders. For instance, there is some research that finds foster youth stepped down from a group home to a transitional living program may be at risk of increased drug use (Narendorf & McMillen, 2010). Increased training to service providers of group care and independent living placement settings in symptoms of substance use disorders may go a long way to enhancing early detection and subsequent need for treatment.

Taken together, emerging adults in child welfare systems are at high risk for both problematic substance use and a poor trajectory into young adulthood, issues which only serve to exacerbate each other. Despite the need for more rigorous epidemiological substance use research with this population, it is clear that once these young people leave foster care, their risk for developing substance use disorders is high. Social service systems would be best served by implementing evidence-based behavioral health screening at several key periods (e.g., entry into care, regularly on a fixed schedule, before exit from care). Such efforts would have great potential to better triage young people into proper levels of care.

BARRIERS TO SUBSTANCE USE TREATMENT

Several studies have reported on lifetime and past-year use of SUD treatment services among foster youth making the transition to adulthood in one state (Courtney et al., 2004, 2005, 2007, 2010, 2011, 2014; Courtney & Charles, 2015; McMillen et al., 2004, 2005; Pecora et al., 2005). For youth at age 17, the past-year rates of substance use treatment range from 3% (McMillen et al., 2004) to 14% (Courtney et al., 2004). Over time, however, there is a decrease in the receipt of substance use treatment. For instance, rates decrease from 8% at age 19 (Courtney et al., 2005) to 4% at age 26. This trend holds up when estimates are based on national data. Recent evidence drawing from a sample of 17-year-olds in foster care in 50 jurisdictions and the District of Columbia suggests that slightly over one-quarter of youth (27%) report having been referred for SUD assessment or counseling at some point in their lives (U.S. DHHS, 2012a); between the ages of 17 and 19, however, this drops to 14% (U.S. DHHS, 2014). A slightly higher percentage of same-aged youth that emancipated from foster care than of youth that remained in foster care reported being referred for substance use assessment or counseling. Given that the transition to adulthood is a critical time for learning positive health behaviors for later in life, it is critical to identify potential barriers that may exist to substance use treatment.

One barrier to accessing services *after* leaving foster care may have to do with the limited opportunities provided to foster youth *during* foster care to understand their behavioral health needs and to be involved in services planning. In a recent focus group study, foster youth described being "pushed" to access mental health services while in foster care even though they did not have a perceived need for help (Sakai et al., 2014). Other evidence suggests that obstacles to sharing information with foster youth may also exist, as some service providers have reported feeling uncomfortable reviewing psychiatric histories with young people in foster care (Havlicek et al., 2012). The lack of open communication about behavioral health needs may partially explain why over 1 out of every 10 foster youth at age 19 that was hospitalized or visited an emergency department reported substance use or emotional problems as the main reason for hospitalization (Courtney et al., 2005).

An additional barrier to service receipt may have to do with marginalization and stigma. In addition to the general stigma associated with misusing substances, several studies describe the ways that foster care contributes to a stigmatized self-identity (Kools, 1997) and an inability to ask for help even when help is needed (Samuels & Pryce, 2008). It may then follow that young people in foster care who are approaching adulthood may not have the skills needed to advocate on their own behalf. Substance use and mental health conditions can also further impede foster youths' abilities to advocate for themselves. This suggests that providing foster youth with information about how and where to obtain substance use treatment may not be sufficient to ensure receipt of help. Active preparation and outreach may be necessary conditions to facilitate access to and receipt of needed treatment. It is also unclear how young people conceptualize and access drug and alcohol treatment programs, which could potentially vary from group psychoeducation to mental health counseling. Given that just under 50% of youth report receiving information about substance use at age 17 or 18 (Courtney et al., 2004), the manner in which youth are asked is important. More detailed understanding is needed about how young people conceptualize the types of services received and whether such services are perceived of as being adequate for addressing needs (Rauktis, Fusco, Cahalane, Bennett, & Reinhart, 2011).

By virtue of their placement into child welfare, foster youth have had at least one, if not ongoing, experience of adverse relationships with adults due to neglect, abuse, and/or abandonment. Attachment serves as the primary foundation for forming healthy relationships (Bowlby, 1969, 1988); unstable and chaotic relationships, therefore, may result in difficulties developing and maintaining healthy and productive alliances with health professionals or other authority figures. Setting and relationship turnover (e.g., school mobility, multiple placements, and temporary caregivers) can perpetuate these challenges. For example, a study of case manager turnover indicated that young people can develop strong attachments to these providers, only to lose that relationship and disrupt the development of a nurturing bond (Strolin-Goltzman, Kollar, & Trinkle, 2010). Over time, foster youth may build up skepticism about the perceived costs and benefits involved in relationship building (Hyde & Kammerer, 2009), including healthcare relationships.

Trust—whether between youth and parents, case managers, therapist, or physicians—is an essential component of healthy relationships. Foster care alumni, given experiences with discontinuity in important relationships, may struggle or be reluctant to develop trust, particularly with healthcare providers whom youth may only see briefly and infrequently (DiGiuseppe & Christakis, 2003; Rubin et al., 2004). Indeed, in a focus group study, foster care staff, administrators, and parents expressed concern about brief interventions (Braciszewski, Moore, & Stout, 2014), a common and successful practice in the general population of emerging adults (Monti et al., 1999) but one whose components involve brief and infrequent meetings. Participants believed that developing a solid working alliance quickly would be very unlikely. Furthermore, if such a relationship were to develop, respondents strongly feared that this could have negative consequences, as the interventionist would soon leave the young person's life, repeating a pattern that the staff and parents were trying to staunch. Regardless of intervention brevity, development of a trusting relationship may present the most significant challenge for the implementation of interventions within the foster care system.

Social support—especially for abstinence from alcohol and drugs—is arguably the strongest predictor of short- and long-term abstinence (Stout, Kelly, Magill, & Pagano, 2012; Kelly, Stout, Magill, Tonigan, & Pagano, 2011; Kelly, Hoeppner, Stout, & Pagano, 2012). However, individuals exposed to adverse events in childhood tend to report smaller social networks (Ford, Clark, & Stansfeld, 2011). Further complicating matters, foster youth have negatively rated suggestions to access such support (Braciszewski, Tran, et al., 2017). Specifically, participants felt that encouragement to use support networks reminded them that few or sometimes no people existed on whom they could rely, subsequently increasing their cravings to use alcohol or drugs. Thus, traditional substance use interventions that push social support as a mechanism of change may further isolate transition-age foster youth.

Treatment engagement can be further impacted by disruptions in the chain from screening to intervention. In states that do not provide systematic screening of health needs, case managers may rely on foster parents or group home leaders to identify the need for healthcare (Simms, Dubowitz, & Szilagyi, 2000). However, these individuals often do not have the legal power to provide treatment consent; rather, biological parents (i.e., in cases where parental rights have not been terminated) can sometimes remain in charge of consent, causing a delay in service access. If consent is granted, the complexity of these cases (e.g., legal involvement, multiple health issues, obtaining health histories) and low insurance reimbursement relative to time invested can serve as a deterrent to receipt of care (Simms et al., 2000). Changes in placements can also lead to a change in provider, further delaying timely assessment or treatment. Even if providers remain the same over time, housing disruptions can negatively impact consistent health monitoring. Results from an analysis of Medicaid claims data suggested that foster care status was associated with decreased continuity of care when compared with similarly insured but non-foster care youth (DiGiuseppe & Christakis, 2003). While the difference in timely receipt of services was not particularly large, the authors concluded that for youth with more substantial needs, this delay could be problematic.

Finally, there is some, albeit limited, evidence that drop-off in SUD treatment receipt may be due to past receipt of services and whether foster youth viewed treatment (and other services) as beneficial. In focus groups with 28 former foster youth with current mental health conditions, themes centered around limited engagement in decision making about mental health services and insufficient support in planning for future needs (Sakai et al., 2014). The lack of control over treatment options exacerbated limited control in other areas during foster care and engendered mistrust of mental health professionals and negative attitudes about seeking help.

In summary, this review is limited in what can be said about the nature, severity, and prevalence of alcohol and substance use disorders among aging-out foster youth. Studies that identify chronic exposure to neglect and child abuse (Havlicek, 2014; Havlicek & Courtney, 2015) along with serious histories of drug and alcohol problems among biological caregivers (Courtney & Charles, 2015; Courtney et al., 2004) nevertheless suggest that young people approaching adulthood in foster care may be at heightened risk for substance use and co-occurring mental health disorders. This may be particularly true when young people with symptoms of trauma enter child welfare systems and these symptoms are inconsistently identified and treated across state child welfare systems (McCarthy et al., 2007). As young people exit foster care through emancipation and face barriers to transitioning to new adult roles, substance use may exacerbate the successful mastery of developmental tasks and contribute to failures and stress (Schulenberg, Maggs, & O'Malley, 2003). Providing group care and independent living service providers with substance use–specific education and training may assist in the identification and/or prevention of alcohol or substance use problems. Recent policy shifts in independent living and healthcare access may also provide new opportunities to increase understanding of behavioral health needs and planning between foster youth and service providers (Courtney, 2009).

SHIFTING POLICY DEVELOPMENTS AND NEW OPPORTUNITIES TO ADDRESS BEHAVIORAL HEALTH NEEDS

Recent policy developments provide a unique opportunity to address the behavioral health needs of children in foster care. These policy changes reflect an evolving understanding of normative transitions to adulthood and growing knowledge of the particular challenges faced by foster youth in the transition to adulthood

(Courtney, 2009). To begin with, the role of the federal government in supporting foster youth shifted dramatically when the Foster Care Independence Act of 1999 (FCIA) established the Chafee Foster Care Independent Program (CFCIP), which allocates federal funds annually to fund a variety of independent living services. The FCIA strengthened the Independent Living Program of 1986 by doubling federal funds provided to states to fund Chafee services targeting education, employment, financial management, and substance use prevention; offering states flexibility in defining eligibility criteria; and allowing states to use up to 30% of funds to pay for the costs of housing (Okpych, 2015). A key function of the FCIA was establishing the National Youth in Transition Database (NYTD) to track cohorts of foster youth as they transition to young adulthood and to record receipt of services funded through the CFCIP. That one of the services funded by the CFCIP is SUD treatment and the NYTD is reporting on referral to and receipt of treatment services suggests that new opportunities may exist for developing better understanding of national patterns of access and use of substance use treatment. This may be particularly useful in exploring the magnitude of and reasons for variation in substance use service receipt within and across states (Courtney & Charles, 2015; Okpych, 2015).

More recently, the Fostering Connections to Success and Increasing Adoptions Act (hereafter referred to as the Fostering Connections Act) of 2008 (P.L. 110-351) gives partial reimbursement to states for the costs of extending foster care to age 21, provided that foster youth are (1) completing high school or an equivalency program; (2) enrolled in post-secondary or vocational school; (3) participating in a program or activity designed to promote or remove barriers to employment; (4) employed for at least 80 hours a month; or (5) incapable of doing any of these activities because of a medical condition. States that opt to extend foster care[1] become responsible for caring for foster youth while promoting connections to work and school (Courtney, 2009). This means that jurisdictions must address substance use disorders that become a barrier to work and school. Under the Fostering Connections Act, jurisdictions may use federal training dollars at an enhanced reimbursement rate to train staff outside of the child welfare system in behavioral health needs. Challenges nevertheless remain in (1) the reluctance of states to extend foster care to age 21; (2) the few evidence-supported models of coordinated care to streamline the transition from child to adult service systems; and (3) the lack of a strong evidence base supporting the effectiveness of services provided to foster youth (Courtney, 2009). This suggests that there is a critical need to understand how substance use treatment is coordinated within and across child and adult service systems. More specifically, answering the following questions is critical:

1) To what extent are funds being used for cross-training purposes?
2) What do substance use treatment services in the adult sector look like with emerging adults in public systems of care as children?

1. As of April 4, 2015, there were 22 states with an approved plan to extend foster care after the age of 18.

3) How do substance use treatment services build support systems around young adults who may be with reliable family in the transition to adulthood?

Given the likely co-occurrence of PTSD and substance use disorders, understanding what types of substance use treatment models are most effective with young people exiting care through emancipation may also be key.

A third change has to do with guaranteed access to health insurance, including benefits to substance use and mental health treatment, under the Patient Protection and Affordable Care Act (ACA). As of January 1, 2014, all states in the United States must extend Medicaid coverage to age 26 for all foster youth enrolled in Medicaid and in foster care on their 18th birthday or enrolled in Medicaid when they age out of foster care if over the age of 18 (Emam, 2014). Youth aging out of foster care are also eligible for benefits from the Early and Periodic Screening, Diagnostic, and Treatment (EPSDT) provisions of Medicaid until age 21. EPSDT benefits include preventative, dental, mental health, and developmental services for youth, and states are required to provide Medicaid-coverable, appropriate, and medically necessary services needed to these youth to improve their healthcare. Together, these benefits have the potential to provide a critical safety net to foster youth to manage health and behavioral health needs. Challenges include ensuring that youth are enrolled through automated systems, training child welfare and Medicaid staff and partners in Medicaid enrollment and re-enrollment of aging-out foster youth, and training child welfare staff to help youth to use their new healthcare coverage (Emam, 2014; Sakai et al., 2014).

A significant number of young people may seek to reunify with their families, however, and potentially lose that connection to healthcare just prior to their 18th birthday. State systems may not be able to respond quickly enough to re-enroll them in foster care, thus reducing their chances to meet eligibility criteria for these benefits. Improved flexibility is needed to bridge this gap, as this particular group of young people may be likely to experience homelessness after becoming categorically ineligible for services in child welfare systems.

These policy developments have occurred in the context of a decreased number of children entering child welfare systems and an increase in the number of children exiting care through reunification, adoption, and guardianship (U.S. DHHS, 2012a). With fewer children entering foster care and remaining on caseloads, the Administration for Children and Families (ACF) has moved toward integrating the goals of (1) safety and (2) permanence of children with enhancing (3) well-being in light of emerging research that has consistently identified that the impacts of maltreatment are concentrated on behavioral, social, and emotional domains. Of the three goals, child welfare systems has tended to focus less on well-being than on safety and permanence (Wulcyzn, Barth, Yuan, Harden, & Landsverk, 2005).

In 2011, the Child and Family Services Improvement and Innovation Act of 2011 (P.L. 112-34) required each state to include in their healthcare services oversight and coordination plan information about treatment of emotional trauma associated with child maltreatment. In a follow-up Information Memorandum issued by the ACF in April of 2012, the U.S. Department of Health and Human Services encouraged child welfare systems to focus on improving the behavioral and socioemotional outcomes for young people who have been exposed to abuse and neglect, through consistent screening and use of evidence-based services (U.S. DHHS, 2012b). This suggests that increasing the information and skills that foster youth have to navigate behavioral health services is a critical part of preparing foster youth to make the transition to adulthood.

In summary, substance use treatment services are currently funded by the Chafee Foster Care Independent Act, but there is variation within and across states in the use of such treatment. The National Youth in Transition Database may ultimately help states to use information on substance use treatment outcomes to improve access to services within and across states. The increasing focus on addressing the well-being of maltreated children in foster care provides new opportunities for targeting interventions prior to and during emerging adulthood. Next, we give consideration to screening and workforce training, program development, and implementation issues related to emerging adult substance use disorders.

IMPLEMENTING SUBSTANCE USE SERVICES FOR EMERGING ADULTS IN CARE

Screening and Training

Given the shifting policy landscape, child welfare agencies should pay special attention to the behavioral health service needs of youth in care who are approaching the age of majority. In particular, routine screening for substance use and mental health disorders should be common practice when working with older youth in out-of-home care. Although the Children's Bureau of the Administration for Children and Families has issued guidelines recognizing the importance of assessing mental health and substance use problems among youth in out-of-home care, the guidelines do not currently specify the timing or the content of screening. A 2004 review of state Child and Family Service Review final reports found that only 16 states had adopted a requirement for screening upon or soon after entry into foster care. Only one state consistently screened all youth entering the child welfare system, while the remainder of states tended to screen youth inconsistently (McCarthy et al., 2007). In 2009, a group of 11 child-serving organizations came to a consensus and developed and endorsed guidelines for child welfare, which call for screening within 72 hours of placement and within 30 days to screen for ongoing problems (Romanelli et al., 2009). These recommendations support a joint policy statement by the American Academy of Child and Adolescent Psychiatry and the Child Welfare League of America, which recommends regular and routine screening as a part of well-child care. Very little is known about the extent to which foster youth are screened for substance use disorders in emerging adulthood.

According to the Substance Abuse and Mental Health Service Administration (SAMHSA, 2011) guide for child welfare organizations, early detection and screening of behavioral health problems should adhere to standards and principles, such as obtaining informed consent from parents, guardians, or young adults who are ages 18 and over, and obtaining informed assent from youth under the age of 18. Youth who are capable of understanding should receive an explanation of what the early identification process is and why it is being done, and given the right to refuse to participate. Providing foster youth with information about the purpose of screenings and being given the right to refuse participation may be especially important from the perspective of young people who describe ways in which drug testing can make them feel untrusted by others, particularly when they have done nothing to warrant testing (Hyde & Kammerer, 2009). Clear, written procedures for requesting consent and notifying youth and/or their caregivers of the results should be available (SAMHSA, 2011).

SAMHSA recently identified and described eight substance use/disorder screening tools with adolescents in a matrix for comparison by target problem, age, and other factors. The age range of tools is from as early as 12 years, in the Personal Experience Screening Questionnaire (PESQ), and as high as 20 years, in the Adolescent Obsessive Compulsive Drinking Scale (A-OCDS) and the Adolescent Alcohol and Drug Involvement Scale (AADIS). Required reading levels ranged from fourth-grade level in the PESQ to the sixth- to seventh-grade level in the Rutgers Alcohol Problem Index (RAPI) and the Drug Abuse Screening Test–Adolescents (DAST-A). Caution is nevertheless warranted given that the use of these eight screening tools has not been studied in child welfare settings (SAMHSA, 2011).

Although screening tools are designed to take anywhere from 5 to 10 minutes to complete, the National Institute on Alcohol and Abuse (NIAAA) in collaboration with the American Academy of Pediatrics developed a two-question screen for problematic alcohol use among 9-year-olds to 18-year-olds (National Institute on Alcohol Abuse and Alcoholism, 2011). One question asks about friends' drinking and the other asks about the frequency of personal drinking. These questions were empirically derived through analysis of a representative survey that included 166,000 youth ages 12 to 18 (Smith, Chung, Donovan, Martin, & Windle, 2010) and multiple longitudinal studies (Brown et al., 2010). If a youth screens positive, he or she can be given a longer evaluation. Analyses indicate that these questions are effective predictors of adverse alcohol outcomes; A recent study with a large and diverse sample of 12-17 year olds shows good reliability and validity though further testing in the general population is still needed (Spirito, Bromberg, Casper, Chun, Mellow, Dean, & Linakis, 2016).

Substance use–specific training may also be useful for professional staff in group care, residential settings, and independent living programs, where there may be reduced levels of supervision and elevated risks for alcohol and substance use (Keller et al., 2010). Helping other service providers, caregivers, and caseworkers learn about some of the warning signs of substance use problems and using these signs to evaluate whether behavior warrants further assessment may also be useful.

Developing Programs that Address Population Specific Needs

Several types of treatment can reduce substance use problems. To our knowledge, there are few existing models that have been tested with emerging adults existing foster care. The Screening, Brief Intervention, and Referral to Treatment (SBIRT) model is an evidence-based practice used to identify and reduce problematic use, abuse, and dependence on alcohol and drugs. The aim of the SBIRT is to prevent unhealthy consequences of alcohol and drug use among individuals who may not have reached the diagnostic level of a substance use disorder, and help those with problematic substance use to enter treatment and stay in it. More specifically, brief interventions are given to individuals showing substance use of moderate severity, while persons with more severe problems are referred to treatment. Although there is evidence supporting the effectiveness of brief interventions for alcohol use among college students in the United States between the ages of 18 and 22 (Carey, Scott-Sheldon, Carey, & DeMartini, 2007), it is not clear whether the SBIRT itself is an effective approach to risky alcohol use among adolescents in acute care settings (Yuma-Guerrero et al., 2012). Less is known about the effectiveness of SBIRT with adolescents or transition-aged youth served in large systems of care. However, the SBIRT was derived from frameworks familiar to child welfare and other systems (e.g., wraparound services, systems of care, gateway provider); thus, with modifications, it could serve as an excellent fit for foster youth. Indeed, in various forms, SBIRT has become the most widely endorsed public health model for addressing the gap in substance use treatment access for both adolescents and adults (SAMHSA, 2013).

Electronic Models of Delivery of Substance Use Disorder Treatment

Although little research has examined how foster youth prefer to access and interact with substance use and/or mental health services, one innovative approach to the delivery of services uses social media and mobile technology for service delivery. One such promising brief substance use intervention is currently being tested with transition-aged foster youth. The aim of Interactive Health Lifestyle Preparation (iHeLP) is to reduce treatment access barriers by using technology to target substance use reduction among youth exiting foster care (Braciszewski et al., 2016). Specifically, foster youth who report potentially problematic levels of alcohol or drug use are first given a 20-minute computerized brief intervention. iHeLP is unique in that an animated narrator delivers intervention content. The narrator, named "Peedy the Parrot," can talk, move, gesture, display emotional reactions, and make empathic reflections that parallel those seen in a person-to-person interaction. Use of headphones and narration by Peedy allows access to content at any literacy level and provides a confidential setting regardless of location. With regard to content, the intervention addresses alcohol and drug use by using an approach consistent with motivational interviewing (MI; Miller & Rollnick, 2012) and the FRAMES (Miller & Sanchez, 1994) approach to brief interventions. FRAMES involves six major elements found in effective, brief clinical trials: (1) constructive, nonconfrontational Feedback, tailored to the individual; (2) emphasis on personal control and Responsibility; (3) provision of nonjudgmental Advice through educational information or suggestions; (4) offering a Menu of options or strategies; (5) displaying Empathy; and (6) promotion of feelings of Self-efficacy.

Upon completion of the computerized portion, all participants provide a "Readiness Ruler" score, based on the following question: "On a scale of 0 to 10, how ready are you to make a change (quit or cut down) in your use of alcohol or drugs?" Responses are then applied to the second component of iHeLP, which involves daily SMS text messaging. Text message content is theoretically grounded in MI as well as the transtheoretical model (TTM; Prochaska, DiClemente, & Norcross, 1992). The TTM posits that behavior change occurs in increments and along stages, including not being interested (precontemplation), considering change (contemplation), getting ready (preparation), starting to change (action), and maintaining change (maintenance). MI and TTM are complementary, as MI is a method of conversation that is particularly effective at the beginning TTM stages of readiness for change (DiClemente & Velasquez, 2002). Individual scores on the Readiness Ruler are anchored by stages analogous to those in the TTM and are highly predictive of drinking outcomes in adolescents (Maisto et al., 2011). iHeLP text messages are tailored to each participant's level of motivation by using content appropriate for that person's current stage of change.

Motivation, however, often fluctuates over time and should be considered when designing motivation-based interventions (Resnicow & Page, 2008). As such, iHeLP asks weekly "poll questions," sent via text message, to assess readiness to change. When participants respond with a score that alters their stage of change (e.g., moving from precontemplation to contemplation), the content of their messages reflects that change. This design allows more up-to-the-minute tailoring of intervention content, rather than relying solely on baseline or follow-up data collected months after the initial interview.

Because so little is known about the preferences and voices of transition-aged foster youth, one major goal of iHeLP development was to incorporate participant feedback at all phases through the use of focus groups, an open trial, and a pilot randomized controlled trial. During the focus group phase, participants were asked to develop their own intervention for problematic substance use. Participants highlighted the need for a nonjudgmental stance, provided feedback about working with service providers, and gave preference for some type of interaction (not necessarily with a human) and respect for autonomy and individuality (Braciszewski, Tran, Tzilos, & Moore, 2014). Participants also provided direct feedback on text message content, while also writing some of the actual messages to be used (Braciszewski et al., 2017).

Next, an open trial was conducted with 17 participants who provided feedback about their experiences. Results from the open trial supported acceptability and feasibility (Braciszewski, Tzilos, Moore, Stout, Bock, et al., 2015). Participants rated the computer as easy to work with, and they viewed the narrator as nonjudgmental. In addition, three times per week, text messages were followed with a question about the relevance or likeability of that day's message. Results indicated a 92% approval rating for the messages. Open-trial participant feedback was incorporated into a final version of iHeLP, which is currently being tested in a small randomized trial. Thirty youth exiting foster care through emancipation have been assigned to iHeLP or a control group. The participants will be followed for 1 year to track intervention effects.

While iHeLP demonstrates promise, there has been surprisingly limited research on harnessing technology to enhance services to foster youth. This suggests that caution is needed. Research is needed that asks several questions: How many youth have access to computers and/or own smartphones? Would technology be useful to young people who lack access to services, such as those residing outside of large urban centers? Are there certain subgroups of youth that would benefit more than others? How can technology be integrated with face-to-face interactions?

Peer Models of Delivery of Substance Use Disorder Treatment

Given the stigma that is associated with being in foster care and/or having a substance use disorder, peer-led approaches to service delivery may also have intuitive appeal to young people in child welfare settings. Reluctance to discuss feelings, to form secure attachments (Samuels, 2009), to rely on others (Samuels & Pryce, 2008), or to let down their guard can hinder engagement in traditional substance use services. To assist foster youth in coping with their experiences, programs may benefit from taking a strengths-based approach. Providing helpers, formal and informal, with supervision and support may be critical, particularly when sharing past experiences of adversity. Currently, very little is known about peer- or alumni-led "helper" approaches with foster youth. Despite the lack of understanding, peer-led approaches may offer critical benefits not only to those being helped but also to the helper (Melkman, Mor-Salwo, Mangold, Zeller, & Benbenishty, 2015). Developing and rigorously testing well-specified peer-led interventions is an important area for future research.

The Need for Trauma-Informed Care

Finally, there is a wealth of evidence that foster youth have extensive maltreatment histories (Courtney & Heuring, 2005), which, at chronic levels, can lead to the development of PTSD. Given the strong relationship between substance use and trauma, it is likely that addressing maltreatment and abuse will be a necessary component of any successful alcohol and drug treatment for this vulnerable group of young adults.

CONCLUSIONS

The lack of current and comprehensive information about substance use disorders among foster youth transitioning to adulthood presents a gap in the existing knowledge base with relevance to prevention and intervention. In the interest of providing guidance for future research and intervention development, we reviewed the research on aging-out foster youth and substance use to gain a better understanding of where to focus the development and implementation of targeted services that will have the most beneficial impact on the lives of youth transitioning to adulthood. These findings suggest a need to focus future attention in three main areas: (1) the transition process from child welfare to adult service systems, (2) coordination of services across public systems of care, and (3) developing evidence-based interventions. Making sure that youth with substance use problems receive treatment, that substance use treatment is coordinated with other service needs, and that services are effective would go a long way toward promoting positive health behaviors in the transition to adulthood.

REFERENCES

Arnett, J. J. (2005). The developmental context of substance use in emerging adulthood. *Journal of Drug Issues, 35*(2), 235–254.

Barth, R. P. (1990). On their own: The experiences of youth after foster care. *Child and Adolescent Social Work Journal, 7*(5), 419–440.

Bowlby, J. (1969). *Attachment and loss,* Vol. 1. New York: Basic Books.

Bowlby, J. (1988). *A secure base: Parent–child attachment and healthy human development.* New York: Basic Books.

Braciszewski, J. M., Moore, R. S., & Stout, R. L. (2014). Rationale for a new direction in foster youth substance use disorder prevention. *Journal of Substance use, 19*(1-2), 108–111.

Braciszewski, J. M., & Stout, R. L. (2012). Substance use among current and former foster youth: A systematic review. *Children and Youth Services Review, 34*(12), 2337–2344.

Braciszewski, J. M., Stout, R. L., Tzilos, G. K., Moore, R. S., Bock, B. C., & Chamberlain, P. (2016). Testing a dynamic automated intervention model for emerging adults. *Journal of Child and Adolescent Substance Abuse, 25*(3), 181–187.

Braciszewski, J. M., Tran, T. B., Moore, R. S., Bock, B. C., Tzilos, G. K., Chamberlain, P., & Stout, R. L. (2017). Developing a tailored texting intervention: A card sort methodology. *Journal of Applied Biobehavioral Research*. doi: 10.1111/jabr.12060

Braciszewski, J. M., Tran, T. B., Tzilos, G. K., & Moore, R. S. (2014). iHeLP: Improving substance use outcomes for foster youth. Poster presented at the Society for Research on Adolescence, Austin, TX.

Braciszewski, J. M., Tzilos, G. K., Moore, R. S., & Stout, R. L. (2015, June). iHeLP: A collaborative approach to substance use prevention for foster youth. Paper presented at the Society for Community Research and Action, Lowell, MA.

Braciszewski, J., Tzilos, G., Moore, R., Stout, R., Bock, B., & Chamberlain, P. (2015). Using technology to prevent substance use disorders in foster youth. *Alcoholism-Clinical and Experimental Research*, *39*, 23A–23A.

Brown, S., Donovan, J., McGue, M., Schulenberg, J., Zucker, R., & Goldman, M. (2010). Youth alcohol screening workgroup II: Determining optimal secondary screening questions. *Alcoholism: Clinical and Experimental Research*, *34*(6), 267A–267A.

Carey, K. B., Scott-Sheldon, L. A., Carey, M. P., & DeMartini, K. S. (2007). Individual-level interventions to reduce college student drinking: A meta-analytic review. *Addictive Behaviors*, *32*(11), 2469–2494.

Courtney, M. E. (2009). The difficult transition to adulthood for foster youth in the US: Implications for the state as corporate parent. Seattle, WA: Society for Research in Child Development.

Courtney, M. E., & Charles, P. (2015). *Mental health and substance use problems and service utilization by transition-age foster youth: Early findings from CalYOUTH.* Chicago: Chapin Hall at the University of Chicago. Retrieved from http://www.chapinhall.org/sites/default/files/CY_MH_DP0515.pdf

Courtney, M. E., Charles, P., Okpych, N. J., Napalitano, L., & Halsted, K. (2014). *Findings from the California youth transitions to adulthood study (CalYOUTH): Conditions of foster youth at age 17.* Chicago, IL: Chapin Hall at the University of Chicago. Retrieved from http://www.chapinhall.org/sites/default/files/Youth%20Report.pdf

Courtney, M. E., & Dworsky, A. (2006). Early outcomes for young adults transitioning from out-of-home care in the USA. *Child & Family Social Work*, *11*(3), 209–219.

Courtney, M. E., Dworsky, A., Brown, A., Cary, C., Love, K., & Vorhies, V. (2011). *Midwest study of the adult functioning of former foster youth: outcomes at age 26.* Chicago, IL: Chapin Hall. Retrieved from https://www.chapinhall.org/sites/default/files/Midwest%20Evaluation_Report_4_10_12.pdf

Courtney, M. E., Dworsky, A. L., Cusick, G. R., Keller, T., and Havlicek, J., (2005). *Midwest evaluation of the adult functioning of former foster youth: Outcomes at 19.* Chicago, IL: Chapin Hall at the University of Chicago. Retrieved from http://www.chapinhall.org/sites/default/files/ChapinHallDocument_4.pdf

Courtney, M. E., Dworsky, A. L., Cusick, G. R., Keller, T. E., Havlicek, J. R., & Perez, A. (2007). *Midwest evaluation of the adult functioning of former foster youth: Outcomes at 21.* Chicago, IL: Chapin Hall at the University of Chicago. Retrieved from http://www.chapinhall.org/sites/default/files/ChapinHallDocument_2.pdf

Courtney, M. E., Dworsky, A. L., Lee, J. A. S., Raap, M., & Hall, C. (2010). *Midwest evaluation of the adult functioning of former foster youth: Outcomes at 23 and 24.* Chicago, IL: Chapin Hall at the University of Chicago. Retrieved from http://www.chapinhall.org/sites/default/files/Midwest_Study_Age_23_24.pdf

Courtney, M. E., & Heuring, D. H. (2005). The transition to adulthood for youth "aging out" of the foster care system In D. W. Osgood, E. M. Foster, C. Flanagan, & G.R. Ruth (Eds.), *On your own without a net: The transition to adulthood for vulnerable populations* (pp. 27–67). Chicago, IL: University of Chicago Press.

Courtney, M. E., Piliavin, I., Grogan-Kaylor, A., & Nesmith, A. (2001). Foster youth transitions to adulthood: A longitudinal view of youth leaving care. *Child Welfare*, *80*(6), 685–718.

Courtney, M. E., Terao, S., Bost, N. (2004). *Midwest evaluation of the adult functioning of former foster youth: Conditions of youth preparing to leave state care.* Chicago, IL: Chapin Hall at the University of Chicago. Retrieved from http://www.chapinhall. org/sites/default/files/CS_97.pdf

Courtney, M. E., Zinn, A., Koralek, R., & Bess, R. (2011). Evaluation of the independent living-employment services program, Kern County, California: Final report. (Report #201113). Washington, DC: Office of Planning, Research and Evaluation, Administration for Children and Families, U.S. Department of Health and Human Services.

Cusick, G. R., Havlicek, J. R., & Courtney, M. E. (2012). Risk for arrest: The role of social bonds in protecting foster youth making the transition to adulthood. *American Journal of Orthopsychiatry*, *82*(1), 19–31.

DiClemente, C. C., & Velasquez, M. M. (2002). Motivational interviewing and the stages of change. *Motivational Interviewing: Preparing People for Change*, *2*, 201–216.

DiGiuseppe, D. L., & Christakis, D. A. (2003). Continuity of care for children in foster care. *Pediatrics*, *111*(3), e208–e213.

Dworsky, A. (2005). The economic self-sufficiency of Wisconsin's former foster youth. *Children and Youth Services Review*, *27*(10), 1085–1118.

Dworsky, A., Napolitano, L., & Courtney, M. (2013). Homelessness during the transition from foster care to adulthood. *American Journal of Public Health*, *103*(S2), S318–S323.

Emam, D. (2014). The Affordable Care Act and youth aging out of foster care: New opportunities and strategies for action. State Policy Advocacy and Reform Center, Washington, DC.

Ford, E., Clark, C., & Stansfeld, S. A. (2011). The influence of childhood adversity on social relations and mental health at mid-life. *Journal of Affective Disorders*, *133*(1), 320–327.

Havlicek, J. (2010). Patterns of movement in foster care: An optimal matching analysis. *Social Service Review*, *84*(3), 403–435.

Havlicek, J. (2014). Maltreatment histories of foster youth exiting out-of-home care through emancipation: A latent class analysis. *Child Maltreatment*, *19*(3-4), 199–208.

Havlicek, J., & Courtney, M. E. (2015). Maltreatment histories of aging out foster youth: A comparison of official investigated reports and self-reports of maltreatment prior to and during out-of-home care. *Child Abuse & Neglect*, *52*(2), 110–122.

Havlicek, J., Garcia, A., & Smith, D. C. (2012). Mental health and substance use disorders among foster youth transitioning to adulthood: Past research and future directions. *Children and Youth Services Review*, *35*(1), 194–203.

Havlicek, J., McMillen, J. C., Fedoravicius, N., McNelly, D., & Robinson, D. (2012). Conceptualizing the step-down for foster youth approaching adulthood: Perceptions of service providers, caseworkers, and foster parents. *Children and Youth Services Review*, *34*(12), 2327–2336.

Hingson, R., Heeren, T., Winter, M., & Wechsler, H. (2005). Magnitude of alcohol-related mortality and morbidity among US college students ages 18–24: Changes from 1998 to 2001. *Annual Review of Public Health, 26*, 259–279.

Hook, J. L., & Courtney, M. E. (2011). Employment outcomes of former foster youth as young adults: The importance of human, personal, and social capital. *Children and Youth Services Review, 33*(10), 1855–1865.

Hyde, J., & Kammerer, N. (2009). Adolescents' perspectives on placement moves and congregate settings: Complex and cumulative instabilities in out-of-home care. *Children and Youth Services Review, 31*(2), 265–273.

Keller, T. E., Salazar, A. M., & Courtney, M. E. (2010). Prevalence and timing of diagnosable mental health, alcohol, and substance use problems among older adolescents in the child welfare system. *Children and Youth Services Review, 32*(4), 626–634.

Kelly, J. F., Hoeppner, B., Stout, R. L., & Pagano, M. (2012). Determining the relative importance of the mechanisms of behavior change within alcoholics anonymous: A multiple mediator analysis. *Addiction, 107*(2), 289–299.

Kelly, J. F., Stout, R. L., Magill, M., Tonigan, J. S., & Pagano, M. E. (2011). Spirituality in recovery: A lagged mediational analysis of alcoholics anonymous' principal theoretical mechanism of behavior change. *Alcoholism: Clinical and Experimental Research, 35*(3), 454–463.

Kools, S. M. (1997). Adolescent identity development in foster care. *Family Relations, 46*(3), 263–271.

Maisto, S. A., Krenek, M., Chung, T., Martin, C. S., Clark, D., & Cornelius, J. (2011). A comparison of the concurrent and predictive validity of three measures of readiness to change alcohol use in a clinical sample of adolescents. *Psychological Assessment, 23*(4), 983–994.

McCarthy, J., Van Buren, E., & Irvine, M. (2007). Child and family services reviews: 2001–2004: A mental health analysis. Washington, DC: Georgetown University Center for Child and Human Development, National Technical Assistance Center for Children's Mental Health and the Technical Assistance Partnership for Child and Family Mental Health, American Institutes for Research.

McMillen, J. C., & Raghavan, R. (2009). Pediatric to adult mental health service use of young people leaving the foster care system. *Journal of Adolescent Health, 44*(1), 7–13.

McMillen, J. C., Scott, L. D., Zima, B. T., Ollie, M. T., Munson, M. R., & Spitznagel, E. (2004). Use of mental health services among older youths in foster care. *Psychiatric Services, 55*(7), 811–817.

McMillen, J. C., Zima, B. T., Scott Jr., L. D., Auslander, W. F., Munson, M. R., Ollie, M. T., & Spitznagel, E. L. (2005). Prevalence of psychiatric disorders among older youths in the foster care system. *Journal of the American Academy of Child & Adolescent Psychiatry, 44*(1), 88–95.

Melkman, E., Mor-Salwo, Y., Mangold, K., Zeller, M., & Benbenishty, R. (2015). Care leavers as helpers: Motivations for and benefits of helping others. *Children and Youth Services Review, 54*, 41–48.

Merikangas, K. R., He, J., Burstein, M., Swanson, S. A., Avenevoli, S., Cui, L., . . . Swendsen, J. (2010). Lifetime prevalence of mental disorders in US adolescents: Results from the national comorbidity survey replication-adolescent supplement (NCS-A). *Journal of the American Academy of Child & Adolescent Psychiatry, 49*(10), 980–989.

Miller, W. R., & Rollnick, S. (2012). *Motivational interviewing: Helping people change* New York: Guilford Press.

Miller, W. R., & Sanchez, V. C. (1994). Motivating young adults for treatment and life-style change. In G.G. Howard & P.E. Nathan (Eds.), *Alcohol use and misuse by youth adults* (pp. 55–81). Notre Dame, IN: University of Notre Dame Press.

Montgomery, P., Donkoh, C., & Underhill, K. (2006). Independent living programs for young people leaving the care system: The state of the evidence. *Children and Youth Services Review, 28*(12), 1435–1448.

Monti, P. M., Colby, S. M., Barnett, N. P., Spirito, A., Rohsenow, D. J., Myers, M., . . . Lewander, W. (1999). Brief intervention for harm reduction with alcohol-positive older adolescents in a hospital emergency department. *Journal of Consulting and Clinical Psychology, 67*(6), 989–994.

Narendorf, S. C., & McMillen, J. C. (2010). Substance use and substance use disorders as foster youth transition to adulthood. *Children and Youth Services Review, 32*(1), 113–119.

National Institute on Alcohol Abuse and Alcoholism (2011). Alcohol screening and brief intervention for youth: a practitioner's guide. Available at: www.niaaa.nih. gov/ YouthGuide.

Okpych, N. J. (2015). Receipt of independent living services among older youth in foster care: An analysis of national data from the US. *Children and Youth Services Review, 51,* 74–86.

Pecora, P. J., Kessler, R. C., O'Brien, K., White, C. R., Williams, J., Hiripi, E., . . . Herrick, M. A. (2006). Educational and employment outcomes of adults formerly placed in foster care: Results from the northwest foster care alumni study. *Children and Youth Services Review, 28*(12), 1459–1481.

Pecora, P. J., Studies, F. C. A., & Casey Family Programs. (2005). *Improving family foster care: Findings from the northwest foster care alumni study*. Seattle, WA: Casey Family Programs.

Perkins, H. W. (2002). Surveying the damage: A review of research on consequences of alcohol misuse in college populations. *Journal of Studies on Alcohol Supplement, 14,* 91–100.

Prochaska, J. O., DiClemente, C. C., & Norcross, J. C. (1992). In search of how people change: Applications to addictive behaviors. *American Psychologist, 47*(9), 1102–1114.

Rauktis, M. E., Fusco, R. A., Cahalane, H., Bennett, I. K., & Reinhart, S. M. (2011). "Try to make it seem like we're regular kids": Youth perceptions of restrictiveness in out-of-home care. *Children and Youth Services Review, 33*(7), 1224–1233.

Reilly, T. (2003). Transition from care: Status and outcomes of youth who age out of foster care. *Child Welfare, 82*(6), 727–746.

Resnicow, K., & Page, S. E. (2008). Embracing chaos and complexity: A quantum change for public health. *American Journal of Public Health, 98*(8), 1382–1389.

Romanelli, L. H., Landsverk, J., Levitt, J. M., Leslie, L. K., Hurley, M. M., Bellonci, C., . . . Jensen, P. S. (2009). Best practices for mental health in child welfare: Screening, assessment, and treatment guidelines. *Child Welfare, 88*(1), 163–188.

Rubin, D. M., Alessandrini, E. A., Feudtner, C., Mandell, D. S., Localio, A. R., & Hadley, T. (2004). Placement stability and mental health costs for children in foster care. *Pediatrics, 113*(5), 1336–1341.

Sakai, C., Mackie, T. I., Shetgiri, R., Franzen, S., Partap, A., Flores, G., & Leslie, L. K. (2014). Mental health beliefs and barriers to accessing mental health services in youth aging out of foster care. *Academic Pediatrics*, *14*(6), 565–573.

Samuels, G. M. (2009). Ambiguous loss of home: The experience of familial (im)permanence among young adults with foster care backgrounds. *Children and Youth Services Review*, *31*(12), 1229–1239.

Samuels, G. M., & Pryce, J. M. (2008). "What doesn't kill you makes you stronger": Survivalist self-reliance as resilience and risk among young adults aging out of foster care. *Children and Youth Services Review*, *30*(10), 1198–1210.

Schulenberg, J. E., Sameroff, A. J., & Cicchetti, D. (2004). The transition to adulthood as a critical juncture in the course of psychopathology and mental health. *Development and Psychopathology*, *16*(04), 799–806.

Schulenberg, J. E., Maggs, J. L., & O'Malley, P. M. (2003). *How and why the understanding of developmental continuity and discontinuity is important*. New York: Springer.

Simms, M. D., Dubowitz, H., & Szilagyi, M. A. (2000). Health care needs of children in the foster care system. *Pediatrics*, *106*(Suppl. 3), 909–918.

Smith, G., Chung, T., Donovan, J., Martin, C., & Windle, M. (2010). Youth alcohol screening workgroup I: Measuring consumption of alcohol as a screener in children and adolescents. *Alcoholism-Clinical and Experimental Research*, *34*(6) 267A–267A.

Spirito, A., Bromberg, J., Casper, C., Chun, T., Mellow, M., Dean, M., & Linakis, J. (2016). Reliability and validity of a two-question alcohol screen in the pediatric emergency department. *Pediatrics*, *136*(6), e20160691.

Stewart, C. J., Kum, H., Barth, R. P., & Duncan, D. F. (2014). Former foster youth: Employment outcomes up to age 30. *Children and Youth Services Review*, *36*, 220–229.

Stout, R. L., Kelly, J. F., Magill, M., & Pagano, M. E. (2012). Association between social influences and drinking outcomes across three years. *Journal of Studies on Alcohol and Drugs*, *73*(3), 489–497.

Strolin-Goltzman, J., Kollar, S., & Trinkle, J. (2010). Listening to the voices of children in foster care: Youths speak out about child welfare workforce turnover and selection. *Social Work*, *55*(1), 47–53.

Substance Abuse and Mental Health Services Administration (SAMHSA). (2011). Identifying mental health and substance use problems of children and adolescents: A guide for child-serving organizations. (No. HHS Publication No. SMA 12-4670). Rockville, MD: Author.

Substance Abuse and Mental Health Services Administration (SAMHSA). (2013). Systems-Level Implementation of Screening, Brief Intervention, and Referral to Treatment. Technical Assistance Publication (TAP) Series 33. HHS Publication No. (SMA) 13-4741. Rockville, MD: Substance Abuse and Mental Health Services Administration.

Substance Abuse and Mental Health Services Administration (SAMHSA). (2014). *Results from the 2013 National Survey on Drug Use and Health: Summary of National Findings*, NSDUH Series H-48, HHS Publication No. (SMA) 14-4863. Rockville, MD: Substance Abuse and Mental Health Services Administration.

U.S. Department of Health and Human Services (2008a). Evaluation of the early start to emancipation preparation tutoring program: Los Angeles County. Washington, DC: Administration for Children and Families.

U.S. Department of Health and Human Services. (2008b). Evaluation of the life skills training program: Los Angeles County. Washington, DC: Administration for Children and Families.

U.S. Department of Health and Human Services. (2012a). Highlights from state reports to the National Youth in Transitions Database, federal fiscal year 2011 (No. Data Brief #1). Washington, DC: Administration for Children & Families, U.S. Children's Bureau.

U.S. Department of Health and Human Services (2012b). Promoting social and emotional well-being for children and youth receiving child welfare services. Information Memorandum, Administration for Children and Families, U.S. Children's Bureau. Washington, DC.

U.S. Department of Health and Human Services. (2014). Highlights from state reports to the National Youth in Transitions Database, federal fiscal year 2013 (No. Data Brief #3). Washington, DC: Administration for Children & Families, U.S. Children's Bureau.

U.S. Department of Health and Human Services (2015). The AFCARS Report: Preliminary Estimates as of June 30, 2014 (Report #22). Washington, DC: Administration for Children and Families. U.S. Children's Bureau.

U.S. Department of Health and Human Services, National Institute on Alcohol Abuse and Alcoholism. (2011). Alcohol screening and brief intervention for youth: A practitioner's guide. Rockville, MD: Author.

White, H. R., & Jackson, K. (2004). Social and psychological influences on emerging adult drinking behavior. Alcohol Research & Health, 28(4), 182–191.

Wulczyn, F., Barth, R.P., Yuan, Y. T., Harden, B. J., & Landsverk, J. (2005). Beyond common sense. Child welfare, child well-being, and the evidence for policy reform. New Brunswick: AldineTransaction.

Yuma-Guerrero, P. J., Lawson, K. A., Velasquez, M. M., von Sternberg, K., Maxson, T., & Garcia, N. (2012). Screening, brief intervention, and referral for alcohol use in adolescents: A systematic review. Pediatrics, 130(1), 115–122. doi: 10.1542/peds.2011-1589

11

An International Perspective

Emerging Adults' Substance Use
Disorder Treatment in Brazil

HELOÍSA GARCIA CLARO, MÁRCIA APARECIDA FERREIRA
DE OLIVEIRA, IVAN FILIPE DE ALMEIDA LOPES FERNANDES,
DOUGLAS C. SMITH, AND ROSANA RIBEIRO TARIFA ∎

INTRODUCTION

Large epidemiological studies in Brazil such as one conducted in 108 Brazilian cities show that alcohol and other substance use is common among Brazilian emerging adults. For example, 78.6% of 18- to 24-year-olds and 79.5% of those ages 25–34 used alcohol at least once in their lifetimes. Substance use disorders are also highly prevalent, with 19.2% of emerging adults ages 18–24 and 14.7% of adults ages 25–34 meeting criteria for substance dependence. Thus, similar to findings in North America, substance use disorders are more prevalent among emerging adults, with only 10.4% of adults over age 35 meeting criteria for substance dependence. Finally, tobacco use is also highly prevalent among emerging adults, with approximately 40% reporting tobacco use (Carlini et al., 2005).

Because of the high prevalence of substance use among emerging adults, it is important to understand the needs of emerging adults who present for treatment. In this chapter, we review the prevalence and etiology of substance use, discuss the Brazilian treatment system, and present findings from a recent study comparing substance use among emerging and older adults.

SUBSTANCE USE PREVALENCE AND ETIOLOGY AMONG BRAZILIAN EMERGING ADULTS

Epidemiology

More than 50% of Brazilian college students drink heavily, having five or more drinks on a single occasion. Furthermore, 37% of these students reported experiencing blackouts. Regarding marijuana use, 17% of emerging adults between ages 18 and 24 and 13.5% of adults between ages 25 and 35 have used it at least once in their lifetime. In comparison, only 5.6% of Brazilian adults age 35 and over report lifetime marijuana use. This same pattern appears for cocaine use, with lifetime prevalence estimates of 4.2%, 5.2%, and 2.1% for those ages 18–24, 25–34, and 35 or over, respectively (Carlini et al., 2005). Lifetime inhalant use is more prevalent among Brazilian emerging adults than among emerging adults in the United States, with 10.8% of persons ages 18–24 and 8.1% of those ages 25–34 reporting inhalant use. This is higher than estimates of past-year prevalence of inhalant use (0.4%) among U.S. emerging adults ages 18–25 (United States Center for Behavioral Health Statistics and Quality, 2016), as well as compared to older Brazilian adults over age 35 (4.3%) (Carlini et al., 2005).

Additionally, clinical studies demonstrate differences in substance use between emerging adults and older adults. For example, one study using a clinical sample in southern Brazil found that people under 39 consume alcohol significantly more often than older adults (Bortoluzzi, Traebert, Loguercio, & Kehrig, 2010).

Brazilian Etiology Studies

Potential reasons for drinking among Brazilian emerging adults include the positive effects of drinking, such as greater self-confidence, sociability, social disinhibition, and to enjoy sex more (Peuker, Fogaça & Bizarro, 2006). These reasons for substance use go hand in hand with peer influences on substance use. Brazilian emerging adults often drink in the company of peers, and it is in this life stage that their curiosity about alcohol and search for pleasure peak (Almeida, 2011).

In addition to peer influences and personal motives for seeking fun, macroeconomic influences also affect emerging adult drinking behaviors. For example, marketing and advertisements targeting emerging adults appear problematic in Brazil. A study focusing on the effects of exposure to alcohol advertisements on alcohol consumption among emerging adults indicated that reducing contact with advertisement has an impact on alcohol intake among this population (Pinsky & El Jundi, 2008). This is concerning, because Brazil is targeted as an emerging market by large alcohol-producing corporations, given recently rising sales (Babor et al., 2010).

Developmental Reasons for Use

The generalizability of emerging adulthood to Brazilians ages 18–29 is still in question. Arnett (2000) proposed the existence of five defining dimensions of emerging adulthood, suggesting that emerging adulthood is a time of (1) heightened *identity exploration*, (2) increased *self-focus* due to fewer familial and occupational demands, (3) *feeling in between* adolescence and full adulthood, (4) *instability* in terms of multiple housing, relationship, and job changes while establishing oneself, and (5) a time of high *optimism about future possibilities*. Arnett (2005) subsequently proposed that most of these dimensions of emerging adulthood would be positively associated with substance use. Some U.S.-based studies have produced mixed findings in this area, and to our knowledge there are no Brazilian studies establishing these developmental dimensions of emerging adulthood as predictors of substance use. One study ($n = 547$), however, did develop and validate a Brazilian Portuguese version of the Inventory of Dimensions of Emerging Adulthood (IDEA), finding that emerging adult constructs appeared more applicable to Brazilians from higher socioeconomic backgrounds (Dutra-Thomé, 2013).

TREATMENT FOR ALCOHOL AND OTHER DRUG USE FOR EMERGING ADULTS IN BRAZIL

Policy Shifts Affecting Substance Use Disorder Treatment in Brazil

The influence of alcohol and other drugs on morbidity and mortality were not recognized by Brazilian public health experts until the late 20th century. In 2003, the Brazilian Unified Health System (BUHS) began a more systematic treatment of the subject in the field of public health, when the Brazilian Health Ministry (BHM) created a document on the Health Policy for Integrated Care for Users of Alcohol and Other Drugs (Brazil, 2004). This document contains guidelines for policy and for structuring and strengthening a support network focused on community care, connected with the health network and social services, with an emphasis on rehabilitation and reintegration of its members. This system, as is the rest of the BUHS, is territory based. That is, a local planning technique and a state policy are used to organize the location and methods of territorial allocation of health services in various geographic and administrative scales (Faria, 2012). There are two main themes worth noting in this 2004 policy. First, it emphasizes that care offered to individuals with substance use disorders should be based on extra hospital services for psychosocial care. Services should involve coordination between the mental health system of care and other health services within the network. These services should make deliberate and effective use of the territory and of the services network, as basic health services are widely spread across the territory and sometimes require coordination with specialty facilities. Second, services are delivered under the guiding principle of harm reduction, which seeks to prevent the consequences of substance use within a public health framework. To achieve this goal, it is important that care take place within the sociocultural environment in which people reside, and that the care structure for alcohol and other drugs is informed by the principles of Brazilian psychiatric reform (BPR) (Brazil, 2004).

Multiple new initiatives for the care of individuals with alcohol and other drug use disorders occurred in the year 2005. Examples include changes in funding mechanisms for having beds for users of alcohol and other drugs in general hospitals (Brazil, 2005b), as well as financial incentives for psychosocial care centers for alcohol and other drugs (CAPSad) that implement harm reduction strategies (Brazil, 2005a). Additionally, other outside health initiatives occurred as a consequence of the National Pact to Reduce Accidents and Violence Related to Harmful Consumption of Alcohol and a shift toward viewing the personal use of drugs as a public health issue instead of a criminal justice issue (Organização Pan-Americana da Saúde, 2001).

All of these policy changes culminated in the development of the Health Care Network (HCN) (Brazil, 2010). The goals of this network are to ensure comprehensive, integrated, and humane care, as well as to enhance the performance of the BUHS in terms of access, equity, clinical efficacy, and economic efficiency. The HCN can be understood as organizational arrangements of health initiatives and services of different kinds (primary healthcare units, outreach actions, centers for psychosocial care, hospitals, specialized centers and so on) that are integrated through technical support systems, logistics, and management. The goal of this integration is to ensure access to care and comprehensive care (Brazil, 2010).

The HCN is based on the understanding of primary healthcare (PHC) as the first level of care. The operative function of primary care is to address the most common health problems, meaning that the services from PHC should be the gateway in the BUHS to all other levels of care. Converging with the HCN principles, specifically in the mental health area, Ordinance No. 3088 from the BHM in December 2011 established the Psychosocial Care Network (PCN), to guide the care of people in the BUHS who suffer from mental disorders and have needs resulting from use of alcohol and other drugs (Brazil, 2011).

The objective of the PCN is to expand access to psychosocial care for the general population, promoting linkage to specialty mental health and substance use disorder (SUD) treatment services. Another goal of the PCN is to ensure coordination and integration of the PCN with the care points of the HCN, to treat people in an integrative way (taking care of their basic health needs, but also urgent and emergency care and specialized care) (Brazil, 2011a).

The services that integrate the PCN within the broader healthcare system include primary healthcare units (with family health strategy), psychosocial care centers for alcohol and other drugs (CAPSad), psychosocial care or mental centers (CAPS), urgent care and emergency rooms in general hospitals, general hospitals' psychiatric and alcohol and other drug services, transitional residential institutions for vulnerable populations, street-based outreach clinics, and other services from the BUHS.

CAPS and CAPSad Services

Currently, the main public institution in Brazil for specialized care for substance use disorders is the CAPSad. CAPS and CAPSad were implemented following the "antimanicomial" movement (i.e., deinstitutionalization), seeking to offer assistance in the area of mental health while respecting and valuing human rights (Brazil, 2011a). CAPS and CAPSad units operate 24 hours a day, 7 days a week, including weekends and holidays (Brazil, 2012). Thus, CAPS and CAPSad offer daily treatment options for individuals and emphasize outpatient care. This is a major policy shift in Brazilian SUD treatment, as inpatient services were a larger part of the system of care until the early years of the 21st century. Thus the emphasis on outpatient treatment by CAPS allows individuals to remain socially connected in their environment and minimizes family disruptions, which was a common experience for those previously experiencing long-term hospitalization (Barros, Oliveira, & Silva, 2007).

CAPs and CAPSad centers employ multidisciplinary staff members to promote psychosocial rehabilitation among their users according to Saraceno's definition (Saraceno, Asioli, & Tognoni, 1994), which was adapted to the needs of alcohol and other drug users (Pinho, de Oliveira, & de Almeida, 2008; Pinho et al., 2009). In this framework, abstinence cannot be the only objective. Thus services follow harm reduction principles to provide individualized treatment and encourage working on patient-defined goals.

The Singular Therapeutic Project

Because of difficulties transitioning to the new models proposed under Brazilian psychiatric reform, especially the massive restructuring of services, the Singular Therapeutic Project was developed. The essence of the Singular Therapeutic Project is the discussion of individualized treatment goals and strategies with the individual suffering from an SUD. These should be based on an individual's characteristics and needs, as opposed to setting the same restricted therapeutic goals for all individuals. The Singular Therapeutic Project matches the comprehensiveness of the BUHS, providing integrated care promoted by the multidisciplinary health team. Working with different professionals, such as mental health nurses, psychiatrists, psychologists, social workers, occupational therapists, physical educators, and arts and crafts educators, it is possible to assist the needs of the alcohol and other drug users more efficiently (Azevedo & Miranda, 2010).

Summary

At the turn of this century, many structural changes occurred in the Brazilian healthcare system to (a) treat SUD from a public health framework using harm reduction principles, (b) coordinate care between behavioral and physical health systems, and (c) move toward greater deinstitutionalization of individuals with SUD. The BUHS currently cares for individuals with SUD mainly through the CAPSad centers. In December 2014, about 2,209 CAPS centers operated in Brazil. Currently, the national coverage is 0.86 CAPS/100,000 inhabitants (Brazil, 2015).

Although these centers were implemented in 2002, studies are now just beginning in Brazil to evaluate their outcomes (Barbosa et al., 2015; Oliveira et al., 2014). We are currently unaware of any studies that speak to the developmental appropriateness of the CAPSad system for the treatment of emerging adults. North American studies have shown differences in both treatment processes and outcomes between adolescents, emerging adults, and older adults (Davis, Bergman, Smith, & Kelly, 2017; Satre, Mertens, Arean, & Weisner, 2003, 2004; Smith, Cleeland, & Dennis, 2010; Smith, Dennis, Godley, & Godley, 2011). Thus, we turn our attention to some preliminary findings on Brazilian emerging adults treated within the CAPSad system.

COMPARING EMERGING ADULTS AND OLDER ADULTS IN SUD TREATMENT

Procedures and CAPSad Locations

We collected data in two states in Brazil, São Paulo (SP) and Minas Gerais (MG). At the end of 2014 when data collection ended, there were 90 CAPSad centers in the state of São Paulo and 40 in the state of Minas Gerais (Brazil, 2015). The 2010 population of SP was 44 million people, and for MG it was 21 million people (Instituto Brasileiro de Geografia e Estatística [IBGE], 2010).

Data were collected from 2013 to 2014 in 15 CAPSad in SP and 14 CAPSad in MG. The sample consisted of 30 randomly selected participants from each CAPSad's active patients list (i.e., currently in treatment). A total of 870 participants were selected, and 688 (79%) were actually interviewed (331 from SP and 357 from MG). Interviews took approximately 40 minutes. The interview was composed of two parts: the first consisted of sociodemographic data, and the second consisted of validated scales to analyze treatment satisfaction and perceived change as well as other variables related to treatment processes in the CAPSad. All interviews were conducted in person by an independent research staff interviewer who was not affiliated with the CAPSad. Attrition was mainly due to not being able to reach participants (who were absent from treatment during the whole data collection period) or participants not signing the informed consent form and not being interviewed. We had eight participants from MG and seven from SP (total of 15) who were excluded from the database because the ID number of the participant did not match across the two data sets (part one and part two of the interviews).

Measures

Age was self-reported, and individuals were coded as being either an emerging adult (18–30) or an older adult (30+). Family income level was measured as a categorical variable (0: amount less than 2 minimum-wage incomes (mw) in the household income; 1: 2 to 4 mw; 2: 4 to 10 mw; 3: more than 10 mw). Education was coded on a 0–4 scale (0, less than basic education; 1, completed basic education and incomplete high school; 2, completed high school; 3, some college; 4, completed university degree and post-graduation). Gender (male = 1, female = 0), ethnicity (1 = White, 0 = non-White), and marital status (1 = in relationship, 0 = single) were all self-report dichotomous variables.

As main dependent variables, we chose three variables related to attitudes toward the treatment and six variables related to attitudes toward drug use. The variables related to the treatment were (a) global satisfaction, (b) perceived change, and (c) perceived helpfulness. Global satisfaction was measured as a continuous variable with scores ranging from 1 (less satisfied) to 5 (more satisfied); perceived change had a score that ranged from 1 (fewer changes) to 3 (more changes). Finally, perceived helpfulness was measured with a dichotomous (yes/no) question on whether the patient considered the number of visits made to the CAPSad to be sufficient.

Drug and alcohol use outcomes were measured with dichotomous indicators measuring the presence of any past-month use of tobacco, alcohol, or illegal drugs. Additionally, participants self-reported the number of days in the past month of marijuana, cocaine, and crack use.

Data Analysis Procedures

We used ordinary least squares (OLS), logistic (LOGIT), and negative binomial regression models, depending on the distributional nature of each dependent variable. Within this framework, we compared emerging adults and older adults on multiple variables, controlling for some important confounding factors including income, level of education, gender, ethnicity, and marital status.

Next we present generalized additive models (GAMs) for both Gaussian (OLS) and binomial (LOGIT) distributions, where we can see how individuals reacted to those same variables along different ages, not just a comparison of the two different groups. GAM is suitable for estimating cross-section nonlinear models, as it is a semi-parametric model, being more general than the generalized additive model (GLM). It is parametric when we assume a distribution for the dependent variable, modeling its average. It is nonparametric when the average is modeled through smoothing functions, which are functions that estimate the functional form of the relationship between the independent variable and the dependent variable. In the next section, we present the data and the main results. More information is available elsewhere for GLM models (McCullagh & Nelder, 1989), count models (Cameron & Trivedi, 1998), and GAM models (Beck & Jackman, 1998; Hastie & Tibshirani, 1990). In short, whereas the GLM models test differences between emerging and older adults using dichotomous measure of age, the GAM models test the functional form of the association between a continuous measure of age (in years) and each of the dependent variables.

Results

PARTICIPANT CHARACTERISTICS

Table 11.1 presents demographic and clinical characteristics of this sample. The sample included 101 emerging adults and 586 older adults, with the majority of participants being male (78%), single (70%), and of non-White racial background (57%). The mean and median ages were close to 44. More than 70% of the sample lived on household incomes smaller than two Brazilian minimum-wage incomes, with just nine individuals having income higher than 10 minimum-wage amounts (the Brazilian minimum wage in 2016 was about $USD 3,300.00/

Table 11.1. CHARACTERISTICS OF SURVEY PARTICIPANTS (N = 688), BRAZIL (2016)

Continuous Variables	Mean (SD)
Age (in years)	43.88 (11.75)
Global satisfaction (5 = most satisfaction)	4.36 (0.48)
Perceived change (3 = most change)	2.60 (0.38)
Days of marijuana use (past month)	1.25 (5.17)
Days of cocaine use (past month)	0.74 (3.60)
Days of crack use (past month)	1.02 (4.38)
Family Income	*n* (%)
<2 Minimum-wage earners (MW)	494 (72%)
2–4 MW	142 (21%)
4–10 MW	43 (6%)
>10 MW	9 (1%)
Education	*n* (%)
Less than basic education (<8 years)	287 (43%)
Incomplete high school (8–12 years)	180 (27%)
Complete high school (12 years)	139 (21%)
Incomplete university degree	35 (5%)
Complete university degree	33 (5%)
Other Descriptive Variables	*n* (%)
% Emerging adults	101 (14.7%)
% Male	541 (76.6%)
% Not single	206 (29.9%)
% White	298 (43.3%)
% Indicating CAPSad services are sufficient (i.e., adherence)	565 (82.1%)
% Any past month use of tobacco	446 (64.8%)
% Any past month use of alcohol	285 (41.4%)
% Any past month use of illegal drugs	151 (21.9%)

year). Thus, the patients served at the CAPSads at SP and MG are mainly low-income citizens. Additionally, about 42% of participants had not completed basic education degrees, with only 10% of the sample having attended some college (5%) or obtaining college degrees (5%).

Regarding treatment variables, the mean perceived change achieved was close to 2.72, indicating a high level of perceived change. Similarly, global satisfaction with services was high, with the median and mean above 4.3. Finally, approximately 82% of individuals indicated that services were sufficient. Overall, participants generally indicated that they had made important changes, were very satisfied with the treatment they had received, and believed they had received enough treatment.

Regarding substance use, more than 60% of individuals had used tobacco in the last month, 41% had used alcohol, and just 22% had used illegal drugs. The other three are count variables of how many days during the last month the individual had used marijuana, cocaine, or crack. These measures come from the 151 individuals who had used any illegal drugs. Almost 90% of the individuals have not used marijuana, 13 have used just once, 26 less than five times, and 25 more than 10 times. Also, 21 had used marijuana daily in the past month. Results are quite similar for the use of cocaine. More than 90% had not used any cocaine in the last month, 23 had used just once, 37 less than five times, 21 more than 10 times, and 7 had used on a daily basis. The results for the use of crack were also similar. Almost 90% of the people had not used crack, 36 had used less than five times, 6 more than 10 times, and 12 had used daily in the past month.

GENERAL LINEAR MODELS—EMERGING ADULTS

Table 11.2 presents the GLM models for treatment process variables, including global satisfaction, perceived change, and perceived helpfulness. The effects labeled "emerging adults" in row one represent the mean difference between the two groups (i.e., emerging and older adults). Emerging adults were significantly less satisfied with the treatment received than older adults, with the difference (0.145 points) representing a small standardized mean difference ($d = .30$). On the other hand, there were no differences between these two groups for the other two variables that measured attitudes toward the treatment. Perceived change and helpfulness from the treatment were statistically the same for both groups. Perceived change for the emerging adults was somewhat bigger (0.016), although not statistically significant. The estimated effect for perceived helpfulness was not trivial (1.4 times higher for older adults), but failed to reach statistical significance.

Substance-related outcomes are presented in Table 11.3. Statistically significant differences between emerging and older adults were observed for illegal drugs and use of marijuana and cocaine. For use of illegal drugs, we can interpret the coefficient as an odds ratios it we take the exponential of the estimated β of the log-odds. This transformation shows that emerging adults are 1.75 times more likely to use illegal drugs than older adults. This may be accounted for by the higher likelihood of marijuana and crack use by emerging adults, also

Table 11.2. GLM Main Results of Emerging Adults, Brazil (2016)

Dependent Variable	Satisfaction	Perceived Change	Helpfulness
Model	OLS	OLS	LOGIT
Emerging adults	−0.145**	0.016	−0.359
	0.062	0.046	0.273
Race	0.004	0.007	−0.136
	0.038	0.031	0.212
Gender	−0.014	0.041	0.272
	0.044	0.039	0.241
Marital status	**0.071***	**0.068****	0.035
	0.040	**0.033**	0.226
Education (1)	−0.011	−0.013	−0.179
	0.045	0.039	0.250
Education (2)	0.004	-0.008	−0.030
	0.050	0.044	0.287
Education (3)	-0.055	0.032	0.275
	0.099	0.060	0.550
Education (4)	−0.034	0.084	−0.438
	0.118	0.065	0.454
Income (1)	**0.105***	0.052	0.170
	0.045	0.038	0.271
Income (2)	0.076	0.042	−0.582
	0.080	0.065	0.399
Income (3)	−0.335	−0.064	−0.311
	0.353	0.104	0.810
Constant	**4.357***	**2.532***	**1.511***
	0.054	**0.044**	**0.276**

OLS, ordinary least squares.
* p-value ≤ 0.1
** p-value ≤ 0.05
*** p-value ≤ 0.01

presented in Table 11.3. There were no differences in the use of tobacco and alcohol, meaning that emerging adults and older adults seem to have the same patterns of use.

GAM Models—Emerging Adults Measured by Continuous Age
Here we present different models estimated by GAM techniques, where we measure the effects of emerging adults without establishing any threshold. That is,

Table 11.3. GLM Substance-Related Outcomes for Emerging Adults, Brazil (2016)

Dependent Variable	Alcohol	Illegal Drugs	Marijuana	Cocaine	Crack
Model	LOGIT	LOGIT	Neg. Bin.	Neg. Bin.	Neg. Bin.
Emerging adults	−0.044	**0.560****	**1.154****	**1.229****	−0.281
	0.224	**0.250**	**0.418**	**0.462**	0.541
Race	−0.152	0.109	0.050	0.351	−0.266
	0.164	0.198	0.392	0.364	0.319
Gender	−0.111	0.318	0.675	−0.223	−0.619
	0.192	0.243	0.484	0.601	0.457
Marital status	−0.111	-0.221	−0.297	0.196	0.151
	0.177	0.215	0.444	0.409	0.406
Education (1)	0.079	0.347	−0.275	−0.034	0.462
	0.196	0.228	0.430	0.434	0.384
Education (2)	0.030	0.019	0.058	**1.172****	−0.127
	0.217	0.271	0.438	**0.475**	0.457
Education (3)	**0.664***	0.636	1.628	1.801	0.190
	0.382	0.434	1.236	0.789	0.824
Education (4)	0.110	0.323	−0.395	0.485	1.281
	0.402	0.498	0.956	0.745	0.824
Income (1)	0.050	0.088	0.097	0.349	−0.571
	0.202	0.242	0.467	0.502	0.420
Income (2)	−0.245	−0.563	−1.448*	**−0.985***	−0.820
	0.355	0.505	0.855	**0.580**	0.570
Income (3)	−0.501	−1.026	−1.682	**−3.436*****	−22.517***
	0.772	0.981	1.416	**0.945**	0.603
Constant	−0.203	**−1.737*****	−0.445	−1.088	0.544
	0.213	**0.272**	0.520	0.754	0.490
/lnalpha			3.504	3.309	3.361
			0.132	0.148	0.129
Alpha			33.241	27.351	28.830
			4.399	4.044	3.727

Neg. Bin, negative binomial.
* p-value ≤ 0.1
** p-value ≤ 0.05
*** p-value ≤ 0.01

GAM models are flexible enough to estimate the exact functional form of the relationship between the independent and the dependent variable without making the stronger assumptions of linearity present at GLM models. Another difference is that we transform the count variables that measure the number of days of marijuana, cocaine, and crack use into dichotomous variables (0 = no use, 1 = used substance in past month). We do that to graphically interpret the functional form of the relationship between age and those variables. The other control variables remain the same.

In Figure 11.1 we present the three models related to the variables of attitudes towards the treatment. At the vertical axes of the two first graphs we present the local effects of age on the dependent variables (global satisfaction and perceived change). As in the third graph the dependent variable, perceived helpfulness, has a binomial distribution (dichotomous indicator), we can interpret the vertical axis as the probability of adhering to the treatment. At the horizontal axes in all three graphs, we present the values of age on our sample (from 18 to 76 years). Since we have fewer data on ages above 65, just 22 cases, the confidence intervals tend to be bigger than on the lower ends of the distribution (i.e., left side of the graphs).

In the GLM models, we found that just global satisfaction was different between these two groups, and there were no statistical differences between groups for both perceived change and helpfulness of the treatment. In the GAM models, findings for global satisfaction and perceived change were replicated. However, the GAM model for treatment helpfulness shows a statistically significant difference between emerging and older adults. As this variable follows a binomial distribution, we interpret the vertical axis as the probability of reporting that the treatment was sufficiently helpful. There is a 40% probability that an emerging adult will answer that the frequency of treatment is sufficient, and for older adults above 60 years old, this probability is much higher, close to 60%, indicating that there is a significant difference across age for helpfulness of treatment. In short, emerging adults are less satisfied with the amount of treatment received when compared to older adults.

In Figure 11.2 we present the three models related to the use of substance: alcohol, tobacco, and illegal drugs. Since all models have a binomial distribution, the vertical axes display probability intervals. In the last section, we found that emerging adults were significantly more likely than older adults to use illegal drugs, and there were no statistical differences for the use of tobacco or use of alcohol.

This result contradicts recent international literature, which notes that in the general population younger adults use significantly more alcohol compared to older adults (Barrickman, 2016; Lau-Barraco, Linden-Carmichael, Braitman, & Stamates, 2016; Osaki et al., 2016). This may simply indicate that in this clinical sample, emerging adults are more likely to present for treatment if they are using illegal drugs. Treatment utilization for alcohol use disorders is low among emerging adults.

For illegal drugs, the findings in the GAM models are consistent with the GLM models. For example, there was an 80% probability of using illicit drugs for a 20-year-old emerging adult in this sample versus a 30% probability for a 60-year-old

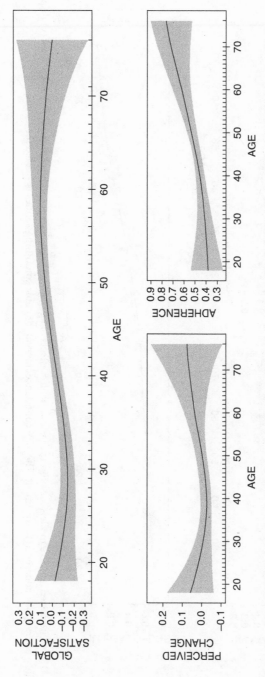

Figure 11.1 Generalized additive models for treatment attitude variables: effects of age on global satisfaction, perceived change, and adherence to treatment. Vertical axes (y) display the values of the local effects of age on each dependent variable for the two first graphs (global satisfaction and perceived change) and display probability intervals for adherence to treatment. The 95% confidence interval for cubic smoothing splines is shaded for all graphs.

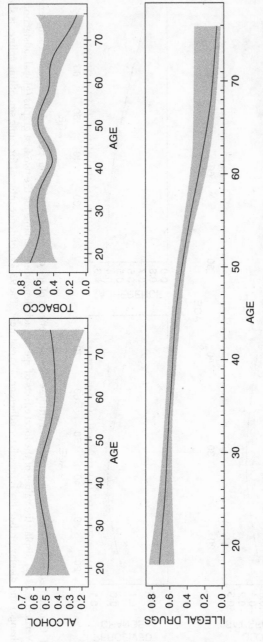

Figure 11.2 Generalized additive models for substance use variables: effects of age on alcohol, tobacco, and illegal drug use. Vertical axes (y) display probability intervals for adherence to treatment. The 95% confidence interval for cubic smoothing splines is shaded for all graphs.

adult. This implies that treatment providers at CAPSad centers should be competent at treating illicit drug use disorders for emerging adults. On the other hand, in the second graph that shows the probabilities of using tobacco the GAM models are inconsistent with the GLM models. The curve was not as linear as the curve observed for illegal drugs use, but there was a clearly tendency toward reduced tobacco consumption at older ages, decreasing from 60% to close to 40%.

Finally, Figure 11.3 shows three graphs related to the use of specific illegal drugs—marijuana, cocaine, and crack. Once more, since all models have a binomial distribution, the vertical axes display probability intervals. In the GLM models, we found that marijuana and cocaine use was different between emerging and older adults, and there was no statistical difference for crack use. In Figure 11.3 GAM analyses reveal that all illegal substances are used more frequently by emerging adults. The differences between groups are quite similar across the three graphs. Emerging adults have a 70% probability of using marijuana, cocaine, or crack, and older adults age 60 and above have a probability ranging from 20% to 40% for each drug.

Implications of Study Findings

Notwithstanding this study's limitations of using nonstandardized measures of substance use outcomes and using a cross-sectional design, this study makes a novel contribution to our limited knowledge of treated emerging adults presenting to Brazilian CAPSad centers. First, we found that emerging adults are less satisfied with treatment services than older adults. Although satisfaction was generally high among emerging adults, it was still lower than that of older adults, and future studies in the CAPSad centers could seek to explain and address these differences.

Our findings are also consistent with other Brazilian and international studies demonstrating that the prevalence of drug use is higher among emerging adults (Carlini et al., 2005; Evans, Li, Grella, Brecht, & Hser, 2013; Galduróz & Carlini, 2007; Leitão Filho et al., 2009). Thus, it may be particularly important to address other health risks associated with drug use among younger adults, such as sexually transmitted diseases (Bonar et al., 2016), and other risky behaviors that are often tolerated more during emerging adulthood (Sussman & Arnett, 2014), such as driving while intoxicated or riding in a car with an intoxicated driver (Arnett, 2002; Miller, Furr-Holden, Voas, & Bright, 2005; Miller et al., 2009).

It is unclear what treatment innovation could be adapted for Brazilian emerging adults that would increase their perception of their needs being met. Although not statistically significant, relative to older adults, emerging adults indicated that they did not receive sufficient treatment. Some authors have suggested that adaptations may be needed to better engage emerging adults in treatment, including being more flexible and using technology-based interventions (Bergman, Kelly, Nargiso, & McKowen, 2015). Additional research with Brazilian emerging adults is needed in this area.

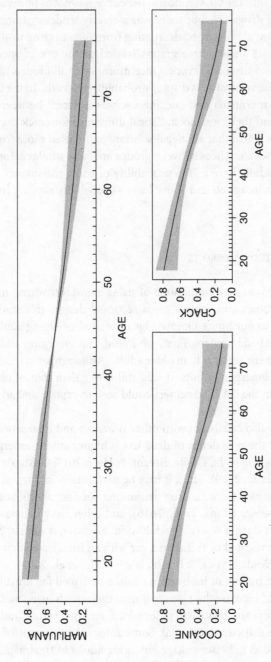

Figure 11.3 Generalized additive models for illegal drug use variables: effects of age on marijuana, cocaine, and crack use. Vertical axes (y) display probability intervals for adherence to treatment. The 95% confidence interval for cubic smoothing splines is shaded for all graphs.

SUMMARY AND CONCLUSIONS

Numerous positive changes to the SUD treatment system have been implemented in the past decade, including a push toward deinstitutionalization, adoption of harm reduction principles, and the establishment of regional CAPSad centers. Yet, more work needs to be done to improve treatment for Brazilian emerging adults, who were found to be less satisfied with treatment and more likely to be using illicit drugs compared to older adults. Additional research with Brazilian emerging adults is needed to improve their treatment outcomes.

REFERENCES

Almeida, N. D. (2011). Uso de álcool, tabaco e drogas por jovens e adultos da cidade de Recife [Use of alcohol, tobacco and drugs by youth and adults in the city of Recife]. *Psicologia Argumento*, 29(66), 295–302.

Arnett, J. J. (2000). Emerging adulthood: A theory of development from the late teens through the twenties. *American Psychologist*, 55(5), 469–480.

Arnett, J. J. (2002). Developmental sources of crash risk in young drivers. *Injury Prevention*, 8(Suppl. 2), ii17–ii23.

Arnett, J. J. (2005). The developmental context of substance use in emerging adulthood. *Journal of Drug Issues*, 35(2), 235–254.

Azevedo, D. M. de, & Miranda, F. A. N. d. (2010). Práticas profissionais e tratamento ofertado nos CAPSad do município de Natal-RN: Com a palavra a família [Professional practices and treatment offered in the CAPSad of the municipality of Natal-RN: Family with the word]. *Esc Anna Nery*, 14(1), 56–63.

Babor, T., Caetano, R., Casswell, S., Edwards, G., Giesbrecht, N., Graham, K., . . . Rossow, I. (2010). *Alcohol: No ordinary commodity: Research and public policy*. New York: Oxford University Press.

Barbosa, G. C., Oliveira, M. A. F. de, Moreno, V., Padovani, C. R., Claro, H. G., & Pinho, P. H. (2015). Satisfação de usuários num Centro de Atenção Psicossocial em álcool e outras drogas [Users satisfaction in the center for psychosocial care in alcohol and other drugs]. *Revista Portuguesa de Enfermagem de Saúde Mental*, 14, 31–37.

Barrickman, J. C. (2016). *Predictors of excessive alcohol consumption among US business travelers*. Minneapolis, MN: Walden University.

Barros, S., Oliveira, M. A. F. de, & Silva, A. L. A. (2007). Práticas inovadoras para o cuidado em saúde [Innovative practices for healthcare]. *Revista da Escola de Enfermagem da USP*, 41, 815–819.

Beck, N., & Jackman, S. (1998). Beyond linearity by default: Generalized additive models. *American Journal of Political Science*, 42(2), 596–627.

Bergman, B. G., Kelly, J. F., Nargiso, J. E., & McKowen, J. W. (2015). "The age of feeling in-between": Addressing challenges in the treatment of emerging adults with substance use disorders. *Cognitive and Behavioral Practice*, 23, 270–288.

Bonar, E. E., Whiteside, L. K., Walton, M. A., Zimmerman, M. A., Booth, B. M., Blow, F. C., & Cunningham, R. (2016). Prevalence and correlates of HIV risk among adolescents and young adults reporting drug use: Data from an urban emergency department in the United States. *Journal of HIV/AIDS & Social Services*, 15(1), 3–28.

Bortoluzzi, M. C., Traebert, J., Loguercio, A., & Kehrig, R. T. (2010). Prevalência e perfil dos usuários de álcool de população adulta em cidade do sul do Brasil [Prevalence and profile of adult population of alcohol users a city in southern Brazil]. *Cien Saude Colet, 15*(3), 679–685.

Brazil (2004). A Política do Ministério da Saúde para a Atenção Integral a Usuários de Álcool e outras Drogas [The policy of the Ministry of Health for the integral care of users of alcohol and other drugs]. *Brasília.*

Brazil. (2005a). Ministério da Saúde. Portaria nº 1.028/GM de 1º de julho de 2005 [Ordinance No. 1,028/GM, July 1, 2005]. Determina que as ações que visam à redução de danos sociais e à saúde, decorrentes do uso de produtos, substâncias ou drogas que causem dependência, sejam reguladas por esta Portaria.

Brazil. (2005b). Ministério da Saúde. Portaria nº 1.612/GM de 9 de setembro de 2005 [Ordinance No. 1,612/GM, September 9, 2005].

Brazil. (2010). Ministério da Saúde. Portaria nº 4.279, de 30 de dezembro de 2010 [Ordinance No. 4.279, December 30, 2010].

Brazil. (2011a). Ministério daSaúde. Portaria nº 3.088, de 23 de dezembro de 2011 [Ordinance No. 3,088, December 23, 2011]. Institui a Rede de Atenção Psicossocial para pessoas com sofrimento ou transtorno mental e com necessidades decorrentes do uso de crack, álcool e outras drogas, no âmbito do Sistema Único de Saúde (SUS).

Brazil. (2011b). Ministério da Saúde. Secretaria de Atenção à Saúde. DAPES. Coordenação Geral de Saúde Mental. Saúde Mental no SUS: as novas fronteiras da Reforma Psiquiátrica [Mental health in SUS: The new frontiers of psychiatric reform]. Relatório de Gestão 2007–2010: Ministério da Saúde Brasília.

Brazil. (2012). Ministério da Saúde. Portaria nº 130, de 26 de janeiro de 2012 [Ordinance No. 130, January 26, 2012]. Redefine o Centro de Atenção Psicossocial de Álcool e outras Drogas 24 h (CAPS AD III) e os respectivos incentivos financeiros.

Brazil. (2015). Ministério da Saúde. Saúde Mental em Dados 12 [Mental health in Data 12]. Ministério da Saúde do Brasil: Brasília.

Cameron, C. A., & Trivedi, P. K. (1998). *Regression analysis of count data* (Econometric Society monographs). Cambridge, UK: Cambridge University Press.

Carlini, E.; Galduróz, J., Noto, A., Carlini, C., Oliveira, L., & Nappo, A. (2005). II Levantamento Domiciliar sobre o uso de drogas psicotrópicas no Brasil: Envolvendo as 108 maiores cidades do país [II Household survey on the use of psychotropic drugs in Brazil: Involving the country's 108 largest cities]. Secretaria Nacional de Politicas sobre Drogas (Ed.)

Davis, J. P., Bergman, B. G., Smith, D. C., & Kelly, J. F. (2017). Testing a matching hypothesis for emerging adults in Project MATCH: During-treatment and 1-year outcomes. *Journal of Studies on Alcohol and Drugs, 78*, 140–145. http://www.jsad.com/doi/pdf/10.15288/jsad.2017.78.140

Dutra-Thomé, L. (2013). *Emerging adulthood in southern Brazilians from differing socioeconomic status: Social and subjective markers.* Available at http://www.lume.ufrgs.br/bitstream/handle/10183/76534/000886149.pdf

Evans, E., Li, L., Grella, C., Brecht, M.-L., & Hser, Y.-I. (2013). Developmental timing of first drug treatment and 10-year patterns of drug use. *Journal of Substance Abuse Treatment, 44*(3), 271–279.

Faria, R. M. de (2012). A territorialização da atenção primária à saúde no Sistema Único de Saúde: perspectivas de adequação aos perfis do território urbano de Pouso Alegre-MG [The territorialization of primary healthcare in the Unified Health

System: Prospects for adequacy to the profiles of the urban territory of Pouso Alegre-MG]. Campinas. Tese de doutorado.

Galduróz, J., & Carlini, E. (2007). Use of alcohol among the inhabitants of the 107 largest cities in Brazil—2001. *Brazilian Journal of Medical and Biological Research*, 40(3), 367–375.

Hastie, T. J., & Tibshirani, R. J. (1990). *Generalized additive models* (Vol. 43). Boca Raton, FL: CRC Press.

Instituto Brasileiro de Geografia e Estatística (IBGE). (2010). Censo demográfico 2010 [Demographic Census 2010]. Rio de Janeiro Retrieved from http://www.ibge.gov.br/home/estatistica/populacao/censo2010/default_sinopse.shtm.

Lau-Barraco, C., Linden-Carmichael, A. N., Braitman, A. L., & Stamates, A. L. (2016). Identifying patterns of situational antecedents to heavy drinking among college students. *Addiction Research & Theory*, 24(6), 431–440.

Leitão Filho, F., Galduróz, J., Noto, A., Nappo, S., Carlini, E., Nascimento, O., & Jardim, J. (2009). [Random sample survey on the prevalence of smoking in the major cities of Brazil]. *Journal of Brasilian Pneumology*, 35(12), 1204–1211.

McCullagh, P., & Nelder, J. A. (1989). *Generalized linear models* (Vol. 37). Boca Raton, FL: CRC Press.

Miller, B. A., Furr-Holden, D., Johnson, M. B., Holder, H., Voas, R., & Keagy, C. (2009). Biological markers of drug use in the club setting. *Journal of Studies on Alcohol and Drugs*, 70(2), 261–268.

Miller, B. A., Furr-Holden, C. D., Voas, R. B., & Bright, K. (2005). Emerging adults' substance use and risky behaviors in club settings. *Journal of Drug Issues*, 35(2), 357–378.

Oliveira, M. A. F. de, Cestari, T. Y., Pereira, M. O., Pinho, P. H., Gonçalves, R. M. D. A., & Claro, H. G. (2014). Assessment procedures of mental health services: An integrative review. *Saúde em Debate*, 38(101), 368–378.

Organização Pan-Americana da Saúde. (2001). Relatório Sobre a Saúde no Mundo. Saúde Mental: nova concepção, nova esperança [World Health Report. Mental Health: new conception, new hope]. Geneva: World Health Organization.

Osaki, Y., Kinjo, A., Higuchi, S., Matsumoto, H., Yuzuriha, T., Horie, Y., & Yoshimoto, H. (2016). Prevalence and trends in alcohol dependence and alcohol use disorders in Japanese adults: Results from periodical nationwide surveys. *Alcohol and Alcoholism*, 51, 465–473.

Peuker, A. C., Fogaça, J., & Bizarro, L. (2006). Expectativas e beber problemático entre universitários [Expectations and problematic drinking among college students]. *Psicologia: Teoria e Pesquisa*, 22(2), 193–200.

Pinho, P. H., Oliveira, M. A. F. de, & de Almeida, M. M. (2008). A reabilitação psicossocial na atenção aos transtornos associados ao consumo de álcool e outras drogas: uma estratégia possível? [Psychosocial rehabilitation in the attention to the disorders associated with the consumption of alcohol and other drugs: A possible strategy?]. *Revista de Psiquiatria Clínica*, 35(Suppl. 1), 82–88.

Pinho, P. H., Oliveira, M. A. F. de, Vargas, D. de, Almeida, M. M. de, Machado, A.L., Silva, A. L. A., & Barros, S. (2009). The psychosocial rehabilitation in the alcohol and other drugs treatment: The professionals' conception. *Revista da Escola de Enfermagem da USP*, 43(SPE2), 1261–1266.

Pinsky, I., & El Jundi, S. A. (2008). O impacto da publicidade de bebidas alcoólicas sobre o consumo entre jovens: revisão da literatura internacional [The impact of alcohol advertising on consumption among young people: A review of the international literature]. *Rev Bras Psiquiatr, 30*(4), 362–374.

Saraceno, B., Asioli, F., & Tognoni, G. (1994). Manual de saúde mental: Guia básico para atenção primária [Mental health manual: Basic guide to primary care]. *Saúdeloucura* (Vol. 9): Hucitec.

Satre, D. D., Mertens, J., Arean, P. A., & Weisner, C. (2003). Contrasting outcomes of older versus middle-aged and younger adult chemical dependency patients in a managed care program. *Journal of Studies on Alcohol, 64,* 520–530.

Satre, D., Mertens, J., Arean, P. A., & Weisner, C. (2004). Five-year alcohol and drug treatment outcomes of older adults versus middle-aged and younger adults in a managed care program. *Addiction, 99*(l0), 1286–1297.

Smith, D. C., Cleeland, L., & Dennis, M. L. (2010). Reasons for quitting among emerging adults and adolescents in substance use disorder treatment. *Journal of Studies on Alcohol and Drugs, 71*(3), 400–409.

Smith, D. C., Godley, S. H., Godley, M. D., & Dennis, M. L. (2011) Adolescent Community Reinforcement Approach (A-CRA) outcomes differ among emerging adults and adolescents. *Journal of Substance Abuse Treatment, 41,* 422–430.

Sussman, S., & Arnett, J. J. (2014). Emerging adulthood: Developmental period facilitative of the addictions. *Evaluation & the Health Professions, 37*(2), 147–155.

United States Center for Behavioral Health Statistics and Quality. (2016). *Key substance use and mental health indicators in the United States: Results from the 2015 National Survey on Drug Use and Health* (HHS Publication No. SMA 16-4984, NSDUH Series H-51). Retrieved from http://www.samhsa.gov/data/.

12

Emerging Issues in the Emerging Adult Substance Use Field

DOUGLAS C. SMITH ■

EMERGING ADULTS ARE A SPECIAL POPULATION

Arguably, emerging adults with substance use disorders are a special population that warrants additional research and clinical attention. To underscore this point, we will describe how well emerging adults fit decision rule criteria for undertaking special efforts for treatment improvement. That is, in Chapter 5, my colleagues and I argued that cultural adaptations of substance use treatment should not be undertaken frivolously, indicating that it was important to justify both resource allocation and the expected reach of such interventions. We described Castro, Barrera, and Holleran Steiker's (2010) criteria for deciding when to take on such adaptations, which require that a population of interest has (a) poorer engagement or retention in treatment, (b) unique risk or protective factors, (c) a unique presentation of the clinical problem, and (d) lower intervention efficacy when generic interventions are used.

The potential reach of substance use interventions for emerging adults is undeniable, as about 20% of admissions to substance use disorder (SUD) treatment are emerging adults. Additionally, if we apply these guiding criteria to the problem of whether we should consider improving interventions specifically for emerging adults, we find that such efforts appear well justified. We recapitulate these findings in the next sections and then use the remainder of the chapter to outline priority research and clinical program development areas.

Emerging Adults Have Poorer Treatment Service Utilization and Retention

As noted in many chapters throughout this book, emerging adults do not regularly access SUD treatment services. National surveys indicate that among those who meet SUD diagnostic criteria, as few as 2.2% of them use specialized treatment services (Substance Abuse and Mental Health Services Administration [SAMHSA], 2015). This is much lower than the estimated 10.8% of individuals across the lifespan that both have an SUD and access specialized treatment. So, generally speaking, emerging adults with SUDs are not accessing treatment to the extent that other age groups are. Treatment use is abysmally low among all individuals in need of SUD treatment, but especially so for emerging adults (Center for Behavioral Health Statistics and Quality, 2016).

So, what about treatment retention? Among those few emerging adults who do enter substance use treatment, do they receive the same dose of treatment as individuals from other age groups? Unfortunately, the answer to that question is a resounding "NO!" Sinha, Easton, and Kemp (2003) found that emerging adults were less likely than older adults to complete treatment. Similar findings emanate from other studies as well (Satre, Mertens, Arean, & Weisner, 2003).

Emerging Adults Have Unique Risk Factors

Although motivation to change may be thought of as a common risk factor for predicting the treatment response of all individuals, emerging adults have both lower treatment motivation (Satre et al., 2003, Satre, Mertens, Arean, & Weisner, 2004, Sinha et al., 2003) and a unique presentation of motivational factors compared to adolescents (Smith, Cleeland, & Dennis, 2010). In a series of two studies, Satre et al. (2003, 2004) showed that motivation to change partially explained outcome differences between emerging and older adults, with a lower percent of the former achieving abstinence at follow-up.

Recently conducted research is also showing that a measure of developmental reasons for using substances can discriminate between emerging and older adults (Smith, Davis, & Dumas, 2016). Specifically, emerging adults were more likely to endorse views that they used substances to cope with the pressure of being an emerging adult (i.e., developmental strain) and also because of expectancies that emerging adults are supposed to drink before becoming full-fledged adults (i.e., developmental expectancy).

Finally, we learned in Chapter 8 that emerging adults derive benefits from AA and other mutual-aid societies in different ways from older adults. First, for emerging adults, the effects of AA on outcomes are less likely to be explained by the increase in pro-abstinence social networks than they are for older adults (Hoeppner, Hoeppner, & Kelly, 2014). Second, emerging adults appear to derive more benefit from AA in terms of reducing their impulsivity (Blonigen, Timko, Finney, Moos, & Moos, 2011). These developmental differences in mechanisms of change imply that different intervention targets may exist for emerging adults. Namely, it may be important clinically to reduce impulsivity and also find creative ways to alter emerging adults' social networks (see Chapter 7).

Emerging Adults Have a Unique Clinical Presentation

Emerging adults are more likely than older adults to use substances other than alcohol (Sinha et al., 2003), less likely to endorse high motivation for abstinence (Satre et al., 2003, 2004, Sinha et al., 2003), and more likely to have social environment and mental health risks (Mason & Luckey, 2003). Despite some commonalities in the course of substance use disorders, their presentation is arguably different from that of older adults.

Interventions Are Less Effective for Emerging Adults

In Chapter 1, we outlined a number of studies showing that when emerging adults' treatment outcomes have been directly compared to those of older adults (Davis, Bergman, Smith, & Kelly, 2017; Satre et al., 2003, 2004; Sinha et al., 2003) or adolescents (Smith, Godley, Godley, & Dennis, 2011), their outcomes are worse. Other studies also show an inverse correlation with age and substance use, indicating that older participants tend to have lower substance use at follow-up. Although there are few studies with enough age variation to make direct comparisons between emerging adults and those from other age groups, those that do generally find differences in outcomes.

SO NOW WHAT? THE QUEST TO IMPROVE INTERVENTIONS FOR EMERGING ADULTS

Drawing on the points just made regarding why emerging adults are a special population, let's now turn our attention to what research and clinical program development areas may be fruitful. In my view, these priorities include improving treatment access and retention for emerging adults, improving the assessment of substance-related problems, actively monitoring the impact of marijuana policy liberalization on emerging adults, and identifying novel intervention targets from research on how emerging adult development influences the onset, course, and treatment response for substance use disorders.

Improving Emerging Adult Access to and Retention in Treatment

Two main approaches have been tried in order to improve emerging adults' access to treatment: (1) burgeoning efforts to develop online and other electronic interventions that are low cost and can be widely disseminated, and (2) existing efforts to integrate substance use disorder screening, brief intervention, and referral to treatment (SBIRT) into mainstream medical practice. On a broad scale, both are logical and highly feasible approaches that should be retained as part of multi-pronged efforts to increase emerging adult substance use treatment utilization. Yet, both may be potentially flawed, requiring specific attention to some implementation details of these approaches as well as supplemental efforts.

Potential Flaws in Electronic Interventions and SBIRT

For example, in Chapter 4 we learned of meta-analyses showing that, for emerging adults, electronic interventions do not always work as well as face-to-face interventions (Carey, Scott-Sheldon, Elliott, Garey, & Carey, 2012). It appears that emerging adults may not be paying attention to electronic content when receiving electronic interventions (Lewis & Neighbors; 2015). So, one important area for improvement may simply be to make the first generation of electronic interventions more engaging and fun for emerging adults. It is unclear if anyone has done a content analysis of all the electronic interventions to determine which of them use engaging game formats or interactive texting and which ones are primarily informational. One potential explanation for the early findings on electronic interventions may simply have to do with the sophistication level of the products in the first generation of these interventions. As technology improves and becomes easier to program, such interventions may produce better outcomes for emerging adults.

How may SBIRT affect treatment utilization for emerging adults? Although there are some studies showing that SBIRT works for emerging adults with non-disordered use, there is virtually no evidence that it increases treatment utilization among emerging adults with diagnosed SUDs. In fact, Glass and colleagues (2015) found no impact on treatment receipt among SBIRT models that focused on the referral to treatment (RT) component of SBIRT. Future research may flesh this out better, but currently, despite widespread efforts to implement SBIRT, there are some reasons why it may not be a panacea for emerging adults' treatment utilization disparities.

Alternative Ideas for Improving Emerging Adult Treatment Utilization

Although I don't have all the answers, I have two broad recommendations for improving emerging adult treatment use. First, interventions should be made more attractive to emerging adults. At the risk of sounding overly common-sensical, let me elaborate on some specific ideas. As noted, maybe it is better to use face-to-face interventions rather than poorly made information-based electronic interventions. If the first generation of electronic interventions for emerging adult substance use disorder treatments are not graphically appealing or are simply behind the curve on existing technology, they may not produce optimal positive outcomes. In fact, they may be discredited, depending on design. These interventions may also mainly be stand-alone brief interventions. It is possible that more emphasis is needed on clinician extender models, defined as electronic interventions that are meant to supplement, not replace, face-to-face therapeutic services. In short, it is probably not enough to just assume that, because emerging adults are from a generation that is comfortable using technology, these interventions are appealing. They need to be carefully tested for acceptability using emerging adult samples, ideally with emerging adult input on how engaging the electronic intervention content appears.

Second, emerging adult–specific programs can be offered in some locations, especially larger, urban communities. To our knowledge, there is no direct evidence that emerging adult–specific programming (e.g., emerging adult–only therapy groups, emerging adult residential treatment unit) would achieve better outcomes than mixed-age treatments. However, indirect evidence provides a solid rationale for considering the development of such programs, including evidence from studies with other age groups showing that age-specific groups produce better outcomes than mixed age-group conditions (Kofoed, Tolson, Atkinson, Toth, & Turner, 1987) and one study showing that emerging adults treated in facilities with a higher concentration of emerging adults (versus primarily adolescent agencies) have better outcomes (Smith et al., 2011). Perhaps it is time to test whether dedicated emerging adult treatment units or groups produce better results than mixed-age services where emerging adults are treated with either predominantly younger adolescents or older adults. It is unclear if the benefits of such emerging adult–specific services would be primarily due to greater identification with other similarly aged clients or to better staff expertise in treating emerging adults, forged from experience working primarily with emerging adults. Either curative mechanism may improve treatment engagement for emerging adults because of increased comfort with service providers and group members.

This brings us to a third potential approach to increasing emerging adult engagement: Providers could be specifically trained in emerging adult life-course issues. Some providers may learn about such issues via on-the-job training in emerging adult–specific agencies, but providers in mixed-aged units may get less experience or have less knowledge about emerging adult developmental issues. Some states have specific licensure requirements for adolescent programs, recognizing that adolescent programs should attend to developmental issues. However, no current entity encourages substance use treatment providers to learn about emerging adult development. Because one in five treatment recipients will be emerging adults, it seems like a prudent training investment. It would be very interesting to test whether emerging adult outcomes would be better if they were seen by providers who received specialized training in the life course issues of emerging adults than when seen by those who did not. It is possible that providers who have specialized training in emerging adult development may be more empathic with emerging adults or may hatch treatment innovations that meet their developmental needs.

Finally, a fourth trend to monitor with regard to emerging adult treatment access is the pending national health care revision in the United States. At this writing, legislators are contemplating changes to the 2010 Patient Protection and Affordable Care Act (ACA). In Chapter 6, we noted how the increased insurance coverage of emerging adults under the ACA has resulted in fewer emerging adults reporting that insurance coverage is a barrier to receiving SUD treatment (Gallup, 2011). Thus major changes to the ACA that result in coverage gaps for emerging adults could make the current underutilization of SUD treatment even worse.

Improving Diagnostic Precision for Emerging Adults

Although we reviewed much emerging adult–specific research support for the current DSM-5 criteria, other research has challenged the notion that we should lower the diagnostic threshold to two symptoms in order to be diagnosed with a substance use disorder. One compelling study refutes the claim that emerging adult treatment utilization by those with alcohol use disorders (AUDs) is, in fact, as low as described in this book (Wakefield & Schmitz, 2015). That is, because treatment utilization is the percent of individuals with a disorder who actually obtained treatment, lowering the threshold for disorder may create the illusion of unmet need. Wakefield and Schmitz (2015) compared treatment utilization rates under two different sets of diagnostic decision rules: (1) the current thresholds of two or more of the DSM-5 symptoms or (2) a "harmful dysfunction" AUD pattern that retained the two or more threshold but required the presence of at least one biological dysfunction (e.g., impaired control or withdrawal) criterion and one social harm criterion (e.g., role failure, giving up activities). Relative to the current DSM-5 categorization, harmful dysfunction criteria lowered the national disorder prevalence rates, lowered unmet treatment need, and correctly identified teens with persistent AUDs over a several-year period.

These findings remind us that there is much at stake in how we conceptualize an SUD. While on the one hand the reduction of the SUD threshold may increase access to covered SUD treatment for individuals only experiencing social harms, on the other hand we need to be concerned about labeling individuals as disordered. This puts us in a particularly sticky situation with emerging adults. Emerging adults have elevated substance use frequency and are likely to experience social harms even if they don't meet the full SUD criteria, and they experience long-term health consequences even if their substance use disorders remit later in adulthood (Haber et al., 2016). Many emerging adults may not be experiencing withdrawal symptoms (see Tables 3.1 and 3.2 in Chapter 3), and there are also problems with measuring impaired control via the longer/larger DSM criterion. Thus, applying more conservative SUD typologies to emerging adults could reduce services aimed at preventing harm from substance use.

Thus, more research is needed on how altering the definitions of SUD would impact emerging adults. Especially needed are studies on how different definitions of cannabis and alcohol use disorders impact prevalence rates, diagnostic stability over time (i.e., persistent throughout and beyond emerging adulthood), and access to treatment and prevention services. Current advocacy efforts to shift public perception about the effectiveness of SUD treatment are based on the conceptualization of SUDs as chronic health problems (McLellan, Lewis, O'Brien, & Kleber, 2000). Diagnostic misclassification of emerging adults with non-chronic SUDs could undermine such efforts and reinforce perceptions that SUD relapse rates are high. In fact, post-treatment relapse rates for SUDs are similar to those for other chronic relapsing health conditions (McLellan et al., 2000). In summary, there remains tension between two worthy goals: (1) reserving the moniker of *disorder* for individuals with serious problems and (2) increasing the public health benefits by expanding intervention services to persons experiencing social harms from use. Practitioners and policymakers should remain steadfast in safeguarding both of these worthy views.

Additionally, more studies are needed on what emerging adults are thinking about when responding to questions about the DSM criteria. In Chapter 3, we discussed several nuances that have already been identified in some DSM-5 items for emerging adults. Specifically, we know that sometimes emerging adults' positive responses to some criteria may not reflect the original concept the criteria were designed to capture. More research is needed comparing different item wordings for these items identified as more prone to misinterpretation by emerging adults. More emerging adult–specific research is also needed on the newly added craving criterion for the DSM-5.

Emerging Adults Account for Much Marijuana and Opiate Use

Marijuana

Times are clearly changing with respect to drug control policies, especially regarding marijuana. With close to 30 states allowing some form of medical marijuana use and 7 allowing full recreational use, we need to get serious about research on how marijuana affects individuals. Emerging adults are at an age when experimentation is most common, and an estimated one in nine of these individuals who try marijuana will progress to having a marijuana use disorder (Hall, 2015). Further, new forms of marijuana use, such as dabbing (i.e., a highly concentrated hit of marijuana), and the increased potency of street marijuana raise concerns about whether the addictive potential of marijuana may increase. Although some still debate whether one can even be addicted to marijuana, recent emerging adult research shows that marijuana withdrawal does exist and does predict treatment response (Davis, Smith, Morphew, Lei, & Zhang, 2016). Further, persistence in marijuana use and marijuana use disorders predict downward social mobility at age 38, even after accounting for a number confounding variables (Cerdá et al., 2016).

So, where do we go from here with regard to emerging adults and marijuana use? First, in the coming years, we should carefully track social attitudes toward use and actual use by emerging adults. Early indicators are that perceived risks from marijuana use are dropping among emerging adults (Salas-Wright, Vaughn,

Todic, & Córdova, 2015). That brings us to our second point, which is that we need to study carefully and longitudinally the health risks of using marijuana. Perceived risks are dropping at a time when we have very limited knowledge about the health risks from marijuana use (Hall, 2015). Although the pro-liberalization advocates focus on lack of health-related impacts (i.e., no overdoses), there are potentially yet-undiscovered health effects that may emerge.

We also need to harness the power of big data to discern what health effects exist across the continuum of marijuana use in the general population. For example, we have dietary alcohol risk guidelines with regard to alcohol use that were developed by the National Instituted of Alcohol Abuse and Alcoholism. These guidelines have gender-specific guidelines that define binge use and both daily and weekly (number of) drink limits. If we continue to pursue liberalization of marijuana policy, clearer guidelines are needed to establish health(ier) limits of marijuana use associated with fewer health and social consequences. Establishing these guidelines will be beneficial for all individuals, but will be especially useful for emerging adults, who consume a disproportionate amount of the marijuana in the United States.

OPIATES

In 2012, emerging adults accounted for about half of all opiate-focused treatment admissions in the United States (Substance Abuse and Mental Health Services Administration, Center for Behavioral Health Statistics and Quality, 2014). There are very recent concerns about the increasing number of heroin overdoses in the United States. Further, emerging adults receiving medication-assisted treatments for opiate use have poorer treatment retention compared to older adults (Schuman-Olivier et al., 2014). Emerging adult opiate users are known to be polydrug users (Catalano, White, Fleming, & Haggerty, 2011) and also to have initiated substance use at an early age (Storr, Westergaard, & Anthony, 2005). Thus, emerging adults with opiate use disorders represent a very severely vulnerable population among those with substance use disorders.

There are three current priority areas for such emerging adults. First, the expansion of medication-assisted treatments (MAT) will benefit emerging adults, who comprise a hefty proportion of all treatment episodes for opioids. Second, we must prevent needless overdose deaths by distributing life-saving drugs such as naloxone to friends and family members of emerging adults suffering from opiate addictions. Finally, we should invest in improving retention among those emerging adults who do receive MAT.

Does Development Account for Poorer Treatment Outcomes?

Over the past 15 years, hypotheses on how developmental processes in emerging adulthood impact substance use are mostly based on Arnett's (2005) five-dimensional model of emerging adulthood (i.e., age of identity development, age of optimism, age of self-focus, age of feeling in-between, age of instability). A number of studies have shown how the dimensions of emerging adulthood are or are not associated with substance use in both general and clinical samples of emerging adults. In Chapter 2, we presented two measures (i.e., the Inventory of Dimension of Emerging Adulthood [IDEA] and the Emerging Adult Reasons for Substance Use [EARS]) that are currently being used in research with clinical samples of emerging adults to see whether they moderate outcomes over time.

To cement the argument that emerging adults are a special population, studies are needed that identify change targets that are both grounded in developmental theory and can be impacted by treatments that are developmentally adapted for emerging adults. Such efforts could be modeled after existing efforts for culturally adapting treatments as described in Chapter 5. Although we critiqued the need for some cultural adaptations in Chapter 5, two things bear mentioning. First, there is empirical support for cultural adaptations, which in general psychotherapy literature produce better results than non-adapted treatment (Benish, Quintana, & Wampold, 2011; Griner and Smith, 2006). Second, emerging adults are such a large proportion of the population receiving substance use disorder treatments that the efforts will likely not have limited applicability.

Very few treatments have been developed that have deliberately attempted to address emerging adult developmental constructs within substance use treatment. Studies are needed that test whether participant characteristic interact with treatment types in predicting treatment response. For example, although studies have found some support for emerging adult age by treatment interactions (Davis et al., 2017), no current study tests whether emerging adults at varying levels of the developmental features respond poorer or better to different treatments. For example, do emerging adults high on identity development benefit from added emphasis in treatment on resolving identity issues relative to a treatment with no focus on identity issues? Alternatively, besides personalized feedback interventions, are there any novel treatment components that can be added to treatments to address emerging adults' perception that it is a "normal" part of the emerging adult experience to use alcohol and drugs (Osberg et al., 2010, Smith et al., 2016)? Finally, would emerging adults high on some developmental constructs (i.e., instability, feeling-in-between) fare better if they were receiving treatment from providers with specialized training in emerging adulthood rather than untrained providers?

CONCLUSION

Emerging adults ages 18–29 represent a special population of SUD treatment recipients because they have poorer treatment engagement, poorer outcomes, a different clinical presentation, and unique risk factors relative to those in other age groups. Innovation is needed in four broad areas: improving treatment access and treatment retention, making the diagnostic criteria more relevant for emerging adults, addressing macro-level trends in marijuana use and opiate use, and deriving and testing developmentally adapted treatments with emerging adults. It is my sincere hope that such efforts will help eliminate the human suffering associated with substance use among emerging adults.

REFERENCES

Arnett, J. J. (2005). The developmental context of substance use in emerging adulthood. *Journal of Drug Issues*, 35, 235–254.

Benish, S. G., Quintana, S., & Wampold, B. E. (2011). Culturally adapted psychotherapy and the legitimacy of myth: a direct-comparison meta-analysis. *Journal of Counseling Psychology*, 58, 279–289.

Blonigen, D. M., Timko, C., Finney, J. W., Moos, B. S., & Moos, R. H. (2011). Alcoholics Anonymous attendance, decreases in impulsivity and drinking and psychosocial outcomes over 16 years: Moderated mediation from a developmental perspective. *Addiction*, 106(12), 2167–2177. doi: 10.1111/j.1360-0443.2011.03522.x

Carey, K. B., Scott-Sheldon, L. A., Elliott, J. C., Garey, L., & Carey, M. P. (2012). Face-to-face versus computer-delivered alcohol interventions for college drinkers: A meta-analytic review, 1998 to 2010. *Clinical Psychology Review*, 32(8), 690–703.

Castro, F. G., Barrera Jr., M., & Holleran Steiker, L. K. (2010). Issues and challenges in the design of culturally adapted evidence-based interventions. *Annual Review of Clinical Psychology*, 6, 213–239.

Catalano, R. F., White, H. R., Fleming, C. B., & Haggerty, K. P. (2011). Is nonmedical prescription opiate use a unique form of illicit drug use? *Addictive Behaviors*, 36(1), 79–86.

Center for Behavioral Health Statistics and Quality. (2016). *Key substance use and mental health indicators in the United States: Results from the 2015 National Survey on Drug Use and Health* (HHS Publication No. SMA 16-4984, NSDUH Series H-51). Retrieved from http://samhsa.gov/data/

Cerdá, M., Moffitt, T. E., Meier, M. H., Harrington, H., Houts, R., Ramrakha, S., . . . & Caspi, A. (2016). Persistent cannabis dependence and alcohol dependence represent risks for midlife economic and social problems: a longitudinal cohort study. *Clinical Psychological Science*, 4(6), 1028–1046.

Davis, J. P., Bergman, B. G., Smith, D. C., & Kelly, J. F. (2017). Testing a matching hypothesis for emerging adults in Project MATCH: During-treatment and 1-year outcomes. *Journal of Studies on Alcohol and Drugs*, 78, 140–145.

Davis, J. P., Smith, D. C., Morphew, J. W., Lei, X., & Zhang, S. (2016) Cannabis withdrawal, post-treatment abstinence, and days to first cannabis use among emerging adults in substance use treatment: A prospective study. *Journal of Drug Issues*, 46, 64–83.

Gallup. (2011, September). *In U.S. Significantly Fewer 18- to 25-Year-Olds Uninsured*. Retrieved from: http://www.gallup.com/poll/149558/Significantly-Fewer-Year-Olds-Uninsured.aspx

Glass, J. E., Hamilton, A. M., Powell, B. J., Perron, B. E., Brown, R. T., & Ilgen, M. A. (2015). Specialty substance use disorder services following brief alcohol intervention: a meta-analysis of randomized controlled trials. *Addiction*, 110(9), 1404–1415.

Griner, D., & Smith, T. B. (2006). Culturally adapted mental health intervention: A meta-analytic review. *Psychotherapy: Theory, Research, Practice, Training, 43*, 531–548.

Haber, J. R., Harris-Olenak, B., Burroughs, T., & Jacob, T. (2016). Residual Effects: Young Adult Diagnostic Drinking Predicts Late-Life Health Outcomes. *Journal of Studies on Alcohol and Drugs, 77*(6), 859–867.

Hall, W. (2015). What has research over the past two decades revealed about the adverse health effects of recreational cannabis use? *Addiction, 110*(1), 19–35.

Hoeppner, B. B., Hoeppner, S. S., & Kelly, J. F. (2014). Do young people benefit from AA as much, and in the same ways, as adult aged 30+ ? A moderated multiple mediation analysis. *Drug and Alcohol Dependence, 143*, 181–188. doi: 10.1016/j.drugalcdep.2014.07.023

Kofoed, L. L., Tolson, R. L., Atkinson, R. M., Toth, R. L., & Turner, J. A. (1987). Treatment compliance of older alcoholics: An elder-specific approach is superior to "mainstreaming." *Journal of Studies on Alcohol, 48*(1), 47–51.

Lewis, M. A., & Neighbors, C. (2015). An examination of college student activities and attentiveness during a Web-delivered personalized normative feedback intervention. *Psychology of Addictive Behaviors, 29*(1), 162–167. doi: 10.1037/adb0000003

Mason, M. J., & Luckey, B. (2003). Young adults in alcohol-other drug treatment: An understudied population. *Alcoholism Treatment Quarterly, 21*(1), 17–32.

McLellan, A. T., Lewis, D. C., O'Brien, C. P., & Kleber, H. D. (2000). Drug dependence, a chronic medical illness: Implications for treatment, insurance, and outcomes evaluation. *Journal of the American Medical Association, 284*(13), 1689–1695.

Osberg, T. M., Atkins, L., Buchholz, L., Shirshova, V., Swiantek, A., Whitley, J., . . . Oquendo, N. (2010). Development and validation of the College Life Alcohol Salience Scale: A measure of beliefs about the role of alcohol in college life. *Psychology of Addictive Behaviors, 24*(1), 1–12.

Salas-Wright, C. P., Vaughn, M. G., Todic, J., & Córdova, D. (2015). Trends in the disapproval and use of marijuana among adolescents and young adults in the United States: 2002–2013. *American Journal of Drug and Alcohol Abuse, 41*, 392–404.

Satre, D. D., Mertens, J., Arean, P. A., & Weisner, C. (2003). Contrasting outcomes of older versus middle-aged and younger adult chemical dependency patients in a managed care program. *Journal of Studies on Alcohol, 64*, 520–530.

Satre, D., Mertens, J., Arean, P. A., & Weisner, C. (2004). Five-year alcohol and drug treatment outcomes of older adults versus middle-aged and younger adults in a managed care program. *Addiction, 99*(10), 1286–1297. doi: 10.111l/j.1360-0443.2004.00831.x

Schuman-Olivier, Z., Weiss, R. D., Hoeppner, B. B., Borodovsky, J., & Albanese, M. J. (2014). Emerging adult age status predicts poor buprenorphine treatment retention. *Journal of Substance Abuse Treatment, 47*(3), 202–212.

Sinha, R., Easton, C., & Kemp, K. (2003). Substance abuse treatment characteristics of probation-referred young adults in a community-based outpatient program. *American Journal of Drug and Alcohol Abuse, 29*(3), 585–597.

Smith, D. C., Cleeland, L., & Dennis, M. L. (2010) Reasons for quitting among emerging adults and adolescents in substance use disorder treatment. *Journal of Studies on Alcohol and Drugs, 71*(3), 400–409.

Smith, D. C., Davis, J. P., & Dumas, T. M. (2016). What's development got to do with it? A new measure of emerging adults motives for substance use. *Alcoholism: Clinical and Experimental Research, 40*, 247A.

Smith, D. C., Godley, S. H., Godley, M. D., & Dennis, M. L. (2011). Adolescent community reinforcement approach outcomes differ among emerging adults and adolescents. *Journal of Substance Abuse Treatment, 41*(4), 422–430. doi: 10.1016/j.jsat.2011.06.003

Storr, C. L., Westergaard, R., & Anthony, J. C. (2005). Early onset inhalant use and risk for opiate initiation by young adulthood. *Drug and Alcohol Dependence, 78*(3), 253–261.

Substance Abuse and Mental Health Services Administration. (2015). *Trends in insurance coverage and treatment utilization by young adults.* Retrieved from: http://www.samhsa.gov/data/sites/default/files/SR-1887/SR-1887.pdf

Substance Abuse and Mental Health Services Administration, Center for Behavioral Health Statistics and Quality (2014). *Treatment Episode Data Set (TEDS): 2002–2012. National Admissions to Substance Abuse Treatment Services.* BHSIS Series S-71, HHS Publication No. (SMA) 14-4850. Rockville, MD: Substance Abuse and Mental Health Services Administration. Available at https://www.samhsa.gov/data/sites/default/files/TEDS2012N_Web.pdf

Wakefield, J. C., & Schmitz, M. F. (2015). The harmful dysfunction model of alcohol use disorder: Revised criteria to improve the validity of diagnosis and prevalence estimates. *Addiction, 110,* 931–942.